D1264393

THERAPEUTIC

EDUCATION

EXPLORATION SERIES IN EDUCATION

...

Under the Advisory Editorship of
JOHN GUY FOWLKES

Therapeutic
Education

Its Theoretical Bases and Practice

∙∙

GEORGE DEVEREUX, Ph.D.

DIRECTOR OF RESEARCH
DEVEREUX FOUNDATION
DEVON, PENNSYLVANIA

HARPER & BROTHERS PUBLISHERS

NEW YORK

THERAPEUTIC EDUCATION:

ITS THEORETICAL BASES AND PRACTICE

Copyright © 1956, by Harper & Brothers
Printed in the United States of America

Library of Congress catalog card number: 56–6098

Dedicated to the memory of
EDWARD YARNALL HARTSHORNE, PH.D.
Instructor in Sociology, Harvard University:
gentleman, scholar, and friend.

CONTENTS

....

Contents

PART FOUR. ORGANIZATIONAL PATTERN

✓ PART FIVE. OBSTACLES TO THERAPEUTIC EDUCATION

How to stimulate, handle, or inspire human beings to behave in a desirable manner may be said to be the basic purpose or function of every teacher. Unfortunately, a given number of human beings at any age level do not behave in a way that is accepted by their associates.

Since the pattern of adult behavior is substantially established during the ages of childhood, adolescence, and early adulthood, the importance of wise treatment of students by teachers during these formative stages of development cannot be overemphasized. All those devoted to the tutelage of children are ever eager to learn ways and means of producing exemplary action by those they teach.

Unfortunately, the lot of the teacher is not that of working exclusively with individuals whose personalities and, therefore, beings are sensitively attuned to the contemporary social environment. Consequently, it is necessary that classroom workers spend much time in the modification and elimination of undesirable habits as well as exerting appropriate effort toward prompting the adoption and development of positive behavior habits.

The field of psychoanalysis has been increasingly widely recognized in the treatment of extreme instances of abnormal behavior. The understanding of this relatively new and admittedly complicated and delicate area of professional endeavor, unfortunately, is not generally appreciated. It would seem that there is an inevitable mutually beneficial relationship between psychoanalysis and education. Indeed, as the author of this volume recently stated, "the techniques and objectives of education and psychoanalysis actually dovetail and complement each other."

Therapeutic Education is an intriguing and striking portrayal of both the theory and practice of dealing with children who need special consideration if they are to develop into dynamic, balanced persons. The rich background of experience along with unusual ability and training are reflected throughout this treatise. This volume should prove invaluable not only to teachers but to all those concerned with the responsibility of encouraging individuals both *not to behave* and *to behave* in given ways.

JOHN GUY FOWLKES

PREFACE

....

The present work seeks to outline the foundations of therapeutic education, and to define its relationship to education as well as to psychotherapy.

The orientation of this work is a deliberately theoretical one, simply because, in the last resort, nothing is more practical than theory. This fact, which has been systematically ignored for many decades, and possibly for millennia, is just beginning to be understood and accepted, chiefly as a result of the fundamental contributions of theoretical physicists to the creation of the fission and thermonuclear fusion bombs.[1] The basis of progress is "pure science."

A basic goal of this work is to present its subject matter relationally, i.e., to establish a nexus between the fields of therapeutic education, education, and psychotherapy, on the one hand, and the broad social and cultural context in which these disciplines unfold themselves and are implemented in daily practice, on the other hand. Many passages which, at first blush, may seem to be mere "asides," or, possibly, gratuitous displays of erudition, actually represent attempts to place the subject matter in its social and cultural matrix. Thus, the exhaustive discussion (Chapter 2) of the history of education, with special reference to the struggle between educators and parents over the right to "indoctrinate" the child, may seem superfluous until one realizes that the social

---

[1] It is said that the "pure scientists" of antiquity criticized Archimedes for his work in "applied science" when he developed war engines wherewith to defend his native city, Syracuse. Likewise, the "pure mathematician" Jacobi criticized Fourier because of the latter's advocacy of applied mathematics. Yet, oddly enough, in the end Fourier's work proved to be useful chiefly in pure mathematics, while Jacobi's discoveries became indispensable for engineers (12).

and parental resistances to the therapeutic education of children (Part V) are direct manifestations and products of this ageless struggle.

The second major purpose of this work is to be actually "therapeutically educational" for those of its readers who prepare to enter the field of therapeutic education. Indeed, work with defective or disturbed children and adults stimulates latent anxieties and represents a genuine challenge for the emotional maturity of the worker. Hence, a book on therapeutic education which refused to take cognizance of the worker's professional and personal problems would be wholly inadequate. These problems, as well as certain difficulties related to the worker's own ethnocentrism, are discussed in Chapters 5, 7, 8, 10, 14, 15, 16, 17.

The third purpose of this book is to interpret the work of the educator to the therapist, and vice versa, with special reference to the organizational setting in which interaction between representatives of these two disciplines takes place (Chapters 4, 12, 13, 17). The relevant passages were inspired by the belief that true teamwork, which is indispensable for the proper care of the exceptional child, cannot be achieved unless the practitioners of various disciplines have a clear and workable understanding of the techniques and goals of their co-workers, especially as these relate to their own field of activity. The attempt to clarify the nature and scope of teamwork, whose most significant phase is the art of cross referrals, required a preliminary clarification of certain basic differences between education and psychotherapy (Part II).

In seeking to make this distinction—as well as certain others, such as between superego and ego ideal, or discipline and punishment (Chapter 8)—it was found necessary to draw our lines of demarcation rather sharply. Hence, some colleagues who read the first draft of this work remarked that our distinctions were perhaps somewhat too specific, since in the world of reality boundaries between various concepts and techniques tend to be a little blurred.

In addition, one psychoanalytic reader stressed that our definition of the difference between superego and ego ideal, while wholly acceptable to him, actually represented a slight innovation in the field of psychoanalytic theory.

It is certainly not our intention to deny that, in the world of reality, much of what passes as psychotherapy includes a generous amount of education *stricto sensu*—and vice versa of course. We also recognize that our way of defining the superego and the ego ideal represents a slight modification of existing views. We feel, however, that neither of these facts impairs the validity of the distinctions which we are making in this work.

Indeed, we hold that we could not even recognize that "real" psychotherapy also necessitates occasional educational measures, and that "real" education often contains a generous admixture of psychotherapy, unless we first differentiated in a perfectly clear-cut manner between psychotherapy and education. Nowhere in this work do we advocate that the psychotherapist should refrain from useful and necessary educational activities, or vice versa. We simply suggest that one should know what one is doing, in order to do it well.

The fact that our definitions of such concepts as development, maturation, humanization and ethnicization (Chapter 1); instruction, indoctrination and education (Chapter 2); psychotherapy, remedial measures and therapeutic education (Part II); or superego, ego ideal, punishment, and discipline (Part III) are somewhat at variance with existing definitions is not a violation of basic scientific procedures. Indeed, none of these concepts denotes a tangible and indisputably circumscribed object, such as a table or an arm. Concepts are simply means whereby one classifies and sorts out (Chapter 4) reality, in order to understand, control, and predict its behavior, for a given purpose. The zoölogist, using biological concepts, lumps together a black *horse* and a white *horse* as legitimately as the painter, interested in balancing colors, lumps together a *white* horse and a *white* sheet drying on the clothesline. Otherwise stated, a concept can be defined in any way one chooses to define it, provided only that the definition chosen proves to be useful in a given context and for a given purpose. The definitions which we propose in this work are those which we deemed most useful for our present purposes. No one who is dissatisfied with them can legitimately argue that they are "inherently wrong." He can only propose definitions of his own, and prove them to be more useful for a sound formulation of the principles of therapeutic education than are our definitions. To take an example at random, it is quite certain that the superego is not a self-contained cerebral function or a definitely localized area of the cortex. It is a logical construct, evolved by grouping together certain psychic functions which, in certain situations, appear to act as though they formed a patterned whole. This, in turn, can be usefully contrasted with various other psychic functions which, in the same context, also seem to form a patterned whole, such as the ego ideal. In brief, we simply claim that the manner in which we constructed our patterned units, denoted by various concepts, is useful for our purposes. No such construct can ever be proved "wrong." It can only be shown to be less useful than some other way of arranging reality.

The proper understanding of the scope, purpose—and shortcomings—of a book requires a knowledge of the various "ingredients" which enter into its composition. These ingredients are, in a sense, largely determined by the writer's interests and areas of competence.

The basic conceptual framework of this book took many years to mature and represents a summation—with special reference to therapeutic education—of a general frame of reference, or scientifically humanistic *Weltanschauung,* which underlies all of the writer's published works in a variety of fields, many of which are superficially—but only superficially—unrelated to the focal topic of this book.

Broadly speaking, the present work represents a synthesis of the writer's training and interest in anthropology, educational sociology, and psychoanalysis. Thus, the writer's interest in therapeutic education is inseparable from his interest in anthropological "culture and personality studies," which investigate the way a culturally neutral or amorphous young organism is transformed into a human being—a *zoön politikon*—and into a citizen as well. This product is indelibly marked by the structural and dynamic peculiarities of the environment in which he was raised and to which, under ordinary circumstances, he is expected to adjust. Indeed, in a very genuine sense, the study of all educational patterns and techniques is logically a branch of the broader study of the impact of culture on personality formation. It analyzes the means whereby man's humanization and ethnicization[2] are brought about.

The educative process has, of course, many constituents, which are often not even thought of as educational, but simply as contingent type-experiences such as each child, or even adult, living in a particular milieu experiences in the course of what may be called an ethnic type-biography (*178*). However, its two main aspects—man's ethnically neutral *humanization* (culturalization and socialization) and man's ethnically definite incorporation into a particular social and cultural pattern (*ethnicization*)—have to be sharply differentiated from his ontogenetically determined and phylogenetically prepatterned *maturation* as a member of the zoölogical *genus homo* and will be so differentiated throughout this work.

Within this broad, but scientifically nonetheless manageable,

---

[2] The term "ethnicization," as used in this book, more or less corresponds to what Kluckhohn calls "culturization" and Herskovits denotes by the term "enculturation." We coined this term for the specific purpose of differentiating between "humanization," which results from the acquisition of Culture *per se*, i.e., from the acquisition of any particular culture, and "ethnicization," which results from the acquisition of the specific and distinctive culture of a given society.

framework the analysis of education *per se* is the equivalent of an analysis of the culturally determined means and instrumental values used in the humanization and ethnicization of the child. Thus, we view all education, including therapeutic education, as a branch, and as an application, of culture and personality studies.[3]

The second source is the writer's interest in the relationship between culture and personality deviations, i.e., in "culture and the abnormal personality studies." Such studies deal with instances in which the broad techniques of humanization and ethnicization "went on the wrong track" and failed to achieve their avowed goals. This can happen either when the child is inherently defective or when existing humanization and ethnicization techniques are inherently ill adapted to the specific and distinctive needs of the individual. In the latter case they lead to demands and expectations which, either because of what they inherently represent or else because of the manner in which they impinge on the individual, create stress. In addition, studies of "culture and the abnormal personality" also deal with the problem of the absolute (psychiatric) vs. the social (adjustment) definition of deviation or defect. This problem, while essentially of paramount importance for psychiatry and anthropology (59) alike, is of relatively secondary importance in the present work.

The third source of the present work is the writer's interest in therapy in the broadest sense, i.e., in all types of attempts to counteract the deleterious impact of inappropriate techniques of humanizing and ethnicizing the individual. This interest led the writer to obtain training in psychoanalysis, so as to enable him to adapt standard psychotherapeutic techniques to the specific, culturally determined, potentialities, needs, and expectations of patients with various backgrounds. The attempt to evolve a Culture oriented, but culturally neutral, psychotherapy has a direct bearing upon problems of therapeutic education, since (cf. especially Part

[3] A recent work on the relationship between anthropology and education (203) appeared too late to be used in the writing of this book.

V) we view children as a "minority" and as members of a "subculture" in any society. It should be specified, however, that the present book is not intended as a contribution to the field of "psychoanalytic pedagogics," which has been so carefully explored by Anna Freud and others. The position taken in this work is that therapeutic education is an autonomous discipline, branching off from education rather than from psychotherapy and having a conceptual framework of its own, to which psychoanalytic theory can make important contributions but which it cannot and should not dominate.

The fourth source is the writer's interest in the sociology of education, which was originally aroused by his friend, the late Dr. Edward Yarnall Hartshorne of Harvard University, whose tragically premature death deprived that science of one of its most creative pioneers. Dr. Hartshorne's influence on the writer exerted itself in the most creative manner—i.e., by means of a nonspecific "stimulus diffusion," as Kroeber calls it (144)—which made the writer aware of the total social dimensions of the educational process (112). The writer's preliminary insights into the focal problems of the sociology of education were first presented in a course which he taught at the University of Haiti (summer session, 1945), as Visiting Professor from the United States under the auspices of the United States Department of State, Division of Cultural Relations.

The fifth and final source is the writer's interest in the social pathology of education, viewed as part of the total problem of social pathology in general. His general theory of social pathology was first presented in a course on social pathology given in the University of Wyoming in 1941–1942 and 1942–1943.

No interest, however genuine it may be, can reach fruition unless three external conditions make possible its actualization and implementation.

1. The opportunity to work in one's field of interest.
2. A suitable indoctrination.
3. A concrete stimulus situation, which serves to trigger the process of factual research and theoretical inquiry.

The opportunity to work in the field of therapeutic education was provided by the generosity of one of the trustees of the Devereux Foundation, who is a research worker of considerable eminence in another field. This trustee insisted that the Devereux Foundation, which operates the Devereux Schools, had reached a stage in its development where research was not only a possibility but a definite public obligation. She generously backed up her views with a gift, which permitted the establishment of the Doctor G. Henry Katz Research Department, named in honor of an eminent training analyst who, ever since 1937, has been guide, philosopher, and friend to the Devereux Foundation and all its staff.

The writer's indoctrination with reference to therapeutic education was a particularly stimulating experience, since—like the intangible process whereby man is humanized and ethnicized—it took place through a process resembling osmosis. Stimuli and insights were transmitted almost imperceptibly, through life in an atmosphere in which the core objective was the optimal application of educational means to therapeutic ends. The gradual growth of insight was not unlike that which every anthropological field worker experiences through his participation in the life of a primitive tribe. Though he may spend his actual working hours investigating linguistics or kinship systems or ritual, throughout his stay in the field national characteristics, the focal themes of the culture, and the patterns of individual conduct and of social life obtrude themselves on him in a variety of ways. Hence, be it but in private conversation, even the most consistently culture-oriented and vocally antipsychological field worker can, if he chooses, not only narrate a variety of typical and revealing incidents but also formulate many shrewd and cogent insights into the psychological processes characteristic of the society which he studied. Thus, even though, for a variety of subjective and environmental reasons, the writer first engaged in clinical research, as defined elsewhere (47, 52), in practice the stimulus-impact of life and work at the Devereux Schools, i.e., in a setting dedicated to therapeutic education, rapidly catalyzed his previous seemingly diffuse and unpatterned interests in this technique and led him to formulate the problems and solutions presented in this work. The nuclearity of therapeutic education in the total structure and function of the Devereux Schools, and the force wherewith this nuclearity impinges upon the participant observer, may best be judged by the fact that, to the writer's surprise, his first major work resulting from his association with the Devereux Schools does not pertain, as might be expected, to the field of clinical research, but to the field of therapeutic education. The impact, repercussions, and echoes of the latter he could not fail to perceive both in his research therapeutic work and in his contacts with all members of the staff, particularly with Miss Helena T. Devereux, Director of the Devereux Schools, who undertook his "indoctrination" at her hospitable dinner table, by interpreting to him the "humanitarian and organizational mores" of the Devereux Schools. While, as stated before, some of the stimuli which focused the writer's research interests upon problems of therapeutic education emanated from the Devereux Schools' entire staff, his chief debt in this regard is to Miss Helena T. Devereux, and also to Drs. J. Clifford Scott and Herbert H. Herskovitz, who gave especially freely of their time and knowledge.

The actual "triggering stimulus," which fuses basic interests and opportunities for work with indoctrination and translates them into action, is also of crucial importance for the understanding of a book's real scope.

The history of any book begins at the point where the long, and often but dimly object-directed, preparation, which forms its background, emerges from a larval stage comparable to "prehistory" and enters the realm of "written history." The prehistory of this book—the story of the many frames of reference and types of experience which, often unwittingly, went into its preparation—were described above. It remains to describe the "triggering stimulus," which crystallized a "supersaturated solution," in order to clarify the scope, purpose, and also the latent or unconscious bias of this book. The instant at which a triggering stimulus impinges upon the writer resembles the moment when a dismayed, mechanically unsophisticated, but perhaps not altogether obtuse, observer, confronted with an array of seemingly disparate partial assemblages, suddenly realizes that they have an implicit pattern; that the engine block in the corner, the generator on the shelf, and all the other parts lying about only wait to be assembled into a car.

This catalytic moment, which led to the formulation of the theoretical framework of this book, came when the writer was confronted with a set of facts which, in terms of customary frames of reference, did not seem to constitute a "statistical population" and appeared to possess no "common denominator" in terms of existing theories. However, since in some obscure manner these facts nonetheless seemed to "hang together," the real problem was to find the common elements: the similarity in the differences, and the difference in the similarities.

This basic stimulus was, strictly speaking, not even a research problem, but one related to administrative matters. Miss Helena T. Devereux, Director of the Devereux Schools, asked the writer to study, for purely practical purposes, a group of fifteen students who, in the opinion of the administrative, educational, and medical (non-psychiatric) staff of the Devereux Schools seemingly failed to benefit from the Schools' program of "dynamic, specialized and individualized education in a therapeutic setting." The staff felt that no "movement" was apparent in any of these students, at least from the non-psychotherapeutic point of view. Since only one of these students was in psychotherapy, it was clear to all concerned that what was "on trial" in this inquiry was not the psychotherapeutic division or program but the basic educational system of the school, and its therapeutic milieu. The choice of the term "on trial" indicates that the investigation was to be focused not on the "failure" of the students but on the "failure" of the school. This, be it said in passing, is a refreshingly novel note in the world of education—and perhaps not only in the educational world.

Thus, this investigation was not assigned to the writer as a "research project." Rather was he called in as an impartial umpire, who, being connected neither with the educational and administrative departments of the school nor with its therapeutic division, had no personal stake in the matter, nor any interest—be it but an unconscious one—in justifying or "whitewashing" anyone. It was therefore felt that he could approach the problem disinterestedly, and could view it simply as an inquiry into policy, or into matters well within the scope of administrative psychiatry *lato sensu*. Fortunately, this "purely practical" investigation, which, from the administrative point of view, represented mere "trouble shooting," readily lent itself to being formulated as a scientific problem, related, on the one hand, to an evaluation of the effectiveness of one type of therapy (educational and milieu therapy) as contrasted with another type of therapy (psychotherapy) and, on the other hand, to the interesting technical problem of appraising the effectiveness of any kind of therapeutic effort not in terms of its "successes" but in terms of its "failures."

On the whole, the study of therapeutic "failures" has been as badly neglected in the past as has been the study of the inadequacies of theory, though as regards the latter reference can immediately be made to Freud's study of "A Case of Paranoia Running Counter to the Psycho-Analytical Theory of the Disease" (93), while, as regards the former, one is readily reminded of a recent book devoted to failures of therapy (*118*). This neglect is regrettable; an analysis of so-called "failures" probably sheds more light upon the potentialities of a therapeutic technique than does the study of successes, because failures reveal both the "level of aspiration" of therapeutic technicians and their creative "divine discontent" which is at the root of all progress (Chapter 7).

Once the problem was reworded in this manner, it automatically led to an inquiry into differences between the therapeutic educator's ideal and realistic levels of aspiration, both of which must be evaluated in terms of the inherent potentialities of that technique. This, in turn, made it necessary to define, as clearly as possible, the distinctive characteristics of therapeutic education, and to determine its natural scope and limits. From then on the ripples, set in motion by this particular concrete problem and followed—in that atmosphere of "gentle bewilderment" (Ives Hendricks) which should prevail not only in psychoanalysis but also in the initial stages of every scientific inquiry—by approximately two interviews each with every student concerned, began to spread almost irresistibly, until the writer had only to write down a conceptual scheme practically clamoring to be put into words.

The case histories cited in this work mostly pertain to students of the Devereux Schools and were obtained either personally or from colleagues and associates. The writer is particularly indebted to Miss Gilda Suglia for some of the best examples of therapeutic education cited here. The case histories pertaining to the students of the Devereux Schools were reviewed and cleared for publication by Dr. J. Clifford Scott, Associate Director for Individual Psychotherapy.

Some of these case histories may seem indelicate to squeamish readers. Such readers should remember that children would not be sent to therapeutic schools in the first place, were it not for the fact that their behavior is "objectionable" to their parents, and also to the community. Squeamishness has no place in the make-up of competent therapeutic educators, and, as stated before, one of the purposes of this book is to help future as well as practicing therapeutic educators to cope with their own emotional problems, so as to enable them to cope with the problems of their young charges. The time is past when a psychiatrist could indignantly reprimand a psychotic patient in a mental hospital for presuming to offend his ears by discussing with him his conflicts and anxieties over his impulse to masturbate.

Once the first draft of a book is completed, it is desirable to ascertain whether one has something to say or is simply talking to oneself. At such times one calls on the scholarship, wisdom, and experience—and heavily taxes the patience—of one's friends and colleagues by requesting them to read one's manuscript critically. The first draft of the present work was read by a number of colleagues, whose painstaking comments were of tremendous value in preparing the final draft.

Richard L. Jenkins, M.D., Chief of Research in Psychiatry, Veterans Administration, and Weston LaBarre, Ph.D., Associate Professor of Anthropology, Duke University, painstakingly read the first draft and offered invaluable and detailed comments, suggestions, and criticisms.

The writer is also indebted to the following staff members of the Devereux Foundation for their critical and helpful reading of the first draft of this work: J. Clifford Scott, M.D., Associate Director for Individual Psychotherpay, Herbert H. Herskovitz, M.D., Staff Psychoanalyst, Calvin F. Settlage, M.D., and Albert S. Terzian, M.D., Staff Psychiatrists, Edward L. French, Ph.D., Associate Director for Psychology, Counseling and Education, Michael B. Dunn, Ph.D., Associate Director and Coordinator of Professional Services, and John M. Barclay, Associate Director for Registration and Development, and Chairman of the Associate Directors.

Although in a very few instances the writer did not follow the advice of his friendly critics, most of the improvements in the manuscript are directly due to the creative suggestions of various friends and colleagues.

Last, but not least, the writer is indebted to Gardner Murphy, editor of the Harper Psychology Series, for bringing this book to the attention of the publisher, and to John Guy Fowlkes, editor of the Harper Exploration Series in Education, for recommending its publication in that distinguished series of works.

GEORGE DEVEREUX

December, 1955
Devon, Pennsylvania

....

PART ONE

BASIC PRINCIPLES

The very tribes poorest in material culture have achieved a whole set of our most modern educational postulates.

KNABENHANS

....

CHAPTER 1

The Meaning of Education for Development

At birth, the child is an undifferentiated conglomerate or continuum of potentialities, which are determined to a variable degree by phylogenetic patterns expressed through, and implemented by, ontogenetic processes. It is simply an immature sample of (zoölogically defined) *genus homo, capable* of becoming human, and, indeed, *needing* the fulfillment and achievement of becoming human, but, as yet, not human in any really functional sense.

In the course of development these potentialities unfold in various ways, some more and some less complexly determined by inherent biological patterns. The processes which activate these potentialities may be divided into three groups. We designate the total process whereby any and all potentialities ultimately find an expression by the neutral term "development," and view it as a non-valuatively defined, more or less unidirectional and irreversible, but always highly individualized process. There are three types of development.

MATURATION

Maturation denotes the total changes in the organism and in its function and behavior which formally (though not causally) may be correlated with, or viewed as functions of, the passage of time.

3

No causal role is attributed to the passage of absolute time (i.e., to the progress of the hands of a clock) since it does not determine directly the complex biological and physiological changes in the growing organism. We simply state that there occur in every young organism certain changes, forming a patterned and connected series, which unfold in the time dimension. These changes include a tremendous variety of phenomena, ranging from gain in stature and weight, myelination, increasing coördination, atrophy of the *palmaris longus* and of the pineal gland, etc., to a variety of more complex behavior patterns, including new autoplastic and alloplastic techniques. In theory, these changes would appear in the same order even in children maturing without any human contact, were it possible to keep them alive in an emotional vacuum which, as Spitz's studies of hospitalism and "anaclitic depression" indicate (*204, 205, 206*), is, of course, impossible. However, the view that this maturational series is phylobiologically prepatterned is confirmed by the fact that no appreciable maturational differences have been observed in infants raised in a great many different cultures, whose variety makes them the logical equivalents of experimentation under controlled laboratory conditions.

HUMANIZATION

Humanization—as stated in a previous publication (*55*)—denotes the acquisition of distinctively human traits, by a systematic, though sometimes nearly unconscious and "automatic," series of controlled experiences, representing a process resembling domestication. It is of the essence of our argument that whereas maturation—as defined above—is a process whose direction, sequence, and overall pattern are biologically predetermined, the process of humanization is primarily a result of experience which, though sometimes not consciously perceived as having such a function, assists in the actualization of biologically inherent potentialities. This actualization represents, at one and the same time, an achieve-

ment and a fulfillment, without which the maturational process *per se* would be nonfunctional, and, possibly, even dysfunctional. Indeed, it is highly probable that a human organism, deprived of opportunities for becoming a human being in more than a strictly zoölogical sense, would actually experience maturation as a self-destructive process.

There are weighty reasons for supposing that the process of maturation itself, not implemented by, and given no outlet in, activity of a functional character, would damage the organism, in the same way in which a car whose engine is raced without a meshing of the gears and without a channeling of the energy into propulsion literally "shakes itself apart." This somewhat startling statement can easily be validated by an analysis of the effects of puberty, which, in the physiological sense, is clearly a product of maturation. Our society more or less takes it for granted that puberty will cause considerable emotional upheavals which, in extreme cases, may trigger delinquency or the onset of an adolescent schizophrenia. We are so deeply imbued with the feeling that puberty—which objectively is nothing more than the opening up of a new range of potentialities clamoring for actualization—is necessarily a stormy period that even anthropologists often fail to point out that in a great many societies puberty does not appear to be in any way a stressful and socially difficult period. The inference seems inescapable that whereas the *fact* of puberty, seen as a biological event, is simply a broadening of the organism's potentialities, the *storminess* of puberty is chiefly a culturally determined phenomenon.

THE MANAGEMENT OF PUBERTY

There appear to exist at least three major social techniques for the successful management of puberty.

1. The simplest and most obvious is to allow puberty to coincide with the onset of sexual life. In such cases the newly developed potentialities are given a suitable and socially approve

organismal outlet and therefore cause only minimal intrapsychic and social stresses and problems.

2. The second procedure consists in granting a socially recognized and approved outlet to the intrapsychic conflicts arising from biological frustrations. The classic example is the social recognition granted to the neuroticism of youths tormented by the onset of puberty. Tribes choosing this solution define the pubescent youth's quest for solitude, and his emotional upheavals and hysterical and/or schizoid behavior as the initial manifestations of budding shamanistic powers. In this instance the "storminess" is, in a way, present but is systematically socialized and exploited for the benefit of society. It is not simply neutralized and made harmless but is actually made to serve socially constructive ends.

Even our own society knew, once upon a time, that the readjustments and neuroticisms of puberty are susceptible—occasionally at least—of producing socially valuable art or at least enthusiasm. Hence, it gave a kind of grudging admiration to the emotionally immature bohemianism of youth, even when it refused to take it seriously. Thus, a Hungarian proverb states: "The more violently the grape juice ferments, the better will be the wine." Another European proverb preaches the same lesson: "Anyone who at fourteen is not a radical has no heart, and anyone who at forty is not a conservative has no brains." Our contemporaries have shown themselves less wise in the management of the young. By withdrawing recognition from his neurotic individualism, they drive the adolescent into the shallow conformism of juvenile delinquency, which is the adolescent rebellion of mass man.[1] The remedy for juvenile delinquency is not a bigger baseball park or more dances. The remedy is social recognition granted to youth's quest for individuality, which implies that the writing of even bad poetry must be more highly valued socially than a sixty-yard run

[1] Almost, but not quite the same, conclusion was reached also by Lindner. Cf. *Time,* December 6, 1954.

on the gridiron. The answer to juvenile delinquency is not PAL (Police Athletic League) but Mozart and Keats. Unfortunately, before this answer can become effective, society too will have to change some of its values.

3. The third solution consists in a kind of "prophylactic maneuver." Its pivot is the initiation rite of puberty. The effect of such rites seems to be twofold: (a) The ritual itself serves to "bind" the emotional and instinctual "push," in the same manner in which obsessive rituals help keep intrapsychic problems under control (*44, 89*). (b) The ritual clearly marks a change in social status, so that the initiated youth finds a whole area of new social outlets for his energies, which, to some extent, divert his attention from the problems created by his budding sexual impulse. Thus, even though Jewish youths do not marry at the age of thirteen, the ritual of the *Bar mitzvah* marks their transformation from boys into men, with all that this transition entails in terms of social, and especially of religious, obligations and rights. In fact, we suspect— without being dogmatic about it—that the relatively new phenomenon of Jewish juvenile delinquency has some relationship to the decreased emotional and functional significance of being a man from the religious point of view after the onset of puberty. We suppose that the Jewish child-rearing techniques and the Jewish way of life which these techniques express are such that unless they culminate in the transition rite of the *Bar mitzvah*— experienced as a deeply significant event—they cannot keep the pubescent Jewish boy on an even keel. The recent decrease in the emotional and functional significance of the *Bar mitzvah* and of ritual manhood is, of course, closely related to the increasing acculturation and secularization of Jewish life in the contemporary world.[2]

When society refuses to use any and all of the three techniques

---

[2] This explanation is, of course, incomplete. Another (supplementary) explanation of Jewish juvenile delinquency will be found in Chapter 9.

just listed for the socialization of the maturational phenomenon of puberty, the process of maturation, denied creative functional outlets, becomes both subjectively and socially destructive.

HUMANIZATION AND CULTURE

In this sense, then, humanization, which is connected with the possession of Culture, *per se,* but *not* with the possession of any *one* culture *in particular,* is more than an achievement. It is, as we stressed above, also—and perhaps even primarily—a fulfillment. Indeed, one of the central themes of this book is that many of the traditional defects of conventional education are directly related to society's failure to view techniques of humanization as ways to self-fulfillment instead of as means simply enabling one to reach "the next stage." They are means of self-realization and not merely of achievement. They are the road to selfhood and not simply to group membership. They are the means whereby one may attain that *creative uniqueness* which should be, but seldom is, the most obvious manifestation of man's fundamental nature. Needless to say, this view is closely related to the theories of John Dewey.

We are still a long way from viewing education as a road to humanization. This is revealed by the recurrent, and completely fallacious, attempt to contrast individualization and socialization. Yet, as MacIver (160) pointed out, maximum individualization and maximum socialization form an indissoluble unity, each presupposing the other and impossible without it. Indeed, no human being would be able to achieve maximum individualization, i.e., the most complete unfolding of his distinctive human potentialities, without the guidance and opportunities offered to him by society. In order to illustrate this point, which is the central theme of Gray's "Elegy in a Country Churchyard," we need only think of the predictable frustrations of a Mozart born into a Central Australian tribe. Conversely, society can derive a maximum benefit only from those individuals who are completely individualized, i.e., who were helped and permitted to actualize and to fulfill most completely their inherent human potentialities. This, perhaps, is the most telling argument against the cult of conformity, regardless of whether it assumes the form of a totalitarian *Gleichschaltung* or of a demand for automatic conformity backed by the pressure of public opinion. The suppression and penalization of individual differences and of spontaneity, which are the end results of the full functioning of human beings, are always deleterious. As stressed elsewhere (50) it is destructively and self-destructively easy and unproductive to sanction and to socialize only uniformities. This leads only to a general degradation of social performance and to a reduction of individual efficiency to the lowest common denominator. Socially and culturally creative socialization consists in the far more challenging and infinitely more rewarding attempt to *socialize differences* and also the end products of individualization and differentiation. This *"socialization of the unique"* is the most creative—and also the simplest—function of a healthy society. It requires, to take a homely example, nothing more than assigning to Mozart the task of writing music, for which he is uniquely and distinctively endowed, instead of forcing him to be a ditchdigger because, like other people, he too has hands which can grasp a spade. Expressed this way, the proposition seems almost naïvely simple, since musical genius is a kind of uniqueness which is generally—and therefore, alas, only lackadaisically—approved of by society. The real scope and real challenge of our thesis becomes apparent only when—to paraphrase Justice Holmes—a person's individualization and differentiation are of a more controversial character.

Many thinkers recognized the creative, catalytic, seminal—and highly irritating—role of the alleged "crank." Of course, in everyday situations the *homme de tout repos*—the average man who performs in an average manner—is much more to the liking of the crowd. Hence society is so structured as to favor the average person and to place the fewest obstacles in the path of those whose uniqueness is minimal. Thus, Linton (*151*) rightly stresses that most social roles can be adequately filled by almost anyone. This does not mean, of course, that these roles were "deliberately" so constructed as to fit mediocrity and to minimize commotions of all kinds. Rather is this a result of the *degradation* of established social roles. Today the blacksmith or the salesman is likely to be a very average man, though the "first" blacksmiths and the "first" merchants were probably highly imaginative and inventive "cranks." An echo of this state of affairs still lingers in many primitive societies. In some primitive groups the smith is, to this day, an exceptional person, either in the positive or in the negative sense. Thus, though in some African tribes the smiths are almost pariahs, they are also credited with important magical knowledge. In other societies the smith is a highly esteemed specialist. The traveling salesman is an almost comical figure among ourselves, but Mbra:o, the old chief of the Sedang Moi village of Tea Ha, who, in his youth, had traded far afield, was credited with the possession of a magical root that enabled him to undertake adventurous and successful trading expeditions into faraway countries. Only when a craft reaches its limits—at least temporarily— does the craft role become stabilized and accessible to mediocrities. Thus, it is hard to realize that today's journalist or writer of magazine short stories is a lineal descendant of Homer or of the Norse singers, who enjoyed a fabulous prestige, performed important social functions, and were practically immune to violence, even in the midst of a brutally savage society, where murder and warfare were minor pastimes. In fact, the relative immunity of "the fourth estate" may well be a distant echo of the immunity of the Greek herald.

It can be argued, of course, that all social roles must be so constructed as to fit the average man, because exceptional men are not always available.[3] This argument is both true and false. It is certainly desirable that important routine functions, such as the making of plows or shoes, should be susceptible of being performed by average men, who constitute the majority of the population. What is deleterious is the contamination of exceptional types of functions by the cult of mediocrity to the point where even social roles calling for unique abilities are often reserved for conformists. This policy was challenged more than 2000 years ago by the Chinese Emperor Han Wu Ti, in an Imperial Rescript worthy of being quoted in full: "Exceptional work demands exceptional men. A bolting or kicking horse may eventually become a most valuable animal. A man who is the object of the world's detestation may live to accomplish great things. As with an intractable horse, so with the unscrupulous man—it is simply a question of controlling. We therefore command the various district officials to search for men of brilliant and exceptional talents, to be OUR generals, OUR ministers, and OUR envoys to distant States" (*111*).[4]

This proclamation is perhaps the most creative and positive affirmation of the social value of individualization and humanization. Its only shortcoming is that it fails to specify that all work is exceptional—or should be, in order to be well done. Indeed, if the various climactic moments in the history of mankind have one characteristic in common, it is the skill with which, and extent to which, individualization was socialized, and differences rather than conformities harnessed to social ends at such times. This is the greatest "common denominator" of Pericles' Athens, Lorenzo de' Medici's Florence, Elizabethan England, etc.

A further point to be made is that even where the routinization of some role or function calls only for average performance, this

---

[3] This is far from true. In times of crisis, there often appear on the social scene competent functional leaders, though, unfortunately, at such times society usually prefers to follow psychopathic "charismatic leaders" (*60*).

[4] The approximate date of this rescript is 140 B.C.

does not imply that, e.g., the assembly-line workers must also be deindividualized in private life and must forgo all self-realization and individualization in every other area of his existence as well. What may be functional conformity on the assembly line may, when transferred to ordinary living, become mere dry rot, undermining the foundations of the healthy personality. We suspect that much rebelliousness, which is nominally directed at occupational or situational routine, is but a displacement of man's revolt against outside attempts to level the inner core of his personality. This is a point to which we will repeatedly return in this book.

The one crucial addition to this thesis which remains to be made is the recognition that maximum individualization and maximum differentiation are creatively socializable at *both extremes* of the scale. We hold that society can benefit not only by the *greatness* of Phryne's beauty, of Aeschylus' genius, of Bayard's valor, or of "honest Abe" Lincoln's integrity. It can benefit also by the *smallness* of the "widow's mite," which the "has not," the emotionally inhibited, and the defective has to offer, and which is one of his chief means of being differentiated and of being individualized.[5] One example suffices to prove this point: Many employers know that certain positions are best filled by the intellectually marginal, who not only find self-fulfillment and satisfaction in occupations which would frustrate normal persons but, at the same time, leave the better endowed available for more challenging positions which fulfill and satisfy their need for (superior) achievement. In addition, such an employment policy also lightens the burden which the existence of the unused—and therefore often ill used—defective imposes on society. In this respect Kanner's "defense of the feebleminded" is well worth a second thought (*130*). This too is a point which will consistently preoccupy us in this book.

[5] Many religions hold that one contribution which those needing alms make to society is the opportunity they provide for others to perform charitable actions.

Throughout the preceding pages we equated "humanization" with the acquisition of Culture *per se,* though not with the acquisition of a particular *kind* of culture. In a sense, we treated "Culture" and the *distinctively human* make-up of man's psyche as two aspects of one and the same phenomenon and, possibly, as co-emergents. It is therefore desirable to formulate somewhat more precisely the basic interrelatedness of these two manifestations of man's humanity (55).

CULTURE AS A CHARACTERISTIC HUMAN TRAIT

In the following discussion we differentiate between *homo sapiens* (*genus homo*) as a biological organism and *man* as a human being.

Homo sapiens is the current end product of an evolutionary process toward a high degree of differentiation and individualization. The principal and uniquely characteristic trait of *homo sapiens*—the "constant of human nature"—is his extreme plasticity and the variability of his behavior.

The aforementioned four characteristics of *genus homo*—differentiation, individualization, plasticity, and variability of behavior—represent a unitary biological potentiality, which is actualized in the acquisition of a distinctively human psyche and of culture.

The possession of a human psyche, and culture are uniquely characteristic of man and further stimulate and expand *homo sapiens'* biologically determined tendency toward differentiation, individualization, plasticity, and variability of behavior.

Although the human psyche and culture are the resultants of a biological potentiality, whose actualization they represent, neither the human psyche nor culture may be thought of as *biological* characteristics of *genus homo*. They must be thought of as distinctively *human* characteristics of *man*.

The human psyche and culture are methodologically and functionally inseparable concepts.

Since culture represents an actualization of a basic biological potentiality of *genus homo,* whenever man functions as a "creator, creature, manipulator, and carrier" (*199*) of culture he satisfies one of his most fundamental needs, which cannot be frustrated without dire consequences for the human psyche and for man's status as a human being. This is cogently demonstrated by Davis' (*25*) study of a girl deprived more or less completely of cultural experiences.[6]

The "culturalization" of man is contingent upon, and is a resultant of, the replacing of the direct and massive manifestation of biological impulses—and especially of aggressive rather than of erotic impulses—by plastic, economical, and accurately context- and goal-adapted behavior. Such behavior has a high survival value and is in conformity with *homo sapiens'* biological potentialities for differentiation and individualization. In other words, *homo sapiens,* in actualizing and in implementing his biological potentialities for differentiated, individualized, plastic, and variable behavior, acquires the status of man and functions as a human being.

It is an illusion that culture constricts behavior. If culture constricted behavior, then culture would not actualize but destroy *homo sapiens'* biological potentialities for differentiation, individualization, plasticity, and variability of behavior, so that the human being possessed of culture would be more *homo sapiens* than *man,* which is obviously a fallacy. In reality culture expands the scope, range, variability, efficiency, and appropriateness of behavior by substituting for massive and impulse-determined motility and affect discharge a partial, specific, and goal-and-context-determined motility and affect discharge.

The cultural frame of reference enables the observer to "structure"—i.e., to understand, control, and predict—the behavior of

---

[6] In so far as any reliance may be placed upon reports of so-called "wolf children" in India, these data also support the views just expressed (*163, 201, 202*).

normal persons. The psychoanalytic frame of reference enables the observer to "structure"—in the above sense—the behavior of abnormal persons.[7]

ETHNICIZATION

We understood by "humanization" the culturally facilitated, but also culturally neutral, unfolding of man's inherent human capacities. This process is thought of as being comparable to domestication. Its manifestations range anywhere from the acquisition of speech *per se*, etc., to high degrees of individualization and differentiation whose precise form is, in that context, deliberately left undefined. By "ethnicization" we refer to an area of controlled and directed experience whose manifest purpose is to polarize, orient, and mold these *a priori* neutral, and articulated but unoriented, capacities, in a particular manner, which is adapted to, and oriented with reference to, the prevailing culture pattern. The process of ethnicization can, thus, be viewed as a process of *directed choice,* causing, e.g., the individual moving toward humanization to express himself—and he must express himself or perish!—either in English or in Hottentot, to point—and point he must!—with his finger as we do or with his lips as a Kiowa does (*145*), etc. Broadly speaking, the categories of channels through which the humanized individual must seek outlets, self-expression, self-fulfillment, and individualization are, by and large, the same in every place. These basic channels correspond, on one level, to what the French sociological school calls *"les catégories de l'esprit humain"* (*165*), to what Bastian has labeled *"Elementargedanken"* (*11*), to Freud's concept of the universal and fundamental uniformity of the human mind, to what Wissler (*233*) sought to translate into cultural terms by calling it "the universal culture pattern"—but not to what Jung obfuscated, through an inability to

[7] This formulation is in accordance with Mach's cautious dictum that there are no laws in nature apart from those which we put into, or ascribe to, nature in the course of our attempts to generalize from our observations of discrete phenomena.

think logically, by the "concept" of archetypes. The *existence* of such categories or channels is the basis of the *humanization* process. Their culturally determined concrete "shape" and "direction" are the basis of the *ethnicization* process.

It is noteworthy that Kroeber (*144*) confessed his inability to do anything with the concept of a universal culture pattern and asserted that the same was true even of Wissler, who had evolved this concept. In our view, this is due to the fact that both of these anthropologists made the mistake of treating the "universal culture pattern" in culturological rather than in psychological terms. Both failed to realize that essentially the same concept—that of *"les catégories de l'esprit humain"*—proved highly fruitful in the hands of the psychologically oriented French sociological school. In fact, these categories of the human mind are the basic structural elements of both culture and the human psyche, and the very foundations of man's humanity. Indeed, culture is a phenomenon which is not only *sui generis* but also implies and presupposes the human mind—and vice versa of course. Thus, on the one hand, these basic categories of man's functioning are the means whereby man humanizes himself, and, on the other hand, they are indispensable for the analysis of any given concrete culture. This latter point is readily proved by the table of contents of any standard ethnographic field report.

The preceding considerations do not imply that the universal culture pattern should be used in a reductionist manner, i.e., as a means of transforming social science into psychology, though it can, of course, be misused that way. In our view, it should be used in a non-reductionistic manner, especially in the analysis of any particular culture in cultural terms. There is nothing methodologically unusual in this view. That which is *content* and *subject matter* on a more fundamental level can, when properly understood, often lend itself to being used as a *classificatory* or *categorizational device* on a less fundamental level. In the same sense, instincts are subject matter and content in biology but are classificatory devices and categories in the analysis of psychological phenomena, which are the subject matter and content of psychology.[8]

It is also important to realize that these channels are quite broad, even within the framework of a particular culture. Hence, culturally acceptable behavior does not necessarily imply a constriction of man's potentialities. It is possible to write good poetry both in English and in Chinese, and raising fine reindeer can be as satisfying as raising prize cattle. Even cultural taboos seldom narrow down the choice to only one possibility, and when this does happen, society usually provides also some means for circumventing the taboo. Thus, in a small Australian tribe, where a complex kinship system greatly restricts an individual's choice of a mate, when a given person cannot find a permissible mate he can resort to a traditional way of getting a "forbidden" mate, without having to suffer serious consequences (224). In fact, the existence and importance of cultural alternatives was specifically recognized by Linton (151). We may therefore say that whereas the acquisition of a particular culture preselects to a certain extent the channels through which man may actualize himself and may gratify his basic needs, in most instances these channels are sufficiently broad, and contain a large enough number of alternatives, not to cripple man psychologically. This point will be discussed in some detail in Chapter 4.

In brief, whereas humanization involves man's acquisition of the essence of cultural behavior and the generalized capacity to attain self-realization by cultural means, ethnicization actually provides him with a battery of means suitable for attaining these goals.

Education fosters simultaneously man's humanization and the

---

[8] A failure to understand this led, in certain approaches to psychoanalysis, to a naïvely biologizing and neurologizing psychiatry.

acquisition of the capacity to use cultural means for self-realization. By teaching the child symbolically—in the form of a "pre-experience"—that which it has not yet experienced in reality, education decreases the impact of new experiences upon the psyche, thus enabling the individual to respond to them with greater specificity and with a greater economy of effort. Above all, it enables man to respond to new reality in a creative and subtly individualized manner. By contrast, mere training or drilling mediates to the individual only crude means for survival, but fails to promote in any way the unfolding of his potentialities as a human being through cultural means. The contrast between creative education and sterilizing training will be one of the major themes of this work.   42159

....

CHAPTER 2

A Historical Sketch of the Nature and Scope of Education

A functional discussion of therapeutic education requires that we view it within the framework of education in general, and as a special development thereof. This necessitates at least a cursory sketch of trends in the development of education, from the viewpoint of social and cultural history. It cannot be our purpose to present here an exhaustive history of education. Rather do we propose to link certain distinctive characteristics of therapeutic education with certain aspects of education in general, some of which are old, while some are extremely modern, though the latter often only represent a return to the sound practices of early times. Furthermore, since our main purpose here is to trace the background of the constituent elements of therapeutic education, we will survey separately the development of three major aspects of the educational process: instruction, indoctrination, and education in the broad sense, viewing the latter as a creative synthesis of the first two. We propose to approach the problem of the nature of education by contrasting "instruction" with "indoctrination."

INSTRUCTION

This word denotes the teaching of certain specialized techniques, either with or without reference to the conceptual framework which forms the theoretical basis of these techniques. We can differentiate between three types of instruction, in terms of the extent to which cognizance is taken of the theoretical background of the skills taught.

1. The training of an automobile mechanic often involves almost no teaching of the principles of physics and is restricted to the transmission of certain purely manipulative skills, and of craft lore or "technical know-how." This type of instruction more or less corresponds to rote learning, except in so far as the spatial and functional relationship between the various parts of an automobile itself serves as a "unifying framework" of a concrete and non-conceptual kind.

2. The training of an automotive engineer usually involves both the teaching of some basic physical principles and the transmission of craft lore and of "technical know-how." However, the conceptual framework taught to engineers corresponds primarily to what Henri Poincaré called "mechanical models," rather than to what he termed "conceptual schemes." Furthermore, this knowledge is not imparted for its own sake, but solely as a means for increasing the effectiveness of manipulations of the "applied science" type.

3. The training of a physicist consists essentially in the transmission of a "conceptual scheme," with little or no reference to craft lore and technical skills. In principle, all of the knowledge is imparted "for its own sake," i.e., for the promotion of "pure science."

We cannot, in this context, undertake to discuss in detail the manner in which craft lore gradually expands into an independent body of principles, corresponding at first to a set of mechanical models (or else to geometrical approaches to problems of pure mathematics) and later on to a conceptual scheme.[1] We may,

---

[1] The orientation of the various national cultures appears to influence even physical scientists. Thus, Henri Poincaré, called "the Prince of Mathematicians," stated that French and German scientists were interested chiefly in conceptual

however, indicate at least in passing that one reason why social scientists find it so difficult to differentiate effectively between "culture" and "civilization" is that they usually fail to grasp the essential nature of the contrast between "pure science" and "technology"—or, to be more precise, between "conceptual schemes" and "craft lore." Hence, though a good many social scientists have discussed the contrast between "culture" and "civilization" in these terms, the only one who tackled this problem with any real consistency is Kroeber (144)—and even his analysis is not wholly satisfactory.

We called the three types of teaching described in the preceding paragraphs "instruction" rather than "education," because the information imparted to the student is fundamentally neutral in terms of the generally prevailing *value system* of our society. Indeed, in instruction of this type even the genuine "value" of simply "knowing something" for its own sake is more or less taken for granted. Thus, it is fairly safe to say that instruction in the physical sciences seldom includes a definition of the role of automobile mechanics, automotive engineers, or physicists in society, or a discussion of the social relevance of their professional acts and discoveries.[2] Even the professional code of most occupations and professions seldom forms a part of the curriculum. In most cases the student is not taught formally either an intraprofessional code

---

schemes, whereas English scientists were inclined to think in terms of more concrete mechanical models. A good example of these two types of orientation is the difference between the early Rutherford-Bohr model of the atom, which one could visualize as a miniature solar system, and the purely conceptual approach to the structure of the atom, which found an interesting expression in Dirac's famous remark that the electron is a differential equation. Similarly, some twenty years ago Jaffe could state that physical science in America was so practical and concrete in its outlook that, even though this country had produced some celebrated experimentalists, only two or three Americans could be called genuine theoretical or mathematical physicists (123). Even as late as the 1940's a very large proportion of the theoreticians whose work made the atom bomb and the hydrogen bomb possible were Europeans: Bethe, Fermi, von Neumann, Szilárd, Teller, etc.

[2] This may explain the agonizing soul searching of atomic scientists after Hiroshima (198).

of ethics or the ethics of his chosen profession in its relation to "society as a client." This is particularly true of those professions which are primarily focused on material objects, though even such "man centered" professions as psychology and anthropology evolved only recently something like a professional code. The one conspicuous exception to this rule is the physician's Hippocratic Oath. We suspect, however, that even the continued sway of this fine and durable code may be attributed primarily to the fact that —despite the early differentiation between Hippocratic (scientific) and Aesculapian ("shamanistic") medicine—the contemporary scientific physician is, in relation to his patients and to the community, in more ways than one a descendant of the primitive healing priest or magician. This is a point of which many thoughtful physicians are fully aware. Thus, John L. Bach, press chief of the American Medical Association, recently declared that the physician "thinks that in order to keep his patient's confidence, he must live up to a superhuman role, and build the illusion that medicine is an exact science and doctors are infallible."[3] Even the psychoanalyst is often tempted to let his patient foist upon him the mantle of supernatural—i.e., magical—wisdom (56, 222). In both of these cases the superhuman pose is made possible not by a recognition of the inherent achievements and potentialities of science but by an often unconscious exploitation of the (nonscientific, though not necessarily also unscientific) social and cultural prestige value of science.

In short, in our terminology "instruction" denotes exclusively the teaching of theories, craft lore, and techniques, relevant only in terms of the body of knowledge and operations which constitute a given discipline, skill, or science, and with little or no reference to the position of that discipline within our culture as a whole, or to the cultural—and not only socioeconomic—relevance of that skill for society as a whole.

[3] *Time,* January 31, 1955, p. 41.

HISTORY OF INSTRUCTION

It is fairly easy to trace the history of instruction in the narrowest sense of the term. Broadly speaking, in primitive society most persons—or at least most families, taken as a unit—are jacks-of-all-trades, and, indeed, must be jacks-of-all-trades since, in a relatively undeveloped technology, no man can produce enough surplus of one type to enable him to barter it for another man's different kind of surplus, particularly where basic staples are concerned. Thus, among the Sedang Moi of Indo-China, the medicine man and the smith—and, to a lesser extent, the trader—are the only specialists, and even they practice their specialty only intermittently or seasonally, and are paid for their work mostly in the form of "luxury items" or "treasure," such as Chinese jars. The rest of the time they work in the fields like everyone else and produce their own food and clothing.

At this stage of development, the parent can usually teach his child everything the child needs for its survival. Hence, instruction tends to take place entirely within the bosom of the family, supplemented to a certain extent by informal instruction within the children's play group or work group.[4]

At a later stage of development, characterized by a more complex technology and by the production of reliably predictable surpluses, true specialization and a basic division of labor, which differs from that obtaining within the family on the basis of sex or age, comes into being. Indeed, no primitive individual is really a jack-of-all-trades in the strict sense of the term, since—though most primitive men more or less know how to cook and most primitive women may, in a pinch, knock over a small kangaroo (188)—there always is some kind of division of labor even within the primitive family. Hence, strictly speaking, the autarkic

---

[4] The role of such groups in the socialization of the child is discussed in Chapters 9 and 10.

unit, and the real "jack-of-all-trades," is not the individual but the family. By contrast, in a true and basic division of labor one individual devotes most, or all, of his energies to one craft or trade, partly because the exercise of that trade produces a reliable and steady surplus and partly because it is so complicated that constant practice is needed to perform it properly. At this stage of development the whole instruction of the child can no longer take place within the bosom of the family. If the child is to learn a special craft, he must often be apprenticed to a specialist, who may be an outsider. For example, when the Maori began to develop their mythology, genealogical science, and magic beyond a certain point, they had to establish schools for the future practitioners of these specialties (16). This, in turn, often leads to appreciable difficulties between the school and the family, which will be discussed in some detail in a later section of this chapter.

INDOCTRINATION

The other extreme, or pole, of teaching is a technique commonly described as *indoctrination,* which we define as the *teaching of social techniques,* with special reference to the characteristic value system of a given society or segment thereof. Actually, indoctrination proper was originally an attempt to adapt a given individual to some specific and self-contained phase of culture: adult life, a cult, a secret society, etc. The indoctrinator took an already ethnicized person, i.e., a full-fledged Englishman or Sioux Indian, and caused him to specialize for the occupancy of a certain status and the performance of a certain role. The current manifestations of this original type of indoctrination are such phenomena as the teaching of a catechism or the indoctrination courses of the armed forces.

THE SIZE OF SOCIETY

The systematic indoctrination of man as a citizen or member of society is, in a sense, a late development. We do not mean, of

course, that the primitive child is not taught by his elders to respect public opinion and to do his part for the welfare of society as
a whole. The point we seek to make is that a *systematic* concern
with man as a "political animal"[5] is a relatively advanced development. Thus, students of Greek intellectual history have pointed
out that, before Socrates, philosophers were more interested in
natural science than in the problem of man as a social, cultural,
and moral being. This may be due to the fact that such a preoccupation becomes necessary only after there is a loosening of
the emotional bonds which hold primitive society together and
insure the loyalty of the primitive to his society and its way of life
(35).[6]

More recently, society developed an interest in systematically
fostering the indoctrination of its citizens in regard to the meaning
of their culture and also in connection with their duties as citizens.
It is quite probable that this phenomenon is a result of a radical
social change.

In the first place, as long as the citizen knows only his own
tribal way of life, and has no outside allegiances, primary affective
loyalties and habits usually suffice to keep him loyal to his group
and its way of life, without his even having to become explicitly
aware of it. Thus, conscious nationalism is so rare among some
primitives that Kroeber (*142*) explicitly stressed how unusual the Mohave Indian's sense of nationality was for a south-
eastern Californian tribe.[7] Thus, the expansion of a society beyond

[5] The expression *zoön politikon* was coined by Aristotle and is usually translated
as "political animal," though Kitto suggests (*138*) that it means primarily an animal whose nature it is to dwell in the city (*polis*).
[6] Socrates and Plato lived at a time when the cohesion of the Greek *polis* began
to decline, and it is not without significance that Socrates, who may be called the
first student of man-as-citizen, was condemned as a "subversive."
[7] Obviously Kroeber did not imply that primitives lacked loyalty to their village
or small group, and that the Mohave differed from their neighbors solely in that
their loyalty belonged not only to the local settlement but to the tribe as a whole.
Rather does he appear to have emphasized the conscious conceptualization of this
loyalty. It is possible, of course, that the need for conceptualizations of this type
arises only when person-to-person affective commitments no longer suffice to hold
society together, simply because society has become too large to enable every citizen

the point where each person can feel a personal sense of obligation to every other citizen, automatically requires a formal indoctrination in tribal allegiances, lest society should fall apart.

CULTURAL CHANGE

The second type of situation which necessitates the systematic indoctrination of the citizen results from major shifts in the orientation of culture. Thus, when there is a mass conversion to some new religion or political philosophy, requiring a rearrangement of the previously existing patterns of loyalties and a reassigning of some persons who were previously members of the ingroup to the outgroup, a systematic indoctrination of the people in the new way of life and in the new pattern of allegiances is almost unavoidable. Thus, to take a current example, in war-torn Indo-China some sects are almost more loyal to their religion and to their priests than they are to Viet Nam, which is their country, and therefore function not only as a religious body but also as a primary political unit, with distinctive loyalties and interests. In some cases this repatterning of loyalties can even go to injudicious extremes. Thus, various members of a certain mission were rightly critical of the fanaticism of one of their group who, after converting the younger members of a primitive village, forced them to eject from it their own aged parents and relatives, who had remained "obdurate" and refused to become converted.

---

to have a personal commitment to every other citizen. In this context it is noteworthy that Greek political thinkers held that in the *ideal* city every citizen should know every other citizen at least by sight. Of course, membership in a nonlocalized clan or kin group can temporarily "pinch hit" for personal commitments, in that it enables a person living in village X to feel a sense of personal obligation or commitment to a fellow member of his clan, living in village Y, whom he never met in person. Such clan loyalties may even transcend tribal boundaries—for example, when the same gens exists in several, politically distinct, tribes. Thus, since Australian gentes are often not limited to one tribe only, almost the first question which an Australian will ask from a chance-met stranger is: "What is your gens?" He does this in order to ascertain whether he has formal positive and negative (incest taboo) obligations toward the tribal alien.

NATURALIZATION

In recent times there came into being also a system of indoctrinating divergently ethnicized aliens with the prevailing culture pattern of their country of adoption. This new type of indoctrination is patterned upon earlier and more segmental types of indoctrination and is exemplified by the course of study which aliens applying for American citizenship have to pursue. In fact, these applicants must learn things about the Constitution and the history of the United States which some uneducated native-born Americans do not know, because they never attended classes in "civics." It is felt, however, that such specific knowledge is not absolutely indispensable to the native-born citizen because—having lived all his life in America and never having been differently ethnicized—he can play the American way of life almost "by ear."[8]

EDUCATION

Education, in the broadest sense of the term, is a creative integration of instruction and indoctrination. Where the instructor teaches—at least in principle—only techniques and the craft lore or theoretical frame of reference underlying these techniques, and where the indoctrinator is chiefly interested in the inculcation of the group's way of life, and of loyalty to that way of life, the educator not only instructs his charges but also indoctrinates them, with regard to both the social and cultural import of the subject matter of his instruction and to the ethos of the culture in general.

ANTIQUITY OF EDUCATION

Strange as it may seem, education proper antedates historically both narrow instruction and narrow indoctrination. Indeed, on the primitive level, education consists in the systematic and rela-

[8] Whether or not the courses designed for, and the knowledge required from, prospective American citizens are truly effective means of Americanization does not concern us here. We simply state that the basic philosophy underlying these requirements is sound.

tional inculcation both of specific techniques and the conceptual schemes pertaining to them and of the cultural value system which forms their matrix. As used here, the term "relational inculcation" means that objective knowledge and the social relevance of that knowledge are transmitted in the course of a single, indivisible educational act. In brief, to a large extent the differentiation between "instruction" and "indoctrination" is almost inapplicable to primitive society. Thus, the Plains Indian youth who is taught archery is told, at the same time, that his skill as a hunter has a social function and will be given social recognition, and the Mohave Indian girl who reaches puberty is, in the same breath, enlightened both about the "facts of life" and about the ethics of being a woman (44). The fact that the Greek smith was a devotee of the god Hephaestus was more than a convenient and aesthetic fiction. It also served to relate both his work and his products to the basic ethos of Greek culture.

This type of education was possible only as long as one and the same person—who was usually the parent—was competent to teach both the principles of a craft and its relevance for living in society.

The attitudinal component of a given technique was further strengthened by the fact that the child who is instructed by its parent is, at the same time, enabled to identify with its parent. Thus, the little Sedang Moi girl, who takes care of her baby brother, fetches water and wood, and cooks the family dinner, feels that she is "just like her mother," while the Sedang boy, laboring near his father in the fields and weaving baskets at his side, can identify with him. At a higher level of technology this becomes impossible, at least on a realistic level.

Case 1: Spurious Imitation

The writer recalls that, in his childhood, he tried to imitate his father, who was a lawyer, by taking obsolete legal blanks from his father's office, filling them out with fictitious data, and conducting imaginary lawsuits. However, he remained painfully aware of the fact that his "legal" games did not contribute to the maintenance of the household and were of no help to his father. By contrast, the primitive child's attempts to imitate its parent are economically productive and therefore enable it to identify more effectively with that parent.

FAMILY VS. EDUCATOR

The moment the instruction of the child is delegated to a specialist, an important development takes place, which transcends in scope the narrow limits of instruction in a specialty. Indeed, the primitive technical expert not only is the objective practitioner of a skill or craft but also has a whole series of professional values and rites related to the practice of his craft. Hence, technical instruction is inevitably accompanied also by a type of indoctrination which is sometimes at variance with the ideology of the pupil's own family and leads to a split or dual identification—with the parents on the one hand and with the teacher on the other hand— which parents sometimes find hard to accept or even to tolerate.

A striking example of this type of split allegiance is the type of training to which "apprentice sorcerers" are subjected in some primitive groups. In many areas there are secret societies of witches, which not only teach the "technique" of magic but also inculcate in the future magician a series of attitudes and loyalties which may be at variance with the ideology and practical interests of the apprentice sorcerer's own family. In some areas the apprentice witch does not really acquire supernatural magical powers until he pays for them by letting a member of his own family be bewitched. Certain tribes even specify that the first victim of the apprentice sorcerer be usually a member of his own family (28).

Little wonder, then, that even the primitive parent may sometimes attempt to force his child's educator to function exclusively as an instructor. Thus, in some backward areas an enlightened chief may send his son to a mission school but insist that the missionaries only instruct him, and refrain from indoctrinating him as well. In fact, we suspect that one reason for the rise of "objective" and "non-valuative" instruction, and even of "pure science" as a distinct phenomenon, may be the pressure which families put on educators who are "outsiders," and whose ideology differs from their own, to provide only instruction devoid of all ideological and attitudinal connotations such as characterize education in the bosom of the family.

In brief, the extrafamilial education received by the child is often at variance with family cohesion and family interests. The traditional antagonism between the family and the teacher is, thus, an ancient one and plays a tremendous role in the history of education. One obvious, though indirect, manifestation of this antagonism is the eternal "town and gown" problem of many of our university towns. In the Middle Ages this problem was temporarily resolved by placing students under the exclusive civil and criminal jurisdiction of the university itself.[9] By contrast, in our own day and age society and the family seek to control the ideological orientation of educational centers and also attempt to reconcile educators and parents by means of Parent-Teacher Association meetings. The problem of relations with the families of students is of major importance also to special residential schools for exceptional children.

DOMINANCE OF THE FAMILY

In this contest between family and educators it is often the family which has the last word, partly because of certain historical facts which form the background of Occidental education. In

---

[9] *Time,* February 21, 1955, p. 56, contains an account of a recent settling of 600-year-old differences between the city of Oxford and the University. The reconciliation was symbolized by the granting of the freedom of the city to the Vice Chancellor of the University, and the bestowal of an honorary degree upon the Mayor of the City.

Rome, which is the fountainhead of many of our formal social institutions, teachers were often Greek slaves or, at the most, Greek tutors, whose "social mass" (30)—or what Army slang calls "squawking power"—was appreciably inferior to that of the parents. This Greek tutor was, in the civic sense, an "outsider," who was expected to teach the young Roman gentleman Greek wisdom but not to transform him into an effete *"Graeculus otiosus."*[10]

In the high Middle Ages the prestige of the teacher was somewhat greater because of the halo of supernatural power which surrounded the monk and the secular priest, though even then the house chaplain—being often an inferior cleric—was more or less treated as a dependent. By contrast, the universities enjoyed a relatively high prestige. In countries where universities were formerly in the hands of ecclesiastics, the university teacher continues to enjoy high prestige, though—also in accordance with ecclesiastical precedent—not necessarily also a high salary. Thus, in England eminent scholars are knighted and in France university professors often become members of the cabinet. But in countries where the universities are of more recent origin and follow the German pattern the professor is often treated as a kind of menial. It is said that in Imperial Germany a mere lieutenant could force a professor to step off the sidewalk and in America the professor is often called "a long-hair" or an "egghead" and—as a bitter academic wit once put it—"occupies a position one step above that of a minister and one step below that of a bootlegger." Only in recent years has the professor begun to "talk back" (158).

The Western world resorted to a variety of means to stave off a "real showdown" about extrafamilial education, with all it involved in terms of ideological differences between family and school.

One of these means was the previously referred to technique of

[10] An idle little Greek, i.e., a sponger.

assigning the technical education of young gentlemen to tutors who were menials or even slaves, and whose ideological teachings could be rigidly controlled. Thus, instruction in manners and deportment was provided by hirelings who did not rate as "gentlemen" themselves, since gentlemanly codes were their stock in trade rather than their personal code.[11] Furthermore, by assigning an inferior position to the tutor, one automatically deprived his possibly deviant ideas of all prestige and much of their persuasiveness.

EQUATING THE EDUCATOR WITH THE PARENT

Another means resorted to was the technique of making various occupations hereditary, so that the child remained under the authority of his parents, who also functioned as his instructors and indoctrinators. In brief, the child often simply became his father's apprentice and disciple. Only later on did the true—i.e., extrafamilial—guild apprentice and university student system come into its own. However, even this system was so closely patterned upon the old teacher-parent system that both the apprentice and the student practically passed from the paternal "manus" (power) to the teacher's "manus." This expedient tended to undermine the family, as an organization partly devoted to the instruction and indoctrination of the young, but preserved at least a kind of familial atmosphere even in the extrafamilial situations of education. The tendency to equate the teacher with the parent is revealed by such expressions as the Latin tag *"in loco parentis"* and by the deep personal loyalty which, in the Brahmanic or Hinduistic culture area, the pupil (*chela*) owed his teacher (*guru*). In fact, this familial type of loyalty to the teacher went so far that in ancient India adultery with the teacher's wife was deemed in-

---

[11] As a child, the writer himself was present when a "lady"—who notoriously treated the governesses of her children as menials—actually slapped the governess, the way servants were still slapped at that time.

cestuous (*171*).[12] The same trend is manifest also in the Chinese custom of using the word "teacher" as a generic term of respect, corresponding to our own use of the word "sir," which, by the way, Victorian children were taught to use when addressing their fathers.[13]

DEGRADATION OF THE CHILD'S STATUS

We know very little about the significance of early forms of extrafamilial education of the child. We may, however, indulge in some speculations which seem plausible and which, as long as they are viewed as speculations rather than as facts or proved theories, are not likely to confuse the issue. We are inclined to suspect that the increasingly low status of children in higher societies, and also the increasing brutality of educational methods (*156*) which go hand in hand with the progress of culture, may be related to the extrafamilial education of children by menials. The status of the child may have become degraded through his association with, and subordination to, a mere menial or slave teacher, who found an outlet for his vengefulness in abusing his masters' children, toward whom he stood in a peculiar relationship: Functioning *in loco parentis*—i.e., as the representative of his own masters—the whip or rod he wielded was his, though the authority behind it was that of the parents. The odd fact that the parents themselves countenanced such methods may reflect both their own ambivalence over the educational "extrusion" of the

[12] This legal principle was far from unrealistic psychologically; witness, for example, a relevant scene in Anatole France's novel *Le Mannequin d'Osier*. We also propose to cite two dreams in Chapter 5, showing that teachers in a therapeutic school are unconsciously defined as parents. Compare also the devotion of the Malay scribe Abdullah bin Abdulkadir Munshi to his teacher (*173*).

[13] The word "sir" is derived from the word "senior," which is basically a "kinship type" of designation. It emphasizes differences between generations, which are most clearly manifest in the family, and also the difference between "older sibling" and "younger sibling." This latter distinction is so important in many primitive kinship systems that some of them lack a generic term for "sibling" or even for "brother" or "sister" and have, instead, only such specific terms as "older brother" or "younger sister."

child from the family and also their hope that a brutal teacher would be less likely to alienate their child's loyalties than a gently persuasive one. Thus, young gentlemen were sent to be trained in knighthood at the court of a great nobleman, because this "stranger" would be more strict with them. The fact that, in this instance, the nominal "teacher" was often of higher rank than the parent does not undermine the validity of our remarks about the relationship between extrafamilial education and the brutality of menial teachers, since even at the court of another nobleman the boy was chiefly instructed by various retainers and menials. On the other hand, the diffusion of emotional bonds which resulted from extrafamilial education probably also had socially beneficial results, by spreading the child's social loyalties and personal commitments over a wider segment of the body social (35). Indeed, it is even possible that such "divided loyalties" to one's family, home town, state, church, school, etc., may be the psychological "cement" which "holds together" the social system, and the institutional fabric of culture as a whole.

SOCIETY AND EDUCATION

In the preceding pages we simply contrasted extrafamilial instruction with intrafamilial indoctrination, as though society as a whole took no interest in the matter. Of course, the family is often so functional and basic a unit of society that, with the few exceptions mentioned above, its orientation tends to conform to the ethos of society as a whole, and vice versa, of course. Hence, the extrafamilial indoctrination of the child tends to be similar to that which it would have obtained in the bosom of its family had its parents been qualified to provide it. This explains why, on the few occasions where teachers deviate from the prevailing sociofamilial ideology, society as a whole tends to react with extreme violence. For example, Socrates was sentenced to death both for impiety and for corrupting the young. Apparently the family can tolerate the "usurpation" of its functions only as long as the "usurper" conforms to the basic code,[14] which is something Socrates failed to do.

Some marginal comments are necessary at this point, lest the tremendous posthumous prestige of Socrates should predispose one to condemn the people of Athens out of hand for their "savagery." As Kitto (138) pointed out, the situation is not quite as simple as all that. For example, two major politicians—one of them being the brilliant psychopath Alcibiades—who were a veritable curse to Athens were known to have been Socrates' disciples and intimates. We might also add that another of his disciples, Plato, advocated in his *Republic* a social and political system wholly incompatible with Athenian or any other kind of democracy. Thus, the Athenians were not altogether unjustified in believing that—despite the civic virtue he displayed on the battlefield—Socrates was fundamentally out of sympathy with the Athenian way of life.

Investigations of the loyalty of teachers to the ethos of their society are, thus, not a new phenomenon. As Socrates was made to drink a cup of hemlock, as Friar Bacon was removed from Oxford and imprisoned by ecclesiastical authorities, so teachers in more modern times were, and continue to be, penalized for deviations from the basic ideology of society. As implied above, this is partly due to the unwillingness of the family to relinquish to those who are only supposed to instruct the young also the right to indoctrinate them. This, however, is not the whole story, and only reflects the darker side of the picture. If one disregards the manner in which some ancient as well as contemporary investigations of teachers are conducted, and therefore takes into consideration the more positive side of the situation, one soon realizes that such

[14] In a different context, Kingsley Davis (24) rightly emphasized that prostitutes are despised because they usurp a familial function in a nonfamilial situation. He also points out that this usurpation places the sex act in a different frame of reference, making it an economic rather than a procreative and affectionate activity. Both points are well taken, though Davis might have advantageously stressed more insistently and more specifically the importance of the ideological deviation of prostitution from the nuclear sociofamilial code.

investigations also reflect an awareness of the social importance of education. Society knows that the educator is more than a mere instructor or "technical drill sergeant" and that, even as he instructs, he inevitably also indoctrinates the young and therefore plays an important role in shaping their outlook.[15] In addition, it is not improper to suggest that, whereas grotesquely theatrical investigations of educators, or, for that matter, of anyone else, are incompatible with the spirit of the democratic system, it is equally certain that every society is entitled to protect itself, its ethos, and its basic orientation, provided they are realistic ones.

SOCIAL CONTROL OF EDUCATION

At this point we must make an important distinction between two types of social control exerted over education outside the family. This distinction is sometimes obscured by the fact that, in both instances, what society seems to be controlling is the inevitable ideological component of every type of instruction. But we must not be induced to ignore the existence of some very important differences, which are of prime importance for the understanding of the nature and scope of therapeutic education. We therefore propose to differentiate between (1) the control of instruction *per se,* and (2) the control of the ideological "orthodoxy" of teaching.

Laws against the spread of knowledge *per se* are fairly ancient and must not be confused with laws which, in seeking to insure ideological conformity, incidentally hamper also instruction. Thus, a Cambridge, Massachusetts, city ordinance once required the removal from all libraries, other than strictly personal and private ones, of all books containing the names of Lenin or Stalin. This would have made the teaching of geography impossible, since

[15] Any teacher of a course in the history of economic or political theory knows how difficult it is, short of lapsing into abject and humiliating public professions of faith in the democratic system, to present the theories of communism or fascism in so objective a manner that he will not be suspected by some of being in sympathy with such ideologies.

every map of Russia shows the location of Leningrad and Stalingrad. Yet, what the councilman who introduced this ordinance aimed at was simply a control of ideological deviations. We propose to discuss here, therefore, only laws which specifically seek to curtail the spread of knowledge. Thus, an Italian princeling once forbade the teaching of reading and writing to the children of poor parents, while in other places the instruction of slaves was prohibited by law. In both of these examples the legislators were not interested—at least not consciously—in controlling ideologies. They simply defined knowledge as power and sought to limit access to this source of power to those interested in maintaining the *status quo*. These laws are therefore comparable to those which forbade serfs to own or carry swords, or limited the right to vote to persons owning a certain amount of property. Fundamentally, our Italian princeling was probably no more opposed to learning *per se*—in fact, for all we know, he may have been a great patron of learning—than feudal society was opposed to war, including civil war. He was simply interested in restricting the "ownership" of the weapon of knowledge to those who had a stake in preserving a system which dated back to the Middle Ages and was rapidly becoming outmoded and nonfunctional. In the same sense, the eighteenth-century French nobility was often quite irreverent and liberal in its outlook, without, however, encouraging the spread of similar attitudes also to their serfs, whose labor supported them. In fact, an arrogant nobleman of that period is said to have remarked of an eminent middle-class thinker: "This fellow wants to philosophize about everything, and does not even enjoy a decent private income." This outlook is also in harmony with Plato's view that slavery is the basis of all freedom, since only if the labor of the slave frees his owner from irksome tasks is the latter truly "free" and able to devote himself to philosophy and government, which are the only tasks worthy of free men (cf. The South African Bantu Education Act).

Of course, the situation is actually more complicated. It is impossible to acquire technical knowledge of any kind without a change in one's outlook, and without experiencing the temptation to think for oneself also on nontechnical subjects. Hence, an interference with the spread of literacy to the poor also represents an attempt to prevent the critical reëxamination of the existing system, because it tends to give rise to subversive ideologies causing social strife. Usually no restrictions are placed on the education of those who, in a pinch, can be counted upon to support the system which insures their continued hold on the rest of the population.

The thesis advanced in the preceding paragraphs can be easily substantiated also with reference to current practices in our society. For example, certain types of information—such as where babies come from—are systematically withheld from the very young, in order to inhibit their sexual activity, which is defined as a prerogative of adult married persons. Likewise, while access to "top secret" data is indispensable to generals and statesmen, information of this type is systematically withheld from the population at large because it might produce disturbances. Thus, while admirals had to know all the distressing details of the disaster at Pearl Harbor, much information was withheld from the public in order to prevent discouragement, for which there was plenty of reason at that time.

In all of these instances, interferences with the spread of knowledge have as their aim the limitation of access to the means of evolving a subversive ideology.

By contrast, in the condemnation of Socrates and of Friar Bacon, as well as in some contemporary investigations, the object of social control is the indoctrinational function of education, rather than merely doctrinal deviations resulting from the acquisition of knowledge, which leads to independent thinking. What is curtailed is not the acquisition of objective knowledge, resulting from instruction, but the manner in which the social function of knowledge is defined.

INDOCTRINATION BY SPECIALISTS

So far we have discussed chiefly the incidental indoctrination of students who, because of the increasing complexity of various technically specialized segments of culture, had to be apprenticed to expert technicians who, at least in principle, were expected to refrain from formally indoctrinating the student. Quite often only if the "outsider" was definitely equal in rank to the child's family was he both permitted and expected to provide indoctrination as well as instruction. Thus, as said before, young gentlemen were sent as pages to the court of some other nobleman to learn both the craft and the ideology of knighthood.

We now propose to turn to another type of extrafamilial education, which resulted from the increasing complexity of religious and other ideological and attitudinal disciplines, making indoctrination by specialists in doctrine both unavoidable and desirable. As stated—at least in passing—in the earlier sections of this chapter, extrafamilial indoctrination is chiefly necessary in times of cultural change, regardless of whether this change is due to a slow internal decay of existing value systems or to the introduction of new ideologies.

In brief, Socrates and Plato could get disciples because Greek rationalism (66) and the functional and *automatic* effectiveness of citizenship in the city-state (138) began to decline, while medieval priests found pupils because the Christianization of Europe required an ideological reorientation of society. As stated before, as long as a culture is unchallenged, its ideology seldom becomes so complex as to necessitate the formal indoctrination of the citizen. This is a point to which we will return in connection with an examination of the role of education—which includes indoctrination—in the present world.

We have already referred to the fact that the increasing complexity of Maori mythology, etc., made the establishment of

schools necessary. The same complexity of law and doctrine led
to the establishment of schools among the theocratic Jews. In both
of these instances the school was an agent of society as a whole.
By contrast, even though Plato's Academy and Aristotle's Lyceum
were highly esteemed, they were private "schools," not genuine
social agencies. Likewise, a school established by the Church in
medieval times was, by and large, not an agency of society as a
whole, though in this instance the situation is somewhat complicated by the fact that, in the official value system of that period,
religious ideas occupied the highest position. However, the town-
and-gown antagonisms of that period suggest that we are not permitted to view these medieval schools as formal agencies of society, in the sense in which the Maori or Jewish schools were
organs of society.

On the whole, the rise of formal social agencies for the indoctrination of all future citizens appears to be a relatively late development.

IDEOLOGICAL ASPECTS OF EDUCATION IN FRANCE

A careful examination of the recent history of public education
in France under government auspices is particularly suitable for
giving us an insight into the attempts of society as a whole to
shape the outlook of the citizenry through educational means.
Sooner and perhaps also more extensively than anywhere else we
witness in France the rise of some of the most significant processes
and attitudes forming the basis of the civilized side of modern life,
against which totalitarianisms of all types are but shadowy reactions. Indeed, it is Athens and not Sparta, Rome and not the bar-
barians, which men remember. Regardless of the fate of modern
democracy in its struggle with totalitarianism, human history will
ultimately be shaped by what happens at the Sorbonne, at Oxford,
and at Harvard, by what transpires in Montparnasse, Bloomsbury,
and Greenwich Village, and not by what arms are produced in the

arsenals of Moscow or Peking. In the long run, the civilizations which influence future civilizations are those which, the more they change, the more they remain themselves. Any improvement made in our system would only make it look and be more like democracy, and would represent its fulfillment. By contrast, any rigid totalitarian system, which has "all the final answers," cannot change without ceasing to be itself, since historically all final and rigid systems are self-abolishing, regardless of what happens on the battlefield.

The trends which characterize the rise of contemporary French civilization are: (1) rationalism, (2) the attrition of regional and class particularisms, and (3) the social implementation of individuality, which is not to be confused with "rugged individualism" of the antisocial and destructive kind.

The rise of public instruction in France was animated by a secular and rationalistic outlook. Its implicit starting point was the assumption that specific indoctrination in any kind of liberal dogma was unnecessary. It was felt that, once man's reason was freed from the shackles of irrationality, traditionalism, willful blindness, and mere ignorance, it would inevitably reach conclusions in complete harmony with the rationalistic outlook of humanitarianism. In this the philosophy of education in France resembled both the Socratic doctrine that knowledge is virtue and Rousseau's view that, contrary to the doctrine of original sin, man is fundamentally decent.[16] Oddly enough, the French republican viewpoint and that of the Italian princeling who forbade the education of the poor, but not that of the rich, have much in common. Both the advocates and the opponents of the spread of knowledge took it for granted that instruction alone can radically shape the

---

[16] A psychoanalytic defense of this thesis, which requires the repudiation of the theory of the death instinct, is relatively easy and was presented elsewhere in some detail (56). The gist of the argument is that the phenomenon of life itself is evidence of the primacy of Eros, since, even if a death instinct (Thanatos) should exist, as long as there is life the forces of Eros necessarily outweigh those of Thanatos.

attitudes and ideologies of the student. They differed only in that the French republic deemed such a change desirable, while the Italian princeling felt it to be harmful. This only shows that the ideology of a period tends to be uniform, even where different practical conclusions are drawn from it by contending interest groups.

This theory was at once the chief strength and major weakness of French public instruction in its early days. Logically unassailable, it failed to take into account neurotic biases, the dead hand of obsolete tradition, and particularistic interests. It was therefore rather successfully challenged by a more traditionalistic point of view, perpetuated within the family as well as within certain traditional institutions of French culture. In fact, familistic values easily lent themselves to being made the fulcra of an antirepublican orientation, with all its implications. For example, the old French family system, which subordinated the wife to the husband, was not at all uncongenial to men, who therefore did not interfere with their wives' antirepublican attitudes. Taken together, attempts to preserve masculine prerogatives within the family, and the feminine traditionalism which it fostered explain why liberal and progressive France was one of the last major nations to grant the vote to women. All this finally led to the paradoxical situation that whereas the middle-class man was usually republican, progressive, and secular to the point of being anticlerical, he let his wife and children go to mass and educated his daughters in convents.[17] In addition, the Army's, and even more the Navy's, cadres of officers were usually quite clerical and sometimes even royalistic.[18]

[17] Cf. the Worms-Clavelin family in Anatole France's four-volume novel: *Histoire Contemporaine.* The father is an anticlerical Jewish prefect, who is the champion of the republican and secular outlook in a provincial district. The mother collects French religious art and sides with the clergy. The daughter is raised in a convent.

[18] Marshal Lyautey, a Lorrainer, found it possible to perform important military functions at a time when France was at war with Germany and Austria, though—

Another interesting characteristic of this period is the change in the outlook of the French nobility, which, as stated earlier, was liberal and irreverent during the reigns of Louis XV and Louis XVI. When the French Revolution deprived it of its leading position in society, the nobility suddenly did an about-face and became extremely traditionalistic and clerical in outlook. Characteristically, this ideological "self-control" or "self-inhibition" of the nineteenth-century French nobility lent "snob appeal" to the antirepublican outlook.

For a while the situation amounted to a stalemate. Public instruction existed side by side with religious schools. The face which the middle-class family turned toward the outside was secular and republican, while the face it showed within the bosom of the family was clerical and conservative. In combination, the two outlooks led to a rather selfish pursuit of gain and political influence, which is the French equivalent of the so-called "robber baron" epoch in American economic history. Thus, until the end of the nineteenth century, French public instruction only instructed, while the French family continued to indoctrinate, the child.

This dual system could function relatively efficiently as long as French society was fairly stable, so that each family clearly understood the ethos of the social subsystem and geographical region to which it belonged and was therefore able to educate its children for the type of conduct and orientation which befitted their predictable station in life. However, owing partly to the above-mentioned pursuit of gain and political influence—which were interrelated, since, in modern society, "deals" with the state are important sources of income—there took place an attrition of regional and class particularisms, culminating in an increased so-

---

as a "loyal Lorrainer"—he felt himself to be the subject of the formerly independent Dukes of Lorraine, whose representative, in 1914–1918, was the reigning Austrian (Habsburg-Lorraine) dynasty. It is impossible for traditionalism to go to more anachronistic extremes.

cial and geographical mobility and in the unification of provinces and classes into a nation. Indeed the peasant family which was previously qualified to raise its children to become good Breton or Auvergnat peasants, whose horizon would be bounded by their village and social class, could not hope to train them now to be primarily French citizens, who might do their compulsory military service in Paris and become factory workers or even prime ministers.

This meant that the state, which had a stake in fostering the effective unification of the nation, had to inaugurate a struggle against the divergent indoctrination of its future citizens both in the bosom of the family and in religious schools. The family was too strong to be attacked frontally. Because of a relatively low standard of living, it was still held together not only by love but even more by innumerable reciprocal needs and services. The absence of canned foods and the expensiveness of eating in restaurants, the fact that it was more economical to darn socks than to buy new ones, etc., made men as dependent on their wives as the difficulty of finding really remunerative jobs made the wives dependent on their husbands. On the whole, it seemed easier to direct the attack at organizations which indoctrinated children in a manner which was at variance with the prevailing official doctrine. This led to the closing of religious schools, the expulsion of teaching and other congregations, and the monopolization of schools by the state.[19]

This struggle against antirepublican, antirationalistic, and antisecular forces does not indicate, however, that the French state actually understood that—owing to various psychological and traditional resistances—the training and unfolding of reason alone

---

[19] This campaign was relaxed to a certain extent after a while, so that, to take a date at random, in 1926 the Catholic University in Paris could give instruction, but its students had to take their examinations at the governmental University of Paris, and received their diplomas from the official "Académie de Paris"—i.e., from the government's Paris district of education.

does not necessarily suffice to indoctrinate the young. The state only sought to prevent the nonrepublican indoctrination of children. Hence, the elementary teachers of the Third Republic were simply taught to think of themselves as the exponents of enlightenment in the provinces. The extent to which they actually functioned in that capacity is shown by two facts. The first of these is the almost proverbial friction between the village teacher and the village priest. The second is the contemptuous habit of referring to a certain type of naïvely rationalistic orientation as "grade-school stuff" (*"primaire"*). A more sophisticated but still uncompromisingly rationalistic outlook was characterized by its foes as *"normalien,"* the *écoles normales* being teachers' colleges. Yet, the term *"normalien,"* when applied specifically to the ideology and cultural sophistication of typical graduates of the "Ecole Normale Supérieure," was a highly complimentary one.[20]

However, in the long run, even this expedient proved insufficient and the French state was compelled to realize that it would have to take a hand in the formal indoctrination of the student in order to shape him into a genuine French citizen. In this, Republican France took its cue from the Jesuits, who were among the first to realize that education can mold personality into a shape which is in harmony with the pattern of society.

A second reason why the French school had to become an instrument not only for the instruction but also for the indoctrination of the young, and why the French family was able to reconquer for the time being some of its indoctrinational functions, and even to impose some of its views upon the public-school system, is related to a twofold nationalistic reaction.

One of these reactions is of a relatively uncomplicated type. It

[20] The Ecole Normale Supérieure is the embodiment of the French republican ideology. It admits only the cream of the crop, on the basis of extremely difficult competitive examinations, and its curriculum is absolutely grueling. Probably no institution of higher learning in the world has more exacting standards. Hence, its graduates form an intellectual elite, and to have been a *"normalien"* is a source of great prestige in France.

simply represents a struggle for the maintenance of traditional
French values by means of an overt opposition to the increasingly
inevitable-seeming drift toward the cultural and political unification of Europe. However, the champions of this reaction, whose
ideology was rooted essentially in the value system of pre-
Revolutionary France, in which classes and regions were highly
differentiated, were obliged, in order to mobilize all of French
public opinion, to take a leaf from the ideology of their republican
opponents. They had to borrow from the spirit of the French
Revolution the conception of France as a unit, and the view that
the many provinces jointly constituted the French nation. This was
paradoxical, since the rest of their ideology was derived from a
period in French history where provincial loyalties often took
precedence over national ones,[21] and where the three estates were
openly at odds with each other. At any rate, one type of nationalistic patriotism in France was of this antirepublican type.

The second type of French nationalism is more complicated.
Beginning with the 1789 revolution, the official doctrine of the
government, which later on became also the intellectual doctrine
of French liberalism, was that France was the champion of mankind and, as Anatole France expressed it, the fellow citizen of
every nation in the world community. Hence, in a sense, the
French liberal viewed the culture of his country as the closest
existing approximation of a supranational, typically "human" culture and defined French citizenship as paradigmatic of, and as a
stepping stone toward, universal citizenship. This viewpoint resembled in more ways than one the Greek conception of the role
of Hellas (109) in the world. However, as they saw it, France's
championship of the cause of humanity as a whole exposed it to

[21] The culturally and ethnically French nobility of Aquitaine fought almost to the
end for its feudal lord, the Duke of Aquitaine, who, as King of England, was the
hereditary foe of the Kings of France. In fact, as late as the early seventeenth century, it was possible for the governor of a French province to raise his province
against the central government and to form alliances with the nation's foes.

to the attacks of all reactionaries and enemies of humanity. Hence, France felt forced to defend itself, if for no other reason than because it represented the interests of humanity as a whole. This led to a highly paradoxical type of antinationalistic nationalism, and to the oddity of a vigorously antimilitaristic and yet warlike spirit.

However, even while assuming responsibility for the education of the young, which includes their indoctrination, the French were reluctant to go about it too pointedly. Hence, it was only in recent years that the name of the "Ministry of Public Instruction" was changed to "Ministry of National Education." This change in designation underscores the fact that a twofold shift took place. The term "public"—which has no national implications and is in accord with the supranational orientation of official French republican doctrine—was replaced by the term "national," and the word "instruction" was superseded by the term "education," which also implies the inculcation of an ideology.

We discussed the French system in some detail because it is more or less paradigmatic of the shift in other European countries from instruction and indoctrination in the family to education in public schools, defined as agencies of society and of the state.

THE ANGLO-SAXON SYSTEM

The shift was less complete in Anglo-Saxon countries—witness the paternalism prevailing to this very day even on the college level. Few things bewilder European students attending an American university as much as does the existence of deans of women, curfews, housing regulations, and the like, which imply that they are still defined as adolescents.[22]

Yet the same "push" toward ideological uniformity is also present in contemporary Anglo-Saxon society and can be conveniently discussed in terms of political developments. Thus, we are wit-

[22] The definition of the student as an "honorary adolescent" is discussed in Chapter 9.

nessing at present a series of "lovers' quarrels" between England
and America, simultaneously with the spectacle of both England
and America calmly relinquishing those portions of their empires
(India, Burma, the Philippines, etc.) which are not suitable for
permanent settlement by culturally Anglo-Saxon colonists.[23] These
phenomena apparently reflect a seesawing between the historically
now impossible desire to remain specifically and exclusively British, or American, and a seemingly inevitable drift, first toward an
Anglo-Saxon Commonwealth and later on toward world government. England has already pretty well reached the stage of being
a culturally—rather than only politically—unified Commonwealth, centering about the North Atlantic, with outposts in temperate Australia and New Zealand and in the semi-temperate parts
of Africa as well.[24]

THE RISE OF TOTAL EDUCATION IN SOCIETY

The point of view we sought to foreshadow in the preceding
paragraphs is that *education, lato sensu, consists in an integration
of technical instruction with familial indoctrination.* Education, in
this sense, existed among most primitives, its executive organ
being the family. Gradually, the expansion of technology and
cultural advancement in general, combined with a breakdown of
hereditary familial occupational patterns and with an increase first
in occupational and then in class mobility, forced the family to
delegate much of its instructional function to outside agencies—

[23] The French approached this problem differently. They sought to turn Africans
into Frenchmen. Hence, the African child attending a French school in its own
country learned history from books whose first sentence began somewhat as follows: "Our ancestors, the Gauls . . ."

[24] We suspect that the rebellious regime in South Africa could not have come
into being before England abandoned the imperial—i.e., colonial—policy of di-
versity in culture and in race and embarked upon an attempt to align all its do-
minions and possessions into a culturally and ethnically Anglo-Saxon British Commonwealth. The same type of local nationalism arose also in the Roman Empire
after important personages from conquered countries began to be granted Roman
citizenship and were even appointed to the Senate.

first in the case of boys and then increasingly also in the case of girls. The broadening social base[25] and increasing size (*144*) of civilized society and of the major religions then brought about a state of affairs in which even an adequately unified and uniform cultural, social, national, or religious indoctrination became impossible within the bosom of the family, which was qualified to indoctrinate its children only with reference to its own subculture or community. This process of social expansion and evolution, by means of an attrition of subgroup ethnicization, parallels, in a sense, certain developments among Plains Indians (*50*), who today, as distinct from what was the case 100 years ago, are primarily Plains Indians and only in the second place *specifically* Crow, Blackfoot, Cheyenne, or Sioux Indians.

The rise of modern public education is, thus, a direct consequence of the decline of primitive familial education, under the impact of social change. It resulted from stripping the family of many of its most ancient, but currently obsolete, functions. Various attempts to "compensate" the family for this loss of function have, on the whole, been unsuccessful. Indeed, it is rather interesting to note that Christianity, which, when it first arose, systematically destroyed the Roman family cults and challenged familial patterns and techniques of religious indoctrination, now champions the very family some of whose major foundations and functions it was the first to undermine in the course of an inevitable process of historical change. (Actually, to be more precise, and therefore also less "culturological," Christianity did this in the course of the inevitable cultural change resulting from the growth and accumulation of new human insights and experiences.) This process then led to a reconstitution of the complete—i.e., primitive —type of total education, integrating instruction with indoctrina-

[25] We denote by this term the process whereby increasingly large segments of society are granted a major voice in the shaping of social policies and trends and which manifests itself in such phenomena as the abolition of slavery and serfdom, the vote for women, compulsory education, and the like.

tion, though outside the family, and now implemented by means of public and "private" schools.

It is now generally recognized that the social role and function[26] of education are at present changing rapidly, both quantitatively and qualitatively.

The quantitative change in society's awareness of the importance of education is reflected by the increasing preoccupation of all governments with matters pertaining to the teaching of the young. Thus, the government of the United States recently established a Department of Health, Education and Welfare, headed by a Secretary holding cabinet rank.

This intensity of modern society's preoccupation with education has many sources. Some of them are obvious, some of them are too complex to be discussed in detail in a work devoted primarily to therapeutic education, and still others are not yet fully understood. We therefore propose to analyze only one of these causal factors, without in any way implying that it is the most important one. We discuss it here simply in the hope that it will enable us to understand one aspect of the social role of education: its relation to population policies as instruments of social action.

Since 1914 the whole world has been preparing itself for the coming struggle for world leadership—or, in the case of smaller nations, for bare survival—such as marks the end of the preponderance of any world power, be it that of Rome, the Holy Roman Empire, France, England, etc. The necessity of girding itself for so decisive a contest obliges each nation to reappraise its assets and to devise means for their augmentation and improvement. Since the quality of the population—both as regards its competence and efficiency and as regards its loyalty and morale—is the principal asset of any nation, governments are necessarily interested in the advancement and socially functional orientation

---

[26] "Function" is the contribution of a given institution, process, or person to the maintenance of the social system and of culture as a whole.

of education[27] and also in using the special qualifications of the individual citizen in an optimal manner.[28]

EDUCATION AND THERAPEUTIC EDUCATION

The preceding, and somewhat elaborate, comments on the history of education are not a simple exercise in erudition. They actually seek to indicate that therapeutic education is bona-fide education, in that it seeks to blend indoctrination with instruction—often in a manner which does not quite please the child's family. We also tried to suggest that true therapeutic education could not have come into being as long as the sole task of any school was to provide instruction pure and simple, leaving indoctrination (i.e., socialization and parts of ethnicization) in the hands of the family. In fact, echoes of this superannuated philosophy still haunt many "schools" for the feeble-minded, where the child is simply trained (instructed or drilled) but is not indoctrinated in any way, owing to the lazily comfortable belief that it is not capable of being indoctrinated.

It is a simple fact that therapeutic education is a modern development. By contrast, the brute drilling of the defective or neurotic child is quite ancient. Thus, we have Elwin's depressing account of a fatal beating given to an idiot Muria child to make it conform. This instance of mere "drilling" is particularly striking and characteristic, since such brutality is normally almost completely out of harmony with the ordinarily good-natured behavior of members of that tribe (80). A similarly nontherapeutically oriented concern with the training of an abnormal child—the future Em-

---

[27] The thesis that the advancement of education is viewed as a means for improving the quality of the population is substantiated by the fact that the fostering of U.S. education is assigned to a Department of *Health,* Education and *Welfare.*

[28] The times when a brilliant young scientist could fall in battle are certainly past. Nor would our government be likely to imitate the example of Athens, which permitted an Aeschylus to fight in the ranks at Marathon, or a Socrates to put on the armor of a hoplite. Nowadays such men would probably be assigned to psychological warfare.

peror Claudius—may be found in the letters of Augustus to his wife Livia, which are cited by Suetonius (*214*). Yet, having been written in a period of relative enlightenment, these letters show at least glimmerings of an incipient interest in the indoctrination, and not only in the instruction, of a seemingly hopeless young person. Nonetheless, the real beginnings of therapeutic education seem to be the efforts of Itard to turn the "wild boy of Aveyron" into a human being, and not only into a performing ape (*122*). However—not unexpectedly—Itard belongs already to the age of enlightenment.

In brief, only if we understand the history of education with special reference to extrafamilial indoctrination can we grasp the significance of therapeutic education for the educational process as a whole. In addition, by viewing therapeutic education in this broad setting, we also obtain an understanding of why it almost presupposes the existence of suitable therapeutic schools. It is usually insufficient to delegate to a special day school the education of problem children. The school in which the "exceptional child" has to be humanized must also provide a suitably therapeutic social setting for the actual implementation of the attitudinal education of the child. In a word, whereas a harshly nontherapeutic day school may be able to ethnicize the child to a limited extent merely by means of instruction, the task of the therapeutic school is chiefly to humanize it. This is, obviously, a task at which the exceptional child's family—which ordinarily undertakes this type of education —has failed, since otherwise the child would not have to be sent to a therapeutic school in the first place.

....

PART TWO

THERAPEUTIC EDUCATION AND PSYCHOTHERAPY

If I keep from preaching at people, they improve themselves. If I keep from imposing on people, they become themselves.

LAO-TSE

CHAPTER 3

Psychotherapy as Education

Therapeutic education is an interdisciplinary science, which seeks to accomplish therapeutic aims by educational means. In order to understand the nature and scope of this science, it is necessary to define, first of all, the meaning of therapy with special reference to the conceptual framework of education.

CORRECTIVE MEASURES VS. PSYCHOTHERAPY

The first point to be clarified is the distinction between corrective or remedial manipulations and true psychotherapy. As viewed in this book, remedial measures consist in attempts to correct certain inadequate activities directly related to (usually conscious) ego functions, in order to bring them in line with some absolutely or statistically "normal" level of performance. The corrective or remedial specialist seeks to influence ego functions by a direct, frontal attack on the symptom itself: The lalling brain-injured child is helped to articulate more clearly; the child with reading difficulties is taught to read more easily. It is known, of course, that the correction of such defects tends to have a favorable effect also on the total personality of the child—for example, by increasing its self-confidence. However, this latter type of improvement has to be viewed as a kind of "bonus" or "windfall," at least from the strictly remedial or corrective point of view. Of course, so clear-cut a distinction between the primary objective of simply improving the articulation of the lalling child, which is required by the conceptual framework of speech correction, and the "accidental" gain represented by the resulting increase in the child's self-confidence, which is outside the objective required by the theoretical framework of speech therapy, should be made only for the sake of conceptual clarity. In practice, the increase in the child's self-esteem is always deliberately and skillfully fostered by the competent speech specialist.

In psychotherapy the situation is somewhat more complicated. Since symptoms, which are usually disturbances of activities belonging to the sphere of the ego, cause the neurotic to seek therapeutic help in the first place, the psychotherapist is, of necessity, interested in them and must ultimately seek to correct them. However, unlike the corrective and remedial therapist, he seldom seeks to influence the symptoms directly or by means of a frontal attack.[1] In fact, he sometimes deliberately refrains from alleviating the symptoms prematurely, even where a sudden "miraculous" cure seems feasible, because certain patients actually need the discomfort which their symptoms cause them, in order to be willing to endure the sometimes extremely painful process of "getting wise to themselves." A further similarity between psychotherapists and remedial or corrective experts is that both seek to help the patient by approaching his problems via his conscious ego functions. In fact, even if the psychotherapist were able to "speak directly to the unconscious" of his patient from the very first moment, it would be undesirable for him to do so in most cases, since the chief purpose of analytically oriented psychotherapy is to help the ego obtain an insight into the unconscious, in order to learn gradually to control and to manage it in an optimal manner.

---

[1] Addicts, acting-out delinquents, and borderline psychotics form a partial exception to this rule.

In brief, the chief difference between psychotherapy and corrective or remedial operations is that remedial work seeks to influence the conscious ego functions directly. By contrast, the psychotherapist seeks first to bring about a fundamental modification of the unconscious portions of the psyche—first and foremost by making them conscious—and holds that this alone suffices to bring about also a permanent improvement in the previously disturbed functions of the ego.

Therapeutic education has many characteristics in common both with psychotherapy and with remedial work. Like them, it seeks to correct activities which belong to the sphere of the ego. Like them, it approaches the patient via his conscious ego. It is only in regard to its relations with the patient's unconscious that therapeutic education differs from the other two meliorative techniques. Thus, unlike the fundamental philosophy of remedial work, the conceptual basis of therapeutic education actually demands that special efforts be made to modify not only defective ego functions but also the unconscious segment of the patient's psyche.[2] However, unlike psychotherapy proper, therapeutic education does not aim primarily at modifications of defective ego functions through a more basic and more extensive modification of the unconscious. Rather does it seek to influence the unconscious through a rectification of defective ego functions. In this respect, at least, therapeutic education has much in common with some of the more external aspects of expertly done supportive, suppressive, or directive psychotherapy. On the other hand, ordinary, nontherapeutic education—or, more

[2] We repeat that we are drawing these sharp distinctions solely in order to achieve conceptual clarity. In actual practice, the boundaries between the various meliorative techniques are always blurred—primarily for the reason that it is wholly impossible to modify even a limited segment of the personality without causing corresponding modifications also in the rest of the psyche. Since these secondary modifications may sometimes be quite harmful, it is desirable that remedial specialists and therapeutic educators should be psychiatrically sophisticated.

precisely, instruction for normal children—has much in common with remedial measures, and differs from them chiefly not in seeking to remedy nonexistent defects or disturbances but in trying to prevent them. It is our thesis that all competent education is a truly prophylactic measure, simply because it provides the child with suitable means for that actualization of its potentialities which is indispensable for its psychic health.

PSYCHOTHERAPY AS UNLEARNING

Let us now examine more closely the nature of psychotherapy in terms of the conceptual framework of education. It will soon become apparent that psychotherapy is, in a sense, the reverse of education and, furthermore, that it is related to education precisely because it is the obverse of the coin of which education is the reverse. Otherwise expressed, there exists between psychotherapy and education the same "complementarity relationship" (Chapter 12) which we have shown to exist also between the sociological and the psychological understanding of a given human action (37). This is to be expected, since education is a form of "sociology in action," while psychotherapy is a kind of "psychology in action."

In the following pages we propose to show that—in a sense—the objective of psychotherapy is to help the patient *un*learn his neurosis. This is true even of psychotherapies which are directive, suggestive, or suppressive, since even in these forms of therapy the suggested or prohibited action is offered to the patient as a substitute for some other action which his neurosis has hitherto compelled him to perform. It is true, above all, of deep psychotherapy, and particularly of psychoanalysis, whose chief and almost sole aim is to help the patient to unlearn. In order to grasp the full meaning of this thesis, we must seek to understand, first of all, that neurosis can be viewed, in one frame of reference, as the result of a certain type of undesirable learning.

NEUROSIS AS UNDESIRABLE LEARNING

We stressed that ethnicization—i.e., education in the most comprehensive sense—guides man's self-actualizing impulses into certain culturally preferred channels and provides devices for their expression and implementation. However, certain idiosyncratic and unforeseen incidents, occurring in the course of ethnicization, may cause some of these channels and devices to acquire certain highly explosive, and usually purely subjective and unconscious, connotations and meanings. It is important to realize that these meanings are usually neither implied nor foreseen by culture itself and are therefore not provided for within the framework of culture. In other words, there usually are few or no specific and standardized cultural means which enable the individual to actualize, to suppress, or to redirect these idiosyncratic connotations in a culturally acceptable and ego-syntonic (self-acceptable) manner. This, in turn, causes the individual to become deviantly neurotic—i.e., neurotic in a manner which is not acceptable to other persons belonging to his culture. In other words, since the neurotic is provided with no cultural outlets for his distorted impulses, he is forced to improvise compromise means for their actualization. These devices, known as "symptoms," instead of facilitating the normal unfolding of humanization and self-realization, inhibit and distort the personality. Furthermore, since these deviant connotations and meanings of experiences and practices are (compensatorily?) subjectively more highly cathected—i.e., charged with more affect or libido—than are their socially cathected standard cultural connotations, symptom formation necessarily takes place in lieu of, and at the expense of, culturally standardized behavior. Hence, as we pointed out elsewhere (47, 53, 55), neurotics and other emotionally disturbed persons are, in a substantive sense, deculturalized (deëthnicized) as well as partly dehumanized individuals. This is a crucial point, to which we will return after giving a concrete example of one type of neurotic behavior which can readily be understood in terms of our scheme.

Case 2: Mysophobia

Cleanliness is, in our culture, a socially highly rewarded form of behavior, and handwashing, as a symbolic act of purification, which removes the blemish of conscious sin from the soul, is an important rite in many religions. There are, however, certain neurotics, hagridden by a dread of germs and of dirt, who wash their hands so constantly and with such compulsive frenzy that, instead of earning the reputation of being particularly cleanly persons, they are considered a nuisance and hence are ridiculed. Consciously, such persons profess to wash their hands solely in order to protect themselves and others from dangerous germs which allegedly lurk in every corner. Unconsciously, however, they are indulging in a kind of private and deculturalized form of purification; its purpose is to remove the marks of some sin, the very nature of which is consciously unknown to them. Yet, when one confronts the mysophobic—who sometimes goes so far as to read books about bacteriology in order to justify his compulsive dread of germs—with this interpretation, he usually strenuously rejects it and insists that he is simply washing off dirt and germs. However, the spuriousness and grotesqueness of such explanations is often strikingly underscored by the fact that some compulsive handwashers hardly ever take a bath, and tend to be untidy also in a good many other ways.

In brief, this type of patient does not use, but simply misuses and abuses, the channels and devices which our culture provides for persons who truly wish to be cleanly, and also those which various religions make available to persons who wish to signify, by means of a symbolic act, their desire to cleanse themselves of a conscious sin.

In fact, we may even say that there exist certain cultural channels which almost inevitably corrupt and distort those who unconsciously use them as means for spurious self-actualization, or, more correctly, for the actualization of their neuroticism. The exercise of power, which, as we repeatedly stressed (*44, 60*), invariably infantilizes man, is one such channel. Normal men may seek leadership but will avoid power just as Cincinnatus did.[3]

THE PSYCHOANALYTIC PROCESS SEEN EDUCATIONALLY

From the educational viewpoint, the psychoanalytic process can be divided into three phases:

1. *The unlearning phase* includes, first, the neutralization and unlearning of attitudes which originally inhibited and distorted the patient's normal humanization and, second, the unlearning of the (now emotionally neutralized) symptoms which served as substitutes for properly ethnicized self-expression and self-realization.

2. *The neutral phase,* which is seldom mentioned in psychoanalytic literature, is one of relative inactivity in that sphere of behavior whose neurotic emotional foundations and symptomatic manifestations have just been unlearned.

3. *The relearning phase* is characterized by new and spontaneous attempts to achieve, first, self-humanization and, then, self-ethnicization.

These three phases characterize both the entire analysis, viewed as a broad and unitary process which modifies the personality structure as a whole, and every stage of the analytic process in which the inhibitions and distortions of some part-function are abolished and replaced by more mature means of self-realization.

THE UNLEARNING PHASE

We specified that, in the course of psychoanalysis, the patient unlearns chiefly those inhibitions and distortions which interfered

---

[3] This view implies that we must differentiate between functional authority and subjective power. Hence, we feel that there can be functional leadership without power, though not without authority. A corollary view is that all power is evil, because it inevitably leads to abuses and excesses. This is precisely what Lord Acton meant when he affirmed that "power tends to corrupt; and absolute power corrupts absolutely."

with his mature self-realization as a human being, as a person, and as a member of a given society living in a certain cultural setting. First he unlearns the idiosyncratic attitudes associated with some activity or function. As he obtains an insight into their true nature, he rejects and reconstructs these attitudes, with the result that the pathological activities and functions (symptoms) through which these attitudes manifest themselves cease to be necessary to him. In other words, he first unlearns certain attitudes and then the activities associated with them. At this point the normal impulse, which was formerly distorted by pathological attitudes and found expression in symptoms, is, for a brief interval, in a state comparable to that in which it exists in the small child. The basic impulse is, at this point, relatively amorphous and does not have at its disposal any established device for its implementation or actualization. This stage is often so brief that it may escape the notice of even the most alert psychotherapist. It therefore deserves to be discussed more in detail.

THE NEUTRAL PHASE

In a sense, at the end of the process of unlearning, there often occurs a kind of "pause," in which the once neurotically utilized impulse is temporarily deprived of outlets and is therefore in a state of "suspended animation." Only after this "pause" can a spontaneous "relearning" take place, in the course of which the previously inhibited or distorted impulse or need is provided with a set of new, and more mature, connotations and meanings, which make possible the evolving or learning of more adequate ways of self-realization, by means of techniques which insure optimal adjustment. Thus, the compulsive handwasher's recovery involves three separate developments. First the patient loses his mysophobia— i.e., his guilt over masturbatory activities and hostile fantasies; then he stops washing his hands. During the next stage he sometimes ceases to wash altogether and occasionally becomes as unself-consciously dirty as a small child. Finally, he relearns—or, at the lowest estimate, begins to implement—the desire for true cleanliness, but this time with different—i.e., culturally realistic—connotations, and by means of culturally approved techniques for keeping clean.

THE RELEARNING PHASE

In the final stage of psychoanalysis there occurs an almost wholly spontaneous development or "learning," in which the basic impulses and drives acquire healthy connotations. This, in turn, makes it possible for the patient to evolve and to learn adequate means for his self-realization as a human being and for a subjectively satisfying adjustment to his social and cultural setting. In brief, at this stage of the analytic process there occurs a *spontaneous* rehumanization and reëthnicization of the patient.

We must stress that even during this final period of emotional growth and "learning" the psychoanalyst does not "teach" his patient anything whatsoever. His objective and tolerant attitude simply fosters the patient's internally motivated "push" toward self-realization and helps him avoid this time the emotional pitfalls into which he stumbled in the course of his first, pathological attempt at self-realization. Hence, he hardly ever interferes with the process of the patient's reëthnicization but simply helps him to "test reality" adequately. That is, the analyst fosters almost exclusively the "learning" of authentic humanization and leaves it to the patient to acquire or to evolve the kind of ethnicization which is most compatible with his distinctive and now mature personality structure. For example, the analysis of a bookkeeper may reveal that he should have become a musician. It will be "up to the patient," however, to decide whether he wishes to become a composer, a music critic, a violin virtuoso, or a jazz drummer.

THE STRIVING FOR HEALTH

An important implication of this scheme is that the human being has an inherent and healthy urge to achieve humanization and emotional maturity, and that neurosis occurs only when external events interfere with the normal unfolding of this "push toward maturity." We stated that when therapy succeeds in stripping the patient's impulses of their neurotic connotations there often occurs a temporary loss of (distorted and/or spurious) ethnicity, now in one segment of his behavior and now in another. Otherwise expressed, the patient is led back piecemeal to a state of ethnic non-differentiation. He becomes something like the "natural man" of the philosopher, and/or like the "potential human being" of the child psychologist—now in regard to sexuality, now in regard to interpersonal relations, etc. This means that the patient is given "a second chance" to start from scratch. Once this point of temporary ethnic nondifferentiation is reached, as far as the analyst is concerned the patient is "on his own." Psychoanalysis restored to the patient nothing more—but also nothing less—than *full access to his real and inherent potentialities* and can therefore leave it up to the patient's natural push toward self-realization to actualize them in accordance both with his personal tastes and inclinations and with the occupational structure of his society. Indeed, the psychoanalyst cannot manufacture a "good memory" for a neurotically forgetful patient, nor does he seek to teach him mnemotechnical devices, as a remedial expert or therapeutic educator might. The psychoanalyst simply helps his forgetful patient to "unlearn" and to get rid of certain neurotic inhibitions, which hold his inherently normal ability to remember in check. This process of unlearning is, actually, doubly beneficial to the patient since, at the same time, the psychic energies which were previously devoted to the destructive task of interfering with the normal capacity to remember also become available for new and more constructive uses. This represents an additional therapeutic gain and an additional step toward optimal and mature functioning. Indeed, one of the most striking results of a successful psychoanalysis is an increased capacity to work and to enjoy oneself.

HOMEOSTASIS

The preceding considerations are based upon the view that the law of homeostasis is applicable also to psychological processes (84). The essential features of this law are based upon the third law of thermodynamics, which postulates that, if a system is disturbed by some external force, the moment the disturbance ceases the system will return to the state obtaining before the disturbance took place, or will move toward the state toward which it would have moved had the external force not disturbed or arrested its progress toward that state. Thus, when severe illness arrests the growth of the child, once recovery sets in, the child usually "shoots up" and eventually attains the size it would have attained had illness not impeded its growth temporarily. Since, like Fletcher (84), we believe that the "wisdom of the mind" parallels that of the body, we feel that, once the pathological factors which inhibited or distorted the process of humanization and/or ethnicization are eliminated, the patient may be relied upon to move "under his own steam" toward that state of maturity, humanization, and ethnicization which he would have reached had his development not been impeded temporarily by a variety of disturbing forces.

At this point it seems desirable to illustrate the three phases of the psychoanalytic process by means of two clinical examples.

Case 3: The Transitory Inhibition of an Incipient Sublimation

A delinquent and schizoid adolescent developed a great interest in medieval architecture and fantasied that he would eventually build himself an old English castle. This escape mechanism was so important to him that he even studied architecture on his own. His therapist did not ridicule this interest but stressed that its purpose was to compensate the boy for the fact that he had never had a real home. After some months of psychoanalysis the adolescent said: "I don't know what is the matter with me. I lost all interest in castles. I cannot even sketch the ground plan of my dream castle any more. I tried to make such a sketch the other day and simply couldn't do it." The therapist made no comment, since it was evident to him that this transitory inhibition was the result of the disintegration of a defensive pseudo-sublimation. Some weeks later this adolescent, who up to that time had planned to become an architect specializing in the building of magnificent private mansions and public buildings, began to discuss seriously the program of a certain School of Architecture, which offered three specialized curricula, homes, industrial plants, and public buildings, and informed the therapist that he had decided to specialize in the building of comfortable and functional middle-class homes. He developed this plan quite realistically and even added some scathing remarks about the showy Greek colonnades of museums and other public buildings. This change of interest was interpreted to him as the result of the transformation of an escapist fantasy into a genuine and practical sublimation. During a subsequent relapse into a state of temporary inhibition this youth stated that he felt like "smashing everything." The inhibition disappeared once more when "building" was interpreted to him as being also a reaction formation against, and a sublimation of, the urge to destroy, which he experienced only when he felt unable to create, and to actualize himself.

Case 4: A Pseudo-Frigid Woman

An emotionally infantile young married woman experienced considerable neurotic guilt over her marital relations and therefore used her sexual compliance or noncompliance chiefly as a kind of "power maneuver"—i.e., as a means of forcing her husband to gratify her various neurotic needs. Yet, despite these neurotic connotations of the sexual act, she was not wholly frigid. When, after months of analysis, the neurotic meaning and neurotic mechanism of her pre-analytic sexual behavior became clear to her, she temporarily lost all interest in marital relations and became practically frigid. Then, "starting from scratch," she gradually evolved a new and healthy interest in sex. From that point onward, not only were her marital relations psychologically more satisfying and even physically more gratifying than they had ever been before, but there took place also a radical improvement in her broader relationship with her husband. This, in itself, was proof of a great deal of new emotional maturity, since—owing to factors wholly beyond her control—her marital situation was a very difficult one.

COMMENT: In this instance the analyst did not help the patient "relearn" sexuality. Rather did he help the patient to unlearn the distorting and inhibiting emotional connotations of neurotic sexual activity. This, in turn, led to a spontaneous transitory loss of sexual interests and skills, until finally the libido, no longer interfered with and distorted by neurotic mechanisms, sought and found new channels and normal techniques for its actualization, in the course of a renewed and now undistorted quest for self-actualization and humanization.

SELF-REËTHNICIZATION

Of course, the patient is not deprived of any guidance whatsoever, even in the course of his spontaneous attempts to reëthnicize himself. However, this guidance is not provided by his therapist. It is provided by culture itself. The patient simply learns to understand the real significance of cultural values and channels and then learns to use in an appropriate manner those culturally provided techniques which he had formerly misunderstood and misused.[4]

EDUCATION IN CHILD ANALYSIS

The psychoanalysis of children is somewhat more complicated. Even the most neurotic adult has already been ethnicized ("educated") in many ways. Thus, though the mysophobic patient

[4] Thus, the patient in question learned to find desirable such sexual values of our culture as monogamy and tenderness, and learned to derive the greatest amount of gratification from those sexual techniques which are deemed "most normal" in our culture. This latter fact need not surprise us, since Róheim stressed long ago that traditional sexual techniques reflect the "national character" of a given group (187). In addition, we indicated elsewhere (54) that in culture area A a sexual technique which is the "normal" one in culture area B may be used to express neurotic needs. In other words, a technique which in culture area B is a means for expressing healthy sexual attitudes may serve as an outlet for neurotic impulses in culture area A, where another type of sexual technique is considered "normal."

(Case 2) grossly misinterprets the culturally established goal of cleanliness and abuses the culturally provided facilities for achieving this goal, he nonetheless "knows" in a way that cleanliness *per se* is socially rewarded, and he is familiar with the proper use of soap and water. Hence, once he is freed from his neurotic inhibitions and biases, he can be relied upon to evolve "spontaneously" a desire for cleanliness and to achieve it by means of culturally provided devices and techniques. The same applies to other types of adult neurotic problems. But the small child may be relatively unaware of the cultural value of cleanliness and may never have learned how to use a toothbrush in a competent and effective manner. His therapy must include also an attempt to educate—i.e., to ethnicize—him. Although this can be done within the psychoanalytic setting itself, it is, on the whole, more desirable that the education of a child receiving treatment be left to the therapeutic educator, who functions within the setting of an analytically oriented therapeutic school. This matter need not concern us further for the time being, since it will be discussed in detail in another chapter (Chapter 5).

Thus, strictly speaking, psychoanalytic therapy in particular is not a learning experience in which the therapist functions as a teacher. The therapist is, on the contrary, a "teacher of forgetting," or of unlearning, and facilitates relearning only in so far as he helps the patient to unlearn neurotic motives, thus making possible the acquisition of healthy ones which lead to self-realization and true humanization.

EDUCATIONAL ACTS IN ADULT ANALYSIS

It would be illusory to deny, of course, that even the most classical Freudian analyst is, now and then, obliged to give his patient some guidance or concrete information; i.e., even he must occasionally function as an educator.

A phobic and obsessive alien became quite fretful because his

analyst systematically refused to provide guidance and information. He complained that he could not figure out why the analyst
provided factual information in one situation and then refused to
provide it in other situations as well. In seeking to answer this
complaint—but not before its dynamics and real meaning were
interpreted to the patient—the analyst formulated for the patient
the following rules governing "educational activities" in the
course of a psychoanalysis:

The giving of concrete information ("teaching") is permissible
under the following conditions:

1. The patient himself is materially not in a position to obtain
unassisted some information which is indispensable to him.

2. The patient is in a position to obtain the needed information, but not rapidly enough to be of use to him in a critical situation. E.g., this alien, who had to write an urgent letter to the
immigration authorities, was given concrete information about administrative regulations.

3. The patient neurotically uses his ignorance of certain matters to justify some line of action or inaction, the neurotic implications of which this justification helps him to ignore. In other
words, in this context one gives the patient the "needed" information so as to make him face the neurotic root of his actions, or of
his inaction. This type of "education" is, of course, dynamically
very different from the purely practical "guide, philosopher, and
friend" position implicit in types 1 and 2 of "educational" activity.
A clinical example may help us to understand this point more
clearly:

Case 5: Neurotic Exploitation of Ignorance

A foreign patient professed to be extremely eager to engage in an
affair with a very willing and quite suitable young woman but alleged
that he could not do so because he did not know what condoms were
called in English and therefore could not purchase any. He also offered

fairly cogent reasons for not asking his associates to tell him the word for contraceptives. Actually, this legitimate, but not at all insuperable, "ignorance" simply served to mask his dread of coitus. When confronted with this evasive use of ignorance as well as with his neurotic dread of sex, he vehemently rejected both confrontations.[5] Hence, the analyst told him the word "condom"—which the patient, not at all surprisingly, "forgot" the moment he left the office. The next day he once more asked the analyst to tell him this word, and even insisted that he should write it down for him. The analyst refused to do this, explaining to the patient that, because of his obsessive preoccupation with "documentary evidence" of all kinds, he would certainly construe this note as a "written permission to engage in sexual relations." The patient then decided to write down the word himself. However, even though his English was more than adequate,[6] he insisted that the analyst should spell out the word, letter by letter, which the analyst agreed to do. After the hour the patient went to a drugstore but, again not unexpectedly, after an agonizing half-hour of indecision turned around without entering the shop and went home. The next day he tried to justify his failure to enter the store by alleging that there were too many other people in the pharmacy at that time, etc. Finally, after repeated confrontations with reality, the patient reluctantly decided to face his dread of sexuality, which he had hitherto strenuously ignored and denied. He explained that since his parents engaged in marital relations, but tabooed all sexual activities for him, he came to define sexuality as an "adult privilege" or "prerogative," to which someone like himself, who felt and acted like an eight-year-old, was simply not "entitled." The analyst then remarked that, since the patient actually wished to remain childish and dependent, he himself obviously felt that the price he had to pay for this dubious "privilege" was the renunciation of all mature sexual self-expression.

COMMENT: This "educational interlude" turned out to be one of the most significant moments in the treatment of this patient. By tearing

[5] This patient compulsively rejected all interpretations and confrontations. He repeatedly told the analyst: "The moment you start to say something, my first thought is to pick flaws in, and to disprove, whatever you may be saying."

[6] This patient tried to conceal his knowledge and his abilities, lest they provide a basis for further demands upon him.

down an imposing façade of rationalizations and resistances, it gave both the analyst and the patient access to some of the neurotic and infantile sources of the patient's sexual inhibitions, the analysis of which required several additional months. However, at the end of that period the patient was finally able to engage, for the first time in his life, and with some measures of success, in sexual relations with a woman who was not a prostitute and whom—at least between intermittent anxiety attacks—he actually liked and respected.

SUMMARY

Genuine psychoanalysis and deep psychotherapy may be thought of as means whereby the effects of a warped ethnicization, resulting from an inhibited, distorted, and arrested humanization, are "unlearned." In restoring the patient's humanity, one simply gives him access to his real potentialities and enables him to become correctly ethnicized. However, in really deep psychotherapy at least, the second—and this time effective—process of ethnicization is not undertaken by the therapist himself. This task is performed for the adult by the social and cultural milieu in which he lives, and for the child by the therapeutic educator, working in close coöperation with the psychotherapist, in a specially structured therapeutic milieu.

The psychotherapist is concerned primarily with the patient's true humanization, through unlearning, while the therapeutic educator is concerned chiefly with the child's correct ethnicization—made possible by the freeing of his human potentialities from its neurotic shackles—by means of learning. The two activities are, thus, complementary. However, the humanization resulting from the activity of the psychotherapist is a *conditio sine qua non* of the effectiveness of the therapeutic educator's ethnicizing activities. This definition, which is meaningful in itself, also serves the very practical purpose of clearly delimiting the operational boundaries between the activities of the psychotherapist and those of the educator.

::

CHAPTER 4

The Differential Tasks of Therapeutic Education

We must now seek to differentiate further between education and psychotherapy, this time not primarily in terms of technical procedures and in terms of what these meliorative devices ultimately can or do achieve but rather in terms of their more fundamental characteristics. Only by means of such an analysis of the basic, and fairly abstract, characteristics which differentiate education from psychotherapy will it be possible to utilize either or both, jointly or severally, in the optimal manner.

PERVASIVENESS OF THERAPEUTIC INFLUENCES

We must recognize from the start that, in practice, the outward effects of the two techniques often resemble each other in many respects. However, these similarities are more apparent than real, since they are largely determined not by some inherent similarity between the two techniques but by the basic characteristics of human beings upon whom the techniques impinge. Man's psyche is not a jumble of disconnected, segmental, and atomistic abilities and performances. Rather is it a tightly integrated whole, within which any change in one area automatically elicits parallel, reinforcing, additional, reactive, or compensatory changes in other segments of the psyche. Thus, the learning of a new skill by purely educational means often increases the subject's emotional security through an increase in self-esteem, etc. Conversely, the lowering of some segmental tension by means of psychotherapy may lead to an improvement in the performance of a previously more or less unmanageable task. Hence, education can often produce effects which usually result from psychotherapeutic efforts—and vice versa. However, we repeat that these similarities obtain primarily between the effects and not between the fundamental characteristics of the two meliorative techniques under consideration.

DELETERIOUS EFFECTS OF TREATMENT

At this point we must issue a warning against the assumption that any improvement in bodily health or in ego functions automatically leads to improvements in the total functioning of the organism. There are, unfortunately, some exceptions to this rule. Indeed, it is one of the functions of symptoms to keep the emotionally sick person in at least some kind of precarious balance. If a ship springs a leak and begins to list forward, one may have to open the sea cocks of the poop to make the ship ride at a relatively even keel, even though this causes the whole ship to ride much lower in the water than it would if the imbalance caused by the initial leak not been corrected. Superficial interferences with symptoms and disabilities can have tragic consequences, as three examples will show:

Case 6: Physical Defect Masking a Psychosis

A patient may suffer much distress because his nose is grotesque or ugly. In order to alleviate his constant and painful preoccupation with his disfigurement, plastic surgery may be undertaken. However, his preoccupation with the ugliness of his nose may actually be a symptom of a severe emotional disturbance. Hence, when he no longer has an excuse to focus his conflicts on his nose, he may "go to pieces" psychologically and become psychotic (*117, 149, 159*).

Case 7: Hysterical Torticollis Masking a Psychosis

A socially fairly well-adjusted and quite rational patient suffered from torticollis—a "hysterical" symptom, consisting in a unilateral contraction of the muscles of the neck, so that the head is twisted sidewise and downward. When, under hypnosis, he was ordered to relax and to bring his head back into the normal position, the patient complied but immediately became completely paranoid, pouring out a stream of delusional material. He did not return to "normal" until the hypnotist withdrew his command and permitted him to develop torticollis once more. In this case the torticollis, which is a hysterical symptom, served to mask and to keep within bounds an underlying paranoia (*191*).

Case 8: Neurodermatitis Masking a Psychosis

It is well known that it is sometimes unwise to tamper, either by purely medical means or by means of hypnosis or suggestion, with neurotically produced skin lesions, or so-called "neurodermatitis," since the suppression of the skin lesions may trigger the overt outbreak of an underlying psychosis (*234*).

In brief, whereas a modification of some aspect of the total psychic functioning of a person aways produces changes also in other segments of his personality, these changes are not always necessarily favorable ones. In fact, in some instances temporarily "unfavorable" changes in the condition of the patient are actually desirable, since they are often caused by the disintegration of symptomatic defenses against underlying conflicts, which hitherto served to keep the personality in some kind of balance. This fact is often stated in the following form: "The patient must get worse before he can get better."

DISINTEGRATION OF NEUROTIC DEFENSES

Sometimes the sick child itself knows that these explosions are stages in its progress toward recovery.

Case 9: Regression Indicates Progress

A twelve-year-old schizophrenic child, of very superior intelligence, tried to explain to his parents in a deeply moving letter that his current "naughtiness," his sudden use of bad language, and his addiction to destructive pranks and to fighting were all part of his improvement and reflected his gradual emergence from the world of fantasy (77).

In short, the disintegration of symptomatic defenses against underlying conflicts often makes possible the treatment of the real cause of the illness, instead of merely that of its symptoms. Of course the management of such "curative aggravations" of the illness requires not only considerable therapeutic skill but also a real ability on the part of the therapist to tolerate anxiety. When a psychiatric resident once asked the staff how much aggressivity he should allow his patient to manifest, the writer replied without a trace of irony, and in dead earnest: "As much as *you* can stand, without being disturbed by it."

Problems of this type beset not only the psychotherapist but also the therapeutic educator, since he too, in modifying one segment of the student's personality, may bring about an eruption of seemingly "more serious" disturbances in another segment of the personality. If he is a highly skilled therapeutic educator, instead of seeking to conceal such "explosions" as signs of "failure," he will immediately call them to the attention of the psychiatric staff, for whom they may represent a long-hoped-for opportunity to get at the roots of the student's problems. Needless to say, these remarks should not be interpreted as a suggestion that the therapeutic educator should deliberately provoke such explosions. Eruptions of the underlying conflict should be neither provoked nor suppressed; they should be neither desired nor dreaded. They should simply be exploited therapeutically when they do take place.

COÖPERATION BETWEEN THERAPISTS AND EDUCATORS

The preceding discussion indicates that education and psychotherapy may produce identical external results—incuding even instances in which the secondary results are, temporarily at least, very "disquieting" ones. However, though both educators and psychotherapists influence not only one segment of the personality but, for better or for worse, also the student's personality as a whole, the process of education and the process of psychotherapy are, fundamentaly, quite different. "A miniature psychotic storm" (20) is for the psychotherapist an opportunity for treatment, while for the educator it is an opportunity for referral to the psychiatrist. In fact, we feel that the fundamental differences between education and psychotherapy can, if well understood, serve as a basis for the most fruitful type of coöperation between educators and psychotherapists. For example, just as the educator has to rely upon the psychotherapist to manage explosive unconscious processes triggered by the educational process, so the psychotherapist may have to call upon the educator to perform important therapeutic functions by strengthening the student's weak ego, and also by curtailing his "acting out" tendencies, since both these defects tend to hamper the progress of psychotherapy.[1]

It should be strongly emphasized that, like ordinary education, therapeutic education also resembles psychotherapy chiefly in its effects, and differs from it in its basic orientation.

THERAPEUTIZABILITY AND EDUCABILITY

This assertion remains valid even if we focus our attention primarily upon the therapeutic effects of education and upon the re-educational aspects of all forms of psychotherapy, which seem to correspond to what Alexander and French call "corrective emotional experiences" (1). In our view, such experiences produce

[1] A more detailed discussion of the proper way of articulating the various meliorative techniques used in a therapeutic school will be found in Chapter 12.

chiefly a favorable change in the pattern of the defenses, through "conditioning," but involve no true gain in insight. Otherwise expressed, those aspects of psychotherapy which resemble reëducation may not be thought of as representing psychotherapy in the strict sense of that term. They do represent, however, means whereby the therapeutizability of the patient—i.e., his capacity to obtain new and meaningful insights into himself—is increased. Conversely, those aspects of therapeutic education which most resemble genuine psychotherapy serve chiefly the purpose of increasing the educability of the child.

The way of increasing the therapeutizability of the patient by giving him certain types of factual information was discussed in the preceding chapter. Examples of quasi-psychotherapeutic educational techniques of helping the child cope with various emotional difficulties, in order to increase his educability, will readily come to the mind of the student of education. Hence, this aspect of the overlap between education and psychotherapy need not arrest our attention any further at this stage of our discussion, since its import is practical rather than theoretical.

MIXED THERAPEUTIC AND EDUCATIONAL TECHNIQUES

We may now return to a further discussion of our fundamental thesis that such mixed "educationally therapeutic" or "therapeutically educational" techniques are possible only because the object at which the efforts of both psychotherapists and therapeutic educators are directed is one and the same. This object is the inadequately developed and insufficiently differentiated and individualized being. The possibility of evolving such mixed techniques is not due to any fundamental relationship between the two component techniques. Indeed, the logical bases of the two techniques are not so closely related as to be even partly undifferentiable. On the contrary, we must at all times be fully aware of the fact that the differences between education and therapy are genuine, effec-

tive, and functional ones. They are definitely not spurious or purely
occupational differences, of the type which William James ridiculed in his well-known quip: "A difference which makes no difference is no difference."

LEARNING VS. UNLEARNING

As stated in the preceding chapter, the most obvious difference
between education and psychotherapy is that the former has as its
goal learning while the goal of the latter is unlearning (in order
to make relearning possible). This way of formulating this genuine difference is admittedly a somewhat crude and heuristic one.
Nonetheless, it does reveal the existence of genuine formal differences between the two techniques, although, needless to say, in a
practical context what counts far more than the existence of formal differences *per se* is the functional import of these formal differences. This is a matter which was discussed in the preceding
chapter and therefore need not be examined further at this
point.

MEMBERSHIP IN A LOGICAL VS. MEMBERSHIP IN AN EDUCA-
TIONAL CLASS

The second obvious, but again chiefly formal, difference is the
manner in which the object of these two meliorative techniques is
defined. The conventional educator—as distinct from the psychiatrically oriented therapeutic educator—directs his efforts in a very
genuine sense not at an individual in the most comprehensive
meaning of that term but at what Bertrand Russell would call
"any" (194) member of a given (logical) class of beings, membership in that class being determined by certain traits common
to all members of that class. Now, it is important to realize that
the characteristics on the basis of which an individual child is assigned to a given class (grade) are often not actual but imputed
characteristics, the imputation being often wholly aprioristic. Spe-

cifically, the often practically, though not logically, legitimate assumption is made that if a child possesses characteristic *x,* which implies membership in a certain *logical* class (e.g., age category), it is "therefore" also legitimate to assign the child to a certain *educational* class (grade) in which it is deemed permissible to make certain educational and behavioral demands on it. Yet such demands would be reasonable and logically valid only if the child possessed, in addition to characteristic *x,* also a certain wholly different characteristic *y.*

INDIVIDUAL VS. AVERAGE PERFORMANCE

Thus, the formal and legal reason why a six-year-old child is sent to the first grade is simply that it possesses the characteristic *x* of being six years old, but not yet seven years old, at the time the school year begins.[2] Then, in this context at least, characteristic *x* (age) is treated as though it were a logically and functionally legitimate basis on which to make certain (educational) demands on the child. In other words, the school acts as though there existed a necessary and logical relationship between age and performance level.

Of course empirical and statistical observations indicate that most (but not all!) six-year-old children also possess the capacity of satisfying the educational demands made upon them on the basis of their age. In other words, because it was found that most six-year-olds are capable of learning certain things, all children who reach that age are sent, without further ado, to first grade and are expected to perform accordingly. This is particularly true nowadays, because the curriculum of the modern grade school is based upon extensive statistical investigations of the average in-

---

[2] Compare in this context the fiction that all thoroughbreds are born on January 1. This means that in a race for yearlings held on December 31, horses 366 days old may be pitted against horses 729 days old. This disparity is not corrected by any type of handicapping, although an age difference of 364 days means more in the case of a young horse than in the case of a young child.

tellectual capacities and educational potentialities of children of various ages. This, however, is simply a matter of empirical experience and statistical standardization, which, in terms of pure logic, definitely does not imply the absolute existence of a necessary and invariant relationship between age and performance.[3]

This point is so important that, at the risk of having to repeat ourselves at least in part, we will elaborate it somewhat further. Experience with many generations of children indicates that the coöcurrence of characteristics x and y (age and a certain performance potential) is statistically sufficiently common and frequent to justify, on a strictly practical level, the developing of certain standardized social attitudes and demand patterns, requiring the possession of characteristic y, in regard to all children demonstrably possessing characteristic x. In other words, the possession of characteristic y (ability) is imputed to all children possessing characteristic x (age). Hence, the demands made on them—e.g., in terms of a curriculum "suitable for six-year-olds"—are made on the basis of this imputation, and not as a result of an actual preliminary attempt to ascertain that each of these individual children does, indeed, conform to the statistical norm and does, in fact, possess also the characteristic y customarily imputed to those who demonstrably possess characteristic x.[4] This means that, in practice, society simply ascertains that a given child is six years of age and thereafter—until proof to the contrary becomes painfully evident —takes it for granted that it also possesses the average educational

---

[3] An example drawn from a radically different context will illustrate this point. Ernest Jones, in his biography of Freud (*129*), emphasizes the perplexities and psychological conflicts experienced by Freud, who in his childhood had to cope with the paradox of being, from the moment of his birth, an uncle to the considerably older son of his paternal half-brother. Though social fiat and practice assigned him to the "uncle" class, his "age linked" level of performance forced him to function on the "younger brother" level in his relationship with his technical nephew. This perplexing situation may have helped him later on to discover the Oedipus complex.

[4] Needless to say, we speak here primarily of old-fashioned schools which do not give psychological tests to their new students.

capacities of the ordinary six-year-old. Putting it in still another way, the demands which are made and the program of education which is imposed upon a child explicitly on the basis of its age are actually, though implicitly, imposed on it in terms of its—often real, but for that reason logically not any less putative and inferential—expected capacity to perform.

We hasten to add that expectations and imputations of this type, made on the basis of absolute, measurable, and sometimes very naïve criteria, which readily lend themselves to classificatory undertakings, are common in every society. They are, in fact, practically indispensable for the smooth functioning of society, being closely related to the whole problem of what Linton called "ascribed status" (*151*)—the ascription of a status and role ("first grader") being made in terms of age, with the expectation that the child will be able to function in that capacity. In the same way, a "masculine" conduct and "male" sexual interests are socially and culturally "demanded" and "expected" from any person who happens to have a certain type of anatomical configuration. When, because of mishaps in the psychic evolution of that person, these demands and expectations are not met—i.e., when the boy acts "sissyish," or the man behaves like a "pansy"—disappointed society becomes extremely indignant.

Old-fashioned parents and unprogressive educators also tend to react with anger to the discovery that a child, assigned to a certain grade on the basis of its readily measurable age, fails to perform as expected. In fact, in many of the "little red schoolhouses" which still form a substantial proportion of our educational institutions the first reaction is that the child must be forced to perform as expected—if necessary "to the tune of the hickory stick" so dear to sentimentalists. This reaction is the inevitable consequence of the initial hypothesis that the child can perform as expected (because, after all, it is six years old) and simply refuses to do so. This type of fallacious reasoning plays a crucial role in the motivation of punitive measures in the old-fashioned classroom, both as regards the mentally inadequate child and as regards the child who misbehaves not because it "wants" to be bad but because its neurosis compels it to misbehave. Only when the failure of "educational" pressures of this type to produce the desired results becomes painfully obvious does the average "old-fashioned" educator —and the "average" is always inadequate in any profession— pause for a "second look," this time at the child's actual and functional characteristic y: its real capacity to perform.[5]

This change in outlook—this shift in preoccupation from the statistically expected level of performance to actual ability—involves two major changes in the educator's general professional "stance": He shifts (1) from concern with the child as member of a *class* (grade), to concern with the child as a unique *person*, and (2) from "class" (i.e., in practice, "grade") assignment in terms of aprioristic expectations based upon *imputed* abilities to a realistic concern with *actual* capacities.

It is important to analyze at this point the "logic" underlying the initial imputation. As stated before, this imputation or expectation was arrived at through an extrapolation to a given individual of the results of empirical experiences with the frequency of the coöccurrence of a readily observable criterion x (age) with a less readily observable (and therefore slothfully imputed) criterion y (level of performance) in a statistical population.

Of course, the high frequency of the coöccurrence of these two characteristics is an empirical fact. However, this fact refers to a "population sample" and not to every individual member of that population. Hence, the extrapolation from the established existence of criterion x (age) to an imputed (and often actually verifiable) criterion y (ability) is legitimate only for the population as a whole, but not for each individual member thereof. In fact, such

[5] This statement is not an exaggeration. Deliberate "naughtiness" is so readily imputed to the child—witness the British axiom that small boys are "nasty little beasts"—that sometimes even organic illness is ignored. Cf. Case 62.

an extrapolation from the statistical population to the individual is both bad logic and bad statistics. It is not the product of scientific reasoning but of a mere "thought habit," whose emotional root is man's misguided desire to generalize, to simplify, and to "coördinate"—to treat all things and all persons as interchangeable. Just as no statistical study of the frequency of collisions can help us predict that John Doe's Ford will actually have a collision because, statistically, it is "his turn" to have one, so no statistical study of the routine coincidence of certain abilities with the sixth year of life in a given population can serve as a basis for imputing certain abilities to an individual six-year-old. If this were permissible, then one would also be entitled to say that a given feeble-minded adult, functioning at the average level of a first-grader, is chronologically six years old. This reasoning is admittedly grotesque, but no more grotesque than is the reverse type of reasoning.

Logically, the attempt to impute a certain capacity to a child on the basis of its age is an expression of a tacit belief in the existence of a certain patterning of criteria. It implies the assumption that these two criteria are logically, and not only empirically, interrelated, and that they form a functional scheme.

We cannot quarrel with this procedure, which is quite standard —and also quite useful—in everyday scientific thinking. What we must do at this point is something altogether different: We must seek to discover the nature of the pattern the existence of which is a tacit presupposition in this whole line of reasoning.

THE REAL CAUSES OF FAILURE

In order to clarify this matter we have to refer back to our initial analysis of what we have called "development," using this term in a general sense. We must specifically ask whether the developmental pattern, which this line of reasoning presupposes, pertains to maturation, humanization, or ethnicization.

It is our view that in most cases the theoretical pattern in terms of which this extrapolation from age to capacity is made pertains to maturation, as this term was defined in Chapter 1. Indeed, the basic assumption—or at least the first assumption—is usually that a six-year-old child's manifest inability to do first-grade work is due to a skewing of its maturational pattern. The first hypothesis which is therefore investigated is that the maturation of the child's intelligence may have lagged—and will presumably continue to lag—behind its chronological age. This view is strongly supported by the distinction which psychologists draw between "chronological age" and "mental age." Only if intelligence tests, which are the first to be administered, fail to reveal such a skewing of the maturational pattern do we begin to investigate the possibility of disturbances, asymmetries, or skewings in the humanization or ethnicization pattern of the child's development by means of psychiatric or sociological interviews and of projective tests. This is a point to which we will have to return shortly.

What concerns us most at this juncture is that the implicit theory underlying educational techniques correlates, in a highly specific manner, maturational, humanizational, and ethnicizational patterns and pattern sequences. In homelier terms, it is assumed that, once a child's psychological maturation has reached a certain stage, it can not only learn to speak (humanization) but learn to speak specifically English, Hottentot, or Chinese (ethnicization). In fact, the progress of maturation, which is a psychobiological concept, is routinely tested by means of its psychocultural (humanization and ethnicization) repercussions. We hasten to add that, at least in the present state of our knowledge, this testing pattern is fully validated by the findings of ethnic psychology, or "culture and personality" studies. Nonetheless, it is quite important that the true nature of this testing pattern be clarified and made explicit. So far as we know, if a child has matured far enough to be able to talk at all, it can be humanized by being helped to talk and can be ethnicized by being taught to speak English or Hottentot, as the case may be.

SORTING AND THE CULTURE PATTERN

At this point we must introduce a concept which seems to be a very crucial and general one: the concept of sorting.

Before we undertake a detailed theoretical analysis of "sorting," we propose to define it for the moment as the establishing of a particular kind of order, which results primarily from systematic exclusions and inclusions and secondarily from an arrangement into a particular pattern at least of the included, and often also of the excluded, sample. For example, we may first separate red balls from white balls and then arrange all the "accepted" red balls into a triangle and all the "rejected" white balls into a square.

The same principles of patterned sorting apply to human behavior.

LANGUAGE AS AN EXAMPLE OF SORTING

The observed fact that any child who can learn to speak at all can learn to speak any existing or made up (Esperanto) language indicates that, theoretically at least, the child's capacity of articulation (sound production) is, for practical purposes, unlimited,[6] or at least extremely large.

Any child can learn French nasalization, Hottentot "clicks," English-American lisping,[7] etc. Its acquisition of one particular phonetic pattern in preference to another, of one vocabulary in preference to another—and, by the way, also of one way of pair-

---

[6] The statement just made emphasizes the importance of the term "for practical purposes." There are sounds which no man can reproduce even remotely. Thus, man can duplicate neither the high-pitched sounds emitted by bats nor the volume of a lion's roar—nor, perhaps, the distinctive sound pattern produced by a person with a cleft palate.

[7] The fact that the English *th*—both in words like "thorn" and in words like "thou"—represents lisping, which anyone, once he knows this, can produce properly, since anyone can lisp at will, was first pointed out by Herzog (*115*). This finding may be helpful in teaching English pronunciation to immigrants.

ing certain sound patterns with certain concepts[8]—thus represents a "sorting" (of its potentialities) in the strictest sense. How durable and tenacious such sound patterns are, once they are established, is shown by the existence of that very common and nearly irremediable defect: the foreign accent. The acquisition of a distinctive pattern of articulation—of a sorting and stabilization of the various possible sound patterns which, both theoretically and practically, any human child can be taught to produce—is a very clear-cut example of sorting. It exemplifies the process of segmental inclusion, with subsequent stabilization and proficiency.[9] This sorting and rank-ordering process even affects those sound patterns which the fundamental phonetic pattern of one language excludes. Indeed, certain lapses from the ideal or conventional sound pattern are deemed less ridiculous and less offensive than others. Thus—perhaps because of historical factors, though this is by no means certain, since the ridiculing of this particular foreign accent antedates the historically rather recent pitched hostility between the French and the Germans—the French deem a Germanic accent the most objectionable of "foreign accents" in French. By contrast, at a time when Charles Boyer was a very popular movie star in America, speaking English with a French (or "Boyer") accent was socially almost at a premium, being thought of as "cute" or "seductive."

What we tried to stress by means of this example—and it deliberately ignores the far too complex problem of the metalinguistic relationship between language and logical patterns (231) (which, by the way, forms no exception to the rule just proposed)—is that man is first and foremost a "sorter," i.e., a being

[8] We mean simply that the sound pattern *to:* signifies "lake" in Hungarian, "breast" in Sedang Moi, and "toe" in English.

[9] In regard to "proficiency," an example already used elsewhere (53) may be cited. The writer once spoke French almost without an accent. Nowadays, when he is obliged to speak French for any length of time, his facial muscles begin to ache from having to articulate so often the now unaccustomed French *u;* since he now speaks mostly English, the muscles he must use in the articulation of this French vowel have become flabby through disuse.

all of whose specifically human and ethnic activities result from a presorting of his behavior (by means of education) and who, by acquiring a special efficiency in sorting in that particular manner, achieves also a greater efficiency in living in a particular milieu. We have only to contrast the proverbial "million years during which a million monkeys would have to pound a million type-writers" before one of them accidentally "wrote" the sign pattern forming the text of a Shakespeare sonnet with the short time it took Shakespeare to "sort" the same letters into the same pattern. This efficiency is admittedly achieved by means of an arbitrary "renunciation" of many inherently possible forms of conduct. For example, the English child, who is taught to speak English, is thereby implicitly made to "renounce" in advance the possibility of ever acquiring a perfect French sound pattern. However, even in the crudest sense, this "renunciation" is largely illusory, since it permits the compensatory achievement of a far greater sorting efficiency within the educationally limited ("taught") universe of behavior modalities.

SORTING IN RELATION TO HUMANIZATION AND
ETHNICIZATION

At this point it is desirable to consider more in detail the implications of the difference between humanization and ethnicization. We indicated above that ethnicization—e.g., learning the English sound pattern—implies, in a sense, a "constriction" of one's total possible vocal behavior modalities, owing to the presorting effects of education. But (and this is the crux of the matter) the presorting of behavioral modalities in the course of ethnicization need not—though, alas, it sometimes does—involve also a "constriction" of the person's humanization. In simplest terms, the self-fulfillment implicit in man's humanization can be attained through a variety of "specific," "restricted," or "presorted" channels, implying a "renunciation" of alternative channels. However, we hold

that the choice of the actual channels of self-realization is unimportant in terms of man's basic humanization. Although the
child who is taught French sound patterns may be thought of as
being forced to "renounce" the possibility of acquiring also a perfect English sound pattern, we deem this "renunciation" inessen-
tial and spurious in terms of the child's need to become human.
The child does need a sound pattern—for economy and efficiency
and also because there is apparently a human need for patterning
per se—but this need, the fulfillment of which enables him to be
human, can be equally well gratified by the English, the French,
or the Hottentot sound pattern, provided, of course, that those
among whom the child lives also use this particular sound pattern.

We deliberately limited the preceding discussion to the fairly
simple matter of sound patterns, since there is still a great deal of
argument over the relative efficiency and expressive capacity of the
various languages. Thus, Greek scholars assure us that the Greek
tongue was an incomparably fine instrument of expression (*116*).
By contrast, missionaries seeking to translate the Gospel into some
exotic tongue are easily exasperated by the seeming clumsiness of
the vernacular. It is, however, open to debate, even for one who,
like the writer, yields to no one in his love of Greek literature,
whether the allegedly superior expressive potentialities of the
Greek language are absolute or simply reflect a suitability of classical Greek for the expression of the type of things we, the heirs of
Greece, were conditioned to seek to express. It is not at all certain
that the Greek tongue would be particularly suitable for expressing the kind of ideas and relationships which the Chinese language
can express.[10] Similarly, though few of us find the English language inadequate for our purposes, an eminent Sinologist, Pro-

[10] We know that many foreign concepts cannot be readily translated into English
and have to be represented by loan words, such as the French *chic* or the German
eingebettet. Likewise, the ponderousness of style which characterizes even some excellent literary translations from the German may not be due to the clumsiness of
the translator but may reflect the profound relationship which exists between syntax
and thought patterns.

fessor Boodberg, assured the writer that some 2500 English words would have to be coined in order to translate certain complex Chinese texts with complete accuracy.[11] Needless to say, the Chinese probably face similar difficulties in translating certain English texts into their own rich and flexible tongue.

Be that as it may, and while being mindful of the frustrations which a young Mozart born into a primitive tribe would probably experience, on the whole we may say that every pattern of ethnicization, i.e., the adoption of the "sorting pattern" of any culture whatsoever, permits a full humanization of every human being.

Thus ethnicization, the chief instrument of which in any culture is education in the broadest sense, may be viewed simply as a means for the inculcation of a particular and selective way of patterning and channeling man's humanization, which his need for self-fulfillment requires. In fact, this sorting process itself, in so far as it presupposes patterned criteria for sorting, is part of man's humanization. We can define man as a sorting animal, i.e., as a being particularly skillful in reversing, in more ways than any other animal, the drift toward entropy in the external world.[12]

It is hardly necessary to state that what represents "sorting" or "order," as against what is "chaotic," often depends largely on the individual's subjective needs and on his preferred "axes" for the organization of reality and experience (53). For example, as any psychologist knows, a set of objects can be sorted into two "legitimate" groups or classes in a variety of ways. In stating that man is a "sorter" and "reducer of entropy" we simply affirm that his

[11] Personal communication.

[12] Entropy is, from the statistical point of view, the most probable, i.e., the least organized and patterned, state of a given system. Any closed system left to itself will drift toward a state of entropy, in which, without any decrease in the energy content of the system, the energy becomes so disorganized and its distribution throughout the system becomes so homogeneous that it can no longer produce any externally perceptible work. We wish to add that the definition of man just offered lends no support to Jeans' view (71) challenged by Donnan and Guggenheim (71), that man is outside the scope of the second law of thermodynamics (law of entropy). In that controversy the writer firmly aligns himself with Donnan and Guggenheim.

sorting operations have that effect within his particular frame of reference.

CATEGORIES FOR SORTING

It is important to stress once more that one and the same "mixed" set of objects can be sorted in many ways and can be fitted into a variety of categories. We suggested elsewhere (53) that four categories are of prime importance for an understanding of the organization of behavior and of experience.

1. *The biological axis* is the axis in terms of which we differentiate, for example, between edible and inedible or between harmless and dangerous creatures, etc.

2. *The experiential axis* is the one in terms of which we differentiate between strangers and persons with whom we are acquainted, etc.

3. *The cultural axis* enables us to distinguish between legal and illegal acts, between those whom we may marry and those whom we may not, etc.

4. *The neurotic axis* may serve as a basis for putting things either into the category of anxiety-arousing objects or into that of anxiety-diminishing or reassuring objects, etc.

Each of these axes, representing a major type of orientation to reality, may serve as a basis for "sorting" reality in a distinctive way, which seems "orderly" and meaningful in terms of itself but may appear chaotic and senseless in terms of a system of sorting based on a different "axis of orientation" or approach to the problem of "sorting out" reality. Thus, from the purely biological point of view, it is legitimate to put an apple and a pig into the same category, since both are edible. However, this way of sorting reality will seem arbitrary and chaotic to a good Mohammedan, whose religion defines the pig as a ritually unclean and therefore "inedible" animal. Our feeling that "all foreigners are crazy" is largely due to the fact that they "sort" reality in a different way. In fact, our principal difficulty in understanding what a neurotic or a psychotic really means is rooted in the fact that his way of classifying reality is based upon a wholly subjective system of categories, with which we are unfamiliar. Not until the "method in his madness" is understood also by the therapist can the latter fully grasp the meaning of his patient's statements and behavior (55).

We need not go here into the intricacies of the logically explosive, and often systematically—i.e., emotionally—misunderstood second law of thermodynamics (or law of entropy). We mention this matter only for the sake of those interested in the philosophical dimensions of the definition of man.[13] What concerns us here is something quite simple:

1. Man is a sorter—as is, to a certain extent, every living organism—and his capacity to sort, and especially to sort in a variety of ways, is an important component of his humanity.

2. Man is also a particular type of sorter, who adheres to certain set systems or patterns in his sorting activities. These patterns or systems are determined by his ethnic affiliation, his life history, etc.

If we disregard Jeans' attempt to define man as a being who reverses the second law of thermodynamics, which is fallacious and which he advanced for another purpose altogether, the definition of man just offered—"man is a particular type of sorter"—is, so far as we know, both a novel and compendious one. We must realize, however, that many novel and compendious definitions of man may be given which, while uniquely defining him, "make no difference," in that nothing can be done with them to promote a further understanding of, and a further inquiry into, matters pertaining either to man himself or to his uniquely characteristic activities. The famous definition "Man is a featherless biped" is of this correct but sterile type.

---

[13] A more detailed discussion of this theory, and of its application to human beings, was presented elsewhere (30).

SORTING AND EDUCATION

Since our definition was developed, or rather is first presented[14] in connection with a discussion of education and psychotherapy, it seems necessary to show what this formulation can contribute to the problem under consideration.

We just stated that behavior and experience can be arranged into four distinct categories or grouped along four special axes: (1) the biological axis; (2) the experiential axis; (3) the cultural axis, and, in special cases, (4) the neurotic axis.

While every form of behavior belongs more or less, both in its origin and in its function, to all of these axes or categories, it is often advantageous to emphasize one of these categories at a time. Thus, in terms of our scheme of developmental analysis, maturation belongs primarily to the biological category, humanization to the experiential one, and ethnicization to the cultural one.

EDUCATION VS. NURTURING

Education, as distinct from (biological) nurturing, has, thus, relatively little to do with maturation, which is primarily an actual, and largely also a self-actualizing, trend of the organism as a whole. Yet it is quite certain that education is in many ways the result of the conceptualization, and not simply of the "raw fact," of biological nurturing. This is clearly shown by the now obsolete French custom of letting the word "to nourish" denote also education, and particularly indoctrination. Thus, during the sixteenth-

---

[14] This distinction has a great deal of functional significance. No idea or definition, no matter how good it may be, belongs to the living realm of science until its functional relationship with the rest of science has been demonstrated, preferably by putting the idea to some constructive use. Indeed, the history of science is littered with "good ideas" which could not be integrated with any particular science and were not susceptible of being put to work until some two thousand years had elapsed. Greek atomic theories are a typical example of such temporarily sterile ideas. In fact, one may legitimately argue that Democritus' atomic theory belonged originally not to the domain of physics but to philosophy. It did not become a part of physics and of chemistry until Western scientists began to think routinely in terms of atoms.

century French religious wars an important bone of contention was whether the young Protestant princes of the Condé family, who fell into the hands of the Catholic King of France, should be nourished (*nourris*) in the Catholic or in the Protestant religion (8). This meaning of the term "nurture" is still far from obsolete in the English language; witness the manner in which it is used even in contemporary "nature vs. nurture" controversies. We therefore feel that "nurturing," which is primarily a physiological process, appreciably influences at least our latent or unconscious conception of, and attitudes toward, education *lato sensu.* Indeed, we not only speak of "devouring books," or of absorbing knowledge," but unconsciously actually conceive of learning as a form of oral incorporation and sometimes even implement this fantasy by means of cultural practices. Thus, among certain North African Mohammedans the prospective pupil has to eat honey and/or sheep or beef brains to strengthen his memory (226).[15] These data help us understand even better why a child who fails to function on the level expected from it on the basis of its age is first examined for maturational deficiencies, and why much of our educational philosophy is but a sophisticated reformulation of basically maturational and nurturational concepts.

Actually, education has more relevance for humanization than for maturation, albeit the relationship is—at least at present—not as direct as would be desirable. In other words, education is still less concerned with humanization—with the unfolding of *"les catégories de l'esprit humain,"* or with the universal culture pattern—than it is with the presorting of potentialities and with providing these potentialities for humanization, which all human beings, including the most feeble-minded, possess to a variable degree, with selected channels for their manifestation, elaboration, and gratification. In a sense, and with due allowances being made

---

[15] Even P. G. Wodehouse's dim-witted Bertie Wooster assumes that his clever "gentleman's gentleman," Jeeves, developed his brain by eating "brain food" containing phosphorus.

for the necessary explanatory overemphasis to which we resort in this context, education often simply "takes it for granted" that the child will talk. It therefore concerns itself very little with the need of the potential human being to have speech at its disposal and emphasizes instead the learning of a particular mother tongue.

We stated above that, for reasons of expository convenience and clarity, we were obliged to overemphasize certain aspects of education. We must now attempt to correct these initially unavoidable distortions. We objected elsewhere (50) rather strenuously to one important defect of Kardiner's scheme of enculturation (131, 132), namely, to its excessive emphasis on techniques of child training, as distinct from the latent—or, in Linton's terminology, implicit—social, cultural, and subjectively parental patterns underlying such training techniques. We asserted that not child-training technique *per se* but the pervasive culture pattern which this technique expresses and implements is what truly molds the personality. This view has since been accepted by Linton (154) himself and appears to be shared now also by Mead (167). In addition, we also specified that the socially most relevant core of the personality cannot be formed, as Kardiner maintains, during the pregenital stage, i.e., at a time when the child perceives all human beings as partial objects, and when the parents are chiefly engaged in *nurturing* the *organism*. On the contrary, we affirmed that this phase of the personality is shaped primarily during the oedipal period, where "three-dimensional" object relations with whole persons—who *educate* the *child*—become possible (50).[16] In stressing the importance of the oedipal stage for the formation of the socially most relevant segment or core of the personality, we did not attempt to minimize the character-molding influences of the pregenital stages and of the experiences they involve. We simply stated—going back, in this respect, to the historical fountainhead of psychoanalytic theory and away from current "fashions in

[16] This view too was accepted by Linton (153) before his untimely death.

pregenitality"—that these latter character traits are socially and culturally of secondary importance and, specifically, that they do not mold the ethnic "basic personality" but chiefly certain segments of the individual's (idiosyncratic) character.

EDUCATION AND THE CULTURE PATTERN

Now, a particular culture pattern may be compared to the "principle" underlying the characteristic "sorting pattern" of a given culture. It consists of a set of what the logician calls "class concepts" (*194*) and differs from culture to culture. The most basic set of class concepts, i.e., the universal culture pattern, is, as Malinowski has shown, in many ways related to man's biological being (*162*), though Malinowski failed to refine his method and terminology sufficiently to differentiate effectively between *homo sapiens* viewed zoölogically and *humanized man* (*55*).

It is a tragic defect of educational theory and practice that little attention is paid to the principles underlying the system whose fragments are taught to the "new member of the social group"— to the *socius in posse*. We have, of course, indicated elsewhere that these principles communicate themselves to the child through the child-rearing techniques, but, in a sense, only by means of a kind of osmosis (*50*). Thus, we tax the resources of the small child very severely by our unconscious expectations that he himself will be able to "sense" the pattern behind the jumble of "cultural nonsense syllables" taught to him by rote through a series of disconnected "do's" and "don't's." Also, once he is provided with the means through which his potential humanness may actualize itself (e.g., the English or Hottentot tongue) he is literally expected to humanize himself.

The intellectually normal child often manages to accomplish this fabulous feat, albeit usually only on a subverbal (or preconscious) level, and thereafter plays the major themes of his culture "by ear." On the other hand, ordinary education confronts the intellectually less alert or emotionally disturbed child with some "cultural nonsense syllables" which he is supposed to learn by rote, but the pattern of which—be it but a mnemotechnical one—he is not able to grasp either implicitly or explicitly.

Now, this underlying pattern, which is made up not only of a set of attitudes but also of an abstract system of logical constructs, cannot be fully grasped via the unconscious *only*. The attitudes of others can, of course, be unconsciously apprehended and may bring into being, through conditioning, a certain patterning of one's own attitudes, in conformity with that prevailing in a given society. However, true humanization and ethnicization also require an apperception of the content of these attitudes, i.e., of the principles which they reflect both severally and in their general patterning, and this implies that intellectual construction has to take place, if not consciously, then at least preconsciously.[17] In other words, they require a degree of intellectual endowment which neither the small child nor the mentally defective adult possesses.

Education, as ordinarily practiced, is thus indictable on two scores:

1. It concentrates its efforts so exclusively on ethnicization that it neglects humanization.

2. It teaches the raw materials of ethnicization without revealing their relational character, i.e., without stressing the nexus between the various items constituting this raw material, on the one hand, or their relation to the basic themes of the culture or to the ethos, on the other hand.

In earlier times there was some kind of—admittedly primitive —"pattern referral" in education. The child was taught, as a matter of course, certain "moral maxims" or "religious principles" which, though often disturbingly at variance with social and cultural realities, represented the themes or patterns of an at least

---

[17] Roughly speaking, the difference between that which is unconscious and that which is preconscious corresponds to that between a "forgotten dream" and a "name that is on the tip of my tongue."

nominally honored segment of sociocultural life. Though mostly "honored in the breach," these were nonetheless viewed as important.

THE INCULCATION OF A SPURIOUS ETHOS

Needless to say, we do not advocate the inculcation of principles which, allegedly to "encourage the child to strive for perfection," actually misrepresent social realities. The teaching of an unrealistic view of the world will only confuse the child who seeks to deal with reality in terms of principles which are at variance with facts, and will burden it with completely irrational guilt feelings because of its inability to live up to an unattainable standard of perfection. An example will illustrate this point.

Case 10: The Misrepresentation of Reality

An analytic patient remembered with great bitterness the attempts of his parents to make him believe a whole series of utterly untrue but lofty-sounding statements about the world. For example, his parents taught him that all adults were wise, honorable, truth loving, and unselfish, though they themselves proved to be neither wise, nor honorable, nor truthful, nor unselfish in their dealings with him. This confused the patient a great deal, since he was unable to reconcile these statements with observed facts, and also made him feel guilty whenever he deviated from these impossible standards of perfection. Of course, by the time he reached puberty, he was at least intellectually able to realize that he had been taught, as he put it, "nothing but a pack of lies." Nonetheless, these unrealistic teachings continued to play an important role in his unconscious motivation and in his emotional expectations. Thus, he recalls being "shocked" and "amazed" when, at the age of thirteen or fourteen, he heard his parents criticize certain other adults whom, in accordance with his parents' earlier teachings, he continued—unconsciously at least—to define as "perfect." In fact, he clung to this illusion so tenaciously that whenever he worked for an even moderately decent employer he would idealize him to such an impossible extent that an ultimate disappointment was inevitable. At that point his extreme devotion to his chief inevitably turned into an equally extreme hatred.

It is quite certain that this extreme idealization of parent surrogates, such as teachers and employers, was fundamentally a very cynical and hostile maneuver. Indeed, he appears to have idealized his superiors chiefly in order to force them to reveal eventually their "feet of clay." This maneuver was repeatedly attempted also in his analysis. He tried to idealize his analyst to such an extent that the effort amounted to a major resistance to analysis, since its ultimate purpose was to manipulate the analyst into a position where he too would have to disappoint the patient's impossibly high expectations. In other words, the patient became what we might call "a collector of disappointments," motivated by an infantile need to find the "perfect parent" and by the monotonously repetitive compulsion to "tear down" and to destroy anyone unworthy of wearing the mantle of perfection which he had foisted on him. He "accepted" his parents' view that all adults—i.e., his parents—are perfect chiefly in order to take revenge on them for having aroused in him expectations which they did not fulfill, by unmasking them as "deceivers" and as "fourflushers with feet of clay." His general attitude was that of the disappointed idealist turned misanthropist, whose professed faith in the goodness of mankind is paralleled by his contempt and hostility for the individual.

While the basic dynamics of this case were obviously much more complex than the above summary indicates, it is nonetheless quite certain that the unrealistic teachings of the parents played an important role in the development of this patient's neurosis.

We do not mean to imply that children should not be taught moral principles. We simply urge that, in the teaching of moral principles, that which *is* should be specifically differentiated from that which *ought to be*. It is one thing to teach a child that people should try to get along with each other and should deal kindly and fairly with their fellows, in order to make life in society a creative instead of a destructive experience. It is quite another matter to tell it that everyone is, in fact, peaceable and kindly—everyone, that is, except the child itself.

TEACHING THE REAL CULTURE PATTERN

We condemn as destructive the practice of teaching misleading principles and of misrepresenting reality to the child and urge instead that the child be taught, as soon as possible, the real "sorting pattern" or "themes" or "ethos" of his culture. We do not believe that such a teaching would ultimately lead to social ossification, provided only that the ethos itself is both functional and realistic.

Unfortunately, we usually fail to teach our children the functional principles underlying the democratic way of life. We do not mean by this, e.g., "lofty preachments" about "equal opportunity for all" which are contradicted by our daily experiences with discrimination and segregation, but the teaching of the realities of our ethos and of principles of responsible citizenship. Mechanically "pledging allegiance to the flag" in the classroom is no adequate substitute for carefully interpreting to the child the basic principles of the Constitution. This is perfectly feasible, since these basic principles, like all great ethical and social principles, are really so simple and fundamental that even a child can understand them. In fact, we suspect that our failure to teach the child the ethos of our society and the principles of responsible citizenship in a democracy is responsible for the current "loss of faith," or, more precisely, decrease in commitment to the democratic system in which we live, by means of which we live, and without which we would be utterly lost and disoriented. It also explains why every kind of totalitarianism which does attempt to inculcate a set of "principles" or "moral maxims"—admittedly nightmarish—seems to be able to mobilize a kind of destructive but fanatical devotion. Now, as the case of our "disappointed idealist" (Case 10) indicates, fanaticism is psychologically necessary only when one seeks to outshout the still, small voice of reason and to persuade oneself that principles "put on a pedestal" by society but ignored in practice are actually operative. By contrast, where the real, functional pattern of a sound society is explained to the growing child, the psychological "security" derived from blind fanaticism is replaced more fully and more satisfyingly by mature enthusiasm, by a freely chosen commitment to a way of life—in brief, by "civic virtue" in the classical sense.[18]

ETHOS AND THE DEFECTIVE

It may be objected, of course, that the child and the defective are not able to grasp the basic principles of the social system and must therefore be taught various rules by rote. It is hoped that the following case history will disprove this view:

Case 11: A Resocialized Defective Psychotic

P. J., the thirty-year-old, feeble-minded (IQ approximately 68), and catatonic son of a widow, belonged to the upper fringes of the lower class and to a socially slightly handicapped minority. When first seen in the schizophrenia research ward of a famous mental hospital, his constantly flushed face displayed a silly grin, his posture was awkward, his clothes were dirty, and the reek of urine, which stained his trousers, was perceptible at a distance of several feet. This person had been imprisoned for a year and a day for arson.[19]

Although he had never been able to emancipate himself from the

[18] We do not assert that the Renaissance and post-Renaissance classical scholar's conception of the average Athenian or Republican Roman as a person endowed with civic virtue is a realistic one, applicable to the majority of the citizens of Athens and of Rome, both of which had notorious traitors and scoundrels in their midst. We do affirm, however, that both Athens and Republican Rome did have the concept of "civic virtue," as distinct from blind fanaticism. Hence, we hold that not fanaticism but civic virtue impelled Aeschylus to fight at Marathon, and Socrates to be the last Athenian hoplite to withdraw before the victorious Spartans on a stricken field. Had Aeschylus been a fanatic, he could not have written his *Persians,* and Xenophon, the pro-Spartan Athenian, would not have praised the civic virtue of Socrates in his "Apology of Socrates."

[19] The relationship between urinary incontinence and fire setting is well known to psychiatrists (99).

tutelage of an extremely possessive mother, he had managed to marry a nagging woman, who led a loose life both before and after her marriage. P. J. had been hospitalized for several years and more or less "got along" in this protected environment, without, however, reaching the point where he could cope also with life outside the hospital. Whenever he was permitted to go home on a visit, he promptly went into another catatonic stupor and had to be brought back to the hospital in an ambulance.

The writer was at that time engaged in a study of the social structure of the schizophrenia ward (36) in which this patient was located. In the course of his interviews with patients he noticed that P. J. was an almost compulsively careful—i.e., highly insecure—person, who was afraid to make careless statements. The writer therefore decided to take advantage of P. J.'s meticulousness and induced him to keep a daily record of everything happening in the ward. He also instructed him to make up a list of rotating cleaning teams, by pairing those patients who were most likely to coöperate with each other.

P. J. was interested in both of these assignments and executed them with commendable care. His daily records of events, as well as the list of pairs of patients which he submitted, were then discussed with him in detail. For example, if he reported that two patients had had a violent argument, an attempt was made to help him obtain some understanding of why and how the altercation had arisen and also of the possible consequences of that incident. His list of pairs of workers was also examined carefully, and he was invited to explain his reasons for, e.g., pairing patient A with patient F instead of with patient N. In other words, a systematic attempt was made to mediate to this feeble-minded and severely psychotic individual some understanding of the way in which the simple world of the ward functioned, and also to provide him with a more general technique for inquiring into the meaning of events in the world in which he lived. This purely educational approach to the patient's difficulties was determined by the writer's belief (29) that one of the major triggering elements in the genesis of schizophrenia is the disorientation of the potential schizophrenic in a complex society and culture. Hence, it was felt that, by helping this patient to understand his milieu and, in a broader sense, by training him to analyze his environment, it would be possible to decrease his social disorientation, which caused him to "give up" and go into a stupor every time he was sent home on a visit. In brief, an attempt was made to mediate to him the "ethos" or "sorting pattern" of the society in which he lived.

This approach to the patient's difficulties yielded such encouraging results that the writer suggested to the psychiatrist in charge of the research ward that the patient be sent home on a trial visit. Although the psychiatrist thought it probable that after a few days at home the patient would relapse into a stupor, as he had done on every previous occasion, and would have to be brought back to the hospital in an ambulance, he agreed to try the experiment, and P. J. was sent home on a visit.

To everyone's surprise, P. J. never returned to the hospital. Instead, he cut the "silver cord" which had tied him to his possessive mother, obtained a divorce from his objectionable wife, got himself a job, and, when last heard from, was still getting along on the outside.[20]

It is felt that, if a feeble-minded catatonic, imprisoned for a crime, hospitalized for years, and handicapped by a mother who sought to infantilize him and by a wife who constantly humiliated him, could be taught to understand some of the basic characteristics of our society, it should also be possible to teach the ethos of our society to intellectually or emotionally handicapped children.

RELATIONAL TEACHING

We cannot but condemn the tendency of old-fashioned education to neglect its duty to help the child humanize itself, and to provide instead only the means (ethnicization) through which the child might express its humanity were it able to humanize itself. An additional shortcoming of old-fashioned education is its failure to teach even these "means" in a relational manner, which would

[20] It has to be stressed that this patient was able to find a job so rapidly chiefly because of the 1940 labor shortage. During a depression he might not have been able to get his foot on the first rung of the ladder and would therefore have had to return to the hospital, probably in a stuporous state.

reveal both the interrelatedness of these cultural techniques and their relation to the central ethos or "sorting pattern" of the culture. Such archaic teaching methods are bad enough in the case of inherently intelligent and normal children. They are simply disastrous in the case of the mentally defective or emotionally unbalanced child.[21]

We did not cite these shortcomings of old-fashioned education simply in order to engage in sterile carping. We did so in order to gain a better understanding of the real tasks of therapeutic education, which must seek to humanize the child by mediating to it the means for the implementation of its human potentialities in a relational manner, of which "project teaching" is a somewhat inadequate example. In fact, we may say that such relational teaching is characteristic of all real education and that sound therapeutic education necessarily presupposes the existence of a sound general philosophy of education. It is, in fact, quite possible that, just as the study of psychopathology helped us to broaden our understanding of normal psychology, so therapeutic education may, in the long run, give new impetus to the development of educational theory as a whole.

[21] A personal experience, of a purely scientific order, may help clarify this point. At the age of eighteen the writer was a fairly accomplished mathematical technician, who could solve partial differential equations quite easily but who, having been taught mathematics "by rote," had no real understanding of the foundations of mathematics. Hence, when he entered college and concentrated upon social science, within two years all his mathematical skills simply evaporated, because nothing he had learned served to "hold together" these atomistically acquired technical skills. By contrast, when Poncelet, one of Napoleon's engineers, was taken prisoner by the Russians and languished without any mathematical books in a POW camp, he decided to reconstruct from memory all the mathematics he ever knew and, in the course of this attempt, discovered an entirely new branch of geometry (12).

4/8/59

CHAPTER 5

....

The Overlap Between Therapy and Education

_____

We stated in the preceding chapters that it is conceptually both possible and necessary to differentiate between therapy and education, and that functionally both may accomplish nearly identical results, since each of these two techniques is what logicians call "a limiting case" of the other. At the same time there is, to a certain extent, also a genuine overlap between the two, in an area where the therapist also seems to function as an educator and the educator also appears to function as a therapist. We have already given some concrete examples of the manner in which factual information may legitimately be imparted to the patient by the therapist, in order to facilitate the course of therapy. This, however, represents only a first approach to this complex problem.

ADDITIVE VS. SUBTRACTIVE PSYCHOTHERAPY

A well-known psychiatrist, Dr. Temple Burling, habitually differentiated between additive and subtractive psychotherapy.[1] At first blush this dichotomy resembles our own distinction between learning and unlearning processes. However, since Burling defines both "additive" and "subtractive" methods as psychotherapy, his conclusions seem to challenge our view that there is a genuine dif-

_____

[1] The writer is obliged to Dr. Richard L. Jenkins both for this information and for the suggestion that he devote a special chapter to the overlap between therapy and education.

ference between education and psychotherapy. Now, Burling apparently includes in his conception of "additive psychotherapy" certain educational efforts which, in our opinion, exceed the limits of what is psychotherapy proper. In other words, Burling's "additive psychotherapy" seems to include a far from negligible amount of "instruction" in the narrow sense.

We do not deny, of course, that the therapist is often obliged to provide concrete instruction. We therefore actually listed the conditions under which the giving of instruction to the patient may become necessary. However, as regards at least the first two types of instruction, such activities, while often necessary and therefore wholly permissible, do not constitute psychotherapy in the strict sense of this term. They are simply instruction in a psychotherapeutic *setting,* and the therapist must be aware of this fact. We are simply reiterating here the very practical maxim that one can do a great many "unconventional" things in a properly conducted psychotherapy as long as one knows what one is doing and why one is doing it—and does not insist that it represents classical psychoanalytic technique. The basic criterion which enables us to determine whether a given procedure or intervention is psychotherapy proper can be stated in very simple terms: Any act or remark which is not wholly subordinated to and directly aimed at facilitating the unlearning of unconscious neurotic attitudes is not psychotherapy, even if it is quite useful and, indeed, indispensable. Hence, when listing the conditions under which "instruction" may be deliberately given we specified that "instruction" must serve one or both of two therapeutic goals:

1. The indirect therapeutic goal of helping the patient to avoid crises which would interrupt his analysis. This type of instruction is exemplified by the giving of information about immigration procedures to an alien patient, who, if he proceeded in an incorrect way from sheer ignorance, would be deported.

2. The specific therapeutic goal of giving information in order

to facilitate the confrontation of the patient with some segment of psychic reality which the patient was hitherto able to "ignore" (scotomize) by exploiting his half-genuine and half-spurious lack of information about a certain point. Telling the patient about a case similar to his own, or about some relevant primitive custom,[2] in order to help him understand his own problem or in order to make him realize that he is not the "only" person on earth so "monstrous" as to be jealous of his son, etc., also subordinates "instruction" to the goal of increasing the patient's capacity to obtain insight into himself.

We recognize, of course, that "accidental instruction" may creep into the psychotherapeutic situation through a variety of crevices. Thus, the foreign analysand's accent may improve through his unconscious imitation of his analyst's diction. An interpretive remark made by the analyst may include some factual bit of information previously unknown to the patient, etc. This type of accidental instruction cannot, however, be viewed as a truly educational activity in psychotherapy any more than the fact that the reader of a detective story often learns something about the law or about police science automatically turns the mystery story into a law book or into a treatise on police laboratory methods.

On the whole, it is our view that, with the exception of the cases listed above, deliberate "teaching" in the course of psychotherapy may be practically desirable but is not therefore essentially psychotherapy. In fact, in many cases the use of educational techniques in psychotherapy is a technical error and represents the kind of "cutting of corners" which, in the long run, can only lead to new and serious resistances and difficulties.

We hold that there is only one kind of "addition" one makes in genuine psychotherapy. In order to understand the nature of this seemingly "additive" procedure, it is necessary, first of all, that we

[2] The writer is indebted to Dr. Paul Sloane for pointing out to him that using primitive customs as illustrative material is technically the equivalent of using clinical examples.

clarify the meaning and purpose of confrontations and interpretations (51).

CONFRONTATIONS

In confrontations the patient is simply made to face the true meaning and contextual significance of his actions or statements. By and large, confrontation consists in stripping pompous oratory of ornamental verbiage which obscures the issue and in translating it into sober declarative sentences. It should be stressed that this "debunking" is not necessarily limited to a revelation of the "ignoble" or "selfish" "real reasons" underlying the patient's loftily worded "good reasons" for having said or done something. It is not restricted to telling a patient who has just boasted of his idealism, which caused him to refrain from some illegal action, that his fear of policemen may have something to do with his display of virtue. It can also involve precisely the opposite type of confrontation with reality.

Case 12: Confrontation with Denied Sublimations

A delinquent adolescent violated school regulations by sneaking out after curfew to have a date outdoors with a girl student. Although the date itself was quite innocuous, he was called to account by one of the administrative heads of the school. During this interview the boy not only made a clean breast of it but even assumed entire responsibility for the incident, although it was known that the escapade had been planned and initiated by the girl. Since his attitude was praiseworthy, he escaped with a simple reprimand—as he knew he would. However, when he told this story to his therapist, he gloated over the "shrewdness" wherewith he had "managed" the situation. Thus, he insisted that he knew in advance that, by being frank about it, and yet "lying like a gentleman to protect the lady," he would escape more severe punishment. He also boasted of his "cunning" and of his "diplomatic" ability to "manipulate" and to "fool" people. Needless to say, he felt much deflated when his therapist, instead of reprimanding him for his "cynicism," confronted him with his compulsive need to make himself appear worse than he was in reality, and to assume airs of tough cynicism in order to disguise both his basic integrity and his neurotic quest for punishment, which was motivated by his unconscious guilt feelings and by his painfully conscious self-contempt. In brief, he was asked why he felt it necessary to pretend that his inherently decent behavior was simply the unscrupulous "confidence game" of a psychopath.

Some weeks later this same youth took a walk in the woods with a group of delinquent boys, who decided to break into an untenanted cabin. The youth in question strenuously opposed the plan of his friends and even followed them into the cabin, pleading with them not to steal anything. It was wholly due to his exertions that the others stole nothing of value from the cabin and contented themselves with taking some worthless junk—a discarded doll and a cup with a broken handle—more or less as "trophies," to prove that they were real "toughs" who thought nothing of breaking and entering. The youth himself took nothing whatsoever from the cabin. Yet, when he told this story to the therapist, he insisted that he too had "broken" into the cabin. When confronted with the fact that he had done nothing of the kind, he said: "Well, I did enter the cabin illegally!" When it was pointed out to him that he had done so only after the others had broken into the cabin, and that he followed them inside only in order to plead with them not to steal anything, he insisted that he was nonetheless technically guilty of breaking and entering and pretended that he had pleaded with the others only because the "crime" was unprofitable and its detection certain. In other words, he denied that he had been motivated by decent impulses and pretended instead that he was simply a "realistic" delinquent, who objected to this unprofitable "crime" only because he felt certain that the police could easily identify them. At this point the therapist once more confronted him with his need to conceal his better impulses by pretending that his actions were motivated exclusively by cunning and selfish shrewdness. He was also shown that the self-depreciation implicit in this pretense was motivated by his acceptance of his parents' low opinion of him, and that he felt unconsciously compelled to "prove them right."

This interpretation was apparently effective, since thereafter the youth gradually began to mention also his better qualities and impulses, and lapsed into self-depreciation and pretended to be a hopelessly tough and cynical person only in moments of transitory anxiety and depression, thus confirming the view we expressed elsewhere that the so-called "instinct-ridden psychopath" is, in reality, a "defense-ridden psychopath" (48).

CONFRONTATION WITH SUBLIMATIONS

The above example serves as a warning against the tendency to assume that confrontations and interpretations necessarily consist exclusively in stressing the patient's antisocial tendencies. On the contrary, it is often very necessary indeed to interpret to the patient his assets rather than his deficiencies. This is particularly desirable in the case of juvenile delinquents, whose self-contempt often assumes appallingly self-destructive proportions. Thus, we described elsewhere the case of a juvenile delinquent who systematically refused to see that his seemingly aggressive acts were primarily self-destructive until one night, while dreaming that he was engaging in an aggressive and forbidden act, he actually fell off the top of a double-decker bunk, smashing up his face quite severely (63).

Statements such as the following are often highly effective, especially in the treatment of juvenile delinquents:

1. You tend to minimize your talents, which are clearly revealed by your vocational aptitude tests, in order not to have to do anything about them.

2. You cannot admit that you are a fundamentally decent person, because you feel obliged to prove by your conduct that your parents were right in calling you "worthless."

3. You assume the role of the "tough guy" and swagger about looking like a hoodlum, simply because you hope that your bearing will intimidate others sufficiently to cause them to refrain from picking a fight with you—and you fundamentally disapprove of fights and are also afraid of them.

4. Your assertion that men constantly pursue you seems to disprove your conviction that you are completely unattractive.

5. You have managed to convince yourself that, because of your sexual escapades, you are the lowest thing on earth: worse than a "gun moll," worse than a shrew, worse than a sadistically gossipy "virtuous" woman. In reality, you are simply what is commonly known as a "bad lot but a good sort." So you might just as well buckle down to hard work in your therapy hour. You are neither hopeless nor unworthy of help.

When offered in the proper context, such confrontations are not simply "supportive therapy," which seeks to bolster the ego. They are examples of dynamic confrontations of the classically psychoanalytic type, since they reveal exactly what psychoanalytic confrontations are supposed to reveal: the spuriousness of defense mechanisms, which are, in a sense, neurotic means of self-deception. Such confrontations are certainly not comparable to supportive psychotherapy, since, instead of seeking to "build up the patient's ego," they get at the root of important resistances to treatment. In addition, like all classical confrontations, they stimulate further associations by threatening existing neurotic "security maneuvers" and by dismantling the protective armor of neurotic defenses. This, in turn, stimulates the urge to develop more mature and more realistic means for dealing with basic human conflicts, tensions, anxieties, and forbidden destructive impulses.

Such confrontations add nothing substantive to the patient's own statements. They simply translate his remarks into a more direct language and place them in their proper context. A confrontation is, thus, little more than a way of telling the patient: "What you are really saying is . . ."

INTERPRETATIONS

Interpretations "add" only one thing to the patient's own productions. This is the missing cloture element of the *Gestalt*—of the verbal or behavioral configuration which has an implicit pattern (*Prägnanz*). This element, by completing the patient's "incomplete" remarks, reveals what he is really trying to say, without knowing it. All such (additive) interpretations are ultimately reducible to statements of the following type: "All you said (or did) *adds up* to . . ." or "what you just said *makes sense only* if we assume that your real feelings or beliefs are . . ." In a sense, an interpretation simply puts together into a coherent configuration the disparate odds and ends which the patient produced piecemeal in the course of his free associations and adds the implicit "missing link." In other words, the interpretation simply reveals the hidden or latent pattern of the patient's productions. The data used are those which were *explicitly* provided by the patient's own remarks and actions, while the "missing link," and the basic configuration which the interpretation reveals, were *implicit* in what he said or did. However, because of his psychic "blind spots" (scotomata) he was unable, without assistance from the analyst, to perceive the missing "cloture element" which gives a meaning to the implicit configuration of his remarks. For example, the analyst may say: "You say you love your brother very much, but every time you speak of him you shift your position on the couch, and assume a stance resembling that of a boxer."

ACCRETIONS IN THE COURSE OF THERAPY

Having clarified the meaning of the terms "confrontation" and "interpretation," we may now discuss more in detail the "additions" made in the course of therapy. Somewhat anticipating our conclusions, we may state at once that these "additions" do not represent "bricks" which the therapist adds to the psychic edifice of the patient. They are simply the products of the patient's spontaneous inner growth which therapy makes possible. Thus, they are not, properly speaking, "additions." They are simply "accretions."

It is our thesis that a sound psychotherapy situation is the equivalent of a laboratory in human relationships, in which the therapist is the guinea pig on whom the patient tries out various ways —both old and new—of dealing with human beings. A simple example will illustrate this point:

Let us suppose that, in some extreme situation, the therapist offers the patient a bit of positive advice, warns him against some action, or threatens to interrupt the therapy if his advice is disregarded or if his demand is not met. (This type of "threat" must be resorted to occasionally in the treatment of addicts and perverts.)

Superficially, if the patient follows the therapist's advice or heeds his warning we may, as a first approximation, assert that this exemplifies "additive" psychotherapy. While this statement is descriptively more or less true, it is dynamically irrelevant to the point of being untrue. It is our view that what is relevant and significant here is not the fact that the patient "took" the advice or prohibition "given" (added) to him by the therapist. What is relevant is that he did, in fact, consent to "take" it. In other words, we maintain that what the therapist "gives" the patient is not an advice or prohibition *per se* but the capacity to accept an advice or prohibition which the patient has often already given himself.

This view is easily susceptible of proof. It happens seldom, if ever, that the therapist's advice or prohibition differs from the advice or prohibition previously given to the patient by his relatives and friends, and sometimes even by his enemies. In fact, it seldom differs from the type of advice or prohibition which the patient himself is, in principle, perfectly capable of giving himself —but is not able to accept or to follow.

The following example will illustrate this point.

Case 13: The Feeling of "Being Driven"

An intelligent patient described himself as "being driven." In order to illustrate what he meant by this expression, he cited the following data: Throughout his life he had a compelling urge to examine the private papers of other persons. This had repeatedly involved him in very real difficulties, many of which led to serious setbacks in his career. In the end the effects of these setbacks became cumulative to the point where his reputation for "nosiness" actually made it difficult for him to get responsible positions of the type for which he was qualified. One day he once more began to poke around in the desk of his chief, who, though notoriously secretive, nonetheless kept in his open desk numerous confidential papers. Even while he was examining his chief's papers, the patient kept admonishing himself as follows: "You fool, what are you trying to do? Don't you have any sense? Don't you know that you are bound to be caught and fired? This may be the last straw. It may be the final setback in your career which means so much to you. Etc." Yet, even while scolding himself, he went right on examining his chief's papers—with dire consequences. Hence, the therapist finally "put his foot down" and made the continuation of the analysis contingent upon the patient's stopping this kind of "acting out," because it was bound to lead to his dismissal from his present position, thereby making the continuation of the analysis impossible. In doing so, the analyst actually did nothing more than restate a prohibition which all of the patient's friends and, indeed, the patient himself had sought to impose on him, to no avail.

Thus, it is not surprising that patients often react even to relatively deep interpretations with a sense of "here we go again" (*déjà vécu*), regardless of how much the interpretation may have "startled" him the moment it was made. In fact, in many cases this "startle reaction" represents the surprise of a "sudden recognition," rather than the surprise of "meeting something alien." Hence, interpretations often elicit the remark: "I have known this all along, but . . ." The patient's impression of being told only something already "familiar" to him[3] is often so explicit that he may complain that he is given no help at all, since he knew all along everything the analyst is telling him. In other instances the

[3] Compare Freud's discussion of "the uncanny" (96).

patient repeats the analyst's statement the next day, as an insight which he himself had reached unassisted. Both of these claims are, in a sense, legitimate, since obviously the analyst could not have formulated his interpretation had its pattern not been *implicit* in the patient's rambling remarks, which contained in an *explicit* form all the components of the pattern, with the sole exception of the "cloture element," which is unconscious.

Thus, the patient's own reactions prove that interpretations add nothing substantive to the patient's psychic content. What is "added" is simply the capacity to listen to oneself both intelligently and with one's emotions—the capacity to register what one is really saying and the capacity to act upon it.[4] Yet, even this "learning" is ultimately a genuine form of "unlearning," since the capacity to "listen to oneself creatively" (to obtain insight into oneself) results from the unlearning of those neurotic attitudes which have hitherto inhibited the actualization of this quite basic human potentiality.

What is incumbent upon us to analyze, therefore, is the "adding" of the capacity to act upon a set of advices, suggestions, and taboos, as distinct from the "learning" of the factual content of these suggestions. We feel that this problem is of importance even for the practice of a strictly supportive or suppressive therapy. We suggested elsewhere (50) that what is being added may be:

1. A sense of the availability of the therapist for the formation of constantly changing libidinal and/or hostile cathexes of sufficient intensity to acquire motivational force.
2. The availability of the therapist for a—preferably temporary —introjection as an auxiliary ego or ego ideal, but—in a well-conducted therapy at least—never as a superego.

[4] Tentatively speaking, it may be possible to analyze also this type of "learning" in terms of the so-called "Yale learning theory," although, again tentatively, it is felt that Dollard himself has not done so *explicitly enough* in his otherwise very insightful studies of therapy as learning (69, 70).

3. A technique for handling conflicts. This requires both the forming of the aforementioned cathexes and the temporary introjection of the therapist as a "psychic auxiliary."[5]

The availability of the therapist for the formation of cathexes
or for introjection is, by and large, made possible by the therapist's
own inner maturity, human warmth, and genuineness. These, we
feel, cannot be "taught." They can only be promoted through
helping the therapist to "grow up," for example, by causing him
to be psychoanalyzed. By contrast, the formulation of a technique
for handling problems of insight, and its mediation to the patient,
is something which may legitimately be viewed as therapeutically
valuable teaching and learning.

EDUCATION IN CHILD THERAPY

This being said, we must recognize that deliberate educational
efforts are not necessarily out of place in therapy, though it is
confusing and undesirable to mislabel such undertakings as therapy. Such a self-deception can only lead to bad therapy and inadequate education as well. The problem of resorting to educational
activities in the course of therapy is particularly acute in the case
of children. Indeed, the adult patient is already a more or less fully
ethnicized person, who "knows" the components of his culture
even if he neurotically misuses them or does not use them at all.
Thus, to return to the fictitious example of the bookkeeper (Chapter 3) who should have been a musician, the analysand is a person
who already knows that music exists, that one can earn a living
as a musician if one is sufficiently talented, etc. By contrast, the
child is as yet incompletely ethnicized and is unfamiliar with the

---

[5] The therapist should not and, if he properly handles his task, cannot be in-
trojected as a supplementary *id*. Indeed, even though he often has to "side" with
the *id* against the abnormally repressive *superego* (morbid conscience, excessive
scrupulousness), he always performs only ego functions—mediating the *id* to the
superego and *ego ideal*. This view is fully compatible with the theory of the basic
immutability of the *id*.

ways and resources of his culture and often even of his language. Children in treatment constantly remind the therapist of this fact —for example, by time and again asking the meaning of various words used by the therapist.[6]

In brief, good child therapy often requires also educational activities, which combine instruction with indoctrination in a relational manner, thus increasing the child's therapeutizability by providing information in order to correct distorted or incompletely developed insights and attitudes. This is especially needed in the following situations:

1. Owing to its youth or neglected education, the child actually did not have an opportunity to learn certain things which it should know at its age. (E.g., words, concepts, attitudes, facts.)

2. Information was deliberately withheld from the child by neurotically rigid adults. (E.g., the facts of procreation.)

3. The child was systematically misinformed. (E.g., "babies are brought by the stork.")

4. There is a definite contradiction between socially sanctioned beliefs and simple common sense. (E.g., society often pretends that black is white, because it *wants* it to be white. Thus, it may be necessary to tell a Southern adolescent, who was taught that Negroes are not quite human, the scientific facts about race.)

5. Society provides only taboos, insteady of positive guidance.[7]

In all of these instances educational activities are both necessary and legitimate. This being the case, there is no need to assuage one's therapeutic conscience by inventing a new definition of psychotherapy, solely for the purpose of making "education in the

---

[6] Needless to say, both children and adults may exaggerate their ignorance and may ask questions whose answers are already known to them, for example, in order to delay some painful interpretation which is obviously in the offing. In such instances not an explanation of the word, or an answer to the question, is called for but an interpretation of the *exploitation* of a *fictitious* ignorance or uncertainty for the purpose of resisting the treatment (Case 5).

[7] The Hebrew theologian and philosopher Martin Buber suggests that one reason why the Ten Commandments are so often violated is that many of them are couched in negative terms ("Thou shalt not . . ."). This, obviously, is an incitement to neurotic rebellion.

course of psychotherapy" appear as "true psychotherapy." Indeed, no medical psychoanalyst who suggests that his analysand should take care of his cold—after interpreting to him why he has not done so already—would call this "psychoanalysis *stricto sensu*." In fact, just as the medical psychoanalyst who happens to give his analysand a prescription realizes that this will have a variety of psychological repercussions and will mobilize transference reactions which have to be taken into account both before and after the prescription is given,[8] so the psychotherapist must realize that any legitimate—but not necessarily psychotherapeutic—intervention in the course of psychotherapy, such as an educational act, will also mobilize a variety of psychological reactions. This does not mean that one should refrain from really necessary "teaching." It does mean, however, that one should consider in advance the effects which this will have upon the course of psychotherapy.

The point we seek to make is really a very simple one. Since it is sometimes necessary to educate or reëducate the child in psychotherapy, one should know and admit to oneself that what one is doing is "education in the course of psychotherapy" and not "psychotherapy proper." Only when one has no illusions about what one is doing is one able to do it well.

A concrete example may help us understand the manner in which, e.g., an adolescent in psychoanalysis can be educated. Our example happens to be one in which all five types of educational deficiencies listed above were in evidence. Not at all surprisingly, it pertains to sexual ethics, which is perhaps the most consistently mismanaged aspect of our culture.

Case 14: Education in Sexual Ethics

I certainly enjoy my dates with Frances. Boy! I am sure learning things! It makes me feel quite sophisticated. But I heard something recently which makes me wonder whether I could not get more out of

[8] No nonmedical psychotherapist should ever suggest that his patient take even an aspirin. In fact, even medical psychoanalysts often refrain from all medical interventions and send the patient to his regular family physician instead.

her. I hear she went "the whole way" with some boys, when she was home last summer. If she did it with them—well, why shouldn't she do it with me too? (Analyst: In other words, you want it as a kind of trophy, to increase your self-esteem and make you feel like a man.) Sure—why not? (Analyst: You mentioned to me that you knew that Frances was a badly disturbed girl last summer.) You mean . . . (groping for words) . . . you mean she did it because she was upset? (Analyst: Yes. It was her sickness that made her do it.) I don't know what to say. I can see that it is not something to make you proud of yourself, if a girl does it because she is sick and not because she loves you. (Analyst: Yes—it is like rolling a drunk.) Well—that *is* a difference. (Analyst: You realize that I am not condemning sex. On the contrary! I am telling you that you would not get out of it everything one can and should get out of it, when it is right.) You mean, of course, that it is more satisfying when the girl does it because she loves you— and not just because she is sick? (Analyst: Yes—and also when *you* do it because you love her and not because you want her as a trophy. She too is a human being—a person—and not a mere utensil or convenience, to be used for your purposes, or for anyone's purposes. Besides, Frances is trying hard to get well.) You mean that it's not fair to tempt her to relapse into her sickness? (Analyst: You know from your own experience that it is not pleasant to be emotionally ill.) I understand—and I am glad you told me this. Why don't people tell you this kind of thing, instead of preaching at you, like my aunt does? She just says it is bad. That is all she ever says. Everything is bad, as far as she is concerned.

PSYCHOTHERAPY AND THE INCULCATION OF SEXUAL ETHICS

Let us now consider in detail why—indirectly at least—some educational activity was necessary in this instance.

It is quite evident that what we had to undertake was not so much education as reëducation, and that the source of the trouble was neither this youth's sexual impulse nor his distinctive psychological make-up as an adolescent, but the attitudes toward sex which his aunt had taught him. These attitudes were based upon some basic misconceptions obtaining in our society about the nature of sex *per se,* and also about adolescent sexual impulses.

Society is greatly—and legitimately—concerned over the casual, and often even promiscuous, affairs of adolescents. It views such acts as proofs of (1) the disruptive "nature" of sexuality *per se,* and (2) the "inherent" sexual irresponsibility of adolescents.

In view of these assumptions, society seeks to deal with adolescent sexuality by repressive means. It utterly fails to realize that the chaotic sexual conduct of some adolescents is not actually evidence either of the antisocial character of sexuality *per se* or of the inherent irresponsibility of adolescents.

Indeed, casual promiscuousness occurs only where the person cannot find real satisfaction in what he is doing and has no sense of total commitment to his partner and to his own actions.[9] We hold that this is not due to any inherent trait of adolescence. Rather is it something systematically taught to the adolescent by society. Only where the growing members of society are taught to differentiate between "sacred" and "profane" love, and to *isolate physiological impulses from personal involvement in the most comprehensive sense,* can there be socially disruptive casual amours. Only then do we meet with pseudo-sexual behavior, in which physiological reflexes—not to be dignified with the label of sexual behavior—are exploited irresponsibly or serve as a means for the "acting out" of hostile or rebellious impulses.

Yet, even the great nonhedonistic religions contain precepts which may serve as a basis for a very different approach to mature sexuality.

Judaism: The Zohar states explicitly that "The pleasure of cohabitation is a religious one, giving joy also to the Divine Presence" (*105*).

Christianity: Even St. Paul, who exalted chastity above mar-

---

[9] It is a psychoanalytic truism that most promiscuous women are either totally or partially frigid. This was already known to the Roman poet who describes one such woman as "exhausted but not satiated" (*"lassata sed non satiata"*).

riage, emphasized the element of tenderness in mature marital acts, by urging spouses to "render due benevolence" to each other.

Mohammedanism: Mohammed believed that the doors of Paradise open themselves wide for the husband whose acts of love give pleasure to his wife.

We therefore hold that, in teaching the adolescent to isolate his personality from his physiological reflexes, we are actually laying the foundation for sexual irresponsibility and promiscuousness. We deem it insufficient for a marriage ceremony to include only the promise "with my body I thee worship," or for doctrine to proclaim only that spouses become "one flesh" instead of also "one soul." Even the primitive Mohave Indians know better than that, and affirm that, when spouses cohabit, both their bodies and their souls are involved in the act. Where there is only a partial involvement, the act cannot culminate in complete psychobiological gratification. It can only result in self-contempt. This explains why Westerners believe that "after such pleasures all beasts are sad," whereas the Mohave affirm that spouses who cohabited the night before "carry themselves proudly and have sparkling eyes"(43). The contrast between the depression of the Westerner and the elation of the Mohave can be understood only in terms of differences in the extent to which the total personality is involved in such acts.

In brief, we feel that the true objective of sex education is not the narrow and futile one of simply inhibiting concrete acts. It is the constructive and effective policy of fostering the capacity to love, which all men possess at least in the form of a potentiality. Our goal should not be simply to prevent frustrating, degrading, and socially disruptive conduct, which would not arise in the first place if we knew how to put the adolescent sexual impulse to a creative use and direct it toward a humanizing goal. Instead, we should educate adolescents for the dignified, creative, and socially constructive role of the loving spouse. An animal puts into its sex acts all it is and all it has and is therefore "without sin." If men put into it less than they are and less than they have—if they are not totally involved in such acts with all that makes them human —then they fall below the animal and, by failing to actualize themselves as human beings, cannot function as decent and mature human beings.

The sole effective means for promoting what men call "morality in sexual matters" is to foster man's capacity to be human and to be involved with all that which makes him human in all of his acts, including his sexual ones. This, rather than a mass of soul-crippling and constricting taboos, is the proper prophylaxis against the socially destructive and personally self-degrading "acting out" of hostile impulses and neurotic conflicts through the medium of genital reflexes, just as the best way of preventing collisions is not to build better *brakes,* but to train more competent *drivers,* who respect the rights of others and know where they are going. In brief, it is easier, more effective, and socially more creative to teach the adolescent to wait for love than it is to make him accept prohibitions against the casual easing of genital tensions here and now. If we expect adolescents to wait, we must make the period of waiting a worth-while one in itself, by defining it as a training period, during which they are helped to attain the emotional maturity needed for obtaining that maximum of totally meaningful gratification from love which, in the words of the Zohar, "gives joy also to the Divine Presence."

Since this is not the manner in which our society trains its adolescents, one must often abandon the rigorously noneducational attitude in psychotherapy. One must help adolescents to unlearn superego-inspired taboos and must reëducate them in terms of the positive principles of conduct which emanate from the ego ideal (Chapter 8). The best way in which this can be achieved is to confront the adolescent relentlessly with all of reality. The case just cited shows how often even minor hints suffice to free the adolescent from the distorted conception of sexuality which had been drilled into him and to liberate his inherent capacity for evolving a healthy and constructive sexual ethic.

In brief, even though the educational and reëducational activities of the child therapist are technically education and not psychotherapy, in the last resort they have definite implications for therapy, by increasing the child's therapeutizability and educability.

PSYCHOTHERAPY IN EDUCATIONAL ACTIVITIES

Just as the psychotherapist is often obliged to educate, so the therapeutic educator's and milieu therapist's work often includes also definitely psychotherapeutic activities. These activities are so numerous and varied in scope that we cannot do more than list a few of them.

LOVING THE CHILD

The therapeutic effect of love was recognized long ago by Ferenczi, who declared that "the unloved child dies." This thesis has since been confirmed by careful studies made in hygenically impeccable but emotionally barren orphanages. For example, Spitz found[10] that only one of a group of babies in a certain ward survived. This happened to be an unusually pretty infant, fussed and cooed over by all nurses and visitors. Today, many hospitals for children assign to certain nurses the task of giving love to the babies, and the "prescription" TLC (tender loving care) is entered in the clinical records of many hospitalized children. Needless to say, this love must be a real one, capable of "bathing" the child in an atmosphere of real tenderness and acceptance. It must be a giving, rather than a narcissistically self-gratifying, love. Real mothering is called for, not a display of how good a mother one is. This rule applies to small children as well as to bigger ones. Its purpose

[10] Personal communication. Cf. also Spitz's significant publications (*204, 205, 206*).

is to build up the child's fragile ego, because the strength of its ego is all that protects the child from being "ground to dust" between the equally tyrannical and equally destructive demands of its id and of its superego. The giving of love is especially important in the case of the intellectually defective or emotionally disturbed child, whose very defect causes it to be deprived of an adequate supply of real love.[11] In this context the situation of the neurotic child is especially worthy of notice. Children become neurotic through being denied the proper kind of love, and, once they are neurotic, it is harder to love them than if they were normal. Nowhere does the adage "Them as has, gits" apply more forcefully— in reverse—than in the case of "exceptional children" of all types.

Needless to say, real love is clear-sighted and does not ignore the child's shortcomings and hostilities. However, it knows how to turn these drawbacks into assets, by reacting to displays of hostility in such a manner that the reaction itself will strengthen the child's ego by an explicit recognition of its potentiality for being good. This is of crucial importance, since no one can work for any length of time with hostile children without realizing how much they want to be good, how severely they condemn their own conduct, how bitterly they despise themselves, and, above all, how much of their misbehavior is an expression of their desperate need to be restrained.

Case 15: Creative Reactions to Hostility

"Trixie"—adopted at the age of six months—is in the middle of her latency period. Her adopted parents were eventually divorced, Trixie remaining with her adoptive mother. This little girl has a rather serious character disorder and does a great deal of "acting out." She has deeply

---

[11] We do not consider the guilt-laden and masochistically "self-sacrificing" pseudo love which some mothers show toward their defective children as real love, since it is compounded of (basically hostile) overprotectiveness and of what the Germans call *Affenliebe,* i.e., of blind and narcissistic pseudo love, emanating from emotionally disturbed or immature mothers.

buried and painful conflicts over questions of loving and being loved, masked by less deeply buried secondary conflicts over sexuality.

A very sensitive and sympathetic teacher gave the writer the following account of her relationship with Trixie.

"I talked to Trixie on several occasions about her bad behavior, because she herself commented on my attitude and seemed unable to understand my acceptance of her conduct. I explained to her that I liked her and that, despite her 'smartness,' I could see a great deal of sweetness in her, which she tries hard to cover up. I told her that the way she acted seemed to imply: 'Well, they are not going to like me anyway, so I might as well be bad.' Although the child seemed a little touched by my remarks, she said she did not really care. I accepted this statement as a fact, but went on to say that I felt that all people—children as well as adults—did care. Hence, because I myself did care, I would continue in my way of thinking. I would continue to believe that, despite her troublesome ways, there was an awful lot in her that was really nice.

"The next day Trixie insisted on sitting beside me, continuing to be a 'little smartie,' but showing improvement. She said she wanted to show me something. This 'something' turned out to be an attempt to bend my finger backward. She was a little surprised by my attitude. She seemed to be gladly disappointed that I did not show that she hurt me and did not display any temper over her intention to hurt me. She did this twice. After she bent my finger twice, I put a stop to it in a friendly but firm manner. A little later I said to her: 'Trixie, you have shown me some of the hurting things you can do. You already know how I feel about you; that I know all the hurtful things that you can do and that you can be mean. But you also know that I feel there is a lot in you that is sweet and good. Having done two hurting things to me—do you think you could do one nice thing to make up for them?' She replied: 'I don't know!' and walked away. Then she came back and asked me if I had a comb. I asked her why she wanted one and she replied that she wanted to comb my hair. After she combed my hair we talked again and she teased some of the other children. Then, suddenly, she kissed me on the cheek, saying: 'That is two nice things.' Ever since, she has behaved nicely in my classes, and has been very affectionate toward me.

"Somewhat later she told me that she was sorry, and had not really meant what she had said a few days earlier when, on being reprimanded, she had declared that she hated the whole staff, and asked me to tell also the other staff members that she had not really meant it. This made me very happy, both for her, and because of what I deeply believe in.

"Five days later I suddenly realized that when I have to scold Trixie she no longer reacts to the reprimand with further 'smartness.' Instead, she seems hurt and once she even cried like a soft little child, all of whose defenses are down. However, her whole attitude indicates that she understands now that my reprimand concerns only a specific act of hers at a specific time, and does not imply that I am rejecting her as a person."

COMMENT: The preceding incidents reveal the manner in which one may cope with a small "acting-out" girl's objectionable behavior by means of loving discipline rather than by punishment (Chapter 8), and by strengthening her ego and her spontaneity rather than by undermining her self-esteem and paralyzing her inner resources.

Several aspects of these incidents deserve special comment.

1. Many children are the first to condemn their own behavior, even if, superficially, they seem defensive about it. The fact that the therapeutic educator, or therapist, does not react with the kind of anger and rejection which the child has come to expect and actually feels that it deserves is often very confusing to the little troublemaker. This observation has been misused for the purpose of justifying punishment, by stressing that the child often becomes anxious if it does not receive the punishment which it seems to be demanding. However, if one punishes the child, one usually only alleviates its guilt feelings over some current concrete bit of "acting out" which, in itself, is but a manifestation of other, more deep-seated, unconscious guilt feelings. Hence, the truly motivating, but deeply buried, guilt feelings are not alleviated—or even reached—by punishment and will therefore continue to motivate further mischief. The teacher, Miss X, handled Trixie's misbehavior differently. Instead of punishing her, she suggested that Trixie make restitution, by doing something nice. In other words, instead of constricting

the girl by imposing a taboo on her and by subjecting her to punishment, which is a passive experience, Trixie's range of behavior was expanded, by showing her that a bad deed can be canceled by a good deed. Instead of establishing a specific and arbitrary taboo, the girl was taught a general principle (the principle of making restitution), and her spontaneity and inventiveness were stimulated by letting her choose the type of restitution she wished to make. As a result, though asked to perform only one kind action, the girl actually made double restitution, by combing the teacher's hair and kissing her as well.

2. The teacher systematically interpreted to the child the fact that disapproval of one specific objectionable act did not imply a rejection of the child itself. She made this explanation convincing by simultaneously taking cognizance of the overt occurrence of bad behavior and of the underlying hunger for affection and desire to be good. How successfully the teacher managed to make this explanation "stick" is shown by the fact that, ever after, she was able to scold the child without eliciting further, reactive, provocativeness. Instead, the girl felt sufficiently loved to allow herself to let down her defenses and show her grief by crying. She would have been unable to do this had she feared that any "show of weakness and vulnerability" on her part would expose her, as a person, to further rejection. Instead, by allowing herself to show grief, she felt "cleansed" and deserving of the teacher's love and acceptance.

We might add in passing that often a seemingly hostile or resistive act actually expresses a great deal of confidence in the person who is being "attacked."

Case 16: Positive Attitudes Behind Overt Resistance

When the analyst tried to interpret something rather painful to an acting-out delinquent, the latter first rejected the interpretation with hostile and sarcastic remarks and then provocatively fell asleep on the couch, so as not to have to listen to the analyst. Two interpretations were offered: (1) "You would not have dared to vent your hostility so openly if you had not felt quite certain that you would not be able to destroy the analyst." (2) "You would not have been able to fall asleep on the couch if you did not feel completely safe in the analyst's presence." These interpretations produced very gratifying results.

Now, the competent therapeutic educator or milieu therapist is unusually qualified to give genuine love and acceptance to the exceptional child, because he does not unconsciously feel "responsible" for the feeble-minded child's defect, and does not have to blame himself for an initial failure to give the neurotic child the kind of love which would have prevented it from becoming neurotic. Last, but not least, the emotionally mature therapeutic educator accepts from the start the fact that his love must not tie the child to him by a "silver cord" but must help it to emancipate itself ultimately from all dependence, including dependence on the educator. In brief, because the educator feels no guilt over the exceptional child's condition, he is often able to love it both more effectively and in a more liberating manner than the child's parents can. What his love may lack in—sometimes narcissistic (9)— parental intensity is usually more than compensated for by its maturity and undemandingness.[12]

These considerations lead directly to the problem of the child's transference reactions toward its teachers and milieu therapists.

TRANSFERENCE

Transference in the broad sense—i.e., behaving and feeling toward X as though he were Y—as well as identification, both patterned upon family relationships, occur, of course, in every school situation, both in the positive and in the negative sense.

The following dream of an adolescent boy shows that he is inclined to treat one of his kindly women teachers as a mother figure, even to the extent of subtly competing for her with his father.

---

[12] It is necessary that the teacher should have a genuine source of narcissistic gratification of his own (65), lest he unconsciously expect the child in his care to gratify what Levy (148) calls a "primary affect hunger."

Case 17: The Teacher as a Good Mother Figure

Pete's parents were divorced while he was in the latency period, the boy remaining with his father. Pete's early development was slow and he was finally enrolled in the Devereux Schools, because of both emotional and organic problems, the latter including poor coördination, speech and hearing difficulties, and intellectual depression. Although the boy is at present in his late teens, his dream has a naïve quality more often found in the dreams of much younger children.

"Dear Miss R.

I had a dream couple of nights ago that I was in [a big city]. I was at my dad's office and I saw you. I was just about to go to [a very large movie]. Dad was giving me extra money. You asked me if you could come along with me. I was surprised so we were on our way. We walked to [the movie] from . . . street on . . . avenue to . . . street on . . . avenue. I payed the way for both of us. We saw a good show. After the show we had lunch together then walked back to my Dad's office. Dad told us to wait at his garage which he own to wait for him and my brother to go to [a suburb] with us. You and I sat in the back together in the car. I'll see you.

Your admirer
Pete

P.S. Let me know what you think of this letter."

The preceding dream is, by and large, positive in its affective tone and reflects the boy's desire to have a mother whom he can have all to himself, at least for a while, and toward whom he may play the masculine role ("I paid for everything") even if the funds for the outing are provided by the father and even though, in the end, the father returns and "takes over" once more.

The following dream shows, by contrast, the extent to which very deep oedipal anxieties and hostilities can be aroused by a very nongiving and "castrative" milieu therapist, who denies the children in her care any sense of warmth and real acceptance. Needless to say, this "therapist" was discharged as soon as her lack of emotional qualifications became apparent.

Case 18: A Milieu Therapist as a Bad Mother Figure

Henry was cyanotic at birth and remained so for several days. He had an orthopedic operation just before the beginning of the oedipal period. He has a chronic brain syndrome which is due to a birth trauma, and a moderate idiopathic mental defect. He is an emotionally unstable personality. His dream, which he related to a friendly male teacher, contains remote echoes of his operation, symbolized by a castrative "attack."

"I dreamed last night that a man came into my room. He scared me to death in my dream. Three times he went for my crotch. Then he went into Mrs. B's room and tried to choke her three times."

It is hardly necessary to state that transferences occur in every school situation. A therapeutic school differs, however, from other schools in that it takes explicit cognizance of transference factors, both by considering them as predictable and important phenomena and in handling them for therapeutic purposes. Thus, Case 37 shows how a skillful teacher handled a boy who, motivated by his transference, sought to "seduce" another teacher into spanking him, the way his mother did. It was likewise a transference phenomenon that this boy—who exhibited his soiling impulses openly at school—was very much concerned over the possibility that his mother might hear of the incident.

This last remark stands in need of further discussion. As the teacher pointed out to the boy, his mother already knew that he had soiling impulses, since that was one of the reasons for his having been sent to a therapeutic school. The boy stressed, however, that he did not wish his mother to know that he also soiled at school. Superficially, this seems to represent little more than an attempt to make his mother believe that he was improving. However, on a deeper and functionally more significant level, his concern meant something altogether different. At school he apparently felt free to manifest his anal expulsive and anal erotic urges more openly than he did at home, because in a transference situation and in regard to a transference object one feels more free to manifest forbidden urges than one does in the "real" situation and toward the "real" object of one's unconscious desires. This, in fact, is one of the therapeutically most valuable aspects of the transference.[13] Hence, the boy was anxious to conceal from his mother the extent to which he "acted out" in the school situation and in connection with his teachers the anal impulses which were primarily directed at her, lest she intuitively become aware of his real feelings toward her.

In brief, a therapeutic educator not only takes cognizance of transference behavior but is also prepared to handle it as such. By contrast, in ordinary boarding schools teachers often do not realize that both the "unreasonable" hostility and the "demanding" affectionateness of children are directed at them not as specific persons but only as substitutes (transference objects) representing the parents. Lacking this insight, the unsophisticated teacher is both unduly angered by the child's hostility and unwarrantably flattered by its caresses and attentions. He is therefore unable to handle such derivative or transference behavior rationally and effectively and is even less able to interpret its real meaning to the child.

The therapeutic school takes cognizance of the children's transference needs and transference problems even in the administrative sense. Thus, a milieu therapist who is unable to give the children the kind of warmth and acceptance which they need—lest they be as bitterly disappointed in the transference situation as they were in the home situation—is seldom kept on the staff. As Case 18, cited above, indicates, a milieu therapist whose behavior was such as to induce severe anxiety dreams in at least one of her charges

---

[13] Similarly, when a man who does not dare to strike the boss "takes it out" on the dog, he is likely to kick the unoffending animal harder than he would have kicked the boss.

was dismissed as soon as her personality defect became obvious. On the other hand, a teacher who is so self-centered and so badly in need of acceptance that he or she is unreasonably flattered by the transference love of a child—or, in other situations, by mere "shows" of affection which are basically seductive or manipulative —is, likewise, not a person qualified to work in a therapeutic school.

In fact, the proper handling of transferences presupposes the thesis that in the therapeutic school situation the most important reality factor is the psychology—i.e., the personality problem— of the child (Chapter 8). This way of defining the reality situation automatically leads to the administrative and personnel policy that a better understanding of the children permits a better selection of teachers since, in the therapeutic school, it is the teacher who must adapt himself to the child's needs and "quirks," instead of vice versa (Chapter 8).

Transference phenomena are not necessarily limited to patients or to children. They are also exhibited occasionally by therapists and educators, and are commonly referred to as "counter transference."[14]

COUNTER TRANSFERENCE

The management of the educational or milieu therapist's own counter transference is one of the most significant of all psychotherapeutic activities in therapeutic education. Again, the complexity of the problem is such that we can mention only some major and recurrent situations, in which the therapeutic educator must creatively control his counter-transference needs.

Love. We referred above to the attempt to win the love of the child because of one's own neurotic need for response, and therefore do not have to discuss this problem in detail.

Favoritism. Both our dislikes and our preferences are deter-

[14] An excellent study of counter transference was published by Gitelson (*103*).

mined by a variety of unconscious motives. We may find a kindly person repulsive because he reminds us of the harsh teacher we had in grammar school, or we may be greatly taken by the looks of a very average girl who reminds us of a generous aunt. Without psychoanalytic help we seldom become aware of the real sources of what Freud calls our "conditions of love," or, more properly, the "prerequisites for being found lovable by us" (91). On the other hand, the attempt to be coldly objective may sometimes cause us to "lean over backward" too far,[15] even to the point where we display excessive severity toward those who "tempt" us to be partial to them. The roots of the preference we show a child are, unfortunately, often too deeply buried to permit us to discover them without psychiatric assistance. However, bearing in mind a general principle of another order is sometimes helpful in such situations. We must realize that each child has different needs. For example, some children struggle to fight off adult interferences while others crave to be leaders. This sometimes leads to bitter clashes within the group. In fact, when the neurotic needs of various children complement each other, real trouble can occur. Thus, psychopathic adolescents sometimes manage to become the leaders of dependent and schizoid youngsters, whom they use as cat's paws.

Case 19: A Devious Troublemaker

An adolescent girl, who had, at the lowest estimate, a very severe character disorder, specialized in making trouble. She herself was never involved in any prank or misdeed but could not even enter a room without causing a commotion of some kind. She had an uncanny ability to detect the weaknesses of others and to manipulate them through their foibles.

When one is tempted to "take sides" or "play favorites," it sometimes helps in clearing away the smoke screen to ask oneself: "How will this privilege or favor affect the other children?" When

[15] Cf. the harshness of the Abbé Pirard toward his favorite, Julien Sorel, in Stendhal's novel *The Red and the Black*.

this question is asked candidly, it never leads to the withholding of a deserved privilege or reward, since the latter can always be justified to the group in a constructive manner. It does, however, inhibit one's tendency to act out one's unconsciously motivated countertransference needs.

Hostile or Envious Giving.   Many persons who were harshly treated in their childhood devote their lives to children. In some instances they do so for healthy reasons, which represent a sublimation of their own early disappointments. They seem to say: "I had it tough. I will therefore see to it that some children are as happy as I was unhappy. That way my own unhappy childhood will not have been in vain." In other cases the sublimation is less complete. The teacher or therapeutic educator seems to say in effect: "I am going to show my harsh and cruel parents how I should have been treated." However, since this sublimation is incomplete, it tends to include also the opposite impulse of "handing on" to the next generation the pain which the teacher suffered in childhood. This leads to destructive ways of over-"loving" or over-"rewarding" the child, which—like all excesses—represent neither real love nor real reward. Such persons sometimes gratify the child to an extent which exceeds the child's capacity to handle its pleasurable excitement. This is a common mistake even in ordinary life; witness the tantrums and crying jags which so often mark the end of a birthday or Christmas party and which are *prima facie* evidence that the child was overstimulated. In other instances the bribe or gift offered is beyond the child's capacity to enjoy and may therefore represent a veiled demand implying a psychic threat. For example, the gift of a real watch to a grossly feeble-minded child may represent for it a demand that it should learn to tell time. The gift of a lipstick or of glamorous undergarments to a severely inhibited girl, who seeks to control her adolescent urges by self-constriction, may be highly threatening to her, since she may unconsciously interpret it as "egging her on" to behave "improperly."

Power. A great deal of neurotic gratification can be derived from making the child increasingly dependent upon the therapeutic educator. For example, there are children who display a neurotic need to be led, and therefore often pretend to be unable to do certain things unassisted. Such a child may be so clever at this stratagem that it will succeed in establishing a permanent pattern of dependency. Of course, such a self-constriction is often achieved only at the cost of becoming pseudo-retarded. Once this pattern is set, the child becomes unable to function anywhere near its real level of ability and requires intensive psychotherapy to start it moving once more in the direction of full self-actualization. The effort required to accomplish this may be considerable, since the child derives a "secondary gain" from having things done for it. One way in which this problem can be handled educationally is to make the child realize that more pleasure may be derived from functioning at the optimum level and in a mature manner than can be obtained from the continued gratification of infantile dependency needs. Hence, whenever a teacher realizes that he derives pleasure from helping a child, he must ask himself whether he is encouraging the child to become dependent on him, thus increasing, rather than decreasing, the child's illness. He must understand that doing for a child what the child itself could do unassisted causes it to develop the attitude that it actually cannot perform these tasks. Of course, it is often easier to do things for a child than to wait patiently while the youngster tries to do it for itself, just as it is easier to "talk above the head" of a child than it is to include it in the conversation. In more general terms, it simply takes more time and self-control to let the child grow up than it takes to make growth seem unnecessary by "taking over." In fact, the adult's habit of "taking over" may be unconsciously interpreted by the child both as a reprimand and as a prohibition against growing up. It amounts to *teaching* the child to be sick, and to rewarding it for its sickness, the way cripples and the insane were sometimes "rewarded" in the Middle Ages, by being appointed court jesters.

This extreme need to make the child dependent on oneself is paralleled by the equally neurotic need of some teachers to repress this impulse to the point where they make impossible demands on the child. This, however, is but another and more roundabout way of forcing the child to come to the teacher for help. The best indication that the teacher is handling his counter transference maturely in this respect is that he demands from the child all the child can do, but not one iota more or less. In addition, such a teacher knows how to make it clear to the child that a reasonable demand made upon it represents a recognition of its ability to do what is expected.[16] In fact, we might even say that the good or bad grades a child makes in a therapeutic school are—within limits—indications of the teacher's success or lack of success in dealing with his own power drives in the counter-transference situation.[17]

"Omniscience." Omniscience and the desire to make oneself interesting often lead to gross violations of the child's right to privacy or to a betrayal of its confidences, and cause adults to become careless of whether or not such violations may become known to the child. Indeed, many adults have the deplorable habit of underestimating the child's intelligence. This is particularly true where retarded children are concerned, since people sometimes discuss them in their presence as though they were deaf or not even present.

Case 20: Reactions to Being Underestimated

An extraordinarily sensitive and alert teacher described as follows the visit of a moron's parents to their son: "Throughout the visit I could not keep my eyes from the boy's face. When anyone was speaking directly to him, his face lit up, so that he looked like a rather handsome

[16] We discussed elsewhere the panicky need of some children and patients to minimize what they actually can do, for fear of having additional—and sometimes unreasonable—demands made upon them (Case 5).

[17] It should be remembered that in a therapeutic school the curriculum is adjusted to the individual child, rather than vice versa.

and alert child of eight. The moment his parents spoke about him, or past him, or over his head, or else kept up a running fire of instructions —of do's and don't's—you could literally see the child's face crumple up before your eyes. His features simply fell apart—he looked ugly, he drooled and his whole posture became as awkward as that of an idiot or imbecile. It was awful!"

In many ways the omniscient attitude is related to the power drive which forces the child into dependency. By talking about a child in its presence, or by "talking over its head," we sometimes force the child to protect itself by learning "not to register" what is being said, thus driving it into further withdrawal. This is almost the same thing as doing things for a child which the child can do for itself.

Anger. The therapeutic educator's ability to control his anger —especially over an occurrence which mobilizes some of his own basic anxieties—is a very important aspect of his professional qualifications. However, in some instances the teacher may be so afraid of his own anger as to over-control it, thereby rendering him incapable of handling the child's aggressions correctly. In overcontrolling himself he will fail to control the child, who may need control quite badly. In some instances even the teacher's genuine and healthy control of his anger may be quite confusing to the child:

Case 21: Explaining Genuine Patience

It scares me that you never scold me when I insult or threaten you. I am not accustomed to this. At home, when I was bad, I "caught" it— but quick. But you just take it on the chin. I am afraid that one day you will finally blow up . . . and what will happen then I shudder even to think of. (Therapist: I am not building up to an explosion. In fact, I am not even angry with you. I realize that the hostility you are showing toward me is not directed at me but at your father, with whom you seek to identify me. You may be lashing out at me—but you are aiming at your father.)

COMMENT: The above example indicates that what is called for is not simply an inhibition of one's anger but a realization that one has nothing to be angry about. Once this insight is achieved, it is possible to interpret it to the child, thus simultaneously resolving the child's worry over the therapist's "confusing" unresponsiveness to attacks and moderating the intensity of its hostilities. Indeed, a hostility directed at its real object is seldom as vicious or unmanageable as one which has been unconsciously displaced or transferred to a substitute object.

Subjective Vulnerabilities. No person, no matter how mature or well analyzed he may be, is equally invulnerable and incorruptible in all areas. All of us have "sensitive spots," which we expect others to respect, in accordance with the adage that "one should not speak of ropes in the house of a man who was hanged." Now, it so happens that children are sent to therapeutic schools and adults to mental hospitals not only because they are objectively quite sick but also because their sickness takes a form which irritates the most vulnerable spots of people. This explains why so many children sent to therapeutic schools have conflicts connected with such "delicate" matters as sex, soiling, and the like. Such behavior in the child also threatens the immature teacher or milieu therapist, who is barely able to control his own impulses in this conflict-laden area of conduct. Hence, he is likely to react to the soiling, sexual "acting out" and aggressivity of the child with anger because it irritates one of his "sore spots." He therefore reacts to it with condemnation instead of with understanding helpfulness. Teachers who can handle such problems in a mature and dispassionate way, *without anger but also without losing control of the child,* are rare indeed. Cases 36 and 37 are worthy of careful study because they show how one should handle in a mature manner situations which irritate the most conflict-laden segments of our personalities. One general principle can be of help to the teacher faced with such situations. He must always bear in mind that the child's offensive soiling, aggressivity, or sexual behavior is often but a neurotic acting out or manifestation of *altogether different* conflicts.

Case 22: Sexual Activity as a Claim of Maturity

The psychotherapy of an adolescent sex delinquent made it obvious that she was very little interested in sex *per se*. It was her way of affirming that she was no longer a child but a young woman, no matter how much her parents insisted on treating her as though she were five years old instead of fifteen. Once this point was made clear to her and once she realized that the school did treat her as an adolescent and not as a child, her sexual "acting out" ceased completely. She no longer needed to display her sexual precociousness in order to "prove" her status as an adolescent, and as a person.

Case 23: Sophistication as a Claim of Maturity

An adolescent girl of superior intelligence, who was not a sex delinquent, displayed a sophistication and a seductiveness worthy of a *femme fatale*. A study of her case made it obvious that this behavior represented a defense against the realization that she had never been treated as a person, but was simply a pawn in the stormy divorce of her parents—in injunctions, counter-injunctions, and even "kidnapings"— which went on for years. She was forced to become prematurely sophisticated and self-reliant because no one provided her with any security or treated her as a person. She became seductive partly because she had seen her mother cajole her father in order to get from him what she wanted, and also because she realized that her father fought for her custody not primarily because he desired the company of his daughter but because he wished—if only to spite his ex-wife—to control the estate which the girl had inherited from a grandparent. Since her sophistication and seductiveness were only symptoms, they were not the proper points at which to attack her psychological illness.

Once the realization dawns upon him that the child's conduct, which irritates him in a "sore spot," has an altogether different meaning—that soiling may reflect a need to remain a baby, that seductiveness is often simply an attempt to get something, that sexual acts may be engaged in solely in order to prove that one is an adult—the educational therapist's anxieties and anger usually abate sufficiently to enable him to devise suitable ways of dealing with the basic problem, instead of warring, in a futile manner, against its indirect manifestations.

Many other types of essentially therapeutic activities in the educational and milieu therapeutic program could also be mentioned. However, most of them fall, in part at least, into one of the above categories. Hence, therapeutic education can effect important improvements by undoing unhealthy attitudes and replacing them with more mature and more creative ones. It represents therapy, in that such efforts tend to correct a pathologically deferred, distorted, or incomplete humanization. Of course, the inculcation of healthy attitudes is also important in ordinary educational practice, which differs from therapeutic education simply the way preventive pediatrics differs from therapeutic pediatrics.

In educating the child therapeutically, the educator must keep his own conflicts out of the picture and must attempt to provide security for the child in terms of the child's own, distinctive needs. Above all, his prime concern must be to increase the child's educability—by means described in Chapter 6—rather than simply its level of actual performance, as in ordinary instruction. To the extent to which the child's educability is increased by these means, therapeutic education may legitimately claim that, in performing primarily educational functions, it also increases the child's therapeutizability.

In conclusion, just as educational activities in the course of psychotherapy are legitimate, but should not therefore be called psychotherapy *stricto sensu,* so important therapeutic activities may take place in the educational context, by admittedly therapeutic means. In each instance one and the same person performs two conceptually distinct operations in a single context, subordinating both activities to psychotherapeutic, respectively educational, goals, depending on whether he is a psychotherapist or an educator. Other distinctions would amount to little more than quarrels over jurisdictional competence.

CHAPTER 6

....

Potentiality Profile vs. Achievement Profile

DIVISION OF LABOR

No person is equally proficient in all areas of performance. At a very primitive stage of cultural development, where no amount of specialization in the area of his maximal skill enables the individual to produce a consistent and reliable surplus, allowing him to obtain by barter the goods and services falling within the area of his minimal proficiency, each person (or family) has to be a jack-of-all-trades. As the level of culture and technology rises, making the production of reliable surpluses possible, specialization sets in. Each person now trades the surplus he produced in his area of maximum proficiency for the surplus others produce in their respective areas of maximum proficiency. In fact, economists stress that it is both socially advantageous and individually profitable for each person to exploit his own best skill. Thus, if John Doe happens to be four times as good a shoemaker and also three times as good a tailor as Richard Roe, despite his double superiority it is advantageous for him as well as for society if he specializes in the manufacture of shoes, and leaves tailoring to Richard Roe.

This specialization leads to a systematic division of labor, and to social polysegmentation, which—as Durkheim pointed out (74) —is a *conditio sine qua non* of social and cultural progress.

THE JAGGED PROFILE

We discussed in Chapter 1 the social advantages to be derived from a constructive utilization of the admittedly limited capacities of the feeble-minded and neurotic. What concerns us here is the factual finding that the profile of the feeble-minded or neurotic individual's performance is quite as uneven and "jagged" as that of any "normal" person. In fact, the performance profile tends to be especially jagged in the case of the "exogenous" (i.e., brain-injured) feeble-minded person.

Many examples of this readily come to mind. For example, the spastic's manual skill may be grossly inferior to his capacity for verbalization, or a bright child may have neurotic reading difficulties and may therefore perform in this respect on a level markedly inferior to its performance in other areas. This view is clearly justified by the whole concept of the "total profile" which was developed in connection with the Wechsler-Bellevue test and other broad techniques for gauging various segments of ability and performance and for reaching a general estimate of the overall pattern of potentialities and performances, as well as in connection with the theory underlying vocational aptitude tests in particular. In fact, the profile approach was found equally applicable to the neurotic, the mentally defective, and the "normal."

We are, thus, faced with the fact that even a feeble-minded child may have relatively well-preserved segmental potentialities and functions. In some instances these segmental abilities are quite remarkable and, in the case of so-called *"idiots savants"* and of some "lightning calculators," may even transcend the routine capacities of "normals."[1]

[1] The thesis that such segmentally superior persons are necessarily either pseudo defectives—i.e., neurotically inhibited individuals—or else schizophrenics is, to say the least, not generally accepted.

SEGMENTAL ABILITIES

Leaving aside, as being more interesting than relevant in this context, many reported cases of brilliantly superior segmental abilities in feeble-minded persons, we will illustrate our thesis by citing the case of a feeble-minded individual whose unusual, though not spectacular, performance in one area can be understood in terms of psychodynamic principles and of social allegiances.

Case 24: Psychodynamics of Segmental Superiority

Peter is a grown man so grossly feeble-minded, and so grotesquely apelike in his appearance, that he has had to be institutionalized ever since he was a child. This man often startles visitors by his ability to recall the exact score of almost every football game ever played by Harvard. This puzzling "feat" loses much of its mysteriousness if, instead of asking ourselves how he can remember so many figures, we inquire into the motivation of his interest in precisely this topic. Peter happens to be a scion of an old and established Cambridge-Groton-Harvard family, who, because of his extreme feeble-mindedness, had to be extruded fairly early in life from his family, while his brothers and male relatives were sent, according to the traditional family pattern, to Groton and to Harvard, where they felt "perfectly at home" and achieved enviable records. Anything on this order was, of course, absolutely beyond this man's potentialities. However, he, like every human being—and one does not cease to be human even if one happens to be grossly feeble-minded—had a deep-seated need to maintain emotional bonds with the family, to experience a sense of "we-ness" and to approximate, be it but in fantasy and in a grotesquely fictitious way, the usual "type biography" of the other members of his family. He therefore developed a pathetic loyalty to Harvard, implemented by means of an absorbing interest in the scores of the Harvard football team, to which he systematically referred as "we."[2] This can be understood as

[2] The writer once analyzed a puny mysophobic, from South Bend, whose great ambition to be a football player manifested itself in his habit of referring to the Notre Dame team as "we."

the manifestation of a primary, nonfunctional identification with those aspects of the ego ideal and family ideal which, while admittedly nonfunctional, and peripheral to the core function and nuclear meaning of that ideal, nonetheless permits at least an illusion of identification and belongingness.[3] We are dealing here with a phenomenon first studied by Freud, who referred in this context to the famous lines from Schiller's Wallenstein trilogy: "The way he clears his throat and the way he spits you have happily imitated, but his genius—I mean his spirit—is not seen on the watch parade."[4] The distinction between truly functional identification and nonfunctional identification with "externals" was discussed with particular cogency by Louisa P. Holt [Howe] (119, 120).

The observation that neurotic mechanisms can be responsible for a segmental high level of performance even in the case of a grossly feeble-minded man will be given due consideration somewhat later in this chapter. What interests us more at this point is the *prima facie* evidence that the performance profile of even such persons is not a straight but a markedly jagged one—just as is that of many nondefectives. As regards the endogenously—i.e., the non-brain-injured—feeble-minded in particular, we hold that the observed deficiency of ability and performance is mostly of a quantitative, rather than, except very incidentally, of a qualitative, kind.

SEGMENTAL ABILITIES AND GENERAL INTELLIGENCE

At this point we venture to advance a hypothesis in the hope that, even if it should prove to be fallacious, it may, by being refuted, stimulate new and more constructive approaches to an understanding of the relationship between the segmental disabilities and overall inadequacy of the mentally defective. The line of

---

[3] In the same way a skinny "ugly duckling" may imitate Veronica Lake's distinctive hairdo, just as minor Austro-Hungarian officials of pre-World War I days imitated the distinctive "mutton chops" of Emperor Francis Joseph I.

[4] This quip, like some other supposedly German witticisms, was actually originated by the French. An almost identical passage may be found in Molière's *Les Femmes Savantes.*

thought about to be presented was set off by a rather naïve observation. One day the writer was watching a film showing mentally defective children in an occupational therapy workshop. He was struck by the fact that when the whole child's image appeared on the screen its posture and movements seemed awkward and poorly coördinated, while when only the working hand and arm were shown, the movements appeared competent and sometimes even graceful. The impression was created that such children could manage one limb at a time but not their entire body.

These observations reminded the writer of the well-known fact that a neural organization of a given complexity can handle effectively just so much "living matter" and no more. Hence, each "ring" or "slice" of an earthworm has to have its own ganglion. Likewise, when the relatively still simple-brained dinosaur came into being, it was obliged to evolve a kind of "auxiliary brain" at the root of its tail in order to coördinate and manage its immense body and limbs.[5]

The relative competence and even gracefulness of the movements of many a mental defective's working hand and the awkward uncoördination of his body posture and total movement pattern suggest that something along this order may also be true of them—perhaps even as regards their segmental abilities. If this line of reasoning is at all valid, the abilities of the mentally defective may be viewed as a kind of mob, lacking a leader who could coördinate its efforts. This, in turn, leads one to ask whether the segmental abilities of the mentally defective are truly as minimal as current tests make them appear. Indeed, just as we suggested in Chapter 1 that no individual can unfold all of his potentialities without the help of society, so no ability may be able to unfold itself with complete functionality unless it is embedded into, and supported by, a well-patterned matrix of other abilities. For exam-

[5] Certain entomologists even suggest that the respiratory system of insects is functionally so restricted in scope that it automatically sets a limit to the size insects may attain.

ple, we may wonder whether feeble-minded "lightning calculators" are not potentially talented mathematicians in whom, owing to lack of support from other abilities, the ability to calculate is "running wild." In other words, we suspect that at least in certain types of genuine feeble-mindedness both the jaggedness of the performance profile and the generally low level of performance are not primarily reflections of inherently low segmental abilities but, on the contrary, the end products of a lack of patterned coordination of the segmental potentialities.

One small example may be quoted in support of this view, which is at present nothing more than a very tentative hypothesis:

Case 25: Liberating a Segmental Ability

A very feeble-minded child had much difficulty in managing its body and was incessantly moving its limbs in a manner which was not understandable in terms of some focal lesion of the nervous system. This child was rapidly helped to achieve a high degree of coördination in doing fine weaving by having those parts of its body which were not needed in weaving partially restrained and immobilized.

SEGMENTAL ABILITIES AND THERAPEUTIC EDUCATION

Leaving aside these speculative ideas, we may now turn our attention to the problem of the practical relevance of exceptional segmental abilities or performances for the planning and patterning of therapeutic educational programs adapted to the special needs of the individual child.

Our first objective must be an appraisal of the social value and practical import of the child's segmental areas of maximum performance. In some cases this segmental ability is of a type which readily lends itself to social utilization. Kanner (130) described a feeble-minded garbage collector who was not only an efficient and well-adjusted city official but also a sober, kindly, and adequate husband and father. In other instances the special capacities of the "abnormal" person are of a type which is not readily utilizable. For example, a defective may sing tolerably well and his musical capacities may be infinitely superior to all his other abilities, though, needless to say, still infinitely below the level at which this segmental talent could be put to self-supportive and socially beneficial uses. The exceptional memory of the man who knew all the Harvard football scores is also a good example of a genuine, but socially not readily usable, ability.

In still other instances the area of maximum performance may be a distinctly undesirable one from the social point of view. Thus, a feeble-minded individual may display an uncanny skill in rigging up booby traps wherewith to harm his fellow patients and the personnel of the institution (216).[6]

Now, where socially readily usable talents are present—and these talents need not be necessarily of a menial type—the therapeutic educator's task is clearly outlined for him and presents no problems of the type which we examine in the present chapter. On the other hand, where socially not readily utilizable special abilities, or outright destructive ones, are present, the therapeutic educator is confronted with genuine problems, requiring him to exert his creative imagination to the fullest extent.

THE CONVERTIBILITY OF TALENTS

The crucial point to be considered here is the much vexed problem of the exclusive specificity or "convertibility" of "talents." We know that some endowments and potentialities are relatively neutral. E.g., a "good memory" can, in principle, be put to a variety of uses. However, even the person who has a "good memory" does not find it equally easy to remember every type of thing. His degree of proficiency will usually be proportionate to the intensity of his motivation or interest, or, as the psychoanalyst puts it, to the

---

[6] According to Richard L. Jenkins, M.D., "the genius of Earlswood Asylum" was probably handicapped in hearing.

extent to which he is able to cathect with libido that which he seeks to memorize, and also the act of memorizing itself. The extent to which he is able to do so will depend, in turn, on a variety of endopsychic factors, such as his unconscious need to obtain certain types of gratification, the extent to which a given achievement lends itself to a binding of his free-floating anxiety or to the sublimation of some of his cruder impulses, etc. In brief, the amount of cathexis will be determined by the compatibility of the goal with various healthy or neurotic unconscious needs and personality patterns. Thus, the memory feats of the man who remembered all Harvard football scores were possible only because of a neurotic[7] hypercathexis of everything pertaining to Harvard, which to him —and in a way possibly also to some average members of his family—was more of a "family resort" than a great university also attended by "outsiders," and not wholly devoted to sports. On the other hand, it is equally certain that, regardless of the intensity of his neurotic preoccupation, he could never have memorized all these scores had he not been the possessor of a fundamentally good memory.

It is of no concern to us for the moment that this "good memory" was, in itself, probably partly a product of the "focusing capacity" so characteristic of some—but definitely not of all—mental defectives. This "focusing capacity" is often due to a decreased ability to perceive things in context and to respond to a variety of simultaneous stimuli, and is, roughly speaking, comparable to the extreme tactile discrimination of the trained blind. An even better example may be the well-known fact that, when one does not have a telescope, one can sometimes see more clearly some relatively distant object by punching a tiny hole in a piece of paper and looking at that object through the hole. One reason for this "increased" visual acuity in a restricted area is that the paper eliminates the things surrounding the object one seeks to see, so that its

---

[7] Needless to say, not every compensatory hypercathexis is neurotic.

details stand out more sharply against the neutral "background" of the paper itself.[8] In brief, the focusing capacity of some mentally retarded persons is, figuratively speaking, the psychic equivalent of a tubular or "gun-barrel" vision, such as one occasionally observes in the sight pattern of glaucoma patients.[9] Psychologically, the whole process can be viewed as the product of a kind of "single-mindedness"—an interpretation which tends to lend additional support to the tentative hypothesis we formulated above, in regard to the relationship between the segmental abilities and the total ability of the mentally defective.

There is even some experimental evidence to support this interpretation. Strauss and Lehtinen (*211*) found that endogenous and exogenous (brain-injured) mental defectives differ in their ability to recognize, e.g., the drawing of a boat if the drawing is overlaid by another design, made up perhaps of a pattern of undulating lines. As a rule, the endogenous mental defective showed a greater ability to recognize the underlying design than did the exogenous (brain-injured) oligophrenic.

Leaving aside this relatively special problem, what does concern us here is the problem of harnessing a "special potentiality" or "talent" to some constructive objective. It is at this point that the problem of the exclusive specificity vs. "convertibility" of potentialities obtrudes itself. This is a relatively little-explored topic, of which much less is known than we know about the "transfer of learning," which lies at the polarly opposite end of the continuum: potentiality↔performance.

Broadly—and also tentatively—speaking, some potentialities seem to be more specific than others. Musical talent appears to be a rather specific one, especially if we are to credit the persistent rumor that two eminent composers, Schubert and Bruckner, were,

[8] In addition, only the central—i.e., the most perfect—portion of the lens is used, and any blunting of vision by the periphery of an imperfect lens is eliminated.

[9] In glaucoma, tubular vision results not from a narrowing of the effective lens but from a narrowing of the sensitive retina due to increased intraocular pressure.

conservatively speaking, far from bright.[10] It also seems to be a fact that no major composer ever displayed real talents in other fields. Thus, the writings of Berlioz, Schumann, and Liszt are tokens of a high general intelligence rather than of special literary talents. The same may be said also of Wagner's libretti, whose literary merit was, for a while, grossly overrated by his admirers. It is also interesting to note that, whereas a good many outstanding mathematicians, such as Bólyai, Einstein, and Teller, acquired a reputation as better than average musicians, the writer knows of no composer of note who excelled also in mathematics. In fact, one may even suggest that the composer's talent is possibly even more specific than is that of the performer, since at least one organist of note—Albert Schweitzer—is, rightly or wrongly, also highly esteemed as a profound thinker. In brief, a musical equivalent of such men as Michelangelo (painter, sculptor, architect, poet) or Leonardo da Vinci (a universal genius) simply does not seem to exist.

Other abilities—particularly "scientific" ones—seem to be more generalized. Thus, an eminent physicist, Leonard B. Loeb[11] once suggested that after Darwin gave an impetus to biological science an unusually large percentage of the best brains of the next generation "went in" for that science, while after Einstein an unusually large percentage of the "best brains" studied physics. The recently reported observation that the average intellectual level of psychiatrists is unusually high even among physicians may, we suspect, be due to the impetus given that science by Freud—and perhaps also by the increasingly acute and challenging problem of neuroticism in society at large. Of course, the fact that the tests used were chiefly verbal ones may also have influenced the results in favor of the psychiatrists.

Thus, while it is probable that a truly outstanding performance

[10] It should be specified, however, that in such cases one cannot disregard, a priori, the possibility of latent schizophrenia.
[11] Personal communication.

in any field can be achieved only by those having specific talents of the required type, many sound achievements can be credited to individuals who chose a given profession because it happened to be a currently very active and progressive one, meeting important social needs.

Unfortunately, despite the importance of the problem of the specificity or nonspecificity of talents, there is little we can add to the preceding remarks. Experimental studies of this important topic are practically nonexistent, and what little work has been done takes almost no account of the role of uniquely idiosyncratic (normal or neurotic) motivation patterns in the actualization of a—possibly relatively neutral—"intelligence" or "general ability" through one means or another. The experimentalist's failure to concern himself with this latter problem in his study of ability must be held responsible for the relative inadequacy of much aptitude testing and vocational guidance work.

All we can be fairly sure of at this point is that more or less specific "talents" can be legitimately differentiated from "abilities," which are somewhat neutral and are therefore susceptible of being put—though not with equally satisfying results—to a variety of uses.

THE EXPLOITATION OF SEGMENTAL ABILITIES

Despite the sketchiness of our understanding of the nature of specific talents and generalized abilities, the general pattern of this problem is sufficiently clear to enable us to formulate at least a broad policy for their management and development by means of therapeutic education. In principle, the following remarks are applicable to normals as well as to neurotics, delinquents, and mental defectives. However, for the sake of simplicity, we propose to deal chiefly with the therapeutic education of the feeble-minded, which may be considered as paradigmatic for the entire field of therapeutic education, mainly for the reason that because the defective intelligence of the feeble-minded is, for him, a source of so many conflicts that he often becomes quite neurotic.

There can be no doubt that the potentialities of the feeble-minded include both "talents" which have a high degree of specificity and a low degree of convertibility, and "abilities" which are "convertible," though not for all purposes or with equal efficiency in all spheres.[12]

The therapeutic educator who wishes to appraise the educability of a mental defective must, first of all, distinguish as best he can—which in practice usually means "by rule of thumb"—between the defective's "talents" and "abilities."

Since it is sometimes more economical to start with the more difficult one of two related problems, we propose to discuss first the situation in which the therapeutic educator is confronted with a specific "talent" which either is not great enough to be harnessed to self-supportive and socially useful ends or is outright destructive, like that of the *idiot savant* who harassed his environment with ingeniously contrived booby traps.

In most instances even a minimal talent should be encouraged and fostered, simply because this gratifies the habitually frustrated defective, increases his self-confidence and venturesomeness, and improves his general emotional adjustment. Once this point is reached, even if the talent remains as specific as ever, so that no real "transfer of learning" can take place, there is often such an increase in the educability and also in the therapeutizability of the defective that further positive advances becomes possible.

The training of such minimal talents, for the purpose of increasing the educability and therapeutizability of the defective, is comparable to the shoring up of the borderline psychotic's tottering ego, by means of supportive psychotherapy, in order to enable him

---

[12] A simple example will help us understand this specification. An ordinary passenger car can be used to pull a freight trailer. However, it will do this job less efficiently than would a tractor or truck of equal price and equal mechanical efficiency and is, in addition, more likely to be damaged by being used for this purpose.

eventually to withstand the stresses and rigors of a regular psychoanalysis, i.e., in order to make him "analyzable." However, just as such an initial supportive psychotherapy—which is not necessarily administered by the analyst himself—must not bolster the borderline psychotic's weak ego to the point where his defenses become sufficiently rigidified to render him almost unanalyzable in a different way, so the training of the defective's minimal talents must stay within reasonable limits. It is certainly not desirable that he should be encouraged to develop so absorbing and obsessive an interest in his one talent that it will prevent him from acquiring also other desirable skills. This is a point to which we shall return shortly.

THE MANAGEMENT OF EXTREME ONE-SIDEDNESS

Difficulties arising from the defective's obsessive and exclusive preoccupation with his one talent or interest can be coped with rather effectively. Special talents, being highly libidinized, have a great "psychological mass" and therefore tend to draw within their orbit, and to become parasitical upon, other abilities which could be put to more profitable uses. Of course, there is nothing inherently abnormal about the fact that a central interest sometimes becomes parasitical upon other interests. For example, an enthusiastic lawyer cannot be called abnormal because he reads like a lawyer, thinks like a lawyer, and brings everything he learns within the scope of his legal interests. Hence, the problem in the case of the mental defective who has one all-absorbing interest is not that he is constantly preoccupied by it, and refers everything to it, but the fact that his resources are so limited that an exclusive preoccupation with his one interest prevents him from acquiring also certain absolutely necessary basic skills.

The educational problem in such cases is relatively simple. Since the talent is not susceptible of being converted and—not being destructive—should be cultivated for the sake of the increase in self-esteem and in educability resulting therefrom, our task is simply to prevent this talent from becoming an all-absorbing pre-occupation which is parasitical upon other more neutral but highly necessary abilities. The careful study of the "neurotic push" moti-vating so obsessive a preoccupation with a single interest, and of the abilities which are drawn, like satellites, within the "field of force" of this interest, as well as an appraisal of the socially more desirable uses to which these satellitized abilities may be put, is among the principal tasks of the therapeutic educator. The next step consists in improvising a set of means whereby the satellitized abilities can be rechanneled, so that, instead of being sources of energy for the parasitical focal interest, they themselves can derive energy and motivating force from it. This, in turn, helps to divert some of the intense "neurotic push" behind that nuclear preoccupa-tion or talent into more useful channels. An example will show how this end can be achieved.

Case 26: Exploitation of an Obsession with Chickens

A rather feeble-minded boy developed an uncontrollable desire to own and raise chickens. Whether this obsessive interest represented a "specific talent" or simply a neurotic obsession, etc., need not concern us here. What is relevant in this context is that this boy's interest in chickens was so pervasive that he refused to talk about anything else, to learn anything not related to chickens, or to do anything, such as at-tending class, which would distract him from his obsessive preoccupa-tion. Finally, an ingenious educator decided to make this hitherto un-manageable interest the pivot of the boy's entire education. He told the boy that he would be given chickens as soon as he made a coop for them and learned enough arithmetic to keep accounts and to bill the school for the eggs which it would buy from him. In other words, an attempt was made to make the boy's obsession the nucleus of a kind of "project teaching" approach. So redirected, this focal obsession suddenly became a source of motivation and of energy for the actualization of other abili-ties which had previously been its satellites. The boy threw himself with great ardor into the work of carpentry and arithmetic classes, and also learned to write well enough to render legible bills. When his hencoop was ready, he was given some chickens, whose eggs he sold to the school at current rates, rendering and collecting bills and keeping rather adequate books. Above all, he ceased to be a management problem and became an appreciably better-adjusted individual. Thus, while there was no attempt to come psychiatrically to grips with his presumably neurotic motivation—which, in many ways, has some of the specificity of talent and may therefore be used to illustrate the problem under consideration—and even though the intensity of his preoccupation with chickens was not diminished, the neurotic interest itself was used as a lever for its own "socialization" and also for the far more important socialization of the boy himself. Of course, the boy continued to view carpentry, arithmetic, and writing simply as means, or as "instrumental values." However, since to the educator they represented actual values, the functional and practical outcome of this maneuver was wholly satisfactory. This example startlingly underscores the therapeutic effectiveness of planned, dynamic, special education. Hence, it cannot be held that therapeutic education "failed" in this case simply because the child's basic obsession was not abolished. Indeed, the eradication of obsessions is a task which lies beyond the inherent boundaries of the therapeutic educative process. In addition, it is not at all certain that the type of intensive psychotherapy which is capable of eradicating an obsession would have been indicated in this case, since the total results obtainable would have represented a rather inadequate return for the time and effort invested in this undertaking.[13]

THE MANAGEMENT OF DESTRUCTIVE ONE-SIDEDNESS

The situation is admittedly more complex where the focal interest is not only initially but fundamentally destructive. However, even the handling of such situations can be patterned upon the technique just outlined. Let us suppose, for instance, that our task is to socialize a booby-trap-making *idiot savant.* In this case rela-

[13] Cf. the sixth of our criteria for the realistic adjustment of educational and therapeutic levels of aspiration, which are discussed in Chapter 7.

tively constructive channels must be provided both for the implementation of the patient's mechanical talents and for the sublimation of his aggressions, preferably in a way which does not require
one to expend energy on first separating the aggressive impulse
from its mechanical implementation. Thus, it should be possible to
divert such a patient's hostilities and talents to the trapping of rats
and of other vermin. It is certainly not enough to provide an outlet
only for the mechanical talent and to ignore the aggressive impulses which are fused with it. Indeed, even though the "genius of
Earlswood Asylum" was also a talented builder of ship models, this
activity did not suffice to divert him from rigging up also ingenious
booby traps, simply because boatbuilding provided no opportunities for the sublimation of his hostility.

In cases where the talent and the aggressivity in the service of
which it is placed cannot be simultaneously diverted into a single
channel, such as the "constructively aggressive" trapping of rats,
three alternative approaches are possible:

1. We can provide one outlet for the talent and another one for
the hostility. For example, the patient could be taught to repair
electrical apparatus and be encouraged to take out his aggressions
on a punching bag.

2. We can provide a suitable outlet for the talent and cope with
the aggression through psychotherapy.[14]

3. In some cases the "talent" itself is so completely fused with
the aggressivity which it serves to actualize that it sooner or later
becomes necessary to attack also the "talent" itself by means of
psychotherapy.

Practically, each of these techniques involves, in one way or another, the "hitching" of neglected abilities and potentialities to a
focal interest or talent. Thus, in the case of the boy obsessed with
chickens, his neglected ability to do carpentry, simple arithmetic,

---

[14] This alternative would not have been particularly useful in the case of the
"genius of Earlswood Asylum" since—probably because of hearing difficulties—it
was difficult to establish verbal communication with him.

etc., was brought within the scope of his focal preoccupation, the gratification of which was made to depend upon the performance of related tasks. In the same sense, if a mentally defective child can sing a little, or wants to sing, but refuses to learn to read, one can sometimes mobilize its latent reading ability by teaching it first to read music, thus bringing reading within the scope of, and relating it to, the focal interest in music.

PATTERNED TEACHING

It would be both dangerously inefficient and degradingly in-human—and these two terms are practically interchangeable in the management of human affairs—to view this technique merely as a kind of "clever trick" which our superior intelligence enables us to play on the defective, allegedly "for his own good." We hold that it is both dishonest and inefficient to try to teach a mental defective disparate odds and ends by relating them artificially to his nuclear interests. Nowhere more than in the case of the defective must we aim at a truly relational and genuinely "person-centered" rather than "problem-centered" education. Nowhere else must we pursue quite so consistently the goal of patterned humanization and ethnicization, rather than of brute training in disparate skills. It is hardly necessary to add that such a "relational" teaching is possible only if the educator himself truly senses the relationship between the various skills which he brings within the scope of the student's focal preoccupation or ability and is convinced that this relationship is not an arbitrary and spurious one.

Above all, the teacher must feel "in his bones" the "humanity relatedness" of that which he teaches. Only then can he convincingly convey to his students—who, though defective, are not necessarily unaware of attempts to deceive them—a sense of the "objective" relationship between the various things which he teaches them. This is especially necessary in the case of the defective, whose chief handicap is precisely his inability to perceive the underlying pattern of things and to relate instrumental values to ultimate goals. That is why great pains have to be taken to explain to the defective the import of intermediate steps for the attainment of ultimate goals and to help him grasp the structural coherence of means-end schemata, which he cannot understand without help. We might add that, in their own way, even the most brilliant neurotics and psychotics labor under a similar handicap, and that, therefore, one of the chief tasks of the analyst is to enable his patients to grasp both the pattern and the consequences of various acts and attitudes.[15]

Needless to say, it is not always easy to convince the defective that the means-end schema offered to him is truly the most expedient one. The proximateness and "force of attraction" of the immediate goal sometimes makes it almost impossible for the defective to improvise the means necessary for attaining it, just as it sometimes makes it impossible for the "acting-out" neurotic delinquent to resist the temptation to "take a short cut" to the gratification of his desires. Similar observations have also been made of animals. For example, Köhler reports that if a dog is separated by a section of wire fencing from a bowl of food placed on the other side of the fence and at some distance from it, the dog will be able to "tear himself away" from the odor of food long enough to go around the fence in order to reach it—i.e., he is able to increase temporarily, and in an efficiently goal-directed manner, the distance between himself and the food, which is his ultimate objective. By contrast, if the food is placed directly against the fence, the intensity of the stimulus often keeps the dog glued to the other side of the fence, in the immediate vicinity of the food, so that he can never reach it (139).[16]

[15] In the course of a particularly successful psychoanalysis probably two interpretations or confrontations out of five consisted in the remark: "What would be the consequences?"

[16] The similarity between this type of behavior and criminal behavior was discussed in some detail elsewhere, with special reference to the high stimulus value of impressions emanating from the proximal segment of the life space, which prevents the criminal from taking "the long view" (33).

A sense of the importance of intermediate steps can be conveyed to a child in a way which is so simple and easily understood that it was found useful in work with both defectives and neurotics. It consists in leading the child to a closed door which opens inward and asking it to open the door. This obviously requires that the child remain at first stationary, twist the doorknob, and then actually withdraw from the door, so as to be able to pull it inward. While the child is performing this simple task, one urges it to note that, under certain circumstances, remaining stationary and even withdrawing from the objective may be an indispensable part of the performance. One can also point out to the child that if one insisted on going outside "in a straight line" this would require the tremendous, painful, and destructive effort of smashing one's way through the door—a simple enough task for elephants, but not for mere men. In brief, while the difficulty of explaining a means-end schema is genuine enough in the case of the feeble-minded, who lives "here and now," it is not insuperable, as the case of the boy obsessed with chickens indicates.

INTELLIGENCE AND THE LINE OF LEAST RESISTANCE

The preceding considerations imply that intelligence is primarily the ability to view the *ergodic*—i.e., the line of least resistance—rather than the *straight line*—which may require one to tunnel one's way through mountains—as the "shortest line" between the need and its gratification. The number of intermediate operations which one is able to perform in order to attain one's ultimate goal, and particularly the ability to perform intermediate operations which require either a great momentary expenditure of effort or else a temporary withdrawal from the ultimate goal, appears to be a rather adequate measure of general intelligence.

It is felt that the definition of intelligence just offered has the advantage of relating intelligence directly both to learning and habit formation and to the influence of the emotions upon the level of performance.

As regards habit formation, this definition of intelligence automatically integrates the theory of the least effort "here and now" with the theory of the least effort "in the long run." Men dig tunnels—i.e., temporarily give precedence to the "straight line" over the "ergodic"—in order to bring about in the long run a state of affairs in which the ergodic and the shortest (straight) line between two points is one and the same. Likewise, painfully and laboriously acquired habits and skills are, in the long run, means whereby both time and effort may be saved. In fact, culture as a whole may be viewed as a kind of ergodic, resulting from the combined efforts of many generations to make the line of least effort also the shortest line between need and gratification.

As regards the influence of the emotions upon the level of performance, the present definition of intelligence not only permits us to take it into consideration but actually requires us to do so. Indeed, the performance of numerous intermediate operations requires the ability to postpone gratification in a goal-directed manner. Needless to say, this is a quality in which emotionally disturbed persons are notoriously deficient.

INTERMEDIATE VALUES

We may now go one step beyond the view that therapeutic education must foster segmental talents in order to increase the defective's ultimate educability and therapeutizability. We feel that, from the viewpoint of the practical therapeutic educator, these objectives are secondary to the further goal of endowing intermediate "instrumental" means with an autonomous value of their own, in a manner almost unrelated to Allport's concept of the "functional autonomy of motives" (2). In other words, an important objective of relational and patterned person-centered education is to help the student or patient to perceive intermediate, instrumental means as "intervening opportunities" in Stouffer's sense (210). He must therefore be taught to endow the successful performance of each intermediate—that is, from his point of view intermediate—task with a value of its own and to cathect these "intermediate" tasks with libido in their own rights. As regards the boy obsessed with chickens, there are many indications, culled from the observations of reliable persons over a period of years, that he has now reached a point where he actually takes pride in the neatness of his bills and in the accuracy of his books and—naturally—also enjoys the profit he derives from the sale of his eggs. With this, we are already in the realm of Veblen's "instinct of workmanship" (220): the capacity to enjoy, to value, and to cathect with libido the means used to attain an end. In other words, we are already in sight of our real and constant objective: the humanization of the "exceptional" child.

EDUCATIONAL INTEGRITY

As we survey in retrospect the various suggested techniques for bringing the achievement profile in line with the potentiality profile, we realize that each of them represents an attempt to "turn the tables" on the defective, and to induce him to transform his foibles into sources of strength. In fact, even our initial willingness to foster one of his segmental, and possibly fairly useless, talents in order to increase his educability in general means, in a sense, that we are turning the tables on him, since we teach him something he does wish to learn, but only for the purpose of making him learn also things in which he, personally, does not happen to be interested.

However, we have already stated that this technique is not to be thought of as a kind of well-intentioned "trick" played on the defective. In other words, therapeutic education is not a kind of intellectual jiu-jitsu, in which a skilled manipulator uses his opponent's own strength to trip him up. On the contrary, one must accept the defective's liabilities and transform them into assets.

This is usually possible, precisely because these defects themselves are a proof of the defective's humanness, since they would not be viewed as shortcomings in an animal. There is a great deal of similarity in this respect between the task of the skilled therapeutic educator and that of the competent psychoanalyst. Both operate on the basis of the assumption that everything the patient or student is or is not, does or fails to do, is potentially grist for their mill. Just as the analyst finds his patient's sullen silence as interpretable as his garrulousness, so the therapeutic educator can—as we saw—base a whole broad educational program upon an initially antieducational obsession with chickens. However, this can be done properly only if one remembers at all times that it is always up to the therapist or therapeutic educator to devise the means whereby defects can be turned into assets, and weaknesses can be made sources of strength. Indeed, were defectives and neurotics able to do this for themselves, they would have no need for our services in the first place.

....

CHAPTER 7

Success vs. Failure in Therapy and Education: The Theory of Adjusted Levels of Aspiration

LAY STANDARDS

Ordinarily, the opinion of the therapeutic or educational team determines whether a given course of treatment was a "success" or a "failure." Except under quite dramatic circumstances—as when a prematurely discharged patient commits some spectacular crime —outside opinion is relatively unimportant, because the expectation of outsiders is often quite unrealistic, and sometimes genuine progress is mistaken for failure. For example, the relatives of a professional man who sustained a severe brain trauma in the war may expect him to resume his previous occupation and to perform at his former level of proficiency. The therapist and the various rehabilitation specialists, who are aware of the brain-injured patient's irreversibly reduced potential, will deem their efforts on his behalf successful if he is enabled to engage in some less exacting occupation and to find contentment in it. Thus, what the therapist calls a success the relatives of the patient sometimes view as a failure. Differences of opinion between therapists and families regarding success or failure are problems which properly belong to the field of psychiatric social work, since they must be dealt with by interpreting to the patient's family the limitations of the patient. This task is sometimes a far from easy one, since, as

163

we indicate later in this chapter, families often make quite unrealistic demands upon their handicapped or mentally defective children.

PROFESSIONAL STANDARDS OF SUCCESS

However, the attempt to interpret the patient's or student's progress to the family cannot be meaningful unless one evaluates first the therapist's or educator's own standards of success or failure. Ideally, the therapist should never be fully satisfied with his results, since his dissatisfaction is an important driving force behind his work. On the other hand, he should not grossly overestimate the potentialities either of his patient or of his type of therapy, lest the patient be retained in the institution or in extramural treatment long after he has reached what represents an optimum for him, i.e., long after he has reached the level at which his greater or lesser capacity for spontaneous growth has been reestablished. We propose to study this problem mainly in terms of the therapist's subjective impression that the treatment was a "failure." Indeed, whereas the analysis of successes provides the best clues to the proper indications for using a given type of therapy, the study of so-called "failures" sheds the most light upon the therapist's level of aspirations, which is our prime concern here. For example, if a therapeutic educator feels that he has failed to help a student, we must seek to discover whether his self-appraisal is actually correct or whether his unrealistically high level of aspiration caused him to expect too much from himself, his student, and his particular technique. In such instances it is often possible to show that, in terms of a more realistic level of aspiration, what had been defined as a failure should actually be viewed as a marked success.

The following case will show in how unprejudiced a manner one must approach the objective reappraisal of "obvious" failures.

Case 27: A Pseudo Failure

Ginny Brown is perhaps the most pathetic little creature the writer has ever seen. She is the hopelessly and irreversibly damaged victim of maternal rubella—emaciated, nearly blind, almost deaf, violent, self-destructive—with an IQ so low that it cannot really be measured. The therapeutic education of this small being, who is almost unmanageable, may strike one at first as a signal failure, until one realizes the simple fact that it is a near-miracle that she has been kept alive at all, and has been prevented from inflicting further irreparable damage upon herself and upon others in her crises of aggressive and self-destructive fury.

The preceding considerations, as well as the case just cited, indicate that one has to differentiate explicitly between absolute and adjusted levels of aspiration.

ABSOLUTE LEVELS OF ASPIRATION

An absolute or perfectionistic level of aspiration is usually a spurious "ideal," reflecting the irrational demands of the superego, which one feels obligated to approximate at all times and under all circumstances, regardless of the inherent limitations of one's technique and also regardless of the quality and potentialities of the human material at one's disposal. From the purely objective point of view, such absolute aspirations are often unrealistic, since one can neither "make bricks without straw" (limitations of the technique) nor fashion "a silk purse out of a sow's ear" (limitations of the human material). However, this realistic insight too can be exaggerated to the point where it becomes both unrealistic and impractical. Indeed, relatively unrealistic aspirations can, in practice, provide motivation for making a maximum amount of effort while one is working at a given task. As an eminent professor of piano in the Budapest Conservatory once expressed it: "Regardless of one's actual limitations, one should always aim at a perfect performance, since otherwise one seldom achieves even mediocrity." Hence, we feel that—within halfway reasonable limits—absolute levels of aspiration are, practically and functionally, not necessarily either harmful or unrealistic. However, the pursuit of perfection must not degenerate into a compulsion. After having aimed at the ideal maximum of results, one must be ultimately capable of tolerating—without experiencing anxiety, neurotic feelings of guilt, or a sense of failure—the practical maximum, whose upper limits are determined by the inherent potentialities of the technique at one's disposal and by the irreversible handicaps of the patient or student whom one treats or works with. Of course, in a few cases the ideal and the practical maximum are nearly identical, and this fact alone makes it both technically and practically desirable to aim, at least in principle, at an absolute ideal of recovery.

In the preceding paragraph we spoke exclusively of the practical maximum of results which can be obtained by applying one specific technique to the treatment of a given student or patient. We must realize, however, that what represents a practical maximum of improvement attainable by means of one technique is not necessarily identical with what can be achieved by means of some other technique, and especially by means of a systematic utilization of all the techniques which constitute the therapeutic pattern of a given institution (Chapter 12). Indeed, the assumption that the practical maximum of progress which can be obtained by means of one's favorite technique automatically represents the absolute maximum of improvement of which a given patient or student is capable is sheer conceit. Quite often a defect which proved resistive to one type of therapy is susceptible of being corrected by the use of another therapeutic technique. We stated in Chapter 6 that it is usually worth while to teach a feeble-minded student something in which he has an obsessive interest, even if this skill is of no great practical use either to him or to society, because it will increase his self-confidence and make him generally more educable and therapeutizable. Likewise, a little timely "first-aid psychotherapy" given to a child who has learning difficulties often increases appreciably his performance in the classroom. In fact, one never quite knows what the practical maximum of improvement may be for a given student or patient until one has utilized every resource of the total therapeutic pattern of a given institution. This insight likewise militates in favor of a temperate and judicious attempt to attain an absolute ideal of recovery. We might almost say that one of the greatest of all therapeutic skills is the art of cross-referral between the various therapists working in a given institution, because only by this means can one bring to bear the full therapeutic resources of that institution upon the student or patient. In practice, this means that one should formulate the absolute ideal of recovery in terms of the combined therapeutic resources of the institution, instead of only in terms of the core technique thereof. This attitude will encourage each individual technician to do his level best for the student and, at the same time, will protect him from too personalized a sense of failure, if even the combined resources of the school or institution do not suffice to achieve an ideally perfect degree of recovery.

It is often useful to delegate the task of formulating and upholding an ideal of total recovery to the administration of the school and to let the various technicians pursue the practical goal of achieving the best possible results by a competent performance of their respective tasks and by means of judicious cross-referrals to other technicians. Such teamwork keeps motivating ideals alive, helps the student, and maintains staff morale at a high level.

ADJUSTED LEVELS OF ASPIRATION

It also seems desirable to let a scientific investigator—who in this context functions as a kind of umpire—evaluate the effectiveness of individual therapeutic techniques, and also of the therapeutic pattern as a whole, in terms of an adjusted level of aspiration, which he must formulate in a manner compatible both with the inherent limitations of the human material on hand and with the limitations of the core technique, the peripheral techniques, and the therapeutic pattern as a whole.[1]

The adjusted level of aspiration is the gauging tool of the scientific observer, by means of which he appraises degrees of success or failure in the approximation of an absolute level of aspiration. It should be stressed, however, that the formulation of the adjusted level of aspiration must, of necessity, always postdate the formulation of the absolute level of aspiration, in that, to speak colloquially, no one knows what can be done by a given means until it has been tried. In fact, we stated elsewhere (56) that even an intrusion of theoretical views into the therapeutic situation can lower one's absolute level of aspiration. For example, one may fail to analyze fully the subjective sources of the patient's self-aggressions if one views them a priori and mechanically as manifestations of the "death instinct" (Thanatos). Even if one happens to believe in this "instinct"—which the writer rejects out of hand, because it is not needed for an understanding of actual clinical data[2]—it would still seem necessary to find out, by means of a searching analysis of the patient's unconscious, why, in his particular case, this supposedly universal "instinct of primary self-destructiveness" is not as effectively held in check by the forces of Eros as it is in other persons.

Six factors have to be taken into consideration in the formulation of a level of aspiration which is realistic both in terms of the

[1] A comparable "adjusted level of aspiration" determines the winner of the mixed classes of the Nassau regatta, where, in a recent race, a small boat which actually came in fortieth won over the thirty-nine larger ships preceding it at the finish line, on the grounds that, in terms of its size and equipment, it did better than the larger ships did in terms of their size and equipment. In other words, the adjusted level of aspiration is a kind of handicapping system.

[2] Cf. in this context Laplace's famous reply to Napoleon: "Sire, I had no need of that hypothesis!" Cf. also Feldman's cogent proof that a paleopsychological explanation of the Oedipus complex is not simply false but chiefly unnecessary (81).

potentialities of the therapeutic pattern as a whole and in terms of the inherent limitations of the human beings who are in treatment.

1. RATE OF MOVEMENT

As regards students or patients capable of improving or of "moving," one must determine whether the progress or "movement" is or is not the optimum rate of movement to be expected in such cases. A commonplace example would be the predictable difference in the length of the analysis of a simple hysteric and of that of an obsessive-compulsive. In the present state of our knowledge, such "standard rates of improvement" can be formulated only on the basis of past experience. One must also realize that certain techniques, whereby "progress" in the external sense may be speeded up, often result in ultimately self-defeating pseudo progress. For example, Freud warned us against the use of techniques whose primary objective is the premature disappearance or radical alleviation of symptoms; this may actually enable the resistive patient to break off treatment, since his chief motivation for undergoing a radical therapy is the discomfort which his symptoms cause him. Similar problems also beset the therapeutic educator. For example, too systematic a mechanical "drilling" (or brute training) of a mental defective may produce "gratifying" results, as far as his parents are concerned, but tends to lead to a permanent "freezing" of whatever spontaneity and capacity for autonomous growth he may possess. "Bearing down" too hard upon a juvenile delinquent may lead to nothing more than a hypocritical compliance with rules, masking an intensification of aggressions and self-punitiveness, which will erupt once more, and with greater violence than before, as soon as he is withdrawn from the school. Even psychotics can be forced and/or cajoled to adapt so well to the simplified and protected environment of the hospital that, later on, special efforts have to be made to induce them to return to extramural life (36). In brief, in many instances ultimate real progress is possible only if there is an initial exacerbation of the symptoms and a seeming—but temporary—deterioration, regression, or relapse of the student or patient. We will only add that, as stated in Chapter 4, sometimes the children themselves realize that the exacerbation of their symptoms is a token of their gradual improvement. In other instances, however, they are frightened by the appearance of new symptoms.

Case 28: Beneficial Exacerbation of Symptoms

A brain-injured girl who, all her life, alternated between a complete suppression of her aggressivity and occasional temper tantrums complained that she acquired in therapy "the dirty nerve" of slamming doors, adding that the first time she did this, when she was angry at her therapist, she cried in the bus all the way home over her behavior. In such instances, it is important for the therapist to explain to the child or patient the real nature of this temporary worsening of his behavior and symptoms.

2. POTENTIALITIES OF THERAPY

A second adjustment has to be made with reference to the optimal level which students or patients may be expected to achieve with the help of the best methods now at the disposal of science. Here again, experience is our guide, even if we derive our criteria from some almost unexpected individual successes, rather than simply from statistical averages. In other words, despite the inherent limitations of one's students or patients, it is sometimes possible to obtain unexpectedly good results by applying available therapeutic or remedial techniques with a great deal of creative imagination and determination. This does not mean, however, that in the final accounting inherent handicaps do not place definite limitations on our efforts. While it is true that a lame man recently became the world's weight-lifting champion, it is quite certain that he could never have become a champion sprinter, no matter how hard he tried. Likewise, even though Demosthenes' extraordinary efforts to master his stuttering enabled him to become one of the great orators of all time, we suspect that his effectiveness as a speaker was due more to the depth and literary quality of his speeches and perhaps also to his impressive "stage presence" than to the perfection of his diction. This interpretation seems plausible in the light of the fact that Churchill's wisdom, wit, and eloquence, as well as his fabulous personal prestige, cause one not to notice his pronounced lisp, which in an orator of lesser caliber would seem distracting.

In seeking to make adjustments in one's level of aspiration, in terms of the optimal results which can be achieved by current methods of treatment, nine practical factors have to be taken into consideration:

1. *Absolute assets vs. absolute handicaps* (e.g., in terms of the preceding examples, creative genius and impressive personality vs. speech defect). We feel that many "surprising" therapeutic results would not seem startling at all had we taken the trouble to ascertain from the beginning not only the patient's handicaps but also all of his assets. In fact, we feel that in diagnostic work the correct appraisal of the patient's assets is, if possible, even more important than is the accurate appraisal of his defects.

2. *Age*—which is often inversely proportional to plasticity—at the time therapy becomes available. On the whole, the older the patient is, the less we can hope to achieve by means of therapeutic procedures.

3. *Total absolute duration* of the handicapped condition. A chronic condition of considerable duration is usually more difficult to treat than an acute condition, whose onset is fairly recent.

4. *The proportion* between the *duration of the illness* and the patient's *age* on beginning treatment. By and large, a patient who has been handicapped most of his life is less good a therapeutic

prospect than is one who has been handicapped only during a relatively small portion of his life. Thus, despite the flexibility of children, a sixteen-year-old who has been severely neurotic for eight years may sometimes be more difficult to cure than a thirty-year-old man whose neurosis began ten years earlier (a 1:2 ratio as against a 1:3 ratio). The percentage of the patient's elapsed life span which his illness covers is often inversely proportional to the results which may still be obtained by means of therapy.

5. *Type of onset of the pathological condition.* A neurotic or psychotic disorder which explodes suddenly is usually more treatable than one whose onset is slow and insidious. Thus, military psychiatrists often speak of "three-day battlefield schizophrenias," which erupt suddenly and with extreme violence and disappear just as suddenly. Such transitory outbursts appear to be highly characteristic also of primitives.

6. *Acuteness vs. chronicity.* Although a schizophrenic on the disturbed ward impresses the layman as far more "sick" than the "burnt-out" and tractable schizophrenic vegetating on a "back ward," there is more hope for the former than for the latter. Indeed, the disturbed state of the "acute" case itself indicates that the patient is still "fighting" his illness, and that his essential personality is not yet wholly engulfed and corroded by his psychosis. By contrast, the "burnt-out" schizophrenic has—so to speak—"given up" the contest and surrendered to his illness. Similar "surrenders to illness" can also be observed in other types of patients.

Case 29: Surrender to Illness

A brain-injured girl, who had severe epileptic seizures, required a year of intensive psychotherapy in order to grasp that she was more important than her seizures—that it was she who had the seizures, instead of the seizures "having her," that she had been mistaken in assuming that "the tail wagged the dog." Only after she understood this was it possible for her to gain some insight into the psychological and physiological tensions which tended to "trigger" her actual seizures.

7. *Absolute duration of the treatment.* This factor is usually of great importance, particularly since it is often only after prolonged treatment or therapeutic education that one is able to appraise correctly both the student's assets and his liabilities.

8. The *proportion* between the *length* of the treatment and the *duration* of the handicap. A disturbance of relatively recent origin can often be treated effectively in a relatively short time.

9. The *proportion* between the *length* of the treatment and the *age* of the patient on entering treatment. By and large, this factor is directly related to the age factor discussed previously under 2. Thus, the psychoanalysis of an eighteen-year-old obsessive, while far from short, is usually less long than that of a forty-year-old obsessive. This is a matter which sometimes has to be explained to a student who is getting impatient. For example, one may tell him that since it took him eighteen years to get into this mess he cannot expect to get out of it in eighteen weeks.

Actually, all of the above factors are closely interrelated and can be distinguished from one another only as what logicians call "analytic variables." Any attempt to adjust one's level of therapeutic aspiration only in terms of one of these factors is bound to lead to gross errors and, hence, to unpleasant surprises and disappointments.

3. INEVITABLE DETERIORATION

Special adjustments in one's level of aspiration have to be made in the case of students or patients whose illness is of such a nature that an automatic, gradual, and irreversible deterioration is inevitable. In such cases the maintenance of the *status quo,* even for a short period of time, or the temporary slowing down of the expected rate of deterioration represents optimal success. Comparable examples from general medicine readily come to mind.

4. SPECIFICATION OF OBJECTIVES: THE DEMAND PATTERN

The adjustment of the level of aspiration in terms of specifications regarding one's objectives is a matter of considerable import and great complexity. The basic fact to be taken into account is that no patient ever ceases to be a member of society and a source of social concern. Otherwise stated, the patient or student will continue to have demands made upon him. Hence, it is one of the principal tasks of the therapeutic educator to see to it that the actual demand-and-expectation pattern confronting the student is compatible with his distinctive abilities, needs, and handicaps (36). One salient characteristic of the therapeutic school environment is, therefore, tolerance. Another is the planned simplicity and unusually great self-consistency of the demand pattern, useful in alleviating the stressful disorientation which occurs when a student, handicapped either by a mental defect or by a neurosis, is confronted with extramural demands which are too much for him. Last, but not least, the demand pattern of the therapeutic school is highly individualized, as the following incident will show:

Case 30: Individualized Leniency

A student in psychoanalysis made the following revealing statement: "I don't know why it is that when I first began to date Jenny the school made us comply with all its regulations, curfew rules and the like, and then ended up by letting us do pretty much as we pleased." The reason for this change in the demand pattern was the fact that the dating behavior of these two students was known to be absolutely irreproachable, being predominantly tender rather than sensual. In brief, the school adjusted its general demand pattern to the actual individual needs and performances of the students in question, particularly since the tender love relationship between these two adolescents was therapeutically valuable to both of them and contributed materially to their emotional stability.

Of course, no school or hospital can operate without a demand pattern (rules), nor—as we know—should it do so, lest it promote, rather than impede, regressions and lapses into total dependency and autism. In addition, the demand pattern must also take into account the realistic needs of both the intramural and the extramural environment. Thus, while it may be theoretically ideal at certain times to allow a student to be destructive, the theoretical advantages of absolute permissiveness are often counterbalanced by the realistic fact that even the best-endowed or most efficiently operated institution cannot afford unlimited losses from breakage. In addition, what may be theoretically ideal for one student may harm other students, either by exposing them to injury or by giving them the idea that they too are entitled to "act out" in their own way, even though, in their case, "acting out" may be theoretically counterindicated. These are realities which the therapist cannot escape and should not even seek to escape. He must accept such basic facts with their true connotations and implications and must not seek to assuage his "therapeutic superego" by beclouding the issue with complicated theoretical verbiage or with self-justificatory arguments against a basic overall policy of tolerance and permissiveness *per se.*

Case 31: Deflating a Spurious Therapeutic Rationale

An example of homely good sense—which refuses to indulge in the creation of verbal smoke screens—will illustrate this point. A superb hospital administrator, after reading a "highfaluting" manuscript about "dynamic approaches" to the "reëducation" of lobotomized patients—seeking to prove, by means of complicated intellectual acrobatics, that the various directives given to postlobotomy patients were "dynamic" —wryly remarked, "I don't see what is so 'dynamic' about telling a patient not to urinate on the floor!" He recognized that, since rules have to exist, the simplest thing to do is to call them "rules," and not something else. In fact, calling a rule a "rule" implies that we recognize that it is simply a practical guide to the formulation of average demand patterns and is therefore susceptible—as Case 30 indicates—of being relaxed or modified in suitable instances. By contrast, if we insist on pretending that a mere point of etiquette is surrounded by a halo of profound psychiatric verities or by an aura of ethical sanctity, we are likely to enforce it even when it is definitely disadvantageous to insist on the "letter of the law."[3]

In other words, some demands have to be made even upon patients and upon students in therapeutic schools, simply because they, like we, live in a real world, in which the resources of hospitals and schools are not unlimited and in which therapists, juvenile courts, and relatives are not paragons of perfection, understanding, and tolerance. To seek to obscure this simple fact by elaborate theoretical smoke screens is brazen escapism, which can only lead to an illusion-laden and purely verbally "realistic" patterning of demands but cannot abolish realistic demands *in toto*. If any "dynamic consideration" is to be raised in this context, it is the very basic and very dynamic fact that reality exists and has to be accepted, though it is incumbent upon the therapeutic educator to mediate this reality to the student, to mitigate its avoidable harshnesses, and to help the student accept and endure those inflexibilities of reality which cannot be escaped.

In concrete terms, all therapeutic schools and therapists must take into account social demands, and particularly the demands of parents, as representatives of society at large. This is a very practical bit of realism, since, if the parents are radically displeased, the child will be withdrawn and will, therefore, not be able to benefit by the other advantages the school has to offer. The cor-

[3] The late Professor Linton once told the writer that he had heard that Gandhi's refusal to wear anything but his "diapers" (dhoti) and a very important Occidental dignitary's insistence that Gandhi should appear before him "suitably dressed" prevented a potentially important meeting between these two major personages. In this instance the matter of "proper dress," which is a point of etiquette and therefore nothing more than an "instrumental value," stood in the way of the realization of a major goal.

rect way of dealing with such realities is to interpret the student's problems to the parents and to help them repattern their more extreme demands. For example, in the case of very defective children the parents may lay undue stress on, and may be unduly delighted by, the "success" implicit in the child's learning to lace its shoes. At the same time, they may be relatively unaware of a far greater achievement which lies behind this limited manifest progress: the fact that the child, defective as it is, has developed a sufficient sense of security to venture into the previously unmanageable seeming world of external reality, even to the point where it dared to undertake the lacing of its shoes. Of course, mere "training," in the brute, simplistic sense, may perhaps also achieve such limited and concrete objectives. However, even if one makes due allowances for the fact that, for reasons of expository convenience, we have drawn the line between education and mere training somewhat too sharply, it is often true that in brute "training" or "drilling" each achievement remains isolated from every other achievement and therefore is not, and cannot be, the starting point for further "successes." Indeed, the learning of certain required manipulations through mere training simply protects the feeble-minded child from punishment or discomfort but does not increase either its self-confidence or its general educability. In dynamic education, on the other hand, even the smallest concrete success is an expression of internal developments and is therefore a starting point for further, and increasingly patterned and consolidated, progress. Thus, the question is not so much "What demands are to be made on the child?" as "What should the wording, psychological-subjective nature, emotional setting, and ultimate goal of the demands be?" In very naïve terms, the problem is simply whether our ultimately worth-while and relevant objective is primarily to train the feeble-minded child to lace its shoes or primarily to enable it to reach a point in a patterned development where the lacing of shoes becomes, in fact, possible.

Hence, the correlating of demand patterns with adjusted levels of aspiration must take place in terms of the educational (dynamic) rather than in terms of the "training" (mechanical) implications and meanings of practical results. As long as one pays attention exclusively to practical performance, one often experiences a sense of failure, which, however, is readily transmuted into a sense of achievement by refocusing one's attention upon the unfolding of the child's potentialities, as reflected in the acquisition of even quite minimal new skills. In brief, the level of aspiration must be adjusted in terms of the prevailing dynamic configuration of the patient's or child's psyche, rather than in terms of his crude, unadjusted performance level. A simple example will show this: Many experienced analysts know that the dreams of paranoid patients often reveal appreciable improvements long before the paranoid pattern actually disappears from their overt behavior. It is not at all surprising that this should be so, since the reality-testing function of dreams has been convincingly demonstrated by Thomas M. French (85, 86, 87). The writer himself systematically—and successfully—fostered an Indian patient's culturally conditioned tendency to test reality, as well as the possibility of recovery, in dream, in order ultimately to promote also behavioral progress in the real world (50).

5. REALISTIC LIMITATIONS

Closely related to the general problem of demands is the type of adjustment in one's level of aspiration which is necessitated by the cost of complying with the inescapable demands of reality. In a society with a particular pattern, structure, or thematic orientation that which, subjectively at least, may seem "therapeutically ideal" cannot always be aimed at or even permitted, because, in another segment of social adaptation, this would lead to gross disharmonies and crises. For example, it is theoretically conceivable that some measure of social maturation could be promoted in the feeble-minded by permitting them to approximate, as closely as possible, normal patterns of functioning. Thus, theoretically at least, one may want to let a moron drive a car since, under normal conditions, where no split-second timing and complex evaluations are required, he could perform quite adequately. However, while such an act of trust may be highly "therapeutic," the moron might get confused in a traffic jam and endanger the safety of others. The maturational value of normal sexual functioning is another relevant example. The defective girl's life pattern of feminine functioning is theoretically just as incomplete without motherhood as is the life pattern of a normal girl. Yet we must renounce this inherently desirable objective because, as Justice Holmes expressed it: "Three generations of imbeciles are enough."[4]

Another problem, intimately related to this type of demand patterning, is created by the defective's limited energy and learning capacity. This obliges one to select carefully the channels into which, and objectives toward which, these limited resources should be directed. Deplorable as it may be from the viewpoint of "ideal therapeutics," it is sometimes basically necessary to direct these limited energies into a channel of lesser natural "talent" and interest, simply because the reality situation demands it. Even a normal musical child prodigy is expected to divert some energy from its violin, and lace its shoes, wash its face, and study arithmetic. In the case of a child prodigy, this does not cause a perceptible lowering of the level of performance in the area of maximum endowment. In fact, the cultivation of all of one's talents tends to expand one's proficiency even in the area of one's maximum competence. In the case of the feeble-minded child, however, some ordinary tasks may actually have to be learned at the expense of achieving something more "spectacular" in some relatively unimpaired

[4] Needless to say, the castration of the feeble-minded, which was extensively practiced in the state institution at Winfield, Kansas (113), is absolutely unjustifiable and inexcusable. By contrast, the question of whether or not the mental defective should be sterilized is open to debate.

but socially less necessary area of functioning. Indeed, as Hans Christian Andersen taught us long ago, even Emperors cannot indefinitely walk around in the nude. However, it is equally obvious that extremely delicate judgment and much good will and good sense must be used to avoid an obsessive preoccupation with the teaching of the many trifling techniques which even the defective child needs. A legitimate preoccupation with socially determined demand patterns should never reach the point where it interferes with true growth in some relatively unimpaired segment of personal functioning. As stated in Chapter 6, this point is of some importance since, even in the case of the feeble-minded child, true growth, encouraged by dynamic education, in a relatively unimpaired area of functioning eventually facilitates growth also in other areas. The same cannot be said of results achieved through mere brute training. In brief, while certain basic demands must be met, even at the cost of deferred—but only deferred—progress in other areas, the real, if sometimes tacit, objective must always be patterned growth, particularly in the optimal and best-preserved areas of the personality. A proper balance in this regard often requires a temporary "calculated renunciation" until very conservatively estimated basic demands are met. Hence, the profile of performance and development which results from such a truly judicious "calculated renunciation" may not be viewed as a true "failure" in terms of an adjusted level of aspiration.

The last point to be made in this context concerns the role of the therapeutic school as a "buffer" between extramural expectations and demands and the child's actual limitations. It is a commonplace observation that feeble-minded children in rural areas, who are not confronted with tasks and demands beyond their limited abilities, are often relatively well adjusted, while the feeble-minded children of parents belonging to the professional classes frequently become emotionally disturbed because the demands implicit in the style of life of their families are wholly beyond their limited abilities. Surprising results can often be obtained quite rapidly by placing such children in a therapeutic school, whose flexible and individualized demand pattern does not tax them beyond their capacities. In such cases the school must sometimes give the parents a realistic picture of the child's limitations in order to help them reduce their unrealistically high expectations, both as regards the potentialities of the child and as regards the amount of improvement the school can hope to bring about. Sometimes this undertaking is far from easy, and requires understanding, wisdom, tact, and genuine sympathy, since what one must tell the parents may be the very unpleasant fact that therapeutic schools are no "miracle workers" and cannot "make a silk purse out of a sow's ear." In some instances parental dissatisfaction with the therapeutic school simply reflects the persistence of unrealistic expectations regarding the child.[5] On the other hand, especially in the case of students capable of living ultimately in the extramural world, the "buffer" role of the school must not be exaggerated to the point where the child is permitted to adjust to a code of conduct so lax and so much at variance with that obtaining on the outside that it is likely to become grossly maladjusted because of its unpreparedness to meet the demands of the world at large.

6. LIMITATIONS IN TERMS OF PROGNOSIS

The final adjustment to be made in one's level of therapeutic aspirations is of a type which, day after day, in small matters and in great ones, every human being is obliged to make. Yet it requires one to make major decisions in terms of certain criteria which humane therapists and devoted educators are particularly reluctant to mention explicitly, although they have to take them into consideration at all times. It is an inescapable fact that the financial resources of even the United States government, or of the best-endowed hospitals and schools, are limited, and that there

[5] Other parental interferences with therapy are discussed in Chapters 14, 15, and 16.

simply aren't enough therapists to meet the needs of our population (170), even if one defines "need" in the most liberal way. Indeed, economists sharply differentiate between "need" and "demand," pointing out that though a hungry beggar has need of food he does not represent demand in the economic sense, since he does not dispose of means wherewith to buy it. This type of need is, obviously, not one which a conscientious therapist or therapeutic organization can simply ignore. On the other hand, there are certain persons whose need for therapy is quite genuine but whose inherent limitations are so great, and prognosis is so poor, that even a large expenditure of time, effort, and money cannot insure adequate "returns" in the form of improvements. Thus, though we know that even very defective individuals can benefit by psychotherapy, we also have to concede that the resulting improvement is often disappointingly small. Of course, as Strecker (212) rightly stresses, in some cases the research value of such therapeutic work can be accepted as an "adequate return." Yet, it is obvious that, by and large, most of one's routine efforts will have to be directed into channels where they will do most good and will bring about the greatest amount of improvement, representing a maximum of return for society. There simply is no way of escaping the painful necessity of asking oneself whether "the game is worth the candle," as long as there are not enough psychiatrists to take care even of those who could most benefit by psychotherapy.

THE HUMAN IMPORT OF THERAPEUTIC EDUCATION

It is at this juncture that the great practical and humane value of therapeutic education—as distinct from its inherent value as a therapeutic technique—becomes most apparent. It is one of the practically most valuable characteristics of milieu therapy, and of dynamically oriented educational programs, that they minimize to an appreciable extent the frequency with which distressing and invidious, though necessary, decisions in terms of "returns" would otherwise have to be made. Indeed, not only do these therapeutic approaches affect everyone coming within their scope but, in addition, those most likely to benefit by such therapies often help "carry along" those from whom little progress could be expected otherwise. However, the greatest benefit to be derived from administering educational and milieu therapy even to the most severely and irreparably handicapped children is of a moral and social, rather than of a purely practical and therapeutic, kind. The integration of such a child into a group, some of whose other members have a better prognosis, serves to remind us at all times that even the most defective child is a human being. This awareness will then safeguard us against the risk of degrading our own status as human beings by forgetting or denying that of the handicapped child. Once we begin to deny the humanity of another person—be it because he is grossly defective or because he does not belong to our race, class, or religion—we make a dent in the armor of democracy through which every other invidious totalitarian abuse can then also insinuate itself. It is but a step from the "purging" of all mental defectives, or all persons of a certain race or persuasion, to the purging of everyone named Smith, or having red hair. Just as no country can survive half slave and half free, so humanity cannot survive half human and half "subhuman."[6]

Provided only that our entire treatment of the irremediably defective child bears witness to our recognition of his membership in the human estate, we cannot accuse ourselves of "failure" if we fail to measure up to—or even fail to formulate—an ideal level of therapeutic aspirations for such children. The final adjustment in our level of aspiration requires us to make due allowances for the necessity of devoting most of our intensive efforts, particularly as regards individual psychotherapy, to patients or students in whose case such efforts are likely to produce adequate returns.

[6] This point was stated magnificently by the French Resistance writer Vercors, in his latest allegorical novel (*221*).

SUMMARY

The preceding considerations represent an attempt to formulate the principles whereby the success and failure of our therapeutic efforts may be objectively appraised, in terms of realistic ego-ideal standards rather than in terms of the absolutistic demands of our therapeutic superego. Explicit recognition is given to the motivating value of ideal, absolute levels of aspiration, viewed here as incentives to maximum therapeutic effort. However, in the objective evaluation of the success or failure of therapeutic education, standards based upon an ideal or absolute level of aspiration can only confuse the issue and may even fail to reveal both the real progress which has been made and, perhaps, also obscurer forms of failure. The objective appraisal of success and failure should therefore be made in terms of a level of aspiration which has been adjusted in accordance with the criteria discussed in this chapter. These criteria are quite general ones and are applicable to any form of therapy or meliorative manipulation, in any setting whatsoever. Hence, they may serve as generalized guide lines also for the formulation of discharge policies, especially in cases which, in ordinary psychiatric parlance, do not represent genuine cures but simply "maximum hospitalization benefit" (MHB). It should be realized, however, that the expression "MHB" actually specifies not maximum possible benefits but simply maximum benefits from hospitalization or, in more general terms, from the use of any particular kind of core technique. Hence, when we state that a patient or student has derived "maximum benefits" from some form of treatment, we do not imply that additional, or different, benefits could not have been obtained by the use of some other technique. In fact, we feel that the admittedly complex concept of "adjusted levels of aspiration" is a suitable basis for the most efficient structuring of a given organization's total therapeutic pattern, which will be discussed in Part Four.

···

PART THREE

DISCIPLINE AND SOCIALIZATION

J'aimerois mieux qu'on ne me fist point
tant de révérences et tant d'honneur et
qu'on ne me fist point fouetter.
LOUIS XIII (*as a child*)

···

CHAPTER 8

Ego Ideal vs. Superego,
Discipline vs. Punishment

The purpose of this chapter is to differentiate formally, psychologically, and sociologically between discipline and punishment, with special reference to therapeutic education. Such a differentiation is highly necessary because the hypocritical desire to give euphonious names to fundamentally objectionable practices tends to disguise the real nature of punishment by calling it "discipline." For example, certain military units which, in more candid times, were called "penal battalions" are now referred to in some armies as "disciplinary units," and the term "correctional institutions" is applied even to prisons which have no obvious therapeutic goals. The state of New York does not even have a Department of Prisons—only a Department of Correction. A psychologically even more interesting example of soothing verbal fictions is that the blind profess to "correct" their Seeing Eye dogs, when they punitively strike them, presumably because they are too dependent on these dogs not to feel guilty for beating them. The neutral term "correction" appears to be psychologically very reassuring to the blind, who dread their own hostilities because the world gives them so few opportunities for manifesting them with impunity.

This last remark enables us to point out a basic defect in the education of all handicapped—and therefore potentially extremely resentful—persons, such as the blind: Since the handicapped are unusually dependent on the normal population and have few opportunities for manifesting normal aggressivity, they are very much afraid of their own latent hostilities. Hence, it would seem highly desirable to employ the handicapped chiefly in occupations suitable for the release of aggressions, just as, in psychiatric hospitals, occupational therapy involving hammering, etc., is now routinely prescribed for many aggressive patients.[1]

The confusion between discipline and punishment is further increased by the lax and ambiguous manner in which the term "superego" is used in contemporary psychoanalytic literature. This is due to the inexplicable and nearly complete disappearance from psychoanalytic terminology of the classical, and extremely necessary, concept of the ego ideal, which, of late, has been consistently used only by Róheim (187) and a few others. These two concepts will have to be discussed in some detail, precisely because of the prevailing tendency to refer the results of both discipline and punishment to superego mechanisms, whereas, as we propose to show, only the latter has any connection with it.

We hasten to add that the definitions of "superego" and "ego ideal" about to be offered are relatively novel ones, though they are not by any means at variance with classical psychoanalytic thought. There can be no logical objection to the reformulation of concepts. The superego, ego ideal, ego, and id are not tangible organs like eyes or feet. Each of these concepts is simply a kind of "shorthand" designation for a *group of psychic functions,* which it is scientifically *convenient* to view jointly, in the form of a

---

[1] This need was unconsciously well understood by the murder mystery writer Baynard Kendrick, creator of a blind detective whose occupation permitted him to find an outlet for his prying impulses, greatly interfered with by his blindness, and for his resentments and aggressions as well. Characteristically, this blind detective has two identical (!) looking dogs: the gentle Schnucke and the savage Dreist.

patterned multiple function. Hence, logically speaking, one cannot ask "What function *belongs* to the superego?" One can only ask: "Which functions is it *convenient* to lump together under the designation of 'superego'?" Anyone wishing to challenge the definitions of superego and ego ideal which we offer cannot simply state: "These definitions are incorrect!" He can only say that he has evolved a scientifically more useful grouping of psychic functions, or, if he feels that our way of defining the superego, etc. is too much at variance with classical psychoanalytic theory (which we do not believe to be the case), he can demand that we employ some other terms for the groups of psychic functions which we describe. Such considerations are commonplace among physicists, who quote with delight and approval Humpty Dumpty's remark that a word means what he wants it to mean.

THE SUPEREGO

One of the most essential characteristics of the superego is that its "vocabulary" is almost wholly restricted to such words as "No!" ("Thou shalt not!") or, at the most, to the sentence: "Don't do it, or you'll be sorry!" The superego shares with the id—and more particularly with the portion of the unconscious containing repressed material which proliferates and assumes monstrous and threatening shapes as a result of repression and while in a state of repression (*92, 94*)—the tendency to think in terms of "either-or" or "black and white," to have relatively tenuous connections with the world of objective reality, to be sadistically absolutistic, and to make impossible demands upon the ego. Furthermore, the superego provides no positive guidance to rational, reality-adequate, and effective behavior. The "guidance" it does provide is of a purely negative type, consisting chiefly of specifications of what the individual may not do, feel, and think. Its realm is that of taboos and avoidances. Its rules and obiter dicta are formulated in terms of enumerative arbitrary exclusions and not in terms of positive, principle-oriented prescriptions. In fact, superego commands are usually not even susceptible of the latter type of formulation. Indeed, the superego comes into being through a series of introjections, triggered by discrete "historical accidents," which, having no pattern of their own, cannot serve as a basis for the formation of a logically coherent or patterned intrapsychic structure or "psychic instance."

We do not deny that the superego does have a spurious kind of pattern. We feel, however, that the simplicity and outright crudeness of the superego—reflected by its restricted and purely negative vocabulary quite as much as by the arbitrariness of its prohibitions and by its known "corruptibility" through "bribes"—reveals that its pattern is a spurious one. We suspect that its "pattern" came into being through Procrustean manipulations, forcibly conjoining sets of inherently disparate and logically incompatible taboos. The violence of the superego further confirms this impression, since we know from daily experience that sound and easily defensible beliefs (58) do not mobilize emotions of such intensity. In brief, the "fanaticism" of the superego is *prima facie* evidence of the artificiality of its pseudo-patterned "solid front," and of the logical vulnerability and spuriousness of its mutually incompatible and grossly unrealistic demands.

The spurious integration of the superego's disparate constituent elements is fully understandable in terms of certain basic psychological principles. It represents an attempt at integration which is comparable to the concretistic and syncretistic integrative attempts of schizophrenics to justify their peculiar spontaneous sorting patterns, or to their offering concretistic and syncretistic—i.e., irrelevant, peripheral, and nonabstractive—explanations of the similarities between groups of objects presented to them in psychological tests.

It could be objected, of course, that the mere fact of the temporal disconnectedness of the "historical accidents" which lead to the formation of the superego does not, in itself, prove that these temporally noncontinuous events are necessarily also logically disparate. Since we actually did imply that these critical events have to be disparate, it is incumbent upon us to account causally for this disparateness. In simpler terms, there must be some reason for the disparateness of the historical events leading to the formation of the superego. We suggest that this objective and/or logical disparateness is far from accidental, and is due to a peculiar kind of psychologically coherent and consistent selectivity.[2]

What, then, psychologically speaking, is the pattern according to which certain historical accidents have been singled out for the "purpose" of serving as starting points for the formation of the superego? The chief characteristic of these accidents is that they were *not susceptible of being understood and mastered by means of ego mechanisms at the time of their occurrence.* Had the child been able, at that time, to master them by means of its ego resources, they would not and could not have provided an impetus for superego formation. As the italicized words indicate, the historical element is of prime importance in this context, since—as the results of any successful analysis indicate—these "historical accidents" are not inherently beyond the mastery of the mature ego. In fact, it would be quite legitimate to paraphrase Freud's well-known definition of the objective of psychoanalytic theory as follows: "Where superego was, there shall ego be!" In this sense, then, that which, in terms of a temporal frame of reference, we had to designate as "historical accidents" can, in terms of the psychoanalytic frame of reference, be designated as "traumata" or, in terms of the *Gestalt* frame of reference, as "conglomerates lacking system-adequate cloture" (51). In simplest terms, from the ego's point of view these "historical accidents," "traumata," or "con-

---

[2] This is not a paradox. A highly coherent psychological process, representing an intellectual effort of almost inconceivable complexity, is needed in selecting ten objects which are truly disparate and which have only one characteristic in common, e.g., that they are all solids rather than liquids.

glomerates lacking system-adequate cloture" are just unfinished business.

The superego is, thus, the residue of such "unfinished business" or "loose ends," which were *pro tem* spuriously "mastered" and provided with "non-system-adequate closure elements."[3] They were "mastered" by using them for purposes of superego formation, instead of being mastered realistically on the ego level. It seems legitimate to state, therefore, that these historically disparate accidents have certain, admittedly rather negative, psychological characteristics in common. They represent the sum total of potentially directive experiences which the infantile ego could not master.[4]

The typical "historical accident" which leads to superego formation involves the introjection of the parents, so that their commands are effective even in their absence. However, the fact that parents and their commands are seldom brutal, dereistic, or incoherent does not contradict the views just expressed, especially since in Chapter 4 we referred to the child's difficulties in grasping the underlying pattern or meaning of what is done to him or happens to him. This elicits a great deal of anxiety and resentment and may turn the child against all commands.

Case 32: The Incomprehensible Rule

A delinquent adolescent, who was in psychoanalysis, felt very angry because he had been campused for smoking in his room. He insisted that he had done no harm, since he was very careful not to cause a fire. When it was explained to him that the existence of such a rule automatically reduced fire insurance rates, he exclaimed bitterly: "Why don't they tell me that? Why do they simply make rules, without explaining and justifying them? That is not the right way to make us

[3] Needless to say, the superego is not only this but also a great many other things, which need not concern us here.

[4] Another example of a logically disparate but psychologically patterned material is, e.g., "the sum total of what I do not know." This, of course, is simply an analogy and implies no similarity between the psychological processes responsible for one's not mastering a given experience and those responsible for one's not knowing either quantum theory or Basque syntax.

conform. That is exactly how my father always acts. He lays down the law, and that is the end of it. He never tries to show me that it makes sense. You cannot learn sensible behavior that way! Now that you have explained this rule to me, I won't smoke again in my room." His anger and bitterness were part of his rebellion against irrational-seeming superego types of command, which had motivated also some of his delinquent behavior. On the other hand, his whole behavior in school showed that he was quite willing to comply with rational demands.

Unexplained commands are so confusing to the child that it cannot master them on the ego level and is therefore obliged to introject them in the form of an irrational superego. In addition, the tendency to "justify" commands by simply saying "Mother knows best" or "You do it because I tell you so" is resented as an indication that the parent considers the child too stupid to make the explanation of a command worth while. This, in turn, undermines the child's self-esteem and impairs or delays the formation of a strong and healthy ego and ego ideal. In other words, even sensible and kindly parents often contribute to the formation of an irrational superego, by issuing unexplained orders and by treating the child as an unreasonable being.

In brief, as regards superego formation, what matters is not whether parental commands are actually sensible but whether the child is helped to understand this fact. Stated in more general terms, the child does not introject the parents themselves, but his perception of them—not what they are in fact but what they seem to him. Unfortunately, what the child often "sees" in its parent is the parent's own superego, and it is this superego-tinged image of the parent which the child then introjects.

There is often little similarity between the real "object" or person which the child sees and the child's emotionally distorted perception of it. Indeed, it does not seem unreasonable to suggest that if a small child cannot be relied upon to form a correct mental image of even emotionally relatively neutral objects—as is shown by the fantastic accounts which children give of even common-place objects and events—it is even less likely to be able to evolve an objectively valid conception of its parents. To take a very elementary example, that which the parent may intend as a "gently restraining" gesture may impress the tiny and weak infant as violent and threatening constraint. In fact, it is easy to show that the child's small stature itself can lead to ways of perceiving reality which differ from the adult's perception of reality and which, if carried over into adult life, represent serious—and possibly even neurotic—distortions of reality.

Case 33: Persistence of Infantile Visual Perception in Dream

A patient had a series of dreams in which quite ordinary objects, such as tables, were always above eye level. He also insisted that, as a child, he saw in his father's sty a pig as tall as a Shetland pony, with legs as thick as a man's calf. He had been wondering all his life what breed this pig belonged to. It was possible to interpret the appearance of tables etc., above eye level as manifestations of this patient's neurotic tendency to define himself, both in dream and in his unconscious, as a small child, for whom a table is actually above eye level. As regards the "gigantic" pig, which also had certain other anatomical peculiarities, its "remembered" mass likewise represents a "carry-over" from the impression which a large pig made on a small child. The other peculiarities of the pig, as the patient "remembered" them, could not be properly understood until he made a drawing of it. Then, after taking a look at what he had drawn, he exclaimed: "That is how I had been taught to draw a pig, without raising my pencil from the paper."

If so great a distortion of perception can occur in the case of a mere pig, it is hardly sensible to expect the small child to have a more rational and realistic mental image of his parents and their actions.

In some instances infantile distortions of perception not only persist throughout life but may even receive cultural implementation. Among many peoples of southeast Asia a person must approach the King crawling and crouching, and must squat in his presence, lest his head tower above that of the King. The same survival of infantile modes of perceiving reality causes us to say that a tall and impressive-looking man has a "commanding presence."

The last factor to be considered here is the great sensitiveness of the child,[5] which causes it to react not so much to the overt behavior of its parents as to their—possibly suppressed—anger or rejection. In brief, the superego is not dereistic and violent because the child has truly brutish parents but because, owing to its own smallness, helplessness, fears, and counter-aggressions, it views them, in one respect at least, as "monsters," just as, for identical reasons, it idealizes them out of all proportion with reality in other respects. In strictly psychoanalytic terms, we view the superego as the psychic instance resulting from the introjection of the "bad" half-parent, as distinct from the loving and food-giving "good" half-parent.

This origin of the components of the superego readily explains why they are logically "disparate" and why they form only a spurious pattern, which is grossly concretistic and syncretistic— and also quite crudely and archaically oversimplified. It also enables us to understand why the dictates of the superego have to consist of "enumerations" of taboos rather than of statements embodying general principles of conduct. This, in turn, implies that the dictates of the superego can only be "memorized" by "rote learning,"—with symptoms serving, perhaps, at least in a limited sense, as arbitrary "mnemonic devices," such as one improvises on a purely subjective basis whenever one has to learn a set of nonsense syllables or a series of numbers.[6]

These considerations explain, in turn, why the superego con-

---

[5] The survival value of this extreme infantile sensitiveness was discussed elsewhere (46).

[6] It is likely that numeral systems—be they decimal, vigesimal, or duodecimal— are, in one sense, chiefly mnemonic devices, enabling one to organize the "nonsense syllables" type of "3–2–7" sequence into a semblance of order, so as to prevent their being "scrambled." Indeed, it is a commonplace that the *one three-digit* number "327" is less likely to become "scrambled" by the person seeking to recall it than is a group of *three one-digit* numbers "3–2–7." This is also one of the chief advantages

stricts, rather than guides, behavior.[7] Rules derived from positive principles permit considerable latitude and actually stimulate spontaneity and inventiveness. By contrast, enumerative prohibitions, not derivable or deducible from coherent underlying principles, can only constrict behavior. Hence, though literary works—representing sublimations—have to conform to aesthetic conventions, they tend to be far more colorful and varied than the often relatively monotonous delusions of psychotics, which usually represent superego derivations. In more general terms, we may contrast the simplicity of the neurotic's or psychotic's inner world with the complexity of the inner world of the normal (47).

In practical, everyday terms, the superego can never motivate ordinary, spontaneously decent behavior. The man who is a slave to his superego can only be compared to the jurist's proverbial "blackguard," who does everything the law does not expressly forbid. This also means that superego demands can never be socially or subjectively beneficial, since they are radically incompatible with true sublimations.[8]

In brief, it is not at all surprising that the superego should be primitive, archaic, and irrational, since it arises in early childhood, through primary introjection and incorporation, as a result of the child's desperate need to handle conflict-laden experiences which its infantile ego is unable to master. The prototype of such tasks is the child's need to curb its hostile impulses, which, precisely because they are being repressed just then, appear to possess a nightmarish violence and intensity and imply and evoke the threat of an equally dreadful punishment or retaliation.

---

of the Arabic positional system (e.g., 19) over the partly nonpositional Roman system (e.g., XIX).

[7] As used here, "to guide" means "to help someone make a real choice." By contrast, the superego pertains only to a "Hobson's choice."

[8] This explains why a certain Catholic priest, who is also a psychoanalytically sophisticated professor of psychology, distinguishes between a functional and normal conscience and a morbidly archaic pathological conscience, or, in other words, between ego ideal and superego.

THE EGO IDEAL

The ego ideal develops much later—probably toward the end of the oedipal period, i.e., at a time when persons are no longer experienced as "black and white" partial objects but as three-dimensional and nuanced objects of some complexity.[9] In very practical terms, it develops at an age when the average child begins to attend school. This gives the teacher an exceptional opportunity to foster the development of the ego ideal, instead of encouraging a further proliferation of superego taboos. Unfortunately it often happens that while the teacher is trying to accomplish this end the child's own parents continue to encourage a further growth of the superego, which often leads to antagonism between the progressive teacher and the strict parent.

Unlike the superego, the ego ideal is not rooted in, and is not made possible by, primary introjection but by an often highly sophisticated functional identification. Its perceptual horizon is large and fully nuanced, and its "vocabulary" is extensive and reality-adequate. Its central theme is the positive injunction: "In such and such a (nuanced) situation, the following (positively worded) line of conduct is proper for a given type of person." Its "definition of the situation" is, thus, based both upon an objective appraisal of external reality and of individual capacities, on the one hand, and upon a code of mature ethics, resulting from sublimation, on the other hand.

This view is strongly confirmed by the commonplace observation that the "code" which the superego-ridden neurotic feels guilty of having violated is invariably an irrational, dereistic, and

---

[9] It is hardly necessary to point out that the ability to perceive complex stimuli in their intricate complexity is, in itself, contingent upon a relatively well-advanced state of ego organization and development. This is indirectly confirmed by the brain-injured patient's need to simplify and to "routinize" his environment, so as to avoid complexities which automatically lead to "surprises." This defensive maneuver was called by Goldstein "the catastrophic reaction" (*104*), and, as we pointed out elsewhere, may be observed even in normals, in situations of extreme stress and unpredictability (*41*).

archaic one, compatible neither with current external reality nor with his current (adult) capacities, needs, and rights. For example, the promiscuous neurotic does not feel guilty of having violated the ego-ideal-inspired rule: "Emotionally mature persons should engage in cohabitation with loved objects only." He feels guilty of having violated the superego-inspired taboo: "Sex is sinful and should be avoided always, at all time, under all conditions, in any shape or form whatsoever, by all persons regardless of age."[10]

The preceding considerations imply that feelings of guilt are basically neurotic. At this point it may be objected that one may feel guilty also over a violation of a mature and realistic code of conduct. In answering this objection, we will leave aside the point that normally mature persons violate such codes much less often than do neurotics[11] and take into consideration only the fact that, people being human, even the most mature occasionally deviate from the standards of the ego ideal. This being said, we hold that there is a fundamental difference between the normal person's regrets over a lapse from a rational code of conduct and the neurotic's feelings of guilt over a deviation from an archaic and irrational code. In fact, it is only an inadequacy of our vocabulary which causes us to say that both experience "feelings of guilt." The point we seek to make is a rather simple one. If a normal individual "slips up" for some reason and does something which he cannot but consider wrong, he will feel regret and will criticize himself for what he has done. The neurotic will go further. He will not only condemn himself for his concrete act, i.e., for what it really

[10] The genuineness of this taboo is revealed by the "panic" of children who discover that their parents engage in sexual acts, and protect themselves against this "shocking discovery" by repressing and denying it (49, 135).

[11] For example, the notion that psychoanalysis encourages promiscuousness is held only by some bohemian pseudo supporters and by some neurotically rigid opponents of psychoanalysis, who know nothing about psychoanalysis and are simply unable to control their own lurid imagination. As we have indicated elsewhere (54), psychoanalytic standards of normal sexual conduct are so unequivocal that many types of sexual conduct which are fully sanctioned even by the most conservative mores have to be viewed as infantile and/or neurotic.

represents, but, in addition, will feel guilty—and perhaps even primarily—for what his concrete act symbolizes for him in terms of his unconscious conflicts. Thus, if a normal person drives at night and, though blinded by the headlights of a car coming from the opposite direction, fails to slow down and therefore runs over a dog, he will feel very unhappy indeed about his carelessness. He will stop and try to see if he can help the dog and, if the animal is hopelessly crippled, will put it out of its misery. The neurotic will react differently. For example, his careless action may mobilize his guilt feelings over all his early infantile hostilities toward his father. Therefore, he may not even stop his car and may flee, as though from the scene of a murder, without, however, ceasing to torment himself over whether he had better go back and find out what happened. In fact, he may even begin to imagine that perhaps he ran over not only a dog but also a person who accompanied the dog and whom he did not even notice "at first"—for the good reason that there was no such person present. If he does stop, he may stand by irresolute, not knowing what to do. The eyes of the hurt dog will evoke for him the stricken eyes of his father, during the latter's last illness, twenty years ago. If the animal is hopelessly hurt, he will not be able to put it out of its misery, because the whole situation mobilizes in him once more all the anxieties which his infantile hostilities toward the father had once aroused, etc. In brief, the normal person will react chiefly and almost exclusively to the real situation, while the neurotic will react to it primarily in terms of what this accident unconsciously means to him: a symbolic fulfillment of his guilt-laden infantile desire to kill his father. Hence, the normal man will feel "guilty" over what he actually did, while the neurotic will feel guilty over what his deed means to him or symbolizes for him.

We are not at all certain that the self-criticism of the normal is dynamically comparable to the self-condemnation of the neurotic, or that the term "feelings of guilt" is legitimately applicable to both ways of experiencing a lapse from one's fundamental code of conduct. Probably a different name should be applied to the self-criticism and regrets of the normal person who violates his rational code of conduct.

We suggest that the feelings of a normal person who failed to live up to the code laid down for him by his ego ideal should be designated as shame. This feeling motivates him to avoid similar trespasses in the future, through better self-discipline, and induces him to perform positive and constructive acts to mitigate both the subjectively and the objectively (socially) deleterious effects of his lapse. However, in making "restitution" he will not operate in terms of the *lex talionis,* inflicting punishment upon himself in the form of "an eye for an eye and a tooth for a tooth." Above all, he will make restitution for what he actually did, not for the "sin" which his harmful act symbolizes for him. To take our preceding example, he may get another dog for the child whose pet he accidentally killed and may befriend the child also in other ways, but he will not make atonement for "having symbolically killed his own father." By contrast, the neurotic who deviates from the dictates of his superego will feel neurotic guilt, will seek to prevent a recurrence by means of self-constricting maneuvers, and will develop socially and subjectively deleterious symptoms for the purpose of symbolically "undoing" the "meaning"—but not necessarily the effects—of his deed. In addition, whereas the rectificatory actions of the normal person are meant to benefit, and do in fact benefit, both himself and the person or group harmed by his objectionable action, the neurotic is exclusively concerned with his own "fall from grace" and need for "salvation." The contrast is, thus, between objective and constructive "enlightened self-rehabilitation" and a purely selfish and socially unproductive "ritualistic atonement" maneuver. Otherwise expressed, the normal person who deviates from the standards of his ego ideal seeks to "square himself" with society and is thereby enabled to "square himself" also with himself. The neurotic who disobeys his superego is only concerned with the mitigation of his own guilt feelings. Hence, his self-pacifying maneuvers, inspired by unsublimated sadomasochism, usually lead only to new symptoms, which make things even worse than they were before, for all concerned. In brief, the normal person's shame is socially beneficial and productive; the neurotic's feelings of guilt are socially useless or even outright harmful.

The preceding considerations are readily applicable to the problem of differentiating discipline from punishment. The first of these two techniques leads ultimately to self discipline, through potentiality-liberating ego ideal mechanisms (true "inner controls"), while the second leads to constriction, through the constraining agency of the superego (derivative external controls).[12]

DIFFERENTIATING BETWEEN DISCIPLINE AND PUNISHMENT

For the purposes of this discussion it is sufficient to list certain very simple rules of thumb whereby genuine discipline may be differentiated from genuine punishment.

THE INTERPERSONAL RELATIONSHIP

In discipline potential equality is not specifically excluded from the interaction between disciplinarian[13] and the one who is disciplined. It is possible, in our sense, to discipline a social equal or even a nominal superior—for example, by offering sensible counterarguments, discussing ignored realistic aspects of the situation,

---

[12] This view is not incompatible with the statement we made elsewhere (30) that, operationally speaking, "proper" conduct is meaningless in the absence of any "policeman" whatsoever. He must be present either in person or else potentially. In that paper we were speaking from the sociological and operational point of view, while here we are speaking from a psychological and functional point of view. Descriptively speaking, "good behavior" can be understood sociologically as the product of the possibility that a policeman may appear on the scene any time, and psychologically by predicating the existence of an "inner policeman" whom, if we wish, we may view as the internalization of an external policeman: parent, teacher, or Officer Donovan. This view is implicit in our analysis of the complementarity relationship between the sociological and the psychological understanding of human behavior (37).

[13] Needless to say, this term is not used here in the conventional sense of "martinet."

imparting new information, etc. No such potential equality, implying reciprocity, is even remotely conceivable in a punishment situation. Mutual discipline is possible. Mutual punishment is, by definition, impossible. Hence, the trauma of punishment can never truly be mastered. At the most, it is simply handed down to succeeding generations—witness a modern Mohave Indian's remark that spanking was used only or chiefly by those Indian parents who had themselves been spanked in American schools (42). In some other instances, the punished child eventually "gets even" by means of some gross and almost ritualistic revenge, whose savagery is increased by the fact that it had to be deferred until the physical decline of the parents put them at the mercy of their now adult child. This mechanism is exemplified by a classical Russian anecdote: "An old peasant exploited and abused his son long after the latter had reached maturity. In the end the son, pushed to the limits of his endurance, lured his father into the orchard and beat him savagely, while dragging him along the path leading toward the fields. When they reached a certain tree, the old man, who, until then, had remained silent, suddenly exclaimed: 'Stop! When I finally dragged my own father down this path, I too stopped beating him at this particular tree. It is enough!' " The sadomasochistic ritualism of this revenge partly explains why punishment can never lead to ego-ideal growth. It cannot do so precisely because the relationship between the punisher and the punished one is, by definition, an asymmetrical and nonreciprocal one and thus precludes the possibility of mastering the trauma on the ego level, by means of functional identification, as distinct from primary incorporation.

THE REALITY FACTOR

Both discipline and punishment presuppose that the child disregarded some aspect of reality. In discipline the reality factor which the child ignored is usually a broad and objective one. It is not limited to one person and is specifically not defined in terms of the (objectively real) idiosyncratic personality make-up of the punisher. It may involve disregard for some segment of physical reality—such as the fact that fire is hot and inflicts painful burns— or else for some segment of rational social reality (*31*), such as the demand that personal and property rights be respected. In mediating this ignored segment of reality to the subject, the disciplinarian functions as an agent of reality and integrates his interpretation of the ignored segment of reality with the concept of reality as such, and also with the proper conceptual framework for a sensible interpretation of reality. By contrast, and regardless of what lip service he may pay to "reality," the punisher often only recognizes, and mediates to the child primarily, one small and far too specific segment of reality, which almost deserves to be ignored: the punisher's own personal conveniences and biases. His demand that the subject should "accept reality" is, thus, often but a polite euphemism for the demand that the subject should adjust to the punisher—to his needs, conveniences, tastes, and biases . . . and even, or perhaps above all, to his neurosis. In this sense, then, the disciplinarian represents "functional authority," whereas the punisher represents only "charismatic power" (*60*). It is worth while to prove, by means of an example, the extent to which discipline, which mediates reality, is more powerful and more influential than is punishment—even punishment pretending to be realistically motivated.

Case 34: Confrontation with Reality as Discipline

A patient, who masturbated compulsively, was caught at it repeatedly in both childhood and adulthood and suffered serious inconveniences as a result of this compulsion. Nonetheless, he strenuously maintained, both in social conversation and in his analysis, that his masturbation was of no concern to anyone, that the punishment he had received was arbitrary, puritanical, and undeserved, etc. When interpretations failed to produce results, the analyst finally asked the patient to outline for him the potential social and biological consequences of a universal adoption of masturbation as the sole outlet for sexual impulses. This simple question profoundly startled the patient, who, after vainly floundering about and trying to find an answer, admitted that this "startling" idea had never occurred to him and that the argument against masturbation implicit in his analyst's question was irrefutable. This simple question marked a crucial turning point in the analysis. From then on the patient began to offer free associations, instead of only defensive rationalizations, in connection with the problem of his masturbation and soon ceased to masturbate altogether.

Unfortunately, sometimes the therapist's or educator's own neurosis interferes with the proper management of such socially prohibited or disadvantageous modes of conduct.

Case 35: Punitive Confrontation with the Punisher's Anxieties

A feeble-minded man, who had spent most of his life in an institution, was carrying on a very constricted and impersonal conversation with a friendly psychiatrist when he suddenly blurted out the question: "Will I go insane if I masturbate?" This question, coming wholly out of context, startled the psychiatrist, who inquired why the man was asking it. The feeble-minded man replied rather timidly that one of the maids—a somewhat neurotically puritanical person—had caught him at it and had warned him that it would make him go insane. He was greatly relieved when the psychiatrist reassured him that this was not true. It is hardly necessary to stress that such a threat, addressed to an insecure and feeble-minded person, was, in itself, likely to produce the very results against which the over-rigid maid had warned him. Indeed, she did not threaten him because she truly wished to discipline him but simply because his behavior disturbed her personally.

In other instances even more extreme measures are resorted to. The writer has it on the authority of a reputable psychiatrist that, in a certain state institution for the feeble-minded, children were castrated as soon as they began to masturbate openly.

Since infantile masturbation, which often arouses neurotic anxieties and conflicts in adults, is usually handled by threats and punishments, it is worth while to cite a case which shows how effectively such matters can be handled through intelligent and creative discipline.

Case 36: The Creative Disciplining of an Exhibitionistic Child

Joe, who had been delivered by Caesarean section, is approaching puberty. He lived with his parents until he was enrolled in the school, where he was diagnosed as a case of early schizophrenia. He seems to have a tolerably good relationship with his parents, since he returned from a vacation in good condition. However, the first day after his return he pretended to hide from the teacher in a teasing way—being all smiles. At the same time, he tried to identify the teacher with his mother, whom he missed, by calling her—except when he felt bashful —"Mummy."

One day, when he was in class with two other children, a girl student was drawing on the blackboard. At that point Joe attempted to exhibit his sex organ. The third student present told Joe to stop it. The teacher heard this and turned around to see what had happened, whereupon the following conversation ensued:

JOE: It is dirty.

TEACHER: No, it is not dirty—but zip up your fly for the present.

JOE: I will do it right there. (*He pretends that he is going to urinate then and there*)

TEACHER: No! If you have to urinate, go to the bathroom.

JOE (*zipping up his fly*):   It is dirty and rude.

TEACHER: It is not a matter of its being dirty or rude. There are certain things which we do not do when we are all living and working in groups. We learn to control the things we want to do. That is part of our growing up. Just because we want to do these things does not make us dirty or rude.

JOE: I like to do it. I like to be dirty.

TEACHER: It is not dirty! Boys get interested in their penis, and, because they cannot show it just any place, they think that it is dirty—but that is not so.

JOE (*picking up a can*): I pee in it.

TEACHER: There is a bathroom right across the hall. If there were no bathroom, and you really had to urinate, you could use the can.

JOE (*acting as though there were urine in the can*): I like to drink it. If I drink it, it will make my tummy sick. [Urine = poison.]

TEACHER: It may make your stomach a little sick. [Urine ≠ poison.]

JOE: I drank it. (*He seems very pleased*)

(*A few minutes later*)

JOE: Suppose I bit my mother on the arm, right there, on purpose?

TEACHER: What will she do?

JOE: Nothing.

TEACHER: She would say something about it.

JOE (*rocking himself*): Am I rocking at home? (*He stops rocking and goes on with his ordinary activities*)

COMMENT: In this instance it was necessary to inhibit an attention-getting device, whose provocative seductiveness was disturbing the other children. Yet a sharp reprimand would have been harmful both to Joe and to the other children, since it would have increased their anxiety over sexuality and the excretory functions. This view is supported by the fact that Joe's whole behavior indicated that he was literally begging to be contradicted when he claimed that his penis was dirty and rude. Thus, while inhibiting the boy's neurotic exhibitionism because of the context in which it occurred, but at the same time denying that sexuality and excretion were inherently objectionable, the teacher both increased the boy's ego strength (which includes an acceptance of one's body and its physiological urges) and helped him to expand his understanding of reality. Indeed, the teacher did not condemn out of hand all interest in the sex organ and in the voiding of urine. She simply asked that the gratification of this interest be postponed, and explained that the capacity to postpone gratification was a means of achieving growth and personal maturity. This way of handling the situation had several advantages. It limited the boy's exhibitionism to a mere "make believe" (symbolic) testing of reality ("What would happen if . . . ?") and therefore protected the other children from being upset by an actual public display of his "urethral prowess." In addition, by not condemning Joe's interest in his organ and its functions, the teacher also reduced the other children's infantile anxieties over their own sexual impulses. In brief, the way this incident was handled increased, rather than constricted, the range of the children's behavior, because, without inhibiting normal sexual activities, the children were taught a new type of activity: the goal-directed and context-determined control of interests. However, Joe had sufficiently intense anxieties over this problem to test the teacher once more. Some days later the following scene took place in the same class.

(*Joe zips his fly open*)

STUDENT: Don't do this. [This is the same student who once before objected to Joe's exhibitionism]

(*Joe grins from ear to ear*)

TEACHER: Joe, you know that you are not to do this.

JOE: It is a rule.

TEACHER: No, it is not just a rule. You remember what we said about customs.

JOE: Yes.

TEACHER: You know how people make up customs as they learn that it is easier and happier for all of us to live together.

JOE: Is it dirty?

TEACHER: No, it is not. You ask me that all the time. You do not quite believe me when I say that it is not dirty, but it really is not. Boys do get interested in their penis and sometimes want to show it.

JOE: Yes, show it to Miss X [the teacher].

TEACHER: I know that Joe has a penis.

COMMENT: While Joe had to reassure himself once more that the teacher really believed that the organ was not dirty, this time he did not come right out and affirm that it was dirty. Instead, he only asked whether it was dirty, and accepted the teacher's negative answer more readily—witness the fact that this last scene was much shorter than the preceding one. It is also noteworthy that Joe seems to have tried to find out whether rules were "just rules" of the "you do it because I tell you so" type, or whether there really was an underlying reason for them. Both the substitution of a question for a direct affirmation and the attempt to verify the logical pattern behind the rule indicate progress, i.e., an expansion of the boy's range of spontaneity and understanding of reality.

The technique of dealing with heterosexual interests of an objectionable nature is shown by the following episode, also involving Joe.

For some time past Joe used to point at the teacher's body, uttering a composite ("portemanteaux") word, which combined an extremely coarse four-letter word for the female genitals with a similar word for coitus. After a while he stopped pointing and uttering this one word and began to say instead, almost as though it were a question: "Stop this **** business." The teacher, who was mature enough not to be threatened by this behavior, always agreed to "stop it," at which point Joe usually giggled. However, one evening he again pointed at the teacher and uttered the same word.

TEACHER (*firmly grasping Joe's hand*): No! [Joe habitually called a restraining hand a "no-pat," thus indicating that even restraint, if exercised in an understanding and warm manner, can be experienced as a kind of "pat."] You know already that you should not do this. You understand that no one is to do that.

JOE: I know. (*A few minutes later*) Can I [perform a deviant, impossible, and hostile act, which revealed his sense of inadequacy as a male]?

TEACHER: No. It is never done. It could not be done.

JOE: It will hurt.

TEACHER: Yes, if anyone tried it, it would hurt. But no one tries to do this.

The rest of the evening Joe was very friendly and well behaved.

COMMENT: The key words in this conversation are "no one." Had the rule been personalized and stated only in the form "you must not do it," the boy would have viewed it as a personalized taboo, representing a kind of discrimination against him, on account of his youth and personal undersirability or inadequacy. The fact that he was told that no one should or could do it did not cause him to feel rejected personally.[14] The rule itself was further clarified by emphasizing two important aspects of reality: that it was impossible to perform the action in question and that it would hurt another person if it were attempted. In brief, while random vulgarity as well as hostile heterosexual interests were discouraged, sexuality *per se* was not rejected out of hand, and the rule was explained and justified. As the following episode shows, the teacher was successful in "putting across" the fact that rules have a rational basis.

Four days after the preceding incident, Joe repeatedly said: "You always explain why something can either be done or should not be done."

The satisfaction Joe derived from this way of disciplining him creatively is revealed by the fact that, for some time afterward, he made many remarks showing his confidence in the teacher: "I want you to shower the boys." (Meaning: "You may be trusted to do so without threatening or ridiculing our masculinity.") "Miss X, don't go home. Sleep in the unit." "Miss X, be a housemother for Mrs. Y's boys," etc. (Mrs. Y was a less warm and understanding person than Miss X. She was also much more obsessively puritanical.)

As the preceding example shows, discipline—as a means for mediating objective reality—leads to self-discipline, through insight and a mastery of reality. Punishment, because it mediates only the "charismatic power" of the punisher—which, though only very segmentally and peripherally, is, of course, also a part of reality—can lead only to constriction, since it does not increase insight and therefore cannot pave the way to a mastery of reality on the ego level.

Needless to say, the preceding sentences do not imply that discipline is always painless. All of us are subject to the "discipline of

[14] Young boys are often keenly sensitive to the fact that women prefer adult men as sexual partners.

reality" and learn how painful it may be to disregard the fact that fire burns, water drowns, ice freezes, bulls gore, etc. However, these painful experiences are not the result of the "sadism" of fire, water, ice, or Brahma bulls. They are consequences implicit in the nature of reality. By contrast, punishment is, in a sense, outside "natural law," in that it is purposive[15] or ideological and always has a sadistic component, which men often seek to disguise by various means.[16]

An interesting example of the very human attempt to lend to penalties the "protective coloring" of "natural law" is the manner in which certain age-class taboos are thought to "function" among the Arunta of central Australia. According to Strehlow (213), the old men find it convenient to impose certain taboos on the young so as to protect their own prerogatives. If a boy happens to violate one of these taboos, he is not necessarily punished for it. Instead, it is held that, because of his trespass, he will simply never mature physically. For example, he will not grow a beard—which makes him permanently ineligible for various adult privileges. Likewise, if an Arunta girl violates the taboos imposed on girls her age, her breasts will remain immature, and she will therefore be forever excluded from the more privileged ranks of adult women. In this instance the partisan interests of a gerontocratic society, which are a very important portion of the social realities of Arunta bands, are assigned the self-vindicating qualities of natural laws in order to disguise their punitive character. Compared to this bit of Arunta "logic," even the hellfire and brimstone punitiveness of the revivalist is a model of realism, since the latter at least does not seek to disguise punishment as biology or physics.[17]

[15] The Brahma bull is not *punitive* but *vengeful*—an important difference.
[16] This view implies a rejection of teleology and "purpose" as basic concepts in the interpretation of nature.
[17] Bettelheim's argument, that subincision and circumcision rites in Australia are nonpunitive and noncastrative (17), is disproved by Elkin's finding that where, under the impact of white culture, these mutilations have been dropped from the initiation rites, the old men are resentful and say that they are forced to surrender their secrets far too cheaply and painlessly to the young (78). Nothing could be more specific.

Of course, in some instances even genuine discipline can be partly unpleasant. However, its unpleasantness does not necessarily mean that it is intended as punishment. It may represent nothing more than an attempt to assist the child's ego to master certain destructive impulses which the child's ego ideal—not superego!—already condemns. Thus, it is discipline and not punishment to ignore a self-dramatizing hysteric, whom this indifference "hurts to the core," because it helps her to regain self-control. It is likewise discipline to restrain a child who, in "building up" to a tantrum—the very prospect of which throws him into a panic—is behaving destructively. In both cases the disciplinarian gives needed support to an important portion of the subject's psyche and, in addition, mediates to the subject the functional reality of social controls. By contrast, a beating—even of the hypocritical "this hurts me more than it hurts you" type—is never discipline. It is only "acting out," and mediates to the child only the shabby reality that it has to take into account the personal sadism, neuroticism, and acting-out proclivity of an irresistibly powerful parent. The inculcation of this *type* of "realism" is, as indicated elsewhere (60), simply a school for future henchmen of dictators—and nothing more.

PUNISHMENT FOR A CONCRETE TRESPASS

Punishment in this instance does not solve the underlying conflict and may eventually become so completely fused with the latter that there will arise a neurotic craving for punishment, yielding all kinds of neurotic gratifications. Thus, J. J. Rousseau, a pioneer in educational theory, describes in his revealing *Confessions* the sexual pleasure he derived from being whipped by his adored foster mother. Such a sexualized reaction to punishment is far from rare and often also creates unnecessary additional problems for the progressive and truly therapeutic teacher, who is obliged to counteract the conflicts, fears, and neurotic desires aroused by other, less understanding, teachers.

Case 37: Increasing Conflicts Through Punishment

Bill is approaching puberty. He is an obsessive-compulsive neurotic who, like all such neurotics, is greatly preoccupied with his bowel movements.

BILL: What would you do if I had a BM in my pants?

TEACHER: Nothing.

BILL: If you saw some BM on the floor, would you suspect me?

TEACHER: It is not a matter of suspecting you. However, now that you told me that you had problems of this kind, I might think of you.

BILL: Yes, that is one of my problems. That is why I came to this school. (*Getting up*) What is "your arse"?

TEACHER: It means "buttocks."

BILL: Miss Z said she would spank my arse if I did it again. Do you agree with her?

TEACHER: Bill, everyone has different ideas on how to help children. I have already told you that I do not believe in spanking, or in other forms of punishment of that type for your problems. I try to understand and help them.

BILL: Miss F asked me if I wanted to be punished. She said that the next time she would punish me. Do you think she really will?

TEACHER: I don't know.

BILL: Will my mother find out if I am doing it?

TEACHER: If it has been one of your problems all along, then your mother already knows it.

BILL: Yes, but will she know that I am doing it here too?

COMMENT: In this situation the teacher not only had to counteract the inappropriate remarks of two other teachers but also had to reduce the boy's own—neurotically sexualized—desire for spanking (i.e., for the vindictive, but erotically pleasurable, stimulation of the very organ whose uncontrolled functioning gave him "sinful" pleasure). At the same time she had to perform the unpleasant, but unfortunately necessary, task of not contradicting another teacher directly, in order not to confuse the boy in regard to his relationship with adults, and also in order to discourage his surreptitious attempts to pit one adult against the other.

We stated that such children often experience spanking as a pleasurably stimulating experience—particularly since, at the same time, it also appeases their conscious guilt feelings without actually reducing the motivational strength of the underlying neurotic conflict. The following conversation will underscore this point:

BILL: Miss Z beat me this morning.

(*Teacher questions the boy about this*)

BILL: You know, it really isn't true. It did not happen at all. Do you think it would be a punishment if she beat me? She threatened to do it. Do you think she will? Do you think it is a crime that, when there are three toilets over there, I still have BM in my pants?

TEACHER: No, I don't think it is a crime. But it is a problem both for you and for the housemother. I think you will learn to understand this, and we, at the school, will help you with it. You will learn to control it.

BILL: My father promised me that I would not be beaten for it here. . . . Should I test Miss Z tonight? I will go to bed with my slippers on. Would she punish me, if I made it look like an accident?[18]

TEACHER: From what I hear, you have done this a number of times before. I therefore doubt that Miss Z could easily accept the explanation that it was an accident.

BILL: I am dying to be whipped!

TEACHER: You like to be whipped.

BILL: I want to be beaten. I hope the test is successful.

TEACHER: Somewhere along the way you got to like whippings.

BILL: They feel good on me.

TEACHER: I know. But I would like to get you to like other things even better. We can help you here with that. Let us try something else. (*Hugs Bill*) Which do you like better?

BILL: That is better.

[18] Slippers in bed are as inappropiate as BM in the pants. The fact that he is trying to make the wearing of slippers to bed appear "accidental"—as BM in the trousers is actually often accidental in the case of a child—casts a great deal of light upon the dynamics of his soiling urge. It is a hostile and provocative act, disguised as an involuntary accident. Cf. also the "pun": "Slipper—slip-up."

COMMENT: The erotic quality of whippings, particularly in the case of an anally fixated obsessive-compulsive, is clearly underscored by the preceding conversation. The manner in which whippings are provoked, by means of "accidents" ("slips") involving slippers or BM's, shows that such "accidents" were probably important attention-getting devices in the early life of this boy. He therefore accepted and then craved whipping, as a substitute for more affectionate forms of attention, which, presumably, were not available. The therapeutic value of the entire conversation is clearly shown by the fact that when nonpunitive attention was given to him, in the form of a hug, he expressed his preference for this more mature form of love. This represents a development, away from infantile anal eroticism and toward more mature and more tender eroticism. In brief, as in all real therapy and discipline, the means used to guide ("discipline") the child served to expand its potentialities, by giving it access to the broader satisfactions available to adults.

The breadth and intensity of adult satisfactions is often minimized, because of the prevailing myth that childhood is the happiest period of life (Chapter 14).

Case 38: The Value of Adult Gratifications

In the analysis of a grown woman, who tenaciously clung to infantile satisfactions, important progress took place when the analyst stressed the number and quality of gratifications available to adults, but not to children.

We suspect that infantile gratifications are craved by adults only if they did not have a sufficient amount of such gratifications in childhood to enable them to expand their capacity for enjoyment.

PRINCIPLE VS. DISCRETE EVENT

Discipline involves the mediation of broad and intelligible reality to the subject. Of course, even the best disciplinarian may sometimes inadvertently use the prohibitory language of punishment and of the superego. However, his students soon come to realize that even when the teacher says: "Do not lie!" he means (and the child "hears") "Speak the truth. *Fiat justitia, ruat caelum!*" Such a disciplinarian relates the child's concrete error or deviation to a broad principle, or to the general structure of physical and social reality. (See Case 36.) By contrast—and regardless of what "pious" mask it may assume—punishment mostly pertains only to some concrete "sin": "I'll teach you to tell me that the vase fell from the mantle all by itself!" We might also add that this distinction between the teaching of general principles and the hammering in of many a discrete individual "don't" also corresponds to what we have defined as the difference between "education" (or teaching) and mere "brute training." (Cf. especially Chapter 7.) We therefore hold that—since, fortunately, abstractions are of various kinds and complexities—even the most retarded human being, whose IQ barely enables him to acquire the rudiments of speech, can be taught, instead of simply being trained, since his (admittedly minimal) capacity for abstraction and concept formation is revealed by his acquisition of at least the beginnings of speech. In fact, even extremely defective children, who do not speak at all and are, in addition, also very severely disturbed, can be "taught" and not only "drilled," provided the attitude of the teacher is logically consistent and is actuated by ego-ideal principles instead of superego taboos.[19]

[19] On the basis of some experience with raising and training dogs, the writer would venture to suggest that even dogs can be taught, and not only drilled. All that is needed is the principle that the dog should be taught things which are necessary for him and not simply things which suit the personal preferences—and exhibitionistic impulses—of his master. It is one thing to train a dog to stay off the highway because he might be run over otherwise and quite another matter to "drill" him in order to show him off to one's friends. Of course, the dog does not "know" intellectually that he is taught to stay off the highway today, so as not to be run over tomorrow. However, he seems to sense the difference between the attitude of the master who teaches him something for his own good and the attitude of the master who teaches him "cute tricks." This view is quite compatible with Bose's interesting paper on the superego of dogs (*19*), though, in our opinion, Bose actually discusses not the dog's superego but—if we may speak somewhat loosely—his ego ideal. Any dog owner knows that there is a great deal of difference between the well-taught dog's need for esteem and the shallow and automatic compliance of the circus dog who is trained only to perform "tricks."

CREATIVE DISCIPLINE

In brief, we hold that the disciplinarian is effective to the extent to which he is an educator—a "guide, philosopher, and friend." This interpretation of discipline is even etymologically correct, since this word is derived from the word "disciple."

Truly competent teachers are fully aware of this, just as they are aware of the fact that effective education involves discipline rather than punishment. In addition, they usually possess considerable insight into the dynamic differences between the exercise of functional authority for the purpose of mediating reality and the exercise of dysfunctional power, which only mediates the personal idiosyncrasies of the teacher to the child. Thus, Mr. Joseph B. Ferdinand, supervisor of the Greenlea unit of the Devereux Schools, once remarked in a conversation that the chief qualification of therapeutic teachers is their ability to adjust their personalities and activities to the make-up of the individual "exceptional" child, instead of demanding that the child adapt itself to the teacher's personality and neuroticisms. We might add that the adaptation of the curriculum and activities program to the individual child's make-up is likewise an indispensable and basic requisite for therapeutic education. This implies, of course, the seeming paradox that, in the case of the "exceptional" child, the basic reality which has to be taken into account is fundamentally the personality make-up and potentiality pattern of the child. Actually, however, this is no paradox at all, since it is the essence of both mental defect and the emotionally determined neurotic handicap that the child's chief "axis for the organization of experience" (53) is, in the case of the defective, usually the biological axis and, in the case of the emotionally ill, the neurotic axis. (Cf. also Chapter 4.)

This *pro tem* way of defining broad reality in therapeutic education does not imply a lack of faith in the human potentialities of the "exceptional" child. The reality of the fact that the determining pattern of such a child's experiences is within the child is recognized—but so is the reality of the axiom that any development of the child's self opens a new road to its humanization and ethnicization. Hence, the crux of the technique of therapeutic education is that it represents the reverse of interpersonal relations characteristic of punitive situations. In therapeutic education it is not the personality make-up of the "person in power"—of the potentially punitive martinet—which serves as a basis for the definition of "reality" and of what is a "punishable offense." Rather is it the idiosyncratic make-up of the "potential victim" in terms of which the situation is defined. Hence, in therapeutic education the very helplessness, sickness, and troublesomeness of the child is the source of its "power" over its adult teachers. This philosophy is closely related to the basic Jewish tenet that charity is not so much a virtue as a duty, because needy persons have a right to it. This view is, needless to say, also in accord with the importance of the role assigned to children and helpless persons in the ethical philosophy of Jesus, who, in this respect, simply elaborated, and gave a compelling and moving quality to, the basic Jewish philosophy of charity, which today animates both therapeutic education and psychotherapy at their best.

CHAPTER 9

....

Socialization and Its Relation to Discipline and Punishment

THE WELL-BEHAVED PRIMITIVE CHILD

In his gently but inflexibly clear-sighted book *Are We Civilized?* (156)—which every civilized person should periodically reread, in order to take stock of himself—the great anthropologist and humanist Robert H. Lowie contrasts the good behavior of the unflogged and unpunished primitive child with the behavior problems of children in higher civilizations. He establishes beyond any doubt that the treatment of children becomes increasingly brutal as civilization "progresses" and that modern, psychologically oriented, education simply represents a return to the wise pedagogical procedures of primitives.

Of course, Westerners often argue that the lenient treatment of the primitive child has many drawbacks.

PRIMITIVE LENIENCY

For example, a psychiatrist suggested that one reason why the South African native is so improvident and lackadaisical in adult life, and so unable to make his way in a harsh and competitive world, is that prolonged nursing and the lenient treatment which he experiences as a child make him an incurable optimist. For a variety of reasons, this line of reasoning is simply nonsensical.

In the first place adaptability, however great it may be, has certain objective limits. There are things which flesh and blood cannot endure. There are, in addition, psychological and ethical limits to what one may expect from man's adaptability. This limit is reached ethically when adaptability degenerates into spineless opportunism and psychologically when the effort to adjust damages the ego.[1] What needs to be interpreted in this context is, therefore, not the South African Negro's "failure to adapt" but the South African white's inadaptability, which is reflected in his inability to deal with his inoffensive Negro fellow citizen except by heaping wanton insult and injury on him. In our opinion the problem of the South African Negro is, thus, not his "unbridled oral optimism." It is the fact that he would be denied reward and recognition even if he were a shrewd, hardbitten, compulsive, and acquisitive person. We therefore hold that what keeps the South African Negro from "cracking up" and going into a severe depression, despite everything that is done to him, is precisely the loving and lenient way in which he is treated as a child. Indeed, as Freud— apparently speaking of himself—pointed out, a man who was his mother's favorite develops enough ego strength not to be crushed by the blows of fate (129).

INTELLECTUAL INHIBITION

Another objection to primitive leniency—which often masquerades as a factual statement about "racial" psychology—comes from unimaginative educators who taught in schools for native children. Their views are based on the finding that the mental development of the primitive child reaches a plateau much earlier than does that of a white child. They point out that whereas, e.g., the small Afri-

---

[1] In this instance, as in many others, the criteria of psychology and those of humanistic ethics are identical.

can child is often an alert and bright pupil, as soon as it approaches puberty its class performance falls below that of white children of comparable age. One conclusion commonly drawn from this observation, which seems accurate, is that the onset of psychobiological maturity occurs earlier in, e.g., the Negro child than it does in the white child. This statement is questionable on many grounds. The most important of these is that much of the world's "colored" population is chronically undernourished and suffers from a variety of endemic diseases, whose cumulative effects may not become apparent until puberty. Hence, the early "leveling off" which characterizes the intellectual development of some "colored" children may not be due to an authentically earlier normal maturation but simply to a pathological premature inhibition of normal development. In brief, what we are dealing with in such cases is not "racial psychology" but the cumulative effect of endemic and deficiency diseases.

PUBERTY RITES

It is, furthermore, quite probable that a variety of sociological and psychological factors also play a role in the sudden premature inhibition of the native child's intellectual development. Perhaps the most important of these was pointed out to the writer by Father André Dupeyrat,[2] who, in addition to having spent twenty-two years as a missionary in Papua, also happens to be a psychologically sensitive and scientifically imaginative anthropologist. He too believes that there is a connection between primitive parental leniency and the sudden "leveling off" observed approximately at puberty but feels that the connection is an indirect one. Unlike certain unrealistic students of this problem, Father Dupeyrat feels that early parental leniency is relevant in this context only in so far as it contrasts with certain experiences at the time of puberty. He finds that the harshness and rigors of puberty rites, which also

[2] Personal communication.

inaugurate a radical change in the patterns of demand made upon the now supposedly mature adolescent, result in an inhibition of its capacity to develop further. In brief, Father Dupeyrat does not feel that the early "leveling off" is due to a spontaneous, normal, and internally ("racially") determined cessation of the developmental process but views this phenomenon as a product of a socially determined psychological inhibition or arrest of development. He denies that at that age the native child has already reached its maximum potential. Instead, he believes that the full unfolding of its potentialities is prematurely halted.

Needless to say, Father Dupeyrat's thesis is both psychoanalytically and anthropologically sound and gives no comfort to those who argue that the lenient treatment of children inhibits their development. Love never inhibits. Only aggression does.

PHYSIOLOGICAL PUBERTY

Another untenable explanation of this "leveling off" process relates the observed mental inhibition of the primitive child to the noninhibition of its sexual interests at puberty. Father Dupeyrat's views seem to have a bearing also upon this point, on which, be it said, Freud more or less contradicted himself. Freud stated on the one hand that whatever civilization gains, it gains at the expense of women (i.e., of mature sexuality) (98), while his more fundamental psychoanalytic theory of sublimation (147) clearly implies that what is sublimated is not mature sexuality but the aggressive impulse, which, in the pregenital stage only, is fused with immature sexual impulses. This latter point is fully substantiated also by K. A. Menninger's unqualified finding that mature sexuality cannot be sublimated (169). This, in turn, implies that any tampering with mature, tender, and responsible sexuality can only lead to its degradation. We are therefore compelled to conclude that the most creative and humane aspects of civilization result from the sublimation of aggressive impulses (including pregenital "sexuality," which contains a liberal admixture of aggression), whereas the seamier side of civilization is derived from the artificial degradation and distortion of mature sexuality.[3]

The thesis that the mental inhibition of the pubescent native child is a direct consequence of the noninhibition of its sexual interests is, thus, untenable. A good reason for this is that e.g., a comparison of the grades of married "GI Bill of Rights" students with those of single students shows that normal sexual gratification is not incompatible with further intellectual growth. These findings are made even more significant by the fact that GI students tend to be older and, thus, are closer to the biologically determined point at which one's development reaches a plateau.[4] In brief, it is quite probable that the belief in the alleged incompatibility of mature sexual interests with the unfolding of one's intellectual potential is derived from theories developed in the Middle Ages, when education was principally a means of becoming a (celibate) priest. In our view marriage is not an obstacle to the unfolding of

[3] Since the psychoanalytic theory of sexuality is consistently misunderstood, we wish to specify that, in psychoanalysis, "sexuality" does not mean simply the urge to cohabit. The sexual instinct is viewed as the biological basis of and the activating energy behind all that is creative, decent, and socially beneficial. The theory of sublimation does not imply that the sexual impulse itself can be sublimated. It implies that aggressive impulses are sublimated through the intervention of the sexual impulse. It is arrant nonsense to say that sex can be sublimated in sports. Sports are sublimations of aggressive impulses, which are guided and restrained by the forces of Eros. The struggle of two teams of football players is a manifestation of aggressivity. The fact that the teams limit this struggle to a contest over the possession of the football, and obey the rules, instead of simply slaughtering each other, is due to the intervention of Eros. Likewise, a surgeon's cutting up of a person is a sublimation of his aggressive impulses, because love and compassion guide his potentially destructive knife. As regards the misconception that psychoanalysis approves of casual fornication, it is held only by the ignorant and by those who are willfully blind because they have an ax to grind. The psychoanalytic theory of mature sexual relations has been stated with perfect clarity by Jesus himself. He forgave the adulterous woman because she loved so much. Psychoanalysts, like Jesus, consider sexual activity normal only if it is an expression of love and respect; casual fornication is viewed as neurotic (54).

[4] Without seeking to minimize the importance of the fact that GI students, being older and usually married, tend to take their studies seriously, we must nonetheless stress that the age at which the unfolding of one's potentialities reaches a plateau is biologically determined and therefore only minimally influenced by existential factors.

one's intellectual potentialities; only dissipation is. The problem of the intellectually prematurely inhibited primitive child is often simply rooted in the fact that, by tribal standards, he is deemed to be more or less ready for marriage, although, because of his Occidental schooling, he is compelled to remain celibate. This incompatibility of his actual social status with the normal and expected social status of other members of his own age group is, presumably, quite traumatic, since it is a socially atypical experience. It is this state of affairs which creates the false impression that the, e.g., Negro adolescent's sexual impulses "arrest" the further development of his intellectual potential.

LENIENCY AND GOOD BEHAVIOR

On the whole, there seems to exist a "one to one" correlation between primitive parental leniency and the good behavior of children. This is in sharp contrast with the observation that Occidental children, raised by "modern" and "psychiatrically sophisticated" parents, are often quite neurotic and maladjusted. In fact, anyone who has been in a home where children are educated in accordance with misunderstood psychiatric theories knows that they are neither well behaved nor—what is even worse—happy and that they manifest an almost pathological amount of uncontrolled aggressivity.

We propose to open our discussion of the relevance of discipline and of punishment for socialization with an analysis of the causes of this seeming discrepancy between two well-documented sets of observation.

It is quite certain that this discrepancy cannot be due to basic differences between "primitive" and "modern" culture. Indeed, in view of the basic uniformity of the human psyche, and above all in view of the fact that during the developmental period the basic (biological) process of maturation plays a decisive role in human psychic functioning, it is safe to say that the children of various tribes resemble each other more than do the adults, who are the finished products of divergent processes of ethnicization (55).[5] Hence, it is hard to see how a method which leads to an early and satisfactory socialization in simpler cultures could lead to emotional turmoil and antisocial behavior in a more complex and more intricately structured one.

WHO DISCIPLINES THE PRIMITIVE CHILD?

The basic factor responsible for the misconception that we are confronted here with a paradox is that Western observers tend to ignore the fact that primitive children are also disciplined, though they are not necessarily punished in our sense. The crux of the matter is that Western observers, in addition to not differentiating between discipline and punishment, allow themselves to be blinded both by their own childhood experiences and by an ethnocentric bias, which causes them to look for primitive disciplinarians in the wrong place. In other words, most observers assume that because primitive parents, parent surrogates, and adults in general do not punish the child to any appreciable extent the young native is permitted to "run hog wild" and experiences no restraint whatsoever. This, as we indicated elsewhere (42), is a complete fallacy.

The primitive child, too, is subjected to discipline. However—and this is the decisive point—discipline is administered by its own age group, or by young people not much older than the child itself. Since the primitive child's functionally effective ingroup is, to a large extent, the "children's society," which is often both a play group and a work group, the pressure put on the child is particularly effective. Indeed, it is well known that the demands and expectations of one's real ingroup are far more effective than are

[5] The only necessary stricture to be mentioned here is that—as stated in Chapter 14 —many primitive children are more genuinely "children pure and simple," while our children's behavior is largely "child*ish*" (and not simply child*like*), because we— more than the primitive—force them to behave in accordance with our unrealistic preconceptions regarding "the nature of children."

pressures which emanate from other segments of society, or even from society as a whole (33), in controlling and directing behavior, at least on the practical level. This specification is of considerable theoretical significance. The structure of society and the ethos of its culture determine precisely what is a given individual's ingroup, just as they determine the fundamental spirit and form of the "demand and expectation patterns" of the ingroup, where its members are concerned. In this sense, then, even though the ingroup is the functional social unit which controls behavior most effectively, this control too is shaped by, and is exercised on behalf of, society as a whole. Viewed in this manner, the ingroup may be defined as the socializing agency of society as a whole.[6]

The second point is that the primitive child is first socialized with reference to the children's group to which it belongs, and only later on with reference to society at large. In other words, its initial socialization consists in learning to adjust as an equal—or at least as a near equal—to other children of approximately its own age group. This, as we stress in Chapter 10, includes functioning now as the pupil and now as the teacher of one's own age mates. Only later on is the child socialized with reference to those much older or appreciably younger than itself, i.e., in terms of a genuine "dominance and submission pattern." Differently expressed, the child learns first to be one of a group of peers and only later on to be a leader or a subordinate. This may perhaps explain why the primitive is often such a "good citizen" in adult life (35).

It could be argued of course that in our society too some children are socialized by their age mates, and that this "gang socialization" sometimes turns them into antisocial adults. While this observation is correct, the general conclusions which some may be inclined to draw from it are false. Indeed, we cannot afford to disregard

---

[6] This is true even of basically antisocial ingroups, such as gangs, whose patterns, as indicated elsewhere, are also molded by the fundamental ethos of the larger society. Of course, in such cases, these ingroup patterns are often negatively determined by the ethos of the society and are manifestations of "social negativism" (31).

certain essential differences between the social position and role of the primitive "children's group" and the status and role of the Occidental "street-corner gang."

A closer examination of these differences may prove enlightening.

THE CHILDREN'S GROUP AS AN AGENCY OF SOCIETY

In primitive society the children's group is a recognized social unit. It has definite social functions, and the task of socializing the child is, more or less explicitly, delegated to it by society itself. Thus, the children's group is part of the manifest, culturally implemented, basic framework of primitive society. It is in the mainstream of the culture (58) and is, moreover, an agent of society and of culture. The primitive child does not join the children's group by fleeing the adults or by "playing hooky." The adults themselves hand the child over to the group, without, however, "extruding" it, even in those cases where relatively young boys and girls are made to move into the dormitory for the unmarried. These facts emerge quite clearly from any good anthropological account of primitive "adolescents' houses" (80).

SOCIAL INTEGRATION OF CHILDREN'S GROUPS

Since the primitive children's group does not exist *contra mundum* but is a recognized association established within the total framework of society, its distinctive standards and specific codes, while oriented primarily to the interests of children rather than of adults, are not in opposition to more general adult social codes, as are the "codes" of adolescent gangs in our own society. In other words, they are not the products of "social negativism" (31) or of "antagonistic acculturation" (64) and do not have as their implicit goal opposition to broad social demands. They are but a first step toward the humanization and education of the child for responsible citizenship.[7] This task is often quite specifically—though not nec-essarily formally—delegated to the children's group by society itself.

COLLECTIVE ESCAPADES

In some instances one function of primitive children's or adoles-cents' groups is to permit a socially organized and controlled "sow-ing of wild oats," both erotic and aggressive,[8] which in our society occurs in the form of private or individualized escapades, or is treated as such even where it is performed by gangs of juvenile delinquents. The distinction we make is similar to that which ob-tains between approved "social drinking" and disapproved "private tippling," or between kissing a friend's wife at a New Year's Eve party and kissing her in private. In some primitive societies the socialization of essentially adolescent "misbehavior" extends even into adult life. Thus, Tahitian society sanctioned the "perpetually adolescent" behavior of members of the "society of the Areoi" (79).[9]

SOCIAL BACKING

Children's and adolescents' societies can count upon the backing of society as a whole. If they get into difficulties, they are not just tolerantly "bailed out" but are actually "backed up" by society, which is a very different matter indeed.

[7] The element of "humanization" as distinct from "ethnicization" enters the picture at this point in the form of an expansion and deepening of all human rela-tions, regardless of what their ethnically determined form may be. This point will be discussed more in detail below.

[8] The sexual activities of juvenile gangs are often quite aggressive.

[9] While there is no real unanimity among Polynesian specialists as regards the details of the traditional behavior of members of this society, it is generally agreed upon that this society was socially sanctioned, enjoyed a great deal of prestige, and required behavior more commonly associated with irresponsible adolescents than with staid adults.

AUTONOMY OF CHILDREN'S GROUPS

Children's societies are, by and large, autonomous, and, in the cases in which they are guided by adults, these mentors are sometimes more like impartial arbitrators than like supervisors deputized by society to keep an eye on the young.

AGE CLASSES

Members of a given children's society often went through life side by side, entering and leaving various age classes or graduated societies either together or at about the same time. This, needless to say, is possible only where the "type biographies" of individuals tend to be relatively similar, because of the limited extent to which occupational specialization prevails in primitive society.

HONORARY ADOLESCENTS

Let us now contrast this with certain types of tolerance and even approval granted to certain privileged adults in Occidental society who, for various reasons, are permitted either to prolong their "irresponsible adolescence" almost indefinitely or else are authorized to behave periodically, and under well-defined conditions, as though they were still adolescents.

PERIODS OF LICENSE

The classical case is that of ritual periods of license, which obtain in primitive and intermediate as well as in civilized societies and affect society as a whole. Australian corroborees, Roman Saturnalia and Lupercalia, the Fool's Feast of the Middle Ages, and the carnivals of certain modern cities specializing in such festivities are good examples of occasions on which—theoretically at least—society as a whole behaves as though it were made up of adolescents.

GILDED YOUTH

In other instances only "gilded youth"—made up of persons who, chronologically at least, are adults but do not have to work—is permitted to behave irresponsibly and sometimes even criminally. St. Augustine states in his *Confessions* that he himself belonged in his youth to such a gang of delinquents, and his contemporary, Apuleius, described in his *Golden Ass* the gangs which infested Hypata in Thessaly. The streets of fifth-century Byzantium were made unsafe at night by distinctively dressed riotous—and occasionally even thieving and murderous—gangs of socially prominent idle young men, and also by the "Green" and the "Blue" factions of circus fans. Such excesses were seldom curbed by the watch. The coarsely violent "bucks" and "Corinthians" of the English Regency were also quite lawless. They sometimes specialized in displaying their personal "valor" by picking fights with famous professional pugilists, with little interference from the "Bow Street runners" (police).

COMMEMORATIVE CONVENTIONS

Even adults are permitted to engage in transitory group misconduct, provided only that this specifically "commemorates" their youthful exploits. The German police dealt leniently with the *Alte Herren* of the various student associations when they had too much to drink and became too riotous when dropping in on their old fraternity. A similar leniency is shown in England to the "old boys" who "cut up" while visiting their former school. In this country the pranks of some veterans' conventions are obligingly overlooked by the police, and not only—as is often assumed—because these veterans bring money into the convention city. Were this the sole reason, equal leniency would be shown to rioting hardware or chemistry conventions, which—significantly in our opinion—seldom get far out of hand. This is probably due to several causes. In the first place, one becomes a member of a hardware or chemistry association after one ceases to be an adolescent, so that such an association is oriented to the (adult) present and to the future, rather than to one's youth, which lies in the past. Indeed, operating a hardware store or being a chemist is more closely related to current and future adult pursuits than is the fact that one fought gallantly but also lived in a relatively irresponsible manner, under circumstances not related to one's adult daily life.[10] In addition, membership in such societies implies no "common past," since one joins them in one's adulthood. No doubt other factors are also operative in causing veterans' conventions and college reunions to be more riotous than professional or occupational conventions.

STUDENTS AS HONORARY ADOLESCENTS

Another privileged group is made up of students, whose prolonged "trainee" status and economic dependence cause them to be treated as adolescents. Even the stuffy officials of Imperial Germany winked at the dueling, drunkenness, and riotous behavior of the *Korpsstudenten,* as long as they wore their distinctive student caps. The French police also look the other way when long queues of Sorbonne students tie up the traffic on the Boulevard St. Michel.

[10] It is striking that, in retrospect, even wounded veterans of the combat infantry often think of the war period as a kind of Roman holiday. Kipling was also quite right in stressing the homesickness of his ex-soldier hero, Terrence Mulvaney, for the Army ("The Big Drunk Draft"). Apparently, regardless of how important certain temporary (draftee) occupations may be, or how long a man belonged to a relatively marginal institution (Regular Army), the fact that such occupations do not form the nucleus of society's routine efforts to survive tends to romanticize them and makes them seem "less serious" than selling dry goods. How much hardship such an occupation entails is of relatively secondary importance. Thus, to the Plains Indian, for whom war was a kind of game, soldiering was glamorous. By contrast, in tribes whose economy is a predatory one, raiding is a definitely adult pursuit. There are even differences between the manner in which "typical" and "atypical" forms of soldiering are defined. Being in the Supply Corps is unglamorous and adult, because the work resembles civilian "drudgery." Being a "cloak and dagger man" or a paratrooper is "glamorous," because it is even more unlike normal civilian drudgery than is being a combat infantryman.

Rioting Oxford and Cambridge students do not come under the jurisdiction of the civil arm of the law but under that of University proctors. As regards America, year after year on the eve of the Big Game with Stanford University the students of the University of California at Berkeley built a bonfire at the corner of Bancroft Street and Telegraph Avenue, so as to bring out the fire department. Then, when the fire trucks arrived, they were overturned, because their color evoked the "cardinal red" of the "enemy" team. This happened so consistently that, instead of calling out the police, the obliging city fathers finally painted the fire department vehicles blue and gold—the colors of the University of California—so as to protect the taxpayers' property.

Society authorizes these groups to define themselves as "associations of honorary adolescents" and grants them a kind of collective immunity for antisocial acts which, if perpetrated by isolated individuals or by socially disapproved groups—such as gangs, whose members are not protected by the social fiction that they are "honorary adolescents"—would invite energetic reprisals. It is important to stress, however, that even "associations of honorary adolescents" do not enjoy unlimited immunity. Their misconduct is defined as "harmless mischief" only under specific conditions. In America, where learning is less esteemed than sports, and student bodies are usually nonpolitical, licensed rioting is limited to football games. Were the students creating a disturbance not for dear old Siwash but, e.g., because of the local school board's refusal to implement the Supreme Court's decision to abolish segregation in schools, we may be sure that the nightsticks would begin to swing very rapidly indeed. In England, too, student misbehavior is tolerated only if it seems to confirm the half-respectful and half-tolerant maxim: "Young gentlemen will have a bit of fun!" Were some young hotheads to erupt from the Oxford Union after a debate over some major issue, and create havoc, neither civil nor University authorities would condone it. Otherwise stated, in order to preserve their immunities as "honorary adolescents" students must renounce any interest and participation in adult pursuits.

STUDENT IMMUNITIES AND EUROPEAN POLITICAL HISTORY

On the continent of Europe the situation is more complex, and the distinction between "a bit of cutting up" and political student riots is less clear-cut. However, even there it is possible to derive the relative immunity of students rioting for political reasons from their traditional right to create havoc "for fun." Hence, the traditional immunities of students played a rather important role in European political history. Indeed, European students did not function as standard bearers of nineteenth-century liberalism simply because their superior education gave them deeper convictions and inspired them with a more ardent and more unselfish spirit of sacrifice. Students could afford to take the risk of rioting for a Constitution, or for universal suffrage, because they, quite realistically, expected a more lenient treatment even from a tyrannical bureaucracy than did workers or small shopkeepers. Tactically speaking, it is as easy to launch the police or mercenary troops against students as it is to launch them against workingmen. What stayed the hand of even the Holy Alliance, or of petty princelings, seems to have been something altogether different. Even such tyrannies had to allow students to riot for political reasons, because it was their traditional privilege—going back to the Middle Ages—to engage in corporate disorderly conduct. Of course, even students were not permitted to engage in armed revolts or to assassinate reactionary officials.[11] This explains why, in a "real showdown," students seldom took it upon themselves to spearhead the populace rising in revolt against oppressive regimes. Thus, as regards *Les Trois Glorieuses*—the three days of street fighting in July, 1830, which led to the dethronement of Charles X of France—we have Stendhal's unimpeachable testimony that the "jackets" of the

[11] Even this statement should be qualified. All liberal nineteenth-century Europe was thrilled when the student Sand assassinated Kotzebue.

bourgeoisie and of students were far less conspicuous on the barricades than were the "blouses" of workers or the "rags" of those
whom Stendhal, a Jacobin with aristocratic tastes, calls, with
grudging admiration, "the canaille." Delacroix's painting of
a scene on the barricades unwittingly offers a similar testimony. It
shows only one main figure wearing a jacket and a top hat, and, not
at all surprisingly, the craggy, ravaged, and haunted face of this
"white-collar" individual marks even him as a "marginal man."
Historians confirm this impression by not assigning a major role
to students in the 1789, 1830, 1848, and 1870 French revolutions.

It is therefore our thesis that, unlike primitive "associations of
adolescents," European "associations of honorary adolescents" did
not enjoy real social backing but only certain immunities. They
were "backed" only when it suited the purposes of a vicious regime,
which could always disavow them when it became necessary to do
so. Thus, German students were used extensively in the "spontaneous indignation riots" of early Nazi Germany, and in the
1920's Rumanian students engaged in pogroms protected (!) by
the police and even by troops. This was very convenient for
regimes which were not strong enough to defy openly certain
major foreign powers, some of whose citizens were also beaten up
in such demonstrations. Had an ordinary rabble injured such
foreign nationals, this might have led to serious diplomatic repercussions. However, the fact that these were student riots effectively
tied the hands of foreign ambassadors, since the right of students to
riot and to molest people was unchallenged in all of Europe.

These observations have a direct bearing upon the problem of
gangs of juvenile delinquents. Quite often the hooliganism of such
gangs is no more destructive than is that of honorary adolescents
engaging in licensed corporate misconduct. Their legal difficulties
are caused by the fact that their corporate existence is not recognized by society, and by the fact that they do not riot under socially
sanctioned conditions. In other words, their misconduct is defined

as anarchic, and not as what Linton (*151*) calls "patterns of misconduct." Hence, even when members of certain conventions maul girls in public, jab them with electric prods, ruin their dresses with water pistols, and manhandle their escorts should the latter be foolish enough to try to protect their girls, they are not arrested, and are invited back the next year. By contrast, adolescent gangs molesting girls are arrested immediately.

There is just a trace of social wisdom in this otherwise completely irrational state of affairs. Socially patterned misconduct usually stays within certain limits, while purely idiosyncratic misconduct often goes to extremes. The well-known rise in the rate of Jewish juvenile delinquency and adult gangsterism tends to support this statement. Ever since their dispersion the Jews have turned inward. To use an expression coined by Lindner,[12] they "suffered out" rather than "acted out" their conflicts. Their illegal acts were crimes of cunning, rather than of violence.[13] In fact, not even legitimate physical activity received an extensive social implementation among Jews.[14] Otherwise stated, Jewish culture provides no socially sanctioned patterns for the expression of even relatively sublimated hostile impulses in the form of sports. Hence, when, as a result of the increasing contact between Jews and Gentiles, the former too developed a tendency to "act out" rather than to "suffer out" their conflicts, they sometimes became even more anarchic than did Gentiles, who have a socialized and culturally implemented tradition of physical violence. While this explanation does not profess to be exhaustive, it does shed some light upon at least one cause of the current increase in Jewish juvenile delinquency and adult gangsterism, and also on the observation that neurotic

[12] *Time,* December 6, 1954, pp. 64–65.

[13] The writer recalls the stunned disbelief of his father—a lawyer who also had a considerable criminal practice—when, in the 1920's, newspapers gave a big play to a Jewish mass murderer in eastern Europe.

[14] The Jewish athletes of the Seleucid period were explicitly criticized by their fellow citizens for their Hellenization. The first Jewish athletes to appear in western Europe were certain famous boxers of the English Regency period, who appear to have detached themselves from the Jewish community.

Jewish children and adolescents sometimes "identify with the enemy" by admiring Hitler, the *Luftwaffe,* or Nazism. Interestingly enough, such children and adolescents, some of whom actually had to flee Nazi Germany under extremely traumatic circumstances, are more often ineffectual dreamers or, at the most, "loud-mouthed phonies" than really aggressive juvenile delinquents. Be that as it may, one thing is certain: Wherever Jews are just beginning to engage in physical "acting out" as a major pursuit, they follow—and exaggerate—gentile patterns. For example, when, in Imperial Germany, Jewish university students, who were excluded from gentile Korps, began to form dueling and beer-swilling associations of their own, they simply imitated the German pattern, since there was no Jewish precedent for such activities.[15] It is precisely this isolation of nonproductive physical "acting" (as in sports)[16] or of physical "acting out" (as in delinquency and gangsterism) from the mainstream and basic matrix of Jewish life which accounts for the complete desocialization or at least extremism of Jews who, as a result of acculturation, turn from "suffering out" to "acting out." This is even manifest in the lawful, but nontraditional, aggressive activities of the Jews. A Jewish unit in Field Marshal Montgomery's African army had a fabulous record of valor, and the fight of tiny Israel against overwhelming Arab forces[17] is also remarkable. However, in the latter case too the detachment of such activities from post-Dispersion Jewish tradition is made manifest by the fact that, in the last days of British occupation and in the early days of independence, there existed embattled semicriminal terroristic groups, such as the Stern gang, which were patterned upon Nazi hoodlumism.

[15] In the early days of the Hitler regime Jews even tried to organize a Jewish-German Nazi party, not, as is commonly assumed, from sheer opportunism, but because of a neurotic "identification with the enemy."

[16] Compare the extraordinary boxing scene in Richard Brooks' *The Brick Foxhole,* New York, Harper, 1945.

[17] The Israeli air force flew ex-Nazi Messerschmitts against Egyptian British Spitfires. If this is a coincidence, it is certainly a striking one!

The preceding considerations suggest that the crux of juvenile delinquency is not so much the nature of the acts committed as the fact that it does not come within the scope of traditionally privileged "corporate misbehavior" and therefore, ipso facto, *gets out of hand by losing all connections with the basic matrix of culture.*

Returning now to our main topic, we believe that primitive society acted wisely when it caused the characteristic rebelliousness of the incompletely socialized child and adolescent to manifest itself through organized or corporate channels. By this device it contributed effectively to the socialization of even basically antisocial impulses. This, as we stress further below, is one of the most arduous, but also one of the most worth-while, tasks confronting any society.

Thus, the good behavior of primitive children is not determined solely by parental leniency and by the absence of punishment administered by adults. It is also, and perhaps even primarily, determined by the discipline administered by the child's own group. As Dr. Richard L. Jenkins kindly pointed out to the writer,[18] even though punishment which has a hostile intent to injure is destructive, the child can benefit even from such a hostile punishment when it comes from a peer, but not if it comes from a person in authority. In brief, we hold that the discipline to which the child is subjected by its peers guides it toward a broader citizenship by making it first a good citizen of the children's group. The second means used for the socialization of hostile and subversive impulses is the sociocultural implementation of adolescent corporate misbehavior.

SOCIALIZATION VS. FAMILIALIZATION

At this point we must seek to forestall the criticism that socialization in the children's group accomplishes only what "familialization" should, in theory at least, also be able to do, i.e., serve as a

[18] Personal communication.

preliminary to a broader "socialization." At this point we have to express a view which runs counter to one of the allegedly most basic—but actually only one of the tritest and, what is more, apparently erroneous—shibboleths of social science: "The family is the basis and basic unit of society."

Overwhelming evidence indicates that, in a very genuine—though naturally not absolute or exclusive—sense, the history of human society may, within limits, be characterized as a struggle between society at large and the family. The nuclear position of the incest taboo, which is one of the truly universal cultural traits (*144*), and the universal insistence on exogamy—be it familial, local, gentile, or tribal—are striking illustrations of this thesis. We certainly do not deny that the family is often the fundamental "brick" of the social edifice, especially in the primitive or *Gemeinschaft* (*215*) type of society. However, it is one thing to state that the family does in fact function as a social brick and quite another to say that it does so function either voluntarily or efficiently. On the contrary, the family may just as easily be viewed as a "trouble unit" (*27*) in society. Just as society must take cognizance of, and manage, the individual's "antisocial" (or, more properly, asocial or nonsocial) impulses, so it must cope with the family's special needs and loyalties, simply because they exist. In fact, the socialization of the family was perhaps a far more difficult task than was, and is, the socialization of the individual. The history of human society is, in a sense, a history of the gradual, socially promoted, breakdown of the primitive and fully functional family. This interpretation can be substantiated by a variety of facts.

1. Linton (*153*) pointed out that the attrition of the extended family (kindred) is accelerated in times of social crisis or transition.

2. Chinese imperial bureaucracy carried on an endless struggle against the disastrous influence of Chinese family loyalties on the individual official, which led to an often unbridled nepotism ap-

proved of by public sentiment. This may explain why Chinese officials were often eunuchs. The struggle of the Catholic Church against ecclesiastical nepotism is of the same order. In fact, there are many indications that one of the chief functional (i.e., ecclesiastic, rather than strictly religious or theological) reasons for the establishment of priestly celibacy under Pope Gregory VII was the need to prevent the rise of a class of married priests, whose family loyalties would have been at variance with the interests of the *ecclesia* as a social body.

3. Reactionary forces systematically exploit the "romantic" or "sentimental" sanctity of the family in order to impede socially valuable progress. Thus, the protection of children against sweatshop exploitation was speciously "interpreted" as an interference with parental rights.

4. At the pathological end of the scale of means whereby man is made into a citizen of a larger society, we have Hitler's well-known attempt to turn German children against their parents, and to cause them to spy on them and denounce them. At the nonpathological, or at least valuatively neutral, end of the scale, we find that practically all movements which seek to increase the size and to broaden the bases of society—which, according to Kroeber (*144*), are basic characteristics of progress—automatically turn the children against their parents. References to this fact may be found even in the New Testament, i.e., at a time when Christianity aimed at a universal society, embracing all men in a single brotherhood.

It is hardly necessary to stress that these remarks do not constitute an indictment of the family *per se*. Indeed, it seems quite probable that the family exists precisely because it meets certain "cultureproof" human needs. Society will always have to take cognizance of these "cultureproof" human needs, just as even antisexual early Christianity, which exalted celibacy above marriage, had to take cognizance of human sexuality, and had to socialize it in two ways: (a) by emphasizing St. Paul's *sexual* definition of marriage, which represents a culture-historical break with the primitive definition of marriage as a primarily nonerotic, and often almost impersonal, arrangement between two kin groups; (b) by defining marriage as a sacrament.

These facts suggest that, from the social point of view, the family can be viewed as an—admittedly unruly—agent of society, whose task is twofold: (a) the socialization of man's sexual impulses; (b) The social channeling of man's apparently fundamental need to form exclusive attachments (object cathexes) of greater than average intensity, even though such intense cathexes, especially if of a sexual nature, are—as Freud indicated (97)— often nonsocial and sometimes even antisocial. This specific channeling of intense cathexes tends to align marriage with such other socially implemented but basically idiosyncratic intense relationships as blood brotherhoods, the group friendships of "age classes" (195), and secret societies (225), etc.

In brief, the social disadvantages resulting from the establishment of such segmental (familial, etc.) loyalties may be simply the price society must pay for the socialization of individual "human nature in the raw," which society at large cannot accomplish directly and by itself. This price is paid by tolerating the socially troublesome aspects of family cohesion, which is but a variety of "subgroup" or "narrower ingroup" loyalties usually formed at the expense of broader social loyalties.[19]

These facts oblige us to contrast the lesser and different socializing capacity of familialization with the major importance of "socialization through membership in a children's group." This view is, actually, less novel than it may seem. Within limits, it harks back to Plato's idea of socializing children by taking them away from their parents. The least that may be said of Plato in this context—and the writer freely confesses that he finds Plato the

[19] The tendency to vote at nominating conventions for a "favorite son," and not for the best man, illustrates this point.

social planner even less congenial than Plato the metaphysician—
is that he was consistent in his views. Having grasped the asocial
aspects of the family and its partly desocializing influence, he
sought to control this "social trouble unit" by advocating the
establishment of totalitarian boarding nurseries. Of course, the
researches of Spitz indicate (204, 205, 206) that this would have
led to a simply appalling rate of infant mortality. However, Plato
lapsed into this error not simply because he knew nothing about
Freud and the psychology of infancy but primarily because he was
so ethnocentric and so ignorant of primitive practices that he took
it for granted that children should be and could only be socialized
by adults. Hence, he did not even envisage the possibility that the
desocializing effects of the family could be counteracted by entrusting the socialization of children to the children's groups, which, unlike Spartan children's groups, can function autonomously, and
not under adult supervision and for adult purposes.

LENIENCY AND SUBSEQUENT NEUROTICISM

A last point to be taken up is one which we have already discussed, at least incidentally, in another context (50). In the early
days of psychoanalysis, when many misunderstandings were
abroad, it was assumed that if children were only raised without
"inhibitions" they would be protected against genuine neurosis in
later life. We stress that we are speaking here of genuine neuroses,
not of developmental neuroses. The latter, as we stated elsewhere
(55) are "uniquely characterized by the fact that they can be 'outgrown' without psychiatric help, i.e., solely by means of the impetus inherent in psychosexual development and maturation. In addition, unlike true neuroses in children, such developmental
neuroses cause no residual pathological distortions of the personality." Eventually it became obvious, however, that mere leniency
did not protect the child against neurosis in later life—witness the
numerous and not altogether inaccurate, though usually viciously

worded, jokes about the neuroticism of the children of analysts. This realization led—even among a few child analysts—to a reaction against educational leniency and even to an outright anti-instinctual orientation (50). Unfortunately, whereas the basic observations on which this "new look" (?) in analytic thinking is based are correct, the conclusions which some persons draw from them are, to say the least, gratuitous. Indeed, it was tacitly assumed that there exists a one-to-one correlation between a permissive upbringing and ultimate neuroticism. Those who drew such unwarranted conclusions failed to consider some extremely simple facts:

NEUROTIC PSEUDO LENIENCY

Many modern parents educate their children "leniently" only because of purely intellectual convictions. Others do so because they are still rebelling against the severity of their own parents. Such a "delayed revolt" is often nothing more than a reaction formation against the more basic impulse to deal equally harshly with one's own children.[20] In other words, the "pseudo-modern" parent's externally and behaviorally correct, but emotionally neurotic and motivationally purely intellectualistic, leniency is one thing, and the non-neurotic, emotionally genuine leniency of most primitive parents is quite another thing. This difference is absolutely fundamental. Children respond far more readily to attitudes than to actions. A failure to understand this point is responsible for Orlansky's (176) and Sewell's (197) misguided criticism of psychoanalytic views regarding the import of traumata suffered in the course of psychosexual development. Both of these "critics" base their conclusions upon data pertaining to manifest parental behavior and upon parental statements, rather than upon a searching—i.e., psychoanalytic—exploration of the unconscious attitudes

[20] A modern Mohave Indian stated that the Indians now spanked their children because they themselves had been spanked in school (42). Similiar remarks are also made by various other, traditionally lenient, primitive parents who had been subjected to Occidental brutality in schools for natives.

and meanings lurking behind the "overt" child-rearing practices of the parents whom they interviewed and whose children they studied.

In brief, it is a sense datum that the overtly "leniently" treated children of psychoanalytically "sophisticated" (?) parents are often highly aggressive, neurotic, and unhappy. This, however, is due to the fact that such children react not to the behavioral, but purely negative, "absence of punishment" but to the implicit and positive seething resentment—or "slow burn"—of their parents, who forcibly hold their counter-aggressions in check, while the children tear the house apart, importune both the parents and their guests . . . and experience no happiness, but only agonizing anxiety and severe guilt feelings in doing so.

It is a hostile dereliction to allow a child to lose control of itself, instead of assisting its attempts at self-control by understanding and patient discipline. It is outright cruelty to allow a child to frighten itself half to death and to force it, in self-defense, to become finally so obnoxious that it will obtain at least punitive restraint.

Of course, the chief reason why creative and kindly discipline is often not forthcoming is that most "lenient" parents, and even a few therapeutic educators and psychotherapists, are afraid of their own aggressions. Unconsciously fearful that they might lose control of themselves while seeking to control the child, they deny it all needed supportive discipline. This point is of such importance that it will be illustrated by means of a detailed example.

Case 39: Supportive Discipline in Child Therapy

A twelve-year-old was sent to a therapeutic school because he had learning difficulties and displayed extremely provocative and immature behavior. The admitting psychiatrist diagnosed him as a severe anxiety neurotic. However, the boy's psychotherapist disagreed with this diagnosis and suggested instead that the boy was either severely autistic and preschizophrenic or else already schizophrenic.

A series of therapeutic interviews, extending over a period of some three weeks, yielded relatively negligible results. In the therapy hour the boy was fidgety, manneristic, systematically uncoöperative and refused even to listen to the therapist's comments. On the other hand he constantly demanded presents of all kinds, including even scientific books from the therapist's personal library, was inquisitive to the point of ransacking the desk drawers, etc. In brief, he was highly provocative and also quite inaccessible. The therapist, whose experience with psychotic children was relatively small at that time, felt that all his gentleness and tolerance did not enable him to establish rapport with this boy. It was evident to him that his interpretations were simply ignored, including the crucially important—and correct—interpretation that the boy was deliberately trying to force people to say "No" to him and to behave punitively toward him.

This stalemate was not broken until the therapist undertook to scrutinize his own reactions to the child, in the belief that, by gaining an insight into his own mounting irritation, he would be able to understand also the boy, and could help him to give up his attitude of mixed provocativeness and withdrawal which had hitherto neutralized all therapeutic efforts.

The crucial insight gained by the therapist was that, in trying to control the overt expression of his irritation, he was diverting needed psychic energy from the positive task of helping the child control itself to the purely negative task of inhibiting his own irritation. Once he understood this point, it became evident to him that he had overestimated the intensity of his irritation and, at the same time, had underestimated his capacity to sublimate it.

This, in turn, increased the therapist's understanding of the child and enabled him to see that the boy was getting extremely anxious because his therapist did not help him control his aggressions and did not even react to them explicitly. This prevented the boy from manifesting his aggressions in a direct form, because he felt that his therapist did not even help him control their indirect expression in the form of mere "irritating behavior."

This last remark reveals how little even an intellectual understanding of technique influences therapeutic work until it is translated into personal terms. Indeed, when the therapist participated in a staff conference, at which a psychiatric resident asked how much aggression he should allow his patient to manifest, it was this therapist who answered: "As much as *you* can stand." In other words, the therapist knew the "right answer" all along and was even able to teach it to others. Yet in this particular instance he was unable to apply it in therapy.[21] In brief, the therapist concentrated on inhibiting his irritation as long as he unconsciously assumed that if he took cognizance of the child's hostility he would feel tempted to react to it punitively. Once he understood this, it immediately became obvious to him that he was perfectly capable of being firm without becoming obnoxiously "adult" and punitive.[22]

During the next hour the therapist systematically inhibited every one of the boy's countless irritating evasions and mannerisms, which, being his means of binding his anxiety and of masking his real hostilities, made any verbal output or show of real emotions both unnecessary and impossible. This policy was pursued relentlessly throughout the hour. It included pulling down the curtain when the boy insisted on looking out the window, the demand that he sit, and not lie in a contorted position, in the chair, and above all the firm request that the boy should stop "talking like Donald Duck"—this being the child's most irritating and therapy-defeating technique.

The boy reacted to this interference with his symptoms with extreme hostility and even rudeness. He defiantly declared that he did not have to tell anyone anything, that he could talk any way he wanted to, that his mother would back him up in all this, etc. He even called the therapist a "liar" on three separate occasions. In brief, he at last replaced mere derivative irritating behavior with overt hostility.

The therapist hewed firmly to the line that the evasive symptoms had to stop then and there. When the boy challengingly asked if the therapist would hit him, the latter replied that he would never hurt the boy in any way. He added, however, that he would use other means

[21] Needless to say, this one lapse was due to various counter-transference factors, which had to be understood before they could be neutralized.

[22] This incident exemplifies the statement that the analysis of a patient should be paralleled by a continuous and concurrent self-analysis of the therapist. See Chapter 17.

to obtain compliance because he realized that the boy did not really wish to be "wicked" and was badly frightening himself with this display of his hostility.

It must be understood that only derivative and disguised hostility was discouraged, in order to help the boy express his real anger. Thus, when a slip of the tongue revealed that "talking like Donald Duck" was simply a substitute for using "bad" and hostile words, the therapist gently told the boy that he could use in therapy all the "bad language" he knew, so long as he did so in plain English.

A brief explanation is necessary at this point. "Donald Duck talk" contains no meaningful words. It is pseudo speech, which only mediates emotions. It was therefore highly suitable for expressing what this boy felt, though not what he thought. It was literally a "song without words," perfectly adapted to the boy's needs, since all he—like Donald Duck—tried to express was anger, fear, and spiteful gloating. In brief, the boy did not have to "squawk" meaningfully in ordinary language because he could squawk literally, like Donald Duck.

Hardly had the therapist authorized the boy to use ordinary bad language when the boy teed off by calling him a liar. Having been offered this outlet for his real thoughts and feelings, and being denied all means of disguising them by means of derivative symptomatic behavior, the boy became overtly hostile and—for a moment—practically acutely schizophrenic. For example, he told the therapist, who is a heavy smoker, that God would punish him for smoking. This was interpreted to the boy as an expression of his wish that the therapist should die of cancer of the lung. Next, the boy began to handle the therapist's books quite roughly and said: "And your books will just disappear—all gone." When asked what this meant, and how it would come about, the boy replied darkly that the books would rot.[23] This was interpreted to him as meaning that he hoped the therapist himself would rot.

The boy was greatly startled when the therapist calmly and explicitly restated these darkly allusive curses. He was also relieved to realize that the therapist was not destroyed by these magical curses and that, even though he had grasped their hostile intent, he did not retaliate.

[23] There had been some talk in an earlier hour about how books too eventually get old and fall apart.

When the boy visibly relaxed after his outburst, the therapist gently told him once more that he need not be afraid to voice his hostility quite openly in the therapeutic hour, since the therapist would not be destroyed thereby and would therefore feel no desire to retaliate. He added that he would continue to help the boy control his aggressions, which frightened him half to death and made him realize that others considered him a "bad boy." Then the therapist smilingly tore off some Christmas seals from a sheet and handed them to the boy—who had previously asked for them but had been refused as a matter of principle —with the remark: "Here are some seals to stick on your Christmas cards." The boy practically jumped out of his chair, came over to the therapist, and, almost leaning against him, handed him an address book, saying: "Write down your address, so I can send you a Christmas card." The writer did so at once and then gave the boy also a small outdated catalogue of steel office files, which the boy had previously demanded in a very provocative manner and which had therefore not been given to him. Although in the course of earlier hours he had managed to extort from the therapist a variety of small gifts—pencil stubs, paper clips, etc.—and had never even bothered to say "Thank you," on this occasion he received this trifling present as rapturously as a normal child might receive a much coveted and valuable gift. He said, "Thank you very much," and snuggled up to the therapist, his usually haunted-looking small face relaxed in a happy smile. The transformation was a truly startling one!

The hour having come to an end, the therapist stood up, placed his arm affectionately around the boy's shoulders, and said: "I like you and I want to help you. I know you frighten yourself with all this. . . . I am trying to help you like yourself." The boy looked intently into the therapist's face and, even though the Donald Duck theme had been dropped more than half an hour earlier, he spontaneously came back to it and said earnestly: "And I will try very hard not to talk any more like a duck." The therapist said: "I know you will, and I will help you. In my room you can say out plainly whatever you want to say."

COMMENT: The first point to be made pertains to the therapist's initial tendency to inhibit his irritation, instead of asking himself why the boy was trying to irritate him. It will be noted that once this point was clarified, anger no longer had to be inhibited, for the simple reason that there could no longer be any anger because it was understood that, in his own sick and unhappy way, the boy was clamoring for non-punitive discipline.

It also becomes apparent that a patient asks for anger and punishment only because he has given up any hope of ever getting real love and discipline. We are therefore less impressed with the overt demands of some schizophrenic patients for a display of the therapist's anger than are Wexler (227, 228), Rosen (192), Whitaker and Malone (229), and Hayward and Taylor (114) and flatly reject any justification of—sometimes physical—punitive behavior toward the patient. It is well to remember in this context a wise comment made by Dr. Mazzanti,[24] who, on being asked by a psychiatric resident whether schizophrenics truly believe in their delusions, replied: "They may be crazy, but they are not foolish." No insane man "in his right mind," paradoxical as this may sound, actually fears love and demands hate. He only fears sick and devouring love and distrusts phony love. Hence, he often asks point blank: "Why should you love me, when you don't even know me?" He prefers aggression only because it is at least an honest sentiment. The question to be asked therefore is not why the patient rejects love and demands punitiveness and anger but why the therapist is not able to love persuasively and undevouringly. The fact that some therapists start with anger and end up with love is, thus, not related only to the "infantilism of the patient who is not capable of enduring mature love." It is also due to the fact that, in the initial "angry stage," the therapist is able to express and get rid of the hostility which all human beings feel toward the mentally ill, whose symptoms are always provocative in one way or another (31).

This brings us to our second point. It seems "obvious" that, by constantly using the word "No" or performing actions having the same implication, the therapist was "punitive," within the meaning of this term as defined in Chapter 8. Such an interpretation of this technique takes no account of the fact that the purpose of these prohibitions, di-

[24] Personal communication.

rected at derivative—i.e., "more acceptable"—symptoms, was the liberation of the real and basic hostility. Thus, even though the child's ears
heard "No, don't fidget," his unconscious mind understood something
different: "Let go with your real feelings!" In fact, we hold that it is
precisely the therapist's refusal to accept the symptoms as a substitute
for the "real thing," and his implicit readiness to tolerate the latter,
which makes possible the emergence of the patient's real conflicts. By
contrast, if a child exasperates its parents and is restrictively punished,
this does not constitute an implicit invitation for the child to voice
openly its oedipal love and hate, which would leave his parents even
more shocked by its "depravity." We suspect that many parents tolerate
the bad behavior of their children so as not to have to find out what it
seeks to "cover up." We feel that no "restraint" is punitive which has as
its goal the liberation of the real, underlying conflict. However, such
restraint cannot be used effectively by anyone who feels angry. It can
only be used where there is real love and acceptance . . . and that is a
love which not even a schizophrenic will fear. This small schizophrenic
boy reacted to a loving restraint, which implied his right to full self-
expression, with almost rapturous happiness. For the first time in his
therapy he was able to be just a child—emotionally not quite twelve
years old perhaps, but at least eight—approaching an adult trustingly,
feeling safe from retaliation and certain that he would be assisted in his
desperate attempts to control himself.

   In brief, what was called for was a disciplinary restraint of the boy's
derivative hostility, as a preliminary to the acceptance of his more basic
real anger. To have denied this boy the discipline he was asking for
would have been as senselessly restrictive as beating him for his symptoms. But the therapist could take this attitude only after he realized
that the boy asked for "help by hate" only because he never knew that
"help by love" could exist. To him, the therapist's initial and inappropriate "angelic patience" seemed to mask a terrible and hypocritical
rage, because that was all the "patience" this boy had ever known.

   Our third and last comment concerns the brief "miniature psychotic
storm" (20). When the boy's provocative acts were inhibited, there
emerged some distinctly magically tinged and actually near-delusional

material. Had these ominous hints been permitted to pass uninterpreted, instead of being firmly brought down to earth and linked up with the real hater and with the real object of this hate, this episode might well have been the acorn from which the mighty oak of a full-fledged delusional system could have grown in due time. When the boy was driven back from his "first line of defenses," composed of neurotically irritating behavior, he fell back upon his "second line of defenses," made up of delusional and magical ideas. However, when this second line too fell and the touch of reality deflated the delusions, there emerged into the open a badly frightened and unhappy little boy, who, unable to control himself, was asking for helpful discipline.

How such pseudo provocativeness can justify anger toward the patient, and even outright physical punishment, is a complete mystery to the writer.

The crux of the whole matter is the emotional spuriousness of all purely negative forms of leniency, and even of certain equally spurious positive-seeming "broad-minded" acts. The example which most readily comes to mind is that certain "modern" parents parade around in front of their children in the nude—i.e., undressed, in the negative sense—"so as to teach them not to be ashamed of their bodies." This "didactic nudity" is actually an unconscious and seductive acting out of counteroedipal impulses, which we analyzed elsewhere in some detail (57) and held to be the effective causes of the rise, and especially of the intensity, of the Oedipus complex. That, however, is merely an aside. The point to be stressed is that such didactic undressing is psychologically completely different from the nonpurposive, unself-conscious, and routine nudity of a customarily naked Kwoma parent (230) and therefore has radically different effects upon the child. This example is paradigmatic of all misguided forms of basically irrational, but formally well rationalized, pseudo leniency or "permissiveness."

An equally important point, to be discussed in detail in Part

Five, is the basic and tenacious, though nowadays often latent, belief of Western adults that "when the chips are down" the child has to obey the adult, and that it can be made to obey. In a society where the punishment of children is socially tolerated, and is highly approved in "spare the rod, spoil the child" circles, even the most "modern" parent knows that, because of his superior physical strength and his capacity to intimidate the child psychologically and also because he has the backing of society—which he would not enjoy in an anti-punitively oriented primitive group—it is he who has the last trump, if he but chooses to play it. The situation is highly reminiscent of the nineteenth-century colonizer's well-known motto about savages:

> Whatever happens, we have got
> The Gatling gun—and they have not!

In other words, it is one thing to inhibit and to renounce, for intellectual reasons, the impulse and the "right" to spank the child, and quite another matter truly not to take blind obedience for granted, and to know that spanking does not represent a socially recognized right but a socially penalized form of bad manners or sin.[25]

LENIENCY AND SOCIAL PRACTICE

The final point to be made is that "lenient" education achieves its maximal effectiveness only if the educational techniques of a given set of parents are congruent with the social practices prevailing in that group. Otherwise they simply create confusion and emotional conflicts in the child. A Mohave and a modern example will show this:

Case 40: Acculturation Pressures vs. Primitive Leniency

A Mohave boy of seven contracted gonorrhea by cohabiting with a girl the same age. Since, in Mohave society, cohabitation between chil-

[25] A journalistic traveler, Richard Katz (*134*), who kept his eyes wide open, reports that if the Balinese mother loses her temper and hits her child the whole village runs to the sanctuary and performs atonement ceremonies to conciliate the soul of the offended child. Cf. also Case 57.

dren is taken for granted even today, this act would not have been penalized even if it had become known to the tribe. However, the fact that this boy contracted a venereal disease caused the matter to come to the attention also of the Reservation authorities, who scolded, reprimanded, and ridiculed the boy but left the "poor girl," who was both the seductress and the source of the infection, unpunished. As a result of these humiliations, the boy became so neurotic that, when the writer asked his Mohave friends to steer him to neurotic children whom he could interview, this boy was among the first to be mentioned.

Case 41: Modern Parents and Conservative Neighbors

A leniently and "progressively" educated girl of ten, living in a somewhat stodgy neighborhood, engaged in relatively innocent sex play with a boy her own age. When the matter became known, the neighbors were so critical of the girl's "depravity" that, all of a sudden, this previously well-adjusted child became quite neurotic.

In order to understand these two incidents, we must once more recall our thesis that an event is traumatic only in so far as it represents a unique, "discriminatory," and culturally deviant experience. In so far, then, as even an emotionally authentic progressive or lenient education represents a socially exceptional experience, causing the spontaneous child to be ostracized in school and in the neighborhood, such an education is traumatic in our society (50, 82). We hardly need to add that if, in addition to this, parental leniency is emotionally spurious, the trauma of such an exceptional upbringing is magnified many times. Thus, there are recurrent stories about unspanked children, who reportedly ask for a spanking, if such a practice is routine for other boys belonging to that group.[26] How true such stories are is a question we cannot answer.

[26] Kipling never forgot—cf. his *The Light that Failed*—the brutal beatings he had received in a boarding school. Yet, in *Stalky and Co.* he rather glorifies canings. He suggests that the boys admired the skill and severity of the just and wise headmaster's canings and felt proud of their ability to endure them without crying. If there is any truth to this fictional account, we may be sure that these boys' attitude was determined by the fact that canings were routine events in the "type biography" of any English public (i.e., private) school boy, who could therefore accept them, and could even glory in them, as long as he felt the punishment to be just. Cf. also the traditional pride of the Marine Corps in its tough top sergeants.

They do, however, reflect at least certain parental attitudes, since, particularly if such tales are true, they must be based upon the reports of "modern" parents, who "control themselves" and do not spank their children. If this inference is correct, it implies the existence of a secondary parental hostility, generated by the inhibition of the primary hostile impulse to lash out at the disobedient or troublesome "brat." One also wonders to just how much ostentatiously non-punitive but deviously sadistic treatment such unspanked "brats" are actually subjected.

In conclusion, we wish to specify that nothing said hereinbefore should be interpreted as a defense of spanking or, indeed, of punishment—as distinct from discipline—of any kind whatsoever. We are firmly convinced that, when a child becomes so troublesome that it simply "has to be spanked" or punished, the persons who really deserve punishment are the parents, because, by defaulting on discipline, they allowed things to get so far out of hand as to make such a brutal solution "necessary."[27]

It is therefore our thesis that, where there is adequate ego-expanding discipline, ego-constricting punishment is never necessary.[28]

[27] It is reliably reported that, when a New York Chinatown boy comes to the attention of the juvenile court, the Chinese community blames his parents for their educational derelictions, apparently on the principle that, since "a stitch in time saves nine," it was up to the parents not to let the situation deteriorate to this point. While due allowance must be made for the self-protective urge of a minority group—also noticeable in the case of the Jews, who created excellent facilities for the nonpublic treatment of Jewish juvenile delinquents—it is quite certain that this group indictment of Chinese parents, rather than of delinquent Chinese sons, reflects a healthy educational philosophy. Cf. also the fact that the recent Philadelphia curfew for adolescents is enforced by fining the parents of the violators.

[28] The conclusions of this chapter seem to be at variance with the views expressed in Dr. Richard L. Jenkins' excellent article on discipline (125). We feel, however, that these differences are more apparent than real and seem to concern only the precise meaning which one should assign to the term "punishment." The real similarity between the two points of view is proved by a letter from Dr. Jenkins, in which this authority affirms that "punishment alone cannot socialize." This is practically the central thesis of the present chapter.

....

Self-Appraisal and Protective Grouping

THE NORMAL AS A PROBLEM FOR THE ABNORMAL

Implicitly or explicitly, resentfully or objectively, vindictively or compassionately, everyone seems to take it for granted that the problems which the defective and the warped create for society are the real crux of the whole matter. The obvious fact that we, the "normals," and our society may represent an even more serious and even more insoluble problem for the deviant seldom enters our minds—at least not in this explicit form. Yet the whole concept of milieu therapy is based on an at least latent understanding of this fact.

We do not speak here only of the unbearable strain which we routinely place on some persons—such as oppressed minorities or soldiers kept in the firing line until they "crack up"—for social reasons, both good and bad, nor of the fact that it is literally possible for one person to drive another to suicide[1] or into a psychosis. In such cases our responsibility for the illness—and hence for the treatment of our fellow men—is clear. As Dr. R. G. Hoskins expressed it: "By society they were broken, by society they must be healed."[2] The point we seek to stress is that the routine of normal

---

[1] Even primitives are aware of this. The Sedang Moi of Indo-China impose a heavy fine on the person whose "oppressive actions" drive another human being to suicide.

[2] Remarks made during a staff research conference at Worcester State Hospital.

society may, in itself, create nearly insuperable difficulties for the defective or for the warped individual. A simple analogy will prove this point. Most of us find the size of our furniture "just right" and therefore we do not stop to think that a dwarf finds it hard to seat himself comfortably in one of our chairs or to handle knives and forks fashioned for persons of normal size. Likewise, an extremely tall person seldom gets a good night's sleep in hotel beds built for average persons and, in addition, must devote an unusually high percentage of his income to buying shoes and clothes, since they have to be custom-made to fit his unusual needs. Last, but not least, street signs are often almost illegible for drivers whose defective eyesight cannot be corrected to 20:20. In simplest terms, it is inconvenient, difficult, time-consuming, and expensive to be even physically non-average. These observations suggest that, since society is actually more "mental" than "physical" in its nature and operations, psychological handicaps or distortions impose an even greater burden on the individual than do physically exceptional traits. For example, the deviant, whose neurosis diminishes his earning capacity, is obliged to pay for a necessarily expensive psychotherapy, so that—to put it colloquially—he "gets it in the neck, both coming and going."

THE SENSE OF FAILURE

The defective or warped person is often painfully conscious of the difficulties created by the fact that he must live in society and compete with "normals." He adopts the criteria of success and the level of aspiration of the more fortunate "normal" person and therefore becomes quite anxious and imbued with a sense of failure when he is obliged to face his inability to live up to these standards and to attain these objectives. In fact, this mechanism is present also in members of oppressed minorities.

For example, it is commonly held that successful dark-skinned Negroes marry girls with lighter skins because a light skin enjoys a great deal of social prestige. While this explanation is certainly correct, it is also quite incomplete. It fails to take into consideration the fact that the systematic rewarding of a physical type which approximates the "Caucasian" standard automatically causes that type to be defined as "beautiful." Thus, conversations with numerous Negro students and physicians convinced the writer that the average American Negro is today almost unable to appreciate the beauty of a dark-skinned girl of a harmoniously African type. The glamour girls portrayed in the fashion plates of Negro periodicals are therefore invariably of the quasi-European and not of the African type. Exactly the same considerations apply to the observation that, in America at least, *"Gentlemen Prefer Blondes."* In England, where blondness is not automatically associated with the physical appearance of the dominant class,[3] it is not automatically also one of the major criteria of beauty. By contrast, since most of the blond women in early nineteenth-century America belonged to the dominant Anglo-Saxon stock, blondness became a characteristic attribute of beauty in America: among dark-haired immigrants, because it suggested prestige-laden Anglo-Saxon origins and among the original English settlers because it differentiated them from immigrant "trash." Certain newspaper practices reveal the extent to which we are ready to infer that a blonde is necessarily also attractive. Headlines—whose purpose it is to stimulate the reader's interest—often read "Blonde is slain," the implication being that the victim, whose picture on another page may reveal her to be barely average in looks, was beautiful. By contrast, the writer has yet to see a headline specifying that the slain woman was a brunette.

It is, of course, legitimate to ask whether a system which puts a

[3] In fact, after 1066 A.D., flaxen blondness was a trait associated with the conquered Saxons, rather than with the often red-haired Norman conquerors. Today the "typical English beauty" is a girl whose blond hair and complexion are derived from her Saxon forebears, while her tall, willowy stature and high-nosed "aristocratic" profile are indicative of Norman ancestry.

premium on certain nonfunctional qualities is actually not "kinder" than one in which prestige is automatically a reward for performance. The writer is indebted to Professor Helmut Schoeck —who is at present preparing a major study on the social psychology of envy—for the suggestion that a person who fails because he belongs to a handicapped minority may suffer less damage to his ego than does a person who has to admit that he failed simply because of his own shortcomings. In our view, this thesis is untenable even on methodological grounds, since it is based exclusively on the study of a single attitude or function: envy. Man's personality is so complex that whereas the study of a single function is both legitimate and necessary, it is impossible to draw from it valid conclusions about the functioning of the personality as a whole.[4] On the contrary, we hold that the sense of failure experienced by the ineffectual person, who comes to realize that he "simply hasn't got what it takes," wreaks less psychological havoc than does the artificial handicapping of inherently able persons who are prevented by social pressures from achieving true self-realization (humanization). The anxieties of the inherently ineffectual person can usually be alleviated by placing him in an environment where he does not have to compete with more talented individuals. This is the fundamental principle on which all milieu therapy is based. By contrast, the artificial handicapping of the gifted person often causes almost irreparable psychiatric damage (50, 68). The latter policy is also far more harmful to society as a whole, partly because it deprives society of the best contributions which such persons could make to its advancement and partly because it is even politically dangerous to drive large groups of talented and resourceful persons into systematic opposition.

Be that as it may, it is quite certain that the defective or warped person is often painfully aware of the difficulties, disappointments,

---

[4] This stricture is also applicable to many "experimental" studies of the validity of psychoanalysis, many of which were summarized by Sears (196).

and humiliations resulting from the fact that he has to live among normals, in a society intended for normal, or at least for adequately adjusted, persons.

Case 42: The Awareness of One's Handicaps

In a moment of intense negative transference, a young epileptic girl with borderline intelligence and moderately though noticeably crippled by spasticity, burst out angrily: "Do you want me to tell you how much I really hate the school? I hate it so much that I am doing all I can to spend the summer with my family, even though I will have to accompany them to the beach, where everyone will see what I look like—what I am!" Then she burst into tears.

This girl's anxiety and humiliation over her crippled condition were the emotions she most consistently sought to deal with by means of repression, suppression, and denial, particularly since—for reasons which cannot be discussed here—they also motivated a great deal of anxiety-arousing hostility. Her suppression of these humiliating thoughts was so systematic that even when the therapist made a direct reference to her condition only very moderately worded and relatively "objective" remarks could be elicited from her regarding this matter. Only in a moment of blind rage, when her limited ego resources were wholly absorbed by the attempt to keep her rage within manageable limits—not an easy task for a girl who saw herself as a potentially terribly destructive person—could she voice both this grievance against life and against normals (one of whom was actually responsible for her condition) and also the agonizing problem which the very existence of normals represented for her.

PROTECTIVE AVERAGENESS

The fact is that the exceptional person—be he exceptional in the positive or negative sense—experiences considerable anxiety over his "apartness." Indeed, it is often highly traumatic to be denied the comforting shelter of "homonomy" in Angyal's sense (3); of conformity, anonymity, homogeneity, and "social invisi-

bility"[5] or at least inconspicuousness. How great this need for
social invisibility really is, and how deeply it affects the behavior
pattern of all men, is seldom adequately recognized and will therefore be illustrated by a few examples:

1. Benjamin Disraeli's flamboyantly brilliant maiden speech
in the House of Parliament was "hooted down" in a manner which
the "Mother of Parliaments" has seldom witnessed before or since.
Hurt to the core, Disraeli thereupon embarked upon a systematic
self-protective program of dull respectability. He succeeded so
well that some years later a fellow Member of Parliament, who
was one of his friends and well-wishers, mentioned to him that a
newly elected country squire of impeccable mediocrity remarked
that Mr. Disraeli was no doubt a most estimable person, albeit
not a particularly brilliant one. On hearing this, Disraeli reportedly heaved a sigh of relief and exclaimed: "At last I have arrived!" (*164*)

2. An eminent British scholar showed one of his most brilliant
American graduate students a letter of recommendation which he
had just written on his behalf. To his great surprise, the younger
man begged him not to refer to him as a "genius," because he felt
certain that this would prevent him from getting the position for
which he had applied.

3. La Fontaine wrote: *Pour vivre heureux, vivons cachés.* (In
order to live happily, we must live in concealment.)

4. Benedict (*14*) and others strongly underscored the Pueblo
Indian's reluctance to "shine" in any way, or to rise above his fellows, lest he be destroyed by envious witches.

Many a primitive's reluctance to have his real—as distinct from
his public—name become known, or to introduce himself by name
to someone new, is paralleled in our society by the practice of
carrying on a long and quite personal conversation with a stranger

[5] As used here, this term denotes the opposite of what sociologists call "social
visibility" and signifies the absence of an objectionable (e.g., skin disease) or of an
arbitrarily penalized (skin color) conspicuousness.

on the train, without introducing oneself. In addition to a number of obvious motives, this practice is also an attempt to cling as long as possible to the protective mask of anonymity and nonspecificity, i.e., to a social façade which provides no toehold for individual- ized hostility—for a "bullet which has our name on it." Once a person's name is known, so that he is uniquely identified, hostility —perhaps in the form of witchcraft—can be focused on him per- sonally.[6]

Society itself is aware of this function of anonymity, which all men both dread and crave, and is therefore highly suspicious of extremes of "social invisibility."[7] In fact, an exaggerated incon- spicuousness practically amounts to extreme conspicuousness. The writer was reliably told that a middle-aged and obviously pros- perous businessman whose name was something like John Smith had had several grotesque misadventures when he tried to register with his young and flashy-looking wife at staid hotels; the room clerks assumed that he was using a phony name while spending a week end with a chorus girl. Conversely, society tends to be sus- picious also of extreme forms of self-identification. Thus, when a somewhat cynical and tactless psychologist was introduced to a very attractive actress, whose name was both unusual and eupho- nious, he asked her point blank whether this was her real name or simply a "stage name."

Now, it is obvious that the conspicuously abnormal person is denied that sheltering anonymity which average appearance and average behavior provide. Much of his energy and thought is therefore absorbed by the hopeless task of masking his "objec- tionable" uniqueness and deviancy, which impair his social eligi- bility as well as his sex appeal. The great industry of cosmetology

[6] It is a common theme in folklore that demons must obey anyone who knows their name.

[7] In a nineteenth-century French novel of adventure a fugitive manages to cross a city where everyone is looking for him by riding in a highly conspicuous carriage, whose very splendor diverts attention from the person riding in it.

caters extensively to persons with such problems: Short men can buy "elevator shoes," tall girls are taught to walk with stooped shoulders and bent knees, flat-chested girls wear pneumatic "falsies," bald men buy toupees, the "ugly duckling" undergoes painful and expensive plastic surgery, neurotics make desperate attempts to conceal their peculiarities under a mask of compulsive and often excessive "normality" (*183*), and the like.[8]

Such maneuvers are psychologically often far from harmless. As we state in Chapter 4, a painful awareness of one's defect can serve to mask an underlying schizophrenia, which erupts as soon as the defect is corrected. This, however, is a point which need not preoccupy us further in the present context.

THE HANDICAPS OF BEING A CHILD

Suffice it to say that problems of this kind arise even in the course of normal development. For example, during the stage of "delegated omnipotence," the child experiences all of its "limitations" (defined in terms of adult standards) in an agonizingly painful manner. The prototypes of this sense of inadequacy and of apartness are the small boy's sense of humiliation over the size of his immature penis and the little girl's distress over her lack of a penis. We need not decide here whether these specific feelings of sexual inadequacy tend to trigger the child's general sense of inadequacy or whether its painful feeling of general immaturity expresses itself most consistently, and with cumulative intensity, in the "small penis" or "female castration" complex. While the former is the more generally accepted interpretation, the latter cannot be discarded a priori, without further study. Indeed, at this particular moment of its development the child begins to form true object relations, with complete instead of only with partial

[8] The writer is indebted to Dr. R. L. Jenkins for the suggestion that, on the basis of the preceding considerations, men should be especially sensitive to some partial lack, women chiefly to a total lack of some quality. The subject is insufficiently explored to enable one to decide whether such a difference actually exists and can be generalized.

objects,[9] and formulates these new relationships in predominantly sexual (oedipal) terms. Hence, the child's preoccupation with its sexual inadequacy may be a survival of its earlier tendency to define human beings as partial objects only. Although this problem is of considerable theoretical interest, we mention it only in passing, since our sole purpose at this juncture is to stress the child's anxiety over all of its limitations, which it defines in terms of adult standards, i.e., in terms of the standards of those who, ultimately, determine its life and fate.

THE GAP BETWEEN TEACHER AND PUPIL

As we see it, education must prevent the gap between teacher and pupil from becoming so great as to discourage the child altogether. At the same time, one must socialize, ethnicize, and above all humanize the child by giving it a chance to identify with a more mature individual. Primitives discovered along ago that these two requirements were by no means irreconcilable. As stated in Chapter 9, they seem to have hit upon the solution of letting their children be educated chiefly in and by a children's group, which contains not only, let us say, five- and six-year-olds but also some seven- or eight-year-old children. The latter, functioning on a slightly higher level than the rest, can educate the younger children, without, however, overwhelming and discouraging them by a display of so superior a performance that the younger ones cannot hope to match it. In fact, in this system even children of the same age educate each other. Each child has certain special aptitudes or picks up odds and ends of information which the other children do not possess. Hence, at certain times, each child has a chance to function as the teacher of its group, only to resume its place among the taught when another child has something new

[9] The term "partial object" denotes, roughly speaking, the tendency to view a human being as intended for one purpose only. To the small child, the mother is simply a milk-giving breast, just as for a factory manager a worker is simply a pair of hands. (Cf. the expression: "all hands.")

to contribute to the education of the group as a whole. Furthermore, since these new skills are usually well within the limits of the average child's abilities, learning takes place without an excessive number of humiliating failures of a type which leave the child who failed with a sense of inferiority and helplessness.[10] Nor is that all. This educational policy affords almost every child the opportunity to cope with the "insult" of having just learned something from a senior whose skills are vastly superior to its own. The child masters this ego injury by identifying with the "aggressor" teacher, not only by actually performing the newly learned operation, but—what is even better—also by imparting this skill to its peers or slightly younger playmates.[11] In other words, each child in turn is given an opportunity to assume an adult role, both as a person who has a given skill and as a person who teaches this skill to others. This gradual downward "seepage" of information, from one age class to the next younger age class, combined with the fact that each child functions alternatingly as teacher and as pupil within its own group, may explain that "continuity in cultural conditioning" which Benedict (15) rightly considers characteristic of primitive society.

SEX INSTRUCTION

It is almost impossible to overrate the importance of this educational device. One of its paradigms is the transmission of sexual knowledge through a series of graduated and overlapping age brackets, instead of directly from adults to children, as is the case in formal "sex instruction." The futility of the latter type of "sexual enlightenment" was recognized by Freud, who emphasized

---

[10] A Veterans Administration psychologist, Dr. Henry Peters, is at present developing a technique of rehabilitating schizophrenics by making them solve graduated problems, partly alone and partly in collaboration with another patient, and never permitting them to fail—even if this requires guidance and direct help from the therapist. So far, the results of this study appear to be quite encouraging.

[11] Similarly, a boy who has just been to the dentist may master this trauma by "playing dentist" with one of his younger siblings.

that children tend to re-repress the information which they obtain in this manner (90). By contrast, among the Mohave Indians (49), as well as among the Sedang Moi, where even actual coital techniques "trickle down" to the youngest generation through a series of sex experiences in which the boundaries between neighboring age groups are repeatedly crossed, children do not re-repress the sex information which they obtain. Parents in our own society are often greatly vexed when the child, after being given a complete course of instruction about birds and bees and the seed daddy planted in mother's body, returns time and again to this topic, asking the same questions over and over again. The parents interpret this as "abnormal curiosity," not realizing that the child actually re-repressed ("forgot") the information which it had received from them.

This phenomenon stands in need of some explanation. There are several reasons why the child is unable to remember the details of the sexual enlightenment which its parents, or some other adult parental figures, provide.

1. The primitive child who gives sexual information to another child is not separated from the latter by the incest barrier and can therefore function both as an instructor in theory and as a partner in practice. This is something which parents cannot do and—as we shall see in a moment—should not even try to do.

2. Even the most objective type of sex instruction is stimulating. The child who instructs another child can, by engaging in childish sex play, gratify some of the desires which the instruction aroused. The parents cannot do this.

3. Due to the incest taboo, which is internalized quite early in life, the sexual instruction given by the parent not only stimulates oedipal desires but also arouses intense oedipal anxieties and guilt feelings.

4. The child is very concretistic in its outlook. It is therefore inclined to view even the most objectively worded parental sex in-

struction as a "revelation" about the parent's own sex life. Since the child is extremely curious about the intimate relations obtaining between its parents and also feels quite guilty about its "peeping" impulses, these supposed "revelations" tend to excite it, and to make it also quite anxious.

5. The child who is instructed by another child is not humiliated by the realization that his "teacher" is much more mature than he is. By contrast, the child who is instructed by an adult experiences an intense sense of failure when it contrasts its own immaturity with the fully developed sexual potentialities of its adult teacher.

In brief, no matter how formal, calm, objective, and scientific the sexual information provided by a parental figure may be, the child tends to experience it as a kind of "seduction," which elicits both ungratifiable oedipal desires and intense oedipal guilt and anxiety. Since the child's ego is not yet sufficiently developed to master this excitement, and the guilt feelings which it arouses, in a mature manner, or, perhaps, even by neurotically isolating the affect aroused by sex instruction from the objective content of that instruction, it deals with its difficulties by simply repressing both. When it returns two weeks later to the same topic, it is not, as parents sometimes assume, "putting on an act" in order to gratify "an unhealthy curiosity." It has truly forgotten (repressed) everything it had been told.

Needless to say, the preceding remarks do not imply that children should be denied sexual information. We simply suggest that the information should "trickle down" to the child through its older playmates. The parents themselves need do nothing more than display a mature, healthy, calm, and poised attitude toward sex, which is neither neurotically punitive nor neurotically seductive. Otherwise stated, actual sex instruction should be provided by older children, while the parents should teach the child a sane attitude toward sex. The latter task is either exceedingly simple or impossibly difficult, depending on whether or not the parents love each other in a mature way. The best way of providing a child with a healthy education in sexual attitudes is to allow it to grow up in a home in which the depth, tenderness, and meaningfulness of the sexual love between the parents pervades the whole atmosphere of the home. Indeed, only parents who love each other can love their children without being either seductive or punitive, and only they can impart to them a mature attitude toward sex. This, of course, is contingent on the parents' own emotional maturity, for which no reading of books about the sexual enlightenment of children and no following of the family psychiatrist's advice can provide a real substitute.

It is unfortunately true that, in rare instances, emotionally ill parents or other adults actually seduce the child while pretending to "enlighten" it (133). In such cases the child does not seem to repress the information it has obtained and may even show a—somewhat superficial—precocious maturity and poise (13). Yet, such a seduction by adults inevitably leads to neurosis in later life, since it cannot help the child to avoid the panicky realization that it is sexually inferior to its adult partner.[12] Of course, such feelings of inadequacy also arise in the course of the so-called "normal" developmental neuroses,[13] but they can usually be overcome without psychiatric help, and leave no permanent scars on the personality.

[12] The paradigm of this "panic of inadequacy" is the small boy's realization that he cannot possibly satisfy his mother and the small girl's fear that she would be torn apart by the "gigantic" organ of the father.

[13] Developmental neuroses, such as minor and transitory phobias, occur in almost all children. They are the manifestations of the child's first and somewhat ineffectual attempts to master, with its limited ego resources, the various instinctual conflicts which arise in the course of its maturation as an organism. If misguided external pressures do not exacerbate these normal conflicts, developmental neuroses are usually "outgrown" without psychiatric help, and solely as a result of the gradual and spontaneous (developmental) increase in the child's ego strength. By contrast, where external pressures exacerbate these conflicts and the parents fail to foster the development of the child's ego, the developmental neurosis cannot be "outgrown." It becomes stabilized and requires psychiatric help (55).

SHARED MISFORTUNE AS PROTECTION

We dwelled at some length on the dynamics of primitive education, and especially of primitive sex education, which in many ways is paradigmatic of all learning. We did so in the hope that it would help us to understand and to justify the milieu therapeutic educational device of forming units and/or classes in which no child is hopelessly and humiliatingly outdistanced by the others. This way of grouping children encourages the individual child not to "throw in the towel" and partly alleviates, at least while the child remains in that therapeutic setting, those of the child's anxieties which have at their root the painful realization of its limitations. Students living in such a therapeutic school are often keenly aware of this fact.

Case 43: An Epileptic Among Epileptics

"In the day school I used to attend I was the only child who had seizures. My spells frightened the other children and caused them to make fun of me. I also had a terrible time keeping up with my studies. Here it is different. There are several other children in my unit who also have such spells. They know what it is like and are therefore sympathetic and helpful. When I have a spell, they don't run away and leave me. They grab me, so that I will not fall and hurt myself, and they take care of me."

In some instances handicapped students unwittingly reveal the extent to which the experience of "shared misfortune" reassures them, even as they seem to rage at another child who is more handicapped than they are.

Case 44: Insight Through Shared Misfortune

I wish they would move Millie to another unit. I hate her. It scares me half to death when she starts having a spell. She yells and she screams and she throws things . . . and then she has a spell. It is terrible. (Therapist: And it frightens you to realize that when you have a spell, you look somewhat the way she does.) That is part of it, though my spells are not as bad as hers. What really scares me is that her having a spell may cause me to have a spell too. I try to hold on as hard as I can. (Therapist: Well, at least you are beginning to realize that it is partly your own frame of mind which triggers off your spells and that you have some control over them.) It sure makes me try hard! (Seems relieved.)

In some instances even the neurotic but intellectually normal student, newly enrolled in a therapeutic school, experiences such relief over not being any longer a person isolated from others by his emotional handicaps that he may grossly overestimate his classmates:

Case 45: Therapeutic Effects of Adjustment to One's Peers

"This is a wonderful place, and the kids are marvellous. They are friendly and nice and smart. I already made many friends among them. I'll have a wonderful time here. The girls are not as stuck up as they were in high school, in my home town. They act friendly and are willing to date you steadily."

Although such extremes of enthusiasm are certainly unrealistic, they do reflect the tremendous relief experienced by this shy and inhibited adolescent when he joined a group of youngsters who—having troubles of their own—did not behave as haughtily toward another neurotic as do normal children in regular high schools. This in itself is a therapeutically extremely valuable aspect of residential schools for exceptional children.

The preceding data indicate the extent to which the child who lives in a therapeutic milieu with children whose misfortunes resemble its own finds security and strength in the realization that it is not a unique, monstrous outcast, nor a hopelessly depraved being, nor the only victim of a cruel fate.[14]

---

[14] Society itself is keenly aware of the soothing effects of shared misfortune. The adage "Misery loves company" expresses an ancient and basic psychological truth, which may even be deliberately exploited by persons capable of imposing their misfortunes on others. Thus, when a neurotic American couple lost a child through

In brief, the observable, and manifestly distressing, self-definition of the "abnormal" person can be alleviated by a planned "protective grouping" of those who share the same misfortune.[15] Hence it is obviously a powerful milieu therapeutic device to group into relatively homogeneous units and classes children with relatively comparable limitations.

MINOR DRAWBACKS OF PROTECTIVE GROUPING

Since there are no "perfect solutions" known to man, we must now seek to investigate also some of the drawbacks of "protective grouping."

LIVING WITH OTHER DISTURBED PERSONS

The most important of these is the fact that the "exceptional" child has to live in the midst of disturbances created by others,

---

death, the parents imposed quite unreasonable restrictions upon their surviving children, and when a relative remonstrated with them on this score, they replied: "Their sibling just died—let them suffer too!" This last remark sheds a great deal of light upon some of the real purposes of funeral mutilations and funeral sacrifices. These rites represent a kind of symbolic or partial death, whose purpose it is to appease the inferential resentment of the person who just died over the fact that others are still alive. Otherwise stated, the mourners impute a kind of "mourning mechanism in reverse" to the dead. The self-pity and resentfulness of Achilles in the underworld (cf. Homer's *Odyssey*, Book XI) is a perfect illustration of this mechanism. The Greek belief that the dead live in a kind of emotional void is thus actually a projection upon the dead of the mourner's own feeling of "being deserted." This is not a mere supposition. The Hopi mourners sometimes slap the corpse, and accuse it of having died solely in order to grieve its relatives (*136*). The same spitefulness toward the dead is also manifest in Mohave funeral rites (*34*). In brief, the mourners derive some satisfaction from imputing to the dead their own state of mind. The mourner's demand for compassion, implemented by the custom of condolences (= shared pain), reflects his need to make others share, or profess to share, his sorrow. This need is sometimes quite intense. The writer knew personally a rather egotistical European woman who, on being widowed, dragged her voluminous widow's weeds all over town, visiting even persons she was barely acquainted with, in order to cast a pall of gloom over every household. Queen Kauna of Nukuoro went to even greater extremes. When she lost her son, she ordered all male children on the island slain, so as to force their mothers to share her grief. Then, still not satisfied, she ordered all pregnant women to abort (*76*). Even animals may be made to "share each other's misfortunes" (*150*).

[15] A whole series of such "shared misfortune" clubs exist: Alcoholics Anonymous, Lonely Hearts clubs, clubs for old people, clubs for unusually tall persons, "We, the Blind," etc.

who are as sick as he. (Cf. Case 44, above). The same is true, of course, also of adult mental patients, who often feel that the constant commotion in some closed ward "would drive anyone crazy." A recovered schizophrenic once told the writer that such disturbances are particularly traumatic for the schizophrenic patient, since he understands, and empathizes with, the unconscious meaning of the "ravings" of other temporarily disturbed patients only too well and therefore feels tempted to "let go" in a similar manner.

Even the average normal person tends to be afraid that close contact with "lunatics" may drive him "mad,"[16] presumably because, as Ferenczi put it, everyone's unconscious understands everyone else's unconscious perfectly.[17] This leads to the inference that the individual's ordinary capacity to function on a conscious ego level actually presupposes a "deliberate" self-protective inhibition of one's "third ear" (T. Reik) or capacity to understand the unconscious of others. We hasten to add, however, that this statement is not meant to lend support to the thesis (100) that ego resistances to the understanding of unconscious material necessarily imply a developmental suppression of alleged "archaic psi-functions" in modern, reality-oriented man.

"Exceptional" children also experience such difficulties; witness, for example, the ease with which one child's convulsive seizure may trigger similar attacks in several others, or the manner in which one child's temper tantrum or exhibitionistic weeping releases similar behavior in others. Such incidents, as even defective children realize (cf. Case 44, above) are traumatic indeed, not only because the other child's behavior is felt to be inherently

[16] Some years ago the writer was asked by an anthropologist planning to go on a somewhat hazardous anthropological expedition to show him classical examples of the major psychoses, so as to enable him to recognize them should he meet with them in the field. However, when he reached the door of a very disturbed ward and heard the shrieks and the commotion, he refused to go in. Yet this man displayed real courage in the field and subsequently proved his psychological sensitiveness by publishing a valuable study on problems of culture and personality.

[17] Most psychoanalysts, but not all psychiatrists, will probably agree with Ferenczi on this point.

threatening, disturbing, and seductive, but partly also because it is a tangible reminder of one's own abnormality.

Case 46: The Handicaps of Others Used as Alibis

An adolescent girl, diagnosed as a severe character disorder, spent an unduly large part of her early therapy sessions ranting and raving about the other adolescents in her unit, or else discussing their problems instead of her own. Although this preoccupation was interpreted to her as a resistance and as an evasion, it did not cease until it was also pointed out to her that she was particularly disturbed by the behavior of those adolescents whose tantrums fascinated her because they resembled her own. The therapist then added that her discussions of the misdeeds of others implied: "My own behavior is made less objectionable by the fact that others also behave in this manner." In support of this interpretation he then cited to her the case of an adult patient who invariably prefaced all accounts of his own "iniquities" with a long list of similar "wrongs" perpetrated by others, in order to persuade both himself and his analyst that he was neither a monster nor an "exception."

The interpretation that she used the "sins" of others to excuse her own was at first rejected out of hand. Gradually, however, an accumulation of confirmatory data led her to understand its relevance and induced her to say that she had resolved to mend her ways. "When I see another kid have a tantrum, I don't want to have to think that I must look just like he does, when I throw a tantrum."

This case indicates that identification with other disturbed persons can have definitely therapeutic effects. In fact, even though a patient's preoccupation with the problems of another patient can be quite a nuisance at times, it may, in a non-paranoid youngster, represent a first attempt to "take a distance" from oneself and to evaluate one's behavior objectively. The interpretation to be offered when complaints against other children become unduly frequent is: "You apparently see yourself in them."

Of course, the children themselves seldom realize how revealing their preoccupation or identification with the problems of other children actually is.[18] Child psychiatrists and educational therapists working in special schools are seldom disturbed by the fact that the children who are brought to the therapy building in a bus sometimes "trade dreams" en route, in the hope of deceiving their therapists. It is perfectly possible to draw correct inferences from such "borrowed dreams," since not the manifest content of the dream itself but the child's associations to the borrowed dream are the data on which the interpretations are ultimately based.

Case 47: Interpreting a Borrowed Dream

A youngster once reported that he had forgotten the dream he had had the night before, adding, however, that he recalled a dream his girl friend had told him. He was quite dismayed when the analyst asked him to narrate this latter dream and to produce associations to it. Not at all surprisingly—at least for the psychoanalyst—these associations to a borrowed dream yielded important, and therapeutically effective, new insights into the patient's own problems. The fact that he did not feel "responsible" for another person's dreams apparently facilitated the production of meaningful associations.

EXTRUSION FROM THE HOME

The second drawback to be considered here is that, in order to live with its peers in a protective group, the child must first be removed from its home and then enrolled in a therapeutic residential school. In order to understand the psychological significance of this transfer, we must briefly explain the meaning of "trauma." In our opinion a painful experience which is a routine occurrence in the lives of most children belonging to a given group is not a trauma, because it leads to the formation of the national or class character through the use of "ready-made" cultural devices as defenses against the anxiety which that painful incident

---

[18] The same is true of adult patients. For example, in the case of the patient who habitually prefaced accounts of his own misdeeds with complaints against others, it was almost always possible to predict what he would reveal about himself when he finally got around to it.

elicits. By contrast, a painful experience which is not typical for children of a given group has to be viewed as a genuine trauma, leading to neuroses, because, since there are no ready-made cultural devices for dealing with it, the child has to improvise its own defenses against the anxiety which such atypical experiences mobilize. In order to grasp this point, we have only to imagine how traumatic it would be for an American adolescent to be circumcised and subincised and also to have his front teeth knocked out, and how neurotic he would become as a result of these operations, and then remember that in central Australia these painful experiences only lead to national character formation, because the alleged "trauma" is both expected and buffered by a set of culturally provided rewards and defenses.[19]

In brief, one reason atypical experiences are traumatic is that they cause the child who is subjected to some unusual treatment to feel "set apart" from its fellows and unjustly discriminated against by fate.

Case 48: The Sense of Apartness

A European of gentile extraction had been circumcised at the insistence of his "progressive" father, a physician, even though in Europe gentile boys are not circumcised as a rule. As a result, he felt "mutilated" and "set apart" from others—and also fearful of being mistaken for a Jew. Hence, he would never allow another man to get a glimpse of his penis. However, when he came to America and discovered that most men in this country are circumcised, he promptly lost his humiliating sense of "apartness" and no longer found it difficult to undress in front of other men. In this connection one is readily reminded of Spock's (207) and Bettelheim's (17) finding that uncircumcised American boys often insistently demand to be circumcised, so as to be like the other boys.[20]

---

[19] This view is compatible both with Róheim's (190) and with Kardiner's (131, 132) theories of national character.

[20] The fact that we cite these factually correct data does not imply in the least that we concur with either Spock's advocacy of circumcision or Bettelheim's depth

The preceding considerations suggest that the transfer of the exceptional child to a residential therapeutic school is likely to be truly traumatic only if children of the same social group or neighborhood are not usually sent to boarding schools.

In America—and perhaps even more so in England—the sending of children to boarding schools is a widespread and "honorific" practice. By contrast, in Europe proper, such a practice is wholly exceptional and is usually resorted to only *in extremis,* as a punitive measure. Thus, a European adolescent once told the writer that, even though his parents were quite sadistic and made his life at home quite miserable, they had only to threaten him with boarding school to "bring him to heel." A similar mentality is reflected in the Javanese proverb: "Though gold should rain abroad and hail should fall in the land of one's fathers: Home is home" (*134*). The point we seek to make is that the "exceptional" English or American child who is sent to a therapeutic residential school does not experience this "rejection" in as traumatic a manner as would a similar child in Europe, where the practice of sending children to boarding schools is less prevalent. Of course, the difference here is one of degree, and not of kind, since even English upper-class boys, who have looked forward to being sent to the "public" (i.e., private) school which all their male forebears attended, have been known to grieve for a while and to feel rejected and homesick. This feeling of rejection is particularly acute in the case of neurotic and delinquent children of normal intelligence but occurs even in high-grade morons and students with borderline intelligence, many of whom keenly realize that they have been extruded from their families. As regards the low-grade defective, the situation is appreciably less complicated. The grossly

psychological "justification" of that practice. We fully agree with K. A. Menninger that circumcision, except when necessitated by actual illness, is an act of aggression against the child and that, unconsciously at least, the child itself so interprets it (*168*). The fact that some children wish to be circumcised is correct. This does not mean, however, that the child's motives for wishing to be circumcised are not extremely neurotic, i.e., masochistic.

defective child's libidinal cathexes are a priori both too tenuous and too unstable to make a transfer from the home to a residential school where it is well treated unduly traumatic, though, owing to its low intelligence, it cannot derive any comfort from the fact that even normal children with a comparable social background are also usually sent to boarding schools.

ADJUSTMENT TO AN OVERSIMPLIFIED ENVIRONMENT

A further "drawback" of life in the protective group made up of one's peers is one which, on closer inspection, turns out to be a definite asset. Even primitive societies are complicated structures, and, as culture progresses, societies tend to become increasingly more complex. As stated elsewhere (29), this implies, among other things: (1) an increase in the absolute number of culture traits and of accumulated cultural "goods"; (2) a more complex hierarchical structuring of society and culture as a whole, so that the relationship of the individual cultural item to the many-layered and increasingly latent and abstract central pattern becomes rapidly obscured, thus causing an apparent decrease in the (ideological) "meaningfulness" of individual cultural items and manipulations[21]; (3) the increasingly segmental participation of the individual in his culture and society, with a corresponding impairment of his integration with society as a whole; (4) the increasingly rapid rate of change of society and culture, which leads to a rapid obsolescence of learned techniques and attitudes.

Everyone knows from personal experience how difficult it is to deal efficiently with the manifold problems of life in a complex society. Some of these problems have become almost proverbial. Thus, jokes about the complexities of income tax returns are today a bona-fide part of American folklore and folk humor. It is not surprising therefore that the uneducated, the child, the men-

[21] A good analogy—but only analogy—is the loss of the sense of achievement which results from working on an assembly line instead of turning out a finished product from beginning to end.

tally defective, or the neurotic should often find himself confronted with situations with which he is simply not qualified to deal, and which confuse him to the point where he will experience acute discomfort and anxiety.[22] Hence, life in a structured, orderly, simplified, and, above all, small "world" or "life space" is bound to decrease the adaptational difficulties of the feeble-minded or neurotic child. Of course, this also entails a decrease in the child's "life scope" and a constriction of its "life space." But the constriction is more apparent than real, since the internally already constricted defective or neurotic is not really able to take full advantage of the entire range of possibilities which life in society at large offers to the normal and well-adjusted person. In addition, it is very important to realize that the "constriction" of the child's life space in a therapeutic school is the result of constructive planning and is therefore not comparable to the arbitrarily, punitively, and destructively constricted life space of prisoners.[23] In fact, the life space of a therapeutic school is not, strictly speaking, constricted. Rather is it so constructed that its size, scope, and variety fit the manipulative and experiential potentialities of the mentally or emotionally handicapped child. It is also noteworthy that the size of most "protective groups" is about that of a native tribe, while the complexity of their social structure and of their culture is comparable to the complexity of a primitive society and primitive culture.[24] This, we think, is a relatively novel observation and supports our thesis (40) that anthropology is an indispensable tool for anyone who wishes to construct a really effective therapeutic milieu genuinely adapted to the needs and po-

[22] Cf. the moving scene in John Steinbeck's *Grapes of Wrath* in which Joad, a dispossessed Oklahoma dust-bowl farmer, is unable to find out who is really responsible for his losing his farm.

[23] The paradox of imprisonment is that we seek to socialize the prisoner by desocializing him. We might as well try to teach a paralytic to walk straight by first breaking his legs!

[24] The one crucial difference, whose implications are hard to formulate, is that whereas the ethos of tribal culture is internal to the tribe, the ethos animating the therapeutic environment is externally imposed.

tentialities of certain categories of "abnormal' or "exceptional" adults or children. We must once more remind ourselves of the fact that normal persons and normal sociocultural processes create far bigger problems for the mentally or emotionally handicapped person than the latter creates for society as a whole. Hence, in many ways the construction of an effective therapeutic milieu necessitates not so much an adequate appraisal of the problem which the abnormal represents for society as a clear and objective understanding of the problem which we represent for him.

DISCRIMINATION AGAINST EX-PATIENTS

Another pseudo drawback of the therapeutic milieu is one which affects most the neurotic and delinquent, somewhat less the high-grade moron, and little or not at all the low-grade defective. We refer to the cruel social practice of discriminating against individuals who have been in mental institutions. This is something which many parents dread so greatly that they often deny their children the help which such institutions could provide, simply in order to save them from the lifelong "taint" of having been "hospitalized." Neurotic, delinquent, and high-grade defective children themselves are often quite aware of this fact and are inclined to worry over it. Hence, the fact that the exceptional children can be enrolled in a therapeutic school, instead of having to be sent to a sanitarium for children or to a children's ward in a mental hospital, often relieves the anxieties of both parents and children on this score. Some very sophisticated exceptional children even wonder whether the people at home realize that the boarding school they are attending is a "special" school, but usually conclude that most people will simply think they were sent to an ordinary, though strict, boarding school.[25]

Children themselves readily sense whether the "school atmos-

[25] This anxiety should not be ridiculed. According to Philadelphia press reports, a girl in one of the regular city schools stabbed one of her classmates because the latter reportedly said that the first girl's cousin was in a "special school."

phere" is real or spurious—even at times when they are quite angry at the school.

Case 49: School vs. Hospital

An older girl, with borderline intelligence, complained bitterly about her having been sent to a therapeutic school. "Why do I have to go to school again? I already graduated from high school. I can show you my diploma. I am through with schools. And why do I have to go to a therapist, on top of being in school? Etc. I hated boarding school, and being here only reminds me of the bad times I had when I was still going to school." None of her remarks indicated that she considered the therapeutic school as anything but a real school.

Of course, "labeling" alone does not suffice (cf. Chapter 11). The therapeutic school must possess a genuine school atmosphere, and its core technique must be a systematic program of therapeutic education. Otherwise it is simply a sanitarium for children masquerading as a school.

ADULT CONTROL

The last and greatest shortcoming of the "society of peers," which in a therapeutic school is implemented by carefully balanced units and classes, is related to the fact that it is controlled and taught by normal adults. The gap between these adults and the neurotic or defective child is, if anything, even greater than is the gap between the normal child and the adult. Fortunately this drawback is less serious in real situations than the preceding sentence seems to imply. In large segments of the mammalian world, as well as in every culture, the young are dependent on the adult of the species for their very existence. Hence, in this sense at least, not even the neurotic or delinquent but intellectually normal child feels "traumatized" or discriminated against just because it is placed in a necessarily invidious position of (temporary) inferiority with regard to its teachers.

To what extent the very real gap between the "exceptional" child and the fostering adult is traumatic, or nontraumatic, will largely depend on the teacher or milieu therapist himself. However, we must also bear in mind that, by the time the exceptional child comes to the therapeutic school, it has often had bitter and disappointing experiences with adults, so that it is likely to be hostile toward the whole "tribe of the grownups."

Case 50: Suspicion of Adults

It makes no difference how you act toward me. I admit you have never done me any harm. But you are an adult and represent authority. I hate authority. I had too much of it, both at home and when I passed through the courts. I could not trust my own mother. How, then, can you expect me to trust anyone else? I won't trust anyone—it would hurt me too much if I were let down in the end, the way I was always let down. (Therapist: And, in order to forestall the desertion and letdown which you expect from everyone under the sun, you literally force people to let you down, by constantly provoking them.) Sure—that way it hurts less. That way it is less like a desertion. It is more like something I myself have brought about. (Therapist: You don't seem to have much confidence in your ability to stand further desertions.) Okay—sure—and so what? (Therapist: I think you are really quite broken up over the fact that your friend Harry had to leave school—but you won't admit it. Instead, you gripe about something else. It is impossible for you to admit that your toe hurts when someone steps on it. You prefer to pretend that your head aches.) Damn the school anyhow! Why did they have to send Harry away? Etc. (Therapist: It seems to me that I was right in saying that Harry's departure hurt you very much. However, since you are unable to admit that anyone can hurt you personally, you complain instead about mankind in general. Everything that happens to you revives your anger against adults.) Sure!

BRIDGING THE GAP BETWEEN TEACHER AND PUPIL

It is probable that more than good will and professional competence is needed to bridge this gap between the child and the adult. More than anything else, the therapeutic educator needs the ability to put himself in the child's shoes and to help it forget the chasm between its limited capacities and the full-fledged competence of the adult, which the child rightly views as the source of the adult's authority over children.

THE USE OF MODERATELY INTELLIGENT BUT MATURE ADULTS

We are tempted to ask whether the gap between the defective child and the adults most intimately associated with it could not be deliberately narrowed. For example, to call a spade a spade, we may perhaps consider the possibility of entrusting warm, reliable, and kindly but not overly bright adults with much of the actual care—though not with the teaching—of children with low intelligence. Some attempts of this nature have been rather successful, precisely because of the warm humanity and lack of intellectual arrogance of some adults of this sort. Indeed, the emotionally secure but intellectually borderline custodial employee is often capable of greater patience and tolerance than is the normal individual, who is more on a "hair trigger" and has—understandably—a certain awareness of his superiority (sometimes constructively sublimated into loving compassion) over his charges. Of course, supervision must, of necessity, be in the hands of very superior adults, who have had excellent training in their respective professional fields. However, the actual day-to-day, minute-to-minute care of the defective child can probably be entrusted quite safely to emotionally well-balanced but not overly intelligent adults—including even former students.

THE USE OF SENIOR STUDENTS

It is occasionally possible to benefit two categories of students simultaneously by giving rebellious adolescent girls with unusually intense maternal and related impulses some responsibility for the care of much younger intellectually or emotionally disturbed children. This enables the adolescent girl to gratify both her maternal cravings and her need to play an adult role.[26] She usually takes excellent care of the small, forlorn beings entrusted to her, partly because she tries to prove thereby that she is indeed an adult and responsible person and partly because, by being permitted to exercise authority, she is enabled to master the "insult" of her own subordination to genuine adults, by identifying with them. Similar mechanisms can also be observed in mental hospitals. Thus, we described elsewhere (36) the case of a well-preserved and athletic paranoid schizophrenic, who was perfectly manageable and very useful as long as he was permitted to dress like an attendant and to give calisthenic lessons to other patients but became quite violent the moment he ceased to be treated as a "member of the hospital staff." In addition, both the girl herself and her little charges benefit from her eagerness to lavish affection upon them. Indeed, adolescents, and especially emotionally disturbed adolescents, are both eager to love and very much afraid of love. Hence, the opportunity to love a small, helpless being, who cannot "hit back" by demanding truly mature love (of which such confused adolescents are incapable) and who does not give mature love in return, is very reassuring to such girls and helps them develop gradually a capacity to give and to receive mature love. Similar observations have also been made in mental hospitals. Rowland (193) notes that relatively well-preserved, but shy and withdrawn, schizophrenics often tend to "make a pet" of some very regressed and deteriorated fellow patient, because loving such a helpless and unspontaneous person neurotically involves no (emotional) risks. Even the most normal adult is more willing to show affection for a strange baby or a stray puppy than for another adult, because the latter may either reject the affection or else reciprocate by giving and demanding a responsible and durable

[26] It is a commonplace that one effective way of dealing with the rebel against all authority is to put him in a position of authority.

type of mature love, which is a frightening prospect indeed for the immature part of ourselves. Indeed, the capacity to love and to be loved is, in many ways, the core of all maturity, and therefore also the quality most conspicuously lacking in, and most anxiously craved by, the neurotic. As Ferenczi expressed it, what thirty years of analytic practice taught him was simply how much people wanted to love, and how clumsily they went about it.

It is also probable that "acting-out" delinquent male adolescents could, when they begin to show improvement, become very useful mentors for smaller aggressive boys. Such adolescents often confess in therapy that they eventually hope to help other children who are in trouble with the law or with society, and, as Case 12 indicates, they occasionally go out of their way to prevent other delinquents, less improved than they are, from violating the rules of the school or the laws of society. The suggestion that delinquent adolescent boys could be used in this manner is based upon the views of Alcoholics Anonymous, which hold that only an alcoholic can really control, influence, and help another heavy drinker. The old adage "It takes a thief to catch a thief" is also pertinent in this context.

Two sets of arguments, one culture-historical and one clinical, may be cited in support of the preceding series of suggestions.

In a good many primitive societies there is a belief that the medicine man knows about physical sickness or mental derangement because he himself was once ill or insane and subsequently managed to socialize the experience of having been a patient. Yakut beliefs are quite specific on this point. In this tribe the proper person to diagnose a certain type of mental derangement is someone who once suffered from the same disorder and is now in a state of remission (180). In other areas (209) it is the healer who is a former "patient." Such anthropological data also make good sense psychoanalytically, since the schizophrenic in remission can usually still understand the symbolic meaning of an

acutely ill schizophrenic's speech and actions, although he is
sometimes reluctant to allow himself to understand it because it
makes him uncomfortable and tends to threaten his precarious
psychic equilibrium.

The clinical argument is the fact that even the ideal future
psychoanalyst need not be, *ab initio,* a model of "normality" and
adjustment. In fact, in the course of the training analysis which
every future psychoanalyst must undergo he usually becomes
somewhat neurotic in the analytic hour itself. This is due to a re-
surgence of all of his previously more or less successfully sublimated, and more or less adequately resolved, conflicts, in all their
pristine intensity. Of course, after these partially sublimated conflicts are analyzed, they are once more sublimated—this time in a
more effective and more lasting manner. Indeed, as Jokl pointed
out (*128*), the analysis of its unconscious sources cannot destroy
a sublimation; it can only strengthen it. It is, therefore, precisely
by becoming aware of his own unconscious conflict that the well-
analyzed person learns to tolerate not only his own problems but
also those of his future patients, and becomes capable of em-
pathizing and of sympathizing with them. In fact, the compulsively "normal" person, whose "normality" is often nothing more
than the product of his neurotic need to seem normal (*183*), is
often a fairly insensitive and rigid person, who is more or less
consciously contemptuous of those who are less successful than
he is in keeping their conflicts out of sight. He is often inclined
to be impatient with and overbearing toward those less fortunate
than himself. By contrast, the person who is aware of his own
conflicts, or became aware of them in the course of his didactic
analysis, tends to be intellectually much less arrogant and also
much less conceited about his own emotional balance. He knows
that even the normal person's stability is not like that of the
Rock of Gibraltar but like that of a storm-tossed but skillfully
navigated ship, which one false maneuver can put in jeopardy.

Of course, we do not advocate that the home unit staffs of therapeutic schools should be chosen exclusively from the ranks of persons of low intelligence or of symptom-ridden neurotics. It is, likewise, not a good policy to hire an epileptic housemother for a unit which houses epileptic children, since the housemother's seizure may set off—through identification and psychic contagion —similar seizures among her young charges. Intellectually or emotionally handicapped children need emotionally stable teachers and milieu therapists, in order to enable them to identify with these employees in a therapeutically effective manner. Yet, on the whole, a very rigid "pseudo normal" person is an infinitely less desirable therapeutic teacher or milieu therapist than is a sensitive person who, as the saying goes, "has problems of his own."

It may be objected, of course, that, since children in a therapeutic school are accustomed to witness the outbursts of other children, they are less likely to be frightened by the temporary irrationality of a therapeutic educator or milieu therapist than would be normal children, unaccustomed to such spectacles. The advocates of this thesis may, perhaps, cite in support of their point of view the fact that temporarily quiet patients on an "acute" or "disturbed" ward are sometimes less upset by the outburst of a currently agitated fellow patient than is the ward staff, which is made up of "normals." This line of reasoning has several defects. In the first place, one reason why the outbursts of a child—or of a patient—do not upset the rest too much is that they count upon the therapeutic educator or milieu therapist—or upon the ward personnel—to handle the commotion effectively. In the second place, the irrational behavior of a disturbed teacher or milieu therapist represents a quite realistic danger for children, because they know that the staff person has authority over them and is physically stronger than they are. Last, but not least, the improvement of the disturbed child is often contingent upon the possibility of identifying itself with a sensible and reliable teacher or housemother. This, in turn, presupposes faith in the stability of the staff member, which outbursts and lack of self-control on his part are certainly unlikely to foster.

In brief, while it is desirable to narrow the intellectual gap between the defective child and those who minister to its needs most of the day, and while it is advantageous to entrust the emotionally disturbed child to a person who is not rigidly and compulsively (pseudo) "normal," in order not to make the exceptional child feel too inferior to those who teach and educate it, it is equally undesirable to put such children in charge of very unstable persons, who blithely act out their conflicts without any awareness of the fact that they are doing so. Above all, the employment of persons with a limited intelligence, or having moderate problems of their own, can be therapeutically safe and effective only if their supervisors are intellectually superior and emotionally mature persons.

CONCLUSIONS

In conclusion, the protective grouping of exceptional children is therapeutically effective, because life among its peers, in a simplified setting, does not force the child to compete with superior children in too complex a setting. The therapeutic effects of protective groupings can probably be further increased by diminishing the intellectual and emotional gap between the exceptional child and those persons who take care of it most of the day, provided only that the personnel in question is adequately controlled and guided by emotionally stable and professionally competent supervisors.

PART FOUR

ORGANIZATIONAL PATTERN

The Sabbath was made for man, and
not man for the Sabbath.

JESUS OF NAZARETH (Mark 2:27)

CHAPTER 11

Core Technique, Organizational Self-Differentiation, and Goal Selection

INDIVIDUALIZATION

Man's quest for differentiation, individualization, and autonomy, which culminates in the achievement of selfhood and uniqueness, is counterbalanced and moderated by his desire to "belong," to be a member of various logical, sociological, and functional classes, and to achieve what Angyal calls "homonomy" (3). Both objectives are necessary for life in society, since complete nondifferentiation would lead to the stagnation and "involution" of society, of culture, and even of the human species, whereas unbridled uniqueness would make behavior unpredictable and life in society impossible. One practical function of custom seems to be to limit—creatively in a healthy society and destructively in a sick one—the unpredictability of human behavior (152) which results from the fact that man, being more plastic than animals and less rigidly governed by simple and stable reflexes, can behave in much more various ways than animals can.[1]

Both the quest for individuality and that for conformity can reach pathological extremes. We will largely ignore in this con-

---

[1] We indicated elsewhere that in mental illness there takes place a regression to simplified and more rigid behavior, which seems "unpredictable" only if we insist on trying to understand in terms of normal human behavior (47).

text various extremes of conformity, since Erich Fromm (*102*) devoted a memorable book to the study of spineless "adjustment" to the norm, which destroys not only the basic values of individuality but also those of culture and society. By contrast, the pathological extremes of spurious individualization have been less fully explored, even by totalitarian social "scientists," since totalitarianism does not fear pathological eccentricities half as much as it dreads normal self-realization, simply because the former also represent a kind of constriction of human individualization.

Although men have differed from each other from the dawn of time and, subjectively at least, were aware of this fact, Mauss (*165*) has shown that the conscious quest for selfhood and its social implementation appeared relatively late on the social scene. Thus, those primitive societies which have a classificatory kinship system heavily emphasize the social or functional equivalence of various persons. For example, in seeking revenge for the murder of his son, the grieving primitive father will find as much satisfaction in killing the brother of his son's murderer as he would in killing the murderer himself, and society as a whole will support him in this. Similarly, when the writer asked one of two cousins married to the same Sedang Moi man whether she felt jealous when her husband showed affection to her cousin and co-wife, the young woman casually replied: "Why should I? She is the same person as myself!" The way she said this clearly indicated that she felt like adding: "What a silly question!" This does not mean, of course, that the grieving primitive father does not know the difference between his son's murderer and the murderer's brother, or that this Sedang wife actually thought that if she ate a meal her cousin and co-wife would also feel satiated. It simply means that certain persons are, by definition, deemed to be socially equivalent, and are trained to think of themselves as interchangeable in a social context. This notion is so deeply embedded in the minds of primitives that in some groups the murdered son's parents actually adopt his murderer, thus replacing their son with a social equivalent and, at the same time, taking revenge on the murderer's kin by depriving them of one of their relatives (35).

It is quite certain that the social implementation of man's quest for selfhood represents progress, particularly if we adopt Kroeber's view (144) that one important characteristic of progress is a shift from "surrealism" to greater realism. Indeed, since it is a hard fact that everyone actually differs from everyone else, the social implementation of this insight—for example, in the form of an emphasis on personal as against collective responsibility—actually represents progress toward a higher degree of social and psychological realism.

REAL VS. SPURIOUS SELFHOOD

We must now seek to differentiate between functional and nonfunctional means of emphasizing one's selfhood and uniqueness. A functional quest for selfhood mobilizes and involves the effective and nuclear functions of the personality, whereas a nonfunctional or spurious quest emphasizes primarily the contingent, external consequences of individualization. This definition is based upon the difference, first described by Freud and creatively elaborated by Louisa P. Holt (119, 120), between genuine (functional and spurious (nonfunctional) identification. In our opinion, the latter is, in a very real sense, little more than a conscious implementation of the "narcissism of small differences." The "distinctiveness" of an object, person, or organization is in the eyes of the spectator, and the quest for distinctiveness is spectator oriented. By contrast, true "differentiation" is an inherent and internal characteristic, resulting from goal orientation.

A simple example will show what we mean. Roughly speaking, a musician may seek to achieve functional differentiation by becoming a superlative performer of Mozart's works, whereas his quest for a spurious and nonfunctional distinctiveness may cause him to adopt as his "trademark" some eccentricity of dress or manner.

Now, it is rather interesting that, whereas the tokens of genuine individualization tend to be highly differentiated, the tokens of mere distinctiveness are often simply insignificant variations on some marginal form of what Linton calls "patterns of misconduct" (151), which, in our opinion, include also all "patterns of deviancy," or even of mere nonfunctional distinctiveness. For example, although the piano virtuoso's long hair deviates from the workaday norm, it does—or did formerly—conform to the "distinctive trademark" of a special class: the virtuosi. Thus, the differences between the haircuts of Liszt and of Chopin were only variations on a very trifling theme and moved within narrow limits. In fact, it was only in later life that Liszt ceased to curl his hair like Chopin and achieved a greater (trademark) distinctiveness by wearing his long hair straight. Even more striking patterns of deviancy are exemplified by certain ethnically unique and culturally specialized ways of being "mentally abnormal," as, for example, "being insane" according to the *latah* or *amok* patterns of the Malay (218) or in conformity with the Crazy-Dog-Wishes-to-Die pattern of the Crow Indians (155), etc.[2]

A social manifestation of this nonfunctional technique of "self-identification" is the process of "antagonistic acculturation" (64), whereby society seeks to differentiate itself deliberately—and often quite superficially—from other societies in order to achieve "distinctiveness." The recurrent Biblical admonition to be different from the neighboring heathen (Leviticus 18:3) is a good example of this trend toward spurious self-differentiation.[3] Likewise,

---

[2] Our description of these syndromes as culturally standardized patterns of "being mentally ill" does not imply a denial of the fact that these patterns exist because they are particularly congenial to the members of a given culture, which is characterized by certain stresses and therefore also by certain standardized "type solutions," or "type defenses," of which such patterned forms of "being mentally ill" are a rather extreme example.

[3] Some of the stormier birth pangs of Judaism, Christianity, and Mohammedanism may have been caused by certain excesses resulting from the need to stress the "distinctiveness" of certain practices which had, as yet, no real doctrinal and ide-

it is definitely known that, in its early stages, Islam made a deliberate effort to differentiate its practices and way of life from those of the "peoples of the Scriptures": the Christians and the Jews (*217*). All these attempts to achieve distinctiveness involve a deliberate and provocative way of "being different" and may therefore be rooted in "social negativism," which is of crucial significance in the genesis of all types of deviations from the norm (*31, 58*).

The data just cited indicate that the desire for nonfunctional distinctiveness animates not only individuals but also social institutions and such organizations as armies (uniform), business firms (trademark), schools (colors of the school), and the like. Organizations of all types seek to gain attention or to "corner the market" by being "just a little different"—even if this difference is a wholly unimportant one and amounts to little more than an attractive or prestige-laden way of "packaging" the product.[4]

CORE TECHNIQUE VS. PERIPHERAL TECHNIQUE

Needless to say, such attempts to achieve mere "distinctiveness for its own sake" are not only *non*functional but outright *dys*functional. They are not rooted in functional individualization and differentiation (*119, 120*) but in a kind of unrealistic "narcissism of small differences" culminating in a meaningless and useless type of "trademark distinctiveness." Otherwise expressed, differentiation is goal directed and therefore functional, while

---

ological foundations. We furthermore suspect that many of the subsequent complexities of the doctrine of these religions were the result of attempts to provide a doctrinal justification for certain originally purely external "trademark" type "distinctive" practices evolved in the course of an antagonistic acculturation. In this context we may profitably contrast the numerous relapses into idol worship among the early Jews—of which the "golden calf" incident is the best known example—with the truly fabulous theological complexities of latter-day Talmudic and rabbinical casuistry (*64*).

[4] For example, it used to be possible to buy quite cheaply, by joining a "club," outstanding records of classical music, played by famous orchestras and recorded by some of the leading firms. However, these records were issued under the label of the "club" and did not name either the orchestras or the companies which actually made the recordings. Hence, they lacked "prestige."

mere distinctiveness is means-directed and therefore mostly non-functional and sometimes even dysfunctional.

We must emphasize, however, that since goals cannot be attained without appropriate means it is quite certain that functional, goal-directed differentiation and uniqueness cannot be achieved without an equally functional differentiation and uniqueness of the means resorted to for this purpose. We propose to show that an effective functional differentiation is achieved by means of a rational selection of one of several cognate techniques, having identical aims, as the *core technique* of an organization. Once this choice is made, other techniques which have the same goal are automatically relegated to a marginal position and may therefore be designated as *peripheral techniques.*

What is "core technique" and what is "peripheral technique" depends, in each case, upon the organization which made this choice—upon its structure, its organizational orientation, and the orientation of its personnel. For example, in a psychiatric hospital concentrating on shock therapy it is this procedure which occupies the position of core technique, while psychotherapy, milieu therapy, occupational therapy, etc., automatically become peripheral techniques. The reverse would be true of a psychoanalytically oriented sanitarium.

PERIPHERAL VS. ANCILLARY TECHNIQUES

At this juncture it is important to differentiate between the peripheralness and the ancillarity of a technique.

It is possible for a definitely peripheral therapeutic technique not to occupy an ancillary position, provided only that it is defined as an important contributory factor in the overall structure, or in the total therapeutic pattern, of a given organization. For example, many hospitals which use chiefly shock therapy consider this technique relatively inefficient without simultaneous psychotherapy, etc., even though they continue to view shock therapy as the effective cause—the *causa causans*—of observed improvements. In other instances a peripheral technique is defined as a "heroic measure," *ultima ratio regum* or "court of last appeal," to which recourse is taken only when the core technique has reached the limit of its effectiveness or has failed to achieve its ends.

We are inclined to believe that a therapeutic organization which assigns an ancillary or subordinate position to any peripheral technique whatsoever is almost always one which seeks to achieve a mere trademark type of distinctiveness and fails to realize that the true, though sometimes latent, objective of institutional differentiation should be a high rate of cures. By contrast, a functionally differentiated—i.e., a truly "distinguished" and not simply "distinctive"—organization assigns to its chosen core technique not an absolute but only a relative nuclearity within a total therapeutic pattern. Such organizations realize that only a nonfunctional differentiation can be achieved by means of the choice of one distinctive core technique, while functional differentiation can be achieved only by the construction of a definite total therapeutic pattern arranged around a chosen core technique. The mere choice of a core technique produces only a socially irrelevant and unproductive organizational distinctiveness, comparable to the trademark practices of organization-oriented structures, which cannot be called true, goal-oriented, service organizations (Chapter 13). By contrast, goal-oriented therapeutic (service) organizations are those which utilize total therapy distinctively patterned around a core technique. This approach corresponds more or less to what Myerson (174) has called "total push" and produces a distinctiveness which is incidental and does not result from the ascription of absolute primacy to a given "core" technique. Instead, it is the product of the type of patterning of techniques and policies which results from assigning variable and relationally conceived degrees of flexible nuclearity to the core technique. In fact, we coined the term "core technique" in order to emphasize that, in an efficient sense, the existence of any kind of "core" automatically presupposes also the existence and implies the importance of other, functionally related, peripheral techniques. As used in this book, the term "core technique," unless otherwise specified, should therefore always be conceived in relational terms, i.e., as implying a certain degree of nuclearity with reference to other major components of the total therapeutic pattern.

SCHOOL VS. HOSPITAL

In practical terms, *it is the assigning of the position of "core technique" to therapeutic education which differentiates the residential specialized school from mental institutions for children, which have other core techniques.* It is, of course, also the ready-made means whereby the self-labeling of such schools is (incidentally) achieved. Above all, it is the criterion in terms of which real objectives are formulated and success and failure are appraised. In fact, the choice of a core technique often also helps one to clarify the nature of one's goals. For example, one does not have to subscribe whole-heartedly to Pareto's somewhat unqualified assertion that, under most conditions, any kind of goal-directed action is better than no action whatsoever (*177*) to realize that a constant awareness of the fact that, e.g., therapeutic education, rather than something else, is the core technique of a certain type of organization is especially useful in situations of crisis, which arise quite frequently in organizations devoted to the treatment of "relatively unpredictable"[5] deviants. In fact, it is an inherent characteristic of certain organizations like special schools, the fire department, the hospital, the police, etc., that they are

[5] We have placed the expression "relatively unpredictable" in quotes, so as to reaffirm once more, be it but implicitly, our previously expressed view (*47, 52*) that actually the mentally abnormal person is more predictable, because fundamentally or regressively "simpler," than is the normal person, provided only that one uses the proper frame of reference for the understanding, prediction, and control of his behavior.

constantly "geared to emergencies." It is the unexpected which represents the focus of their efforts, as contrasted with the "routine-geared" work of such organizations as factories, in which emergencies are simply disturbing and exceptional interludes. Hence, an awareness of the core technique and distinctive therapeutic pattern of a "trouble-oriented" organization is of crucial importance in facilitating the making of decisions, in the handling of emergencies, and in formulating the overall policies and goals.

When a crisis arises in a special residential school for "exceptional" children, it helps one to take immediate action if one knows that, the core technique being therapeutic education, the first measures to be tried should be therapeutically educative ones. Indeed, anything which helps focus effort in a crisis is beneficial, as long as it does not lead simply to a "restriction of choice-alternatives," characteristic of some rigid organizations, in which one technique has an absolute, instead of only a relational, core position. Where a true relational nuclearity of the core technique obtains, there is actually no constriction of choice-alternatives but merely a gradation thereof, in terms of their respective proximity to, or distance from, the focal core technique. This in itself permits, in situations of crisis, a judiciously graduated appeal to, and utilization of, the whole range of peripheral techniques, in accordance with the overall therapeutic pattern.

This patterning of the total therapy also has organizational advantages. It facilitates the allocation of credit—or discredit—for so-called failures of the system. In other words, just as in a primarily psychoanalytic institution both the praise for the patient's progress and the blame for his failure to progress are laid mainly at the door of his analyst, so, in a therapeutically educational organization success or failure with a given child is defined chiefly in relation to the performance of the educational system. The more the actual administrative and organizational pattern is congruent with the structure of the therapeutic pattern, the more effectively and responsibly the organization functions. This point will be discussed in Chapter 13 in some detail.

One advantage of this functional self-labeling for the residential school for "exceptional" children deserves special mention. We refer to the fact—also mentioned in Chapter 10—that many parents are loath to send their children to definitely psychotherapeutic sanitaria, in order to protect the child, as well as the family, from the odium attached to the word "insanity." In addition—as we stressed in Chapter 10—the child itself feels less "set apart," and less "hopeless," if it is both nominally and factually incorporated into a school system, as are other children, instead of being subjected to experiences unlike those of its non-handicapped age mates. The specifically traumatic character of deviant life experiences is one of the pivotal arguments of Chapter 10. Hence, we may say with a certain measure of confidence that the more genuinely—and not only nominally or euphemistically—a residential school is primarily a school, whose core technique is (therapeutic) education, the more beneficial, at least in this respect, it will be to the child, whose enrollment (as distinct from hospitalization) does not hopelessly divert its life experiences from the "type biography"[6] of its age mates and former associates.

SUCCESS VS. FAILURE IN TERMS OF THE CORE TECHNIQUE

Last, but not least, the choice of a core technique and of a total therapeutic pattern will determine also precisely what may be called a "success" and what must be conceded to represent a "failure"—and why. Thus, in a neuropsychiatric veterans' hospital the patient's failure to graduate from high school may not

[6] We denote by this term the fictional biography of an imaginary person who is "typical" of his group, and whose "life history" is constructed so as to explain the process of national character formation in that group, as well as to illustrate the major themes and practices of that culture. Interesting American Indian "type biographies" were published by some of the most eminent American anthropologists (178).

be legitimately viewed as a failure of that particular type of institution, since graduating its patients from high school is not directly related to the hospital's implicit and explicit goal structure.

By contrast, a great deal of confusion regarding "success" and "failure" can arise from a reluctance or an inability to define two points with absolute clarity:

1. What does, e.g., a school dedicated to the practice of dynamic, specialized, and individualized education expect from itself, and what, accordingly, does it define as a "failure"?

2. What are the objective limits and the natural, "efficient" scope of the core technique, and how can the natural limitations of any core technique be constructively supplemented by peripheral techniques?

These points are discussed in some detail in Chapter 7, in which we stress that, subjectively speaking, the effectiveness of, and indications for, a technique can be appraised in terms of its successes, whereas self-proclaimed—though not always realistic—failures provide more revealing clues to the aspirations of the practitioner of the core technique than to the inherent potentialities and limitations of the technique itself.

A concrete example may now be given, which will show how this self-definition determines the practices of a school which the writer was able to study at first hand.

CORE TECHNIQUE OF THE DEVEREUX SCHOOLS

The core technique of the Devereux Schools, operated by the Devereux Foundation, is therapeutic—i.e., dynamic, specialized, and individualized—education, in a therapeutic milieu. Hence the school views therapeutic education both as the efficient cause of the improvements noted in the students and as the chief "culprit" if a student seemingly fails to make progress. Milieu therapy, in turn, is defined as a contributory cause, which makes a maximal or optimal impact of the core technique possible. Thus, from the theoretical point of view, the self-definition of this organization as a "school" is legitimate.

Let us now examine to what extent this self-definition is in harmony with reality.

Though licensed by the Commonwealth of Pennsylvania Department of Welfare, as if it were a psychiatric institution or a general hospital, this organization defines itself as a specialized residential school for children, adolescents, and young adults who, were such a school not available, would have to be placed in conventional mental hospitals or in "schools" for the feeble-minded and the like. This self-definition of the school has existed since its founding and is so clear-cut that, for a long time, the school did not even have an intramural psychiatric staff. When a student needed psychotherapy, special consultants were called upon to administer this treatment—often extramurally—just as is done in other schools and colleges. When, owing to the expansion of the school, there was enough demand to justify the appointment of full-time psychiatrists to the staff, a department of psychiatry, staffed exclusively by qualified analysts and by psychiatrists who are undergoing training in psychoanalysis, came into being. However, even the creation of such a department did not modify the basic objectives and total functional (therapeutic) structure of the school. It represented a purely practical shift from peripheral extramural to peripheral intramural individual psychotherapy.

This self-definition of the school remained unchanged as its student body grew from two pupils to some 600. Hence, to this day, the school has systematically refused—and will presumably continue to refuse—to erect a building comparable to a "closed ward," or even to provide a single room which could be made to serve as such. There simply is not a single "locked" room in the entire school, and, for all we know, there may not even be a room which would readily lend itself even to a temporary use as a "locked ward." When a student becomes especially disturbed, one of the following solutions is adopted:

1. The disturbed student may be temporarily transferred from a relatively free and unstructured unit—which we may think of as the equivalent of a "progressive school"—to a more rigid and highly structured unit, which, figuratively speaking, may be compared to a "military academy." While these similes are very inadequate indeed, they do underscore the fact that, regardless of the often considerable differences between the various home units, they all partake to an equal extent of the characteristics of a school, and nothing but a school. The term "school," as applied to any of these units, is, thus, not a "face-saving" device, like calling euphemistically even some poorly organized and barely disguised special prisons for juvenile delinquents "reform schools."[7] It reflects a substantive reality.

2. More severely, but also only transitorily, disturbed students are temporarily housed in the infirmary, which likewise has no "closed ward" facilities and is much like any other school infirmary. Such a transfer therefore simply diminishes the disturbed student's opportunity to importune others, by temporarily removing him from his regular unit. At the same time it also alleviates his situational problems, by removing him from group competition or from situations where intense heterosexual or homosexual temptations are present.

3. When the disturbance is extremely severe and is likely to be of some duration, the school, being a school, handles the situation much as any school or college would handle the sudden psychotic "break" of one of its students: The child is temporarily transferred to a nearby private sanitarium or, if the disturbance is extreme, to one of the best local psychiatric hospitals, in which one of the school's part-time intramural psychiatrists is also a

[7] Needless to say, we do not speak here of certain excellent and humane reform schools.

member of the staff. Such transfers once more underscore that the creation of a psychotherapy department within the school did not imply a restructuring of its therapeutic pattern. It was simply a procedural measure, motivated by considerations of efficiency and involving nothing more than a shift from peripheral extramural to peripheral intramural individual psychotherapy. It should also be emphasized that, just as in other schools, such decisions are taken by the school psychiatrists in a completely unself-conscious manner. Their position is that, the problem having ceased to be a primarily educational one, it is now necessary to handle it primarily psychiatrically, until an educational approach once more becomes possible.

In the preceding pages we attempted to differentiate between the educationally oriented treatment pattern of residential schools and the psychotherapeutically oriented treatment pattern of psychiatric institutions for children, which include deservedly respected child research centers, wards in famous psychiatric hospitals and sanitaria, etc. Our discussion had as its focus solely the problem of differences in the orientation of these two types of service organizations, both of which are functionally differentiated and not simply "distinctive." No attempt was made to draw invidious or valuative comparisons between the two types of orientation. The more extensive discussion of the educationally oriented treatment pattern of residential schools is fully justified by the fact that our topic is therapeutic education and not child psychiatry.

....

CHAPTER 12

The Overlap and Articulation of Techniques in the Therapeutic Pattern

In earlier chapters we repeatedly stated that each technique, however excellent it may be, has certain limitations which can often be compensated for by supplementing it with other forms of treatment. We must not imagine, however, that the boundaries between the indications for, or the applicability of, the various therapeutic techniques are perfectly clear-cut. In fact, as shown in Chapter 5, even the actual procedures of psychotherapy and education overlap to a certain extent. As Dr. Richard L. Jenkins expressed it, "overlap is inevitable and the difference tends to be in the *balance between* the two" techniques.[1] In brief, there are, in every respect, numerous overlaps, which may be quite extensive, as regards both theory and practice. Sometimes several techniques actually have a common conceptual background, as, for example, clinical psychoanalysis and psychoanalytic pedagogics.

THE FUNCTIONAL SIGNIFICANCE OF BOUNDARIES

It is sometimes rather difficult to determine the limits of, and the boundaries between, the various techniques. In many instances such boundaries seem quite arbitrary and shift back and forth as

[1] Personal communication.

science progresses. In actual practice, one's orientation and personal choice—largely reflected in the selection of one technique as *the* core technique—determine how much of the area in which there is an overlap (theoretical or technical) will be defined as belonging primarily, or even exclusively, to the domain of the core technique, instead of to that of a peripheral technique, or, what is better, to both.

Such situations are by no means unique and are not limited to the applied sciences. We sought to demonstrate elsewhere that there is a great deal of overlap between the respective domains of the two explanatory principles which form the basis of the so-called "nature vs. nurture" controversy (37), and indicated that the extent to which one chooses to use one, rather than the other, of these principles is determined partly by one's orientation and by the objectives which such an orientation implies and partly by the law of diminishing returns. Indeed, a very peculiar situation arises when one seeks to interpret or to handle in terms of one's focal thesis or technique certain phenomena and problems which are increasingly remote from, and peripheral to, the nuclear body of facts from which one's central thesis was derived and to which one's preferred technique was applied successfully in the first place. For example, it is easier to offer a convincing psychoanalytic explanation of a neurosis than it is to interpret in exclusively psychoanalytic terms the peculiarities of the Sioux kinship system or the philosophy of Kant. It is also easier to cure a neurotic by means of psychoanalysis than it is to stop a world-wide economic depression by exclusively psychoanalytic means, even though economic depressions too do not exist in a psychological vacuum. In theoretical terms, as one moves into these more and more peripheral areas, the increase in the amount of effort one has to make to interpret facts in exclusively psychoanalytic terms is likely to be greater than the added insights one gains may warrant. The effort may have to increase in geometrical progression in order to cause insight to increase in a simple arithmetical progression. When one attempts to extend the applicability of a certain theory or technique beyond its natural boundaries one sometimes ends up with a display of intellectual acrobatics or "fireworks" instead of with sound science and logic. We hasten to add that these cautionary remarks are applicable to all attempts to push any kind of theory or technique beyond its natural limits. One can be just as foolish in trying to view mental processes exclusively in terms of brain structure and brain chemistry as one can be when one tries to interpret the behavior of a person with a brain lesion in exclusively psychoanalytic terms.

The preceding considerations indicate that it is undesirable to push too far the exclusive applications of a given therapeutic technique. No amount of psychotherapy can make a brain injury disappear or abolish its influence on thought, feeling, and behavior. However, this does not mean that we cannot profitably give psychotherapy also to brain-damaged patients or children, since every brain damage produces secondary psychological disturbances, which are sometimes agonizingly painful. Thus, we repeatedly referred to the fact that the feeble-minded children of educated parents sometimes become quite neurotic and possibly even psychotic because, owing to their intellectual defect, they cannot meet the demands made upon them. In fact, one of the two chief purposes of therapeutic schools for the feebleminded is to prevent children from becoming psychotic (the other major goal being to safeguard them from becoming permanent "custodial" cases, vegetating in a world of dull and meaningless routine). In other types of brain injury or defect there may occur various other secondary psychological disturbances—sometimes denoted by the term "neurophrenia" (67)—which are also amenable to psychotherapy.

In short, there is sometimes a great deal of difference between what a given technique can legitimately claim as its province and what, in a kind of self-deluding grandiosity, it professes to be able to do, all by itself.

TYPES OF OVERLAP

It is desirable to differentiate between areas of effective, authentic, and spurious overlap. In the following pages we will, for the sake of simplicity, discuss primarily areas of overlap between two techniques, because the overlap between two explanatory principles can be analyzed in almost identical terms.

1. The area of *effective overlap* is often quite small. It covers situations which can be handled equally well by either of two techniques. The effective boundary of a given technique is the point at which the increase in effort ("cost") equals the added results ("income") which are obtained.

2. The area of *authentic overlap* is somewhat larger. It covers situations in which desirable results continue to be achieved by one of two techniques, even though the use of the other technique would be more advantageous. The authentic boundary of a given technique is at the point where the total effort ("cost") equals the total results ("income") obtained.

3. The area of *spurious overlap* is often very large—and also quite artificial. It covers situations where only minimal and relatively unimportant results are obtained—or are merely claimed to have been obtained—by the use of a given technique. The spurious boundary of a given technique is the point where the total effort ("cost") is smaller than the total results ("income") obtained. In such instances arguments that one obtained genuine results tend to sound "phony" and strained and may seem scientific only because of the way in which they are worded.

It is self-evident that the inflated boundaries of the area of spurious overlap are not suitable limits to which to push the application of any core technique, however excellent it may be in itself. This point is too obvious to stand in need of proof.

As regards the rather narrow area of effective overlap, it is, ideally, the one which should mark the limits of the application of any technique, be it a core technique or a peripheral one. However, as we shall see in a moment, certain indirect gains may be derived from using instead, as one's practical limits, the boundaries of the area of authentic overlap.

SIGNIFICANCE OF THE CORE TECHNIQUE

An organization which used the boundary of effective overlap as the limit for the application of its core technique would be a more or less undifferentiated one. Its objectives would be relatively vague and its evolution a somewhat haphazard and often non-goal-directed one. This may be a distinct disadvantage, e.g., in that the difference between therapeutic schools and mental hospitals would disappear. We therefore feel that the core technique should be used, in preference to a peripheral technique, in the whole area in which these two overlap authentically, instead of only in the area where the two overlap effectively. Indeed, the added "increment of cost" resulting from this therapeutic policy is more than compensated for by additional indirect returns in the form of organizational coherence, goal-directed specificity of effort, etc. The following example is a good illustration of such indirect gains. There are moderately neurotic or "difficult" children who could be effectively treated in a psychiatric hospital but whose parents are reluctant to hospitalize them because they fear that having been in a "booby hatch" might handicap the child in later life. If there were no therapeutic schools, some of these children would be kept home and would be denied any professional help whatsoever.

The advisability of using primarily the core technique throughout the area of authentic overlap is suggested by the very existence of a core technique, regardless of what it may be. An organization possessing a core technique will—and should—seek to apply it to the limits of its productive capacity, i.e., to the point where the total cost in effort equals, but does not exceed, the total returns. Thus, in a therapeutic school for neurotic, defective, or delinquent children the first attempt to deal with crises will and should involve the use of primarily educational and secondarily milieu therapeutic techniques. Only at the point where these techniques fail to produce total results at least equal to the total effort invested in their application will and should there be an appeal to a peripheral technique, such as psychotherapy. This policy is both natural and sensible, and usually meets with everyone's approval.

RESORTING TO PERIPHERAL TECHNIQUES

The question now arises: As the peripheral technique "takes over," is there, or should there be for maximum effectiveness, a change in orientation? We must remind ourselves that the peripheral technician "takes over" precisely at the point where the core technique began to operate at an actual loss, i.e., at the boundary of the authentic overlap of the core technique with the peripheral technique. Hence, in seeking to evaluate the possible need for a shift in "relative spheres of competence" during emergency psychotherapy, we must remember that this therapy takes place in an educational setting, and that, once the crisis is over, education will once more have to come into its own.

This being said, we nonetheless feel that during the actual period of both "first aid" and intensive psychotherapy the limits within which the educational core technique is applied must shrink somewhat, while those within which psychotherapy is used must expand correspondingly. In more formal terms, at such times the area for the application of therapeutic education includes that of effective overlap, while for psychotherapy it includes that of authentic overlap. Otherwise stated, at such times the educational or milieu therapeutic program should not go beyond the point where each extra bit of effort brings in at least an equal additional return whereas the psychotherapy program should include the whole area in which its total effort equals the total results it obtains.

TEAMWORK IN A CRISIS

Needless to say, a great deal of effective communication and coöperation between the psychiatrist and the therapeutic educator is needed in a crisis situation. For the time being, the therapeutic educator must take his cues from the psychotherapist and adjust his program and his demands on the child to the program and demands of psychotherapy. On his part, the psychotherapist must interpret his work to the educators and milieu therapists and suggest ways of coördinating current educational and milieu therapeutic efforts with the immediate goals of psychotherapy. He must also help the educators and milieu therapists to cope with the specific problems arising from the fact that the child is in psychotherapy. He must prepare them for "acting out" of various types and must outline for them the educational means to be used as buffers for these special forms of acting out (Chapter 13).

Coöperation in a crisis, which reverses usual patterns of action, makes great demands on all therapeutic technicians. It calls for a real understanding of, and respect for, the techniques of others. The psychotherapist in particular must not forget that, from the educational point of view, his technique represents an emergency measure. Hence, while having his day, he must not lapse into those illusions of omniscience and omnipotence which we characterized elsewhere as "analytic megalomania" (56).[2] On his part, the therapeutic educator must not yield to the very human tendency of resisting as long as possible the realization that, temporarily at least, his core technique is "out of its depth," lest he delay the referral of the child to the psychotherapist until long after his

[2] The risks of therapeutic grandiosity were also discussed by Dr. Robert Waelder, in his 1954 Presidential Address to the Philadelphia Association for Psychoanalysis (222).

own core technique has begun to operate at a loss.[3] Such unfortu-
nate delays are sometimes caused by the mistaken belief that a
crisis, i.e., a temporary decrease in returns, represents a "failure,"
which no one likes to confess. However, such "failures" are often
purely imaginary ones, in that they often reflect not a deficiency
or inadequacy of the technician but an inherent limitation of his
particular technique, which is no more omnipotent than any other
technique known to man.

After so many theoretical considerations, it might be helpful to
use a very simple and homely example to illustrate the point we
seek to make. It is well known that in many cases a permanent alleviation of stomach ulcers is not possible without deep and prolonged psychotherapy, and preferably psychoanalysis. Hence, in
suitable cases, where the ulcers are not bleeding so badly that an
immediate operation is needed, the internist, without ceasing to
prescribe proper medical care, may refer the patient to a psychotherapist without experiencing a totally unwarranted sense of
failure. On the other hand, a psychoanalyst may find that his patient's ulcers are suddenly so much worse that they require surgery.
In such a situation he will refer his patient to a surgeon, without,
however, permanently discontinuing his own ministrations. Furthermore, like the internist who made the original referral, he too
will make such a referral without any sense of "failure."

THE COMPLEMENTARITY RELATION BETWEEN CORE
TECHNIQUE AND PERIPHERAL TECHNIQUE

This homely example clearly underscores the "complementarity

[3] This problem is probably especially acute in organizations where the hierarchical rank ordering of techniques is out of line with the pay scale of the practitioners of the several techniques (cf. Chapter 13). In concrete terms, in a residential school the less-paid educational therapist is often slightly reluctant to concede
that his core technique is temporarily out of its depth and to call in the more highly
paid psychiatrist, who practices what, in a school, is a peripheral technique. By
contrast, in a sanitarium, where the core technique is psychiatry and the highest-
ranking technician is the psychiatrist, referrals for supplementary therapy to, e.g.,
educational therapists are more easily made because they do not threaten the psychiatrist's organizational status.

relationship" (*stricto sensu*) between the core technique and peripheral techniques. It is a hard fact that human beings are extremely complicated creatures, whose problems and ailments usually involve many levels of functioning. Regrettable as this may seem to those who prefer logical neatness to the fascinating complexities of reality, few patients are "obliging" enough to see to it that all their troubles arise in the area with which their regular therapist is most competent to deal. On the other hand, and fortunately for all concerned, it is also a fact that the amelioration of difficulties on one level usually produces also improvements on other levels. Hence, the patient's current condition and not his regular therapeutic technician's field of specialization and major interest must determine the type of primary care he should receive. In other words, in real crisis situations it is the patient's condition, and not the orientation of his current therapist, which will determine what—at that moment—is or should be the "core" technique and what the "peripheral" technique. Hence, as stated in Chapter 11, the concepts "core technique" and "peripheral technique" must always be defined in relational terms, and in sufficiently flexible a manner to allow, in a crisis, a previously and routinely "peripheral" technique to take over, for the time being, the role and function of the regular "core" technique.

In summary, the relative boundaries of the various techniques must be defined elastically, in terms of the patient's current condition, and always without any sense of failure. The problems which one's legitimate and understandable involvement with one's preferential technique create can, if one is a responsible therapist, always be neutralized by one's dedication to the real and sole objective of a service profession: the interests and welfare of the patient.

....

CHAPTER 13

Therapeutic vs. Organizational Pattern

In Chapters 11 and 12 we distinguished between core technique and peripheral technique in strictly logical and non-valuative terms. We emphasized that the peripheralness of a technique need not imply that it is actually also ancillary to the core technique, at least not if the nuclearity of the latter is defined in purely relational terms. In brief, we indicated that, in a functional therapeutic pattern, the various techniques are coördinated with rather than subordinated to the core technique.

In the present chapter we will seek to analyze further certain implications of the distinction between core technique and peripheral technique, with special reference to the congruence or non-congruence of the therapeutic pattern with the organizational pattern of the school or psychiatric institution for the treatment of intellectually or emotionally handicapped children. It will soon become apparent that here, too, we must adopt a wholly non-valuative attitude, since the analysis of the relationship between the therapeutic and the organizational pattern specifically requires a non-valuative interpretation of the criteria whereby the core technique may be differentiated from peripheral techniques.

We will continue to refrain from assigning coefficients of relative "merit" or "value" to the various techniques constituting the therapeutic pattern of an organization. Instead, we will seek to recognize objectively the position which various techniques do, in fact, occupy in a given therapeutic pattern, and to interpret the significance of these structural or positional realities for the understanding of the functional realities of the organizational pattern.

VALUE HIERARCHY AND SOCIAL STRUCTURE

Actually, the problem which interests us at this point is simply a special case of a much broader problem, which has long preoccupied social scientists and particularly social anthropologists. We refer to the congruence of the value hierarchy of a given culture with the structure of society. A simple example will show what we mean.

The culture of the Middle Ages assigned a higher coefficient to religious values than to secular ones and rated economically productive pursuits fairly low in the scale of values. This value hierarchy was implemented on the social level by the superordination of the Church to kings and feudal lords, who were, in turn, superordinated to the third estate, which was engaged in economically productive work. Of course, we are describing here the ideal scheme of the Middle Ages. In reality, the lines were far less clearly drawn, since the Pope was also the temporal ruler of the Papal States and considered some kings and lords his vassals. Conversely, certain bishops and abbots who held feudal lands were, in the feudal scheme, the vassals of the King. In addition, kingship itself had many religious connotations, one of which was the thesis that kings ruled by the grace of God, so that submission to them was not only a feudal but also a religious duty.

The fact that boundaries were somewhat blurred in practice did not undermine the principle that, ideally, religious, sociopolitical, and economic values and the estates (church, nobility, business class) corresponding to them were absolutely distinct, even if they did influence each other, and that the blurring of boundaries in practice was due to human frailty rather than to an inherent imperfection of the ideal value hierarchy and social system. Passing disturbances in the system, such as the struggle between Emperor and Pope, the captivity of the Popes in Avignon (France), the raising of armies and the forming of political alliances by the Papacy, the influence of kings upon the appointment of bishops and of cardinals, the struggle of cities against their feudal lords, peasant revolts (Jacqueries), etc., did occur, of course. However, they seem to have occurred chiefly when the "feudal contract" was broken unilaterally,[1] and the system as a whole continued to hold undisputed sway. Its fundamental principles were not seriously challenged until the economically productive citizenry was capable of challenging the nobility.[2] At this point the social system had to be modified to the point where it reflected more adequately the new balance of power between the three estates. Needless to say, society as a whole refused for a long time to give explicit recognition to this new state of affairs. It sought to disguise it by covering up the change with the mantle of feudal fictions. One example is the creation, in France, of a second category of nobility, made up of the chief law officers of the third estate. These men were granted titles of nobility but continued to be referred to as the *noblesse de robe* (nobility of the judicial robe) in order to differentiate them from true feudal nobility, known as the *noblesse d'épée* (nobility of the sword). The revision of the ideological hierarchy of values was even slower, so that, even in countries where the clergy became wholly subordinate to the state, which

[1] It is interesting to note that Jacqueries do not seem to have been motivated primarily by too harsh an exploitation of the peasant by his own lord. Most Jacqueries occurred when, because of his absence or his military weakness, the lord was unable to fulfill his part of the "feudal contract" and failed to protect his serfs against exploitation by others than himself.

[2] This rise in the power of the cities had many causes: the improvement of means of production, the accumulation of wealth through trade, the increasingly rapid circulation of money, the greater availability of precious metals and therefore of ready cash, and, last but not least, changes in the technology of war, which made it possible for the infantry of the cities to resist mounted knights, whose armor no longer provided adequate protection against the English longbow, the improved crossbow, and the newly invented firearms.

paid its salary, or where—as in England—the temporal ruler was also the head of the Church, religion continued to outrank, at least by courtesy, any other value.[3]

Of course, in many instances it is not the hierarchy of values which shapes the structure of society but social structure which "idealizes itself" in the form of a value system. To take an interesting example almost at random, Krader recently published a cogent analysis of the molding of the Buryats' conception of the supernatural world, and of their value hierarchy as well, by the Buryat social system (*140*).

THERAPEUTIC AND ORGANIZATIONAL PATTERN

These considerations serve to indicate that the question of the compatibility or incompatibility of the therapeutic pattern with the organizational pattern is a problem of major importance, closely related to some of the major problems and processes of society and culture as a whole. Just as no culture can survive if it is not supported by a suitable social structure, and just as no social system can operate satisfactorily if it is grossly at variance with the basic culture pattern, so the compatibility of the therapeutic pattern ("culture pattern") of a given school or institution with its organizational pattern plays a major role in determining whether the therapeutic pattern can be implemented to a sufficient extent to make the organization functional.

METHODOLOGICAL CONSIDERATIONS

In seeking to analyze the question of the congruence or noncongruence of the therapeutic pattern with the organizational pattern, we propose to ignore the problem of whether the actual

[3] A peculiar manifestation of this state of affairs is the fact that, since the Book of Common Prayer of the Church of England can be revised only by an act of Parliament, it is possible for Catholic, Nonconformist, Jewish, or agnostic Members of Parliament to vote on what prayers the members of the Church of England should utter.

structural arrangement of the techniques constituting the therapeutic pattern reflects some possible and planned ideal rank ordering of these techniques, or whether it simply "grew like Topsy," as a result of a series of unique historical "accidents" which, in their totality, constitute the developmental history of an organization. Indeed, one may agree or disagree with the value system which assigns a nuclear position to head-hunting in Naga culture, or to the concept of a covenant between God and man in Jewish religion, without changing thereby the actual structural arrangement of Naga culture or Jewish religion. Furthermore, one can analyze the functional consequences of a particular value system without knowing whether the value system itself is a reflection of the social structure or whether—as in the case of medieval society —the latter is a reflection of a value system.

What is incumbent upon us here is to quest for quite a different type of understanding. We must undertake an analysis of the dynamic consequences of the nuclearity of one technique and of the peripherality of other techniques within a total therapeutic and organizational pattern. Actually, wherever a patterning of multiple techniques exists, much confusion is bound to arise if one refuses to recognize the structural realities of this pattern or seeks to obscure its implications by awarding nonfunctional "prestige coefficients" to the practitioners of the several techniques in accordance with some extra-organizational scale of values, which is incompatible with the actual structure of that organization's therapeutic pattern. The need to establish a conformity between the therapeutic and the organizational pattern is particularly acute in organizations devoted to therapeutic education.

THE PATTERN OF PSYCHIATRIC HOSPITALS

An understanding of the special problems of such organizations will be facilitated by a preliminary analysis of the situation prevailing in psychiatric sanitaria and mental hospitals. In principle, the core technique of such institutions is some procedure traditionally associated with practitioners of medicine: individual psychotherapy, shock therapy, lobotomy, etc. Around this core technique are grouped peripheral techniques traditionally associated with nonmedical practitioners: clinical psychology, physiotherapy, occupational therapy, etc. Coördinated with both of these groups of techniques, but somewhat extraneous to them, are techniques directed not at the nuclear objective of the organization, i.e., at the care of patients, but at the maintenance and expansion of the organization itself. These latter operations are performed by persons who may or may not be physicians but who, whether they are physicians or not, do not function in a medical capacity, except incidentally. They constitute the hospital's administrative staff.

In such institutions the physicians and their nonmedical therapeutic associates direct their efforts at an objective which, in a very significant sense, is extra-organizational or, more properly, meta-organizational. This objective is the treatment of patients who are not, strictly speaking, a part of the organization itself, although the organization professedly exists only for their sake. By contrast, the hospital administration directs much of its efforts at the organization itself, which remains, however, an instrumental objective, subordinated to the nuclear objective of therapy. In this respect the hospital differs radically from, e.g., business organizations, whose prime objective is, strictly speaking, intra-organizational in character, since it is concerned with the growth, continuity, and profitableness of the organization itself.[4]

SERVICE ORGANIZATIONS VS. NONSERVICE ORGANIZATIONS

It is our thesis that only the first type of organization—as typified by hospitals—may be legitimately defined as "service organiza-

---

[4] The fact that the profits may go to the shareholders is irrelevant in this context, as is shown by Burnham's analysis of the "managerial revolution" (*21*). Besides, in a sense the shareholders too may be deemed to be—segmentally at least—a part of the organization itself.

tions." Only they pursue an extra-organizational goal and seek to expand the organization solely for instrumental purposes, i.e., for the purpose of providing better care for more patients. It is of no concern to us in this context that there exist also some hospitals which are primarily "moneymaking propositions" and thus deviate functionally from our definition of hospitals as "service organizations." This is best proved by the fact that such profit-oriented hospitals usually go to great length to assume the protective coloring of humanitarianism, in accordance with La Rochefoucauld's dictum: "Hypocrisy is the homage which vice renders to virtue." In fact, few things reveal more clearly the true objectives and real nature of a given social institution than the hypocritical maneuvers of certain other organizations which advance the claim that they, too, belong to the same category. For example, institutions with goals based on humanitarian mores enjoy so much prestige that even wholly self-directed organizations which cannot by any stretch of the imagination be defined as "service organizations" often claim that they seek to "serve the public." Although they sometimes do, in fact, serve the public—for example, because they sell indispensable goods or services—their "public service" is but an instrumental value for them; their real goal is the preservation of the organization itself. Conversely, one should not forget that instrumental values, even when animated by truly meta-organizational objectives, have such a functional autonomy of their own that, even in the "ideal" hospital, there are bound to arise purely "organizational mores" (223), which sometimes interfere with the fullest implementation of the organization's ultimate objective, the latter being formulated in terms of "humanitarian mores." Thus, sometimes an initially and perhaps only nominally instrumental pattern acquires, in the course of time, the functional autonomy characteristic of "organizational mores," occasionally to the point of actually hampering the optimal implementation of nuclear therapeutic goals. The therapeutically unsatisfactory occupational status of nurses seems to be the result of this type of undesirable development (65).

Despite such regrettable accidental by-products of organizational self-perpetuation, our distinction between service and nonservice organizations remains valid. Indeed, the mere existence of an explicit meta-organizational goal (i.e., therapy) radically affects even the most "organizational mores bound" service organizations. It functions—as the French express it—as an *idée-force,* which motivates the organization to pursue objectives based on humanitarian mores.

In nonservice, self-directed organizations the hierarchy of the organizational structure usually corresponds closely to the hierarchical structure of the techniques utilized. The highest and best-paid employees are the administrators; the next in rank and pay are the manipulators of productive ideas (engineers); and so forth. By contrast, with the possible exception of the chief administrator, manager, or superintendent, in hospitals and sanitaria the best-paid and highest-ranking employees are the physicians, who—like the managers of business firms—implement the real goals of the organization. Of course, hospital managers need not necessarily be physicians, and one occasionally finds such administrators who are not. They are, however, an exception to the rule. Usually even those hospital managers whose sole task is to run the hospital smoothly tend to be physicians, precisely—though this is seldom stated explicitly—because it is structurally important for the organization to be consistent in the categorization and rank ordering of its technicians and in the systematic emphasizing of the true objective of the organization. In the case of hospitals, this objective is therapy, i.e., a technique traditionally associated with physicians. This legitimate and basic reasoning is often obscured by unnecessary attempts to justify the appointment of physicians to such administrative positions by alleging that only a "physician turned administrator" can really operate the hospital on medical lines and in accordance with medical objectives. The fact that this line of reasoning is spurious can be shown in many ways. For example, one cannot help being impressed with the efficiency wherewith some veterans hospitals are administered by "lay" managers. In such cases, it suffices that the medical responsibilities be vested in the clinical director, who is a physician. It is also evident that good universities would not offer training in hospital administration to nonmedical persons if there were no demand for them or if they were unable to function satisfactorily in such positions.[5] Hence, it is sufficient to justify the appointment of physicians to hospital managerships in terms of the desirability of maintaining a real congruency between the hospital's "table of organization" and its hierarchy of values and objectives.

Much insight into the functional relationship between humanitarian and organizational mores may be gained by asking a simple question: Why is it deemed necessary to cite spurious reasons in order to justify the appointment of medical superintendents when there are perfectly valid and functional reasons for this policy? The answer seems to be that the good reasons seem somehow more "presentable" than the real ones. Otherwise expressed, it seems more "respectable" to justify the appointment of medical superintendents in terms of humanitarian (medical) mores than in terms of organizational ones. In our opinion this quest for "respectability" is entirely unnecessary. It is quite certain that even the most idealistically humanitarian organization must have certain organizational objectives, which it cannot ignore lest it lapse into chaos and thereby abolish its own usefulness to mankind. It is, of course, a fact that the strictly medical training of the superintendent is largely "wasted" in that administrative position. However, we feel that it is "wasted" in a good—though admittedly intra-organizational—cause. It can be viewed as part of the price one

[5] This type of arrangement may also be found in nonservice organizations. Thus, the manager of a factory does not have to be an engineer.

pays for making the structural and hierarchical pattern of the organization congruent with that of its techniques and objectives. This, we feel, is a valid and desirable undertaking.

The preceding considerations suggest that a purely goal-oriented analysis of the hospital as an institution cannot justify attempts to mask the real (organizational) reasons for the appointment of medical superintendents. On the other hand, an organization-oriented analysis, which stresses such factors as morale, organizational integrity, and soundness, suggests that there is at least a limited need for such a "fiction," which—except in so far as any fiction is undesirable, particularly since it often ends up by being taken for reality—is not outright harmful.

THE PATTERN OF THERAPEUTIC SCHOOLS

As a rule, hospitals find it relatively easy to coördinate their therapeutic pattern with their "table of organization," particularly since tradition itself militates in favor of such a compatibility. By contrast, the task of establishing some kind of congruence between the therapeutic pattern and the occupational hierarchy in special schools devoted to therapeutic education is far from easy, so that the balanced and realistic management of such schools can be a real challenge for competent chief administrators.

An institution devoted to therapeutic education, such as a residential school for "exceptional" children, closely resembles sanitaria and mental hospitals in some respects: it is a genuine service organization animated by humanitarian mores, its organizational "means-end schema" is but an instrument, and its self-perpetuation as an institution is but an instrumental value. On the other hand, the residential school differs from sanitaria in that its organization-oriented pattern differs from its goal-oriented pattern. In concrete terms, the table of organization of the residential school, which implements the rank ordering of the professions and of rates of pay, is, for many reasons, often at variance with its "therapeutic pattern," which reflects the structure of its procedural pattern and ultimate goals.

The principal cause of this state of affairs is that the occupational hierarchy and pay scale of every institution must, of necessity, be in line with the laws of supply and demand, i.e., with the basic structure of the prevailing labor market and with the basic prestige coefficients of various occupational categories.

In order to simplify matters, let us ignore for the moment the purely administrative personnel of institutions for therapeutic education and focus our attention instead solely on the practitioners of the several therapeutic techniques used in such schools. We pointed out that in mental hospitals the men and women engaged in the practice of the core technique—the physicians—are also the persons who have had the most extensive—and expensive—education, enjoy the greatest intramural and extramural prestige, and receive the highest pay. By contrast, in institutions devoted to therapeutic education the practitioners of the core technique—the educators—and the practitioners of the secondary core technique, which aims at making possible a maximum impact of the primary core technique by means of the creation of a therapeutic milieu— the housemothers, counselors, supervisors, and other therapeutic educators in the broad sense—are individuals who, on the whole, have had a less long and less expensive education than the school psychiatrists, enjoy less intramural and extramural prestige, and can command appreciably less pay. This is a basic fact, determined by the structure of the labor market and by the traditional extramural rank ordering of the prestige of various occupations.[6]

[6] A formal and really exhaustive analysis of the pattern of occupational prestige coefficients is long overdue. It is quite certain that such an undertaking will be beset with many difficulties, both objective and subjective. The principal objective difficulty will probably prove to be the fact that the current prestige coefficient of some occupations is a relic of earlier times and no longer reflects social realities. The chief subjective difficulty may turn out to be the paradoxical position of the scientist— who undertakes such a study—in our prestige pattern, and which is mirrored in the well-known quip: "In America, the professor ranks one step above the minister and one step below the bootlegger."

THERAPEUTIC PATTERN VS. PRESTIGE OF TECHNICIANS

In other words, the therapeutic educator is usually confronted with the paradox that whereas his technique is the chief instrumental "value" of the organization, and the nucleus of its self-definition, he himself, as a practitioner of this technique, is organizationally ranked below the practitioners of certain peripheral techniques, such as psychotherapy or clinical psychology, which have a greater extramural market value and prestige, though not necessarily a greater degree of genuine social nuclearity.[7]

We hasten to add that this fact often helps smooth over a situation which, from the administrative point of view, is potentially explosive. Indeed, no organization, however large, complex, and self-contained it may be, can exist in a social vacuum. Hence, the ideologies of the extramural world, its value patterns and choice hierarchies, continue to affect even the most tightly organized intramural world and to influence its personnel. This explains why, if one questions the core technicians of special schools directly, they sincerely profess to see nothing wrong in the fact that the staff psychiatrists, practicing a technique which, in this particular organization, is peripheral, enjoy a greater prestige and receive higher pay than do therapeutic educators. Hence, intra-organizational clashes explicitly caused by this discrepancy are almost unheard of, not because the individual educator feels that, in a pinch, the organization would find it easier to replace him than to replace a psychiatrist, but because he, too, implicitly accepts the occupational prestige coefficients prevailing in society at large.

[7] This last point is of some importance. Functionally, though not in terms of prestige or income, the traditionally underpaid educator is probably more nuclear in Western society than is the therapist. By contrast, some anthropologists have felt (186) that primitive society can be largely defined as a "therapy oriented system" —though even in primitive society the therapist is sometimes very poor (23). It is therefore possible to suggest, at least tentatively, that the high prestige of the medical man in Western society represents a survival from primitive times, when the healing shaman did, in fact, occupy a nuclear position in the social scheme.

EDUCATOR VS. THERAPIST

What difficulties do arise are, superficially at least, caused by "current problems" of a more or less "technical" character. Needless to say, the term "superficially" is not intended to imply "spuriously." We simply mean that even conscious and functional problems, which definitely call for decisions of a technical kind, often derive much additional impetus from extraneous, nonfunctional, and unconscious sources. Otherwise stated, while the problems giving rise to such clashes are genuine enough, the affect which they elicit is often subjective and narcissistic in origin. One is reminded here of Bertrand Russell's witty remark that the light generated by a discussion is usually inversely proportional to the heat which it generates.

Such difficulties arise even in less complex organizations. The frictions between the experienced chief nurse and the junior medical staff are almost proverbial in medical circles. These frictions, like those arising in residential schools, usually originate in the course of objective attempts to deal with various crises which call both for technical therapeutic decisions and for administrative ones. The latter often affect a variety of staff members and therefore represent a "crossing" of various "chains of command." Such "crossings" are hard enough to deal with even in an institution whose table of organization is congruent with the structure of its therapeutic pattern. In therapeutic residential schools, where, as stated above, such a complete congruence does not exist, the situation is even more difficult, and its management calls for much administrative wisdom and tact.

Another source of intra-staff difficulties is related to the feeling of therapeutic educators and milieu therapists—and of psychiatric nurses as well—that in some ways they know more about the student than does the psychiatrist, who, at the most, spends only an hour a day with the student or the patient. It is, of course, perfectly true that the therapeutic educator, milieu therapist, and nurse do know a great deal more about the daily activities and routine behavior of the student than does the psychiatrist, and that their knowledge is actually both valid and important. However, at the same time it is necessary to specify that this knowledge pertains chiefly to the student's ego functions (behavior) and does not, *ipso facto,* include also an insight into his psychodynamics, unconscious impulses, and defense mechanisms.

The situation is comparable to that which obtains in anthropological field work. The white settler or missionary, who spent twenty years with a native tribe, knows everyone personally, and is familiar with countless customs and incidents, is sometimes amazed at the "presumptuousness" of the newly arrived anthropologist, who proposes to make an exhaustive study of "his" tribe in, let us say, a year. He does not understand that the anthropologist can actually perform this task, simply because he knows how to arrange facts into patterns and how to interpret concrete occurrences as manifestations of a broader social process. Thus, the planter or the missionary may know of twenty cases of suicide, while the anthropologist may hear of only five. However, unlike the "old settler," the anthropologist will be able to fit these five cases into the total pattern of the culture and to elucidate the position of suicide in the moral code, religion, literature, and law of the tribe, etc., simply because he is trained for this type of work and has suitable conceptual tools at his disposal for the analysis of the social and cultural meaning of an incident or practice. However, it would be the height of self-defeating arrogance for the anthropologist to turn a deaf ear to the practical advice of the old settler or to refuse to draw upon the latter's inexhaustible store of information about the natives.

In the same way, even though the psychiatrist has special qualifications for understanding what really goes on inside the student, he would make his own work unnecessarily difficult were he to ignore the daily reports of educators, milieu therapists, and the like. Indeed, information about what the student actually does outside the therapy hour is often invaluable to the psychiatrist. Above all, much unnecessary friction and many professional "jealousies" will be eliminated if the psychiatrist not only reads daily reports about the student but also takes the trouble to let teachers, housemothers, unit supervisors, etc., know that their reports are read, put to therapeutic uses, and appreciated.

TEAMWORK AND THE STUDENT

On the other hand, and in the last resort, the psychiatrist must be guided chiefly by what he himself observes, partly because people show more of their real, though unconscious, selves in the therapy hour than in everyday situations[8] and partly because every human being is entitled to tell his own story and to have his day in court. Thus, it seems best to see a prospective student, whose parents wish to enroll him in a residential school, or a student referred to the psychiatrist as a potential candidate for therapy, before one reads or hears anything about him. Then, after one has listened to the student's own story, without preconceived ideas about him, one can read everything there is in his file and write one's final report. Furthermore, the psychiatrist will do well to read carefully the daily reports about every student whom he is treating, without, however, bringing up in the therapy hour any incident which the student himself does not mention first. Nothing is lost by such a discretion, since the very fact that the student refuses to mention, e.g., the fight he had with another boy may help one to understand his reactions to fighting, and also to gain insight into his resistance to therapy. In addition, by not mentioning spontaneously what one read in the daily reports, the therapist

[8] This is less true of students living in a therapeutically educational milieu, such as a residential school, than of patients living at home or in an ordinary school. Indeed, a residential school is therapeutic to the extent to which it permits the student to "take off his mask" also outside the formal therapy hours.

increases the student's confidence in his objectivity and impartiality by not giving the discouraging impression that, no matter what he may say to the therapist, the opinion of the latter will be swayed by what other adults said about the student. This is a particularly delicate matter in the case of adolescents, who are very "touchy" about being treated as "children" and about being "spied upon" by adults. The matter is of so great an importance to some students that they often deliberately refrain from mentioning in the therapy hour even quite spectacular incidents, which must have come to the therapist's attention, simply in order to test to what extent their therapist is truly unprejudiced toward them and is willing to abide by the fundamental principle that the therapy hour belongs exclusively to the patient. Under these conditions it is better to be overcautious than to be overly trusting.

Case 51: A Student Tests His Therapist

In one instance a youth, who was not in therapy with the writer, asked for an interview and reported that he and another youth, who was in treatment with the writer, had done something strictly forbidden, without, however, getting caught. Although the act was a relatively serious one, the writer did not bring it up directly in the therapy hour. He only gave the student an opportunity to mention it spontaneously, if he himself chose to do so. The writer's reason for not mentioning this matter openly, despite its importance, was the remote possibility that the first student might have been sent to him by his own patient, in order to test his discretion and objectivity. Although it turned out in the end that this was not the case, nothing was lost by not bringing up the matter as soon as the writer heard about it, because the patient's silence on this point was, in itself, important for an understanding of his resistances.

CONFLICTS BETWEEN THERAPISTS AND EDUCATORS

Another potential source of conflict between therapeutic educators and psychiatrists is the fact that the former have to bear the brunt of the therapeutized student's "acting out"—or "acting up"—which is caused by a mobilization of his old anxieties as a result of the gradual undermining, through growing insight, of his anxiety-binding symptoms. Thus, it is understandable why even the experienced teacher or housemother occasionally feels that more account should be taken of his or her difficulties with students who are in therapy. This feeling leads to resentments which find an outlet in a variety of attitudes and activities such as: (1) "passing the buck" and assuming an attitude of total passivity, which finds expression in constant demands for guidance, even in matters which any educational or milieu therapist is well qualified to handle; (2) overt or tacit criticism of the doctor; (3) interference with the management of the patient, representing the reverse of the "passing the buck" mechanism; (4) complete impersonality, which includes a refusal to provide the type of emotional support which the patient needs and which only the therapeutic educator is in a position to give (65). Etc.

TRUSTWORTHINESS VS. TEAMWORK

As a rule, elementary good sense is often able to reduce such difficulties to a minimum. While the therapist must rigorously adhere to the principle that any personal material revealed by a patient—be he an adult or a child—is, without any exception whatsoever, absolutely confidential, it is both legitimate and necessary to "issue a storm warning" to the educational and milieu therapy staff when the student leaves the therapy hour in a particularly explosive frame of mind. This does not require that one reveal the causes of the student's current tension. It is enough to warn the educational staff that "a storm is brewing" and to make practical suggestions as to how it should be managed. The educational therapist is grateful for such suggestions and also appreciates being warned to prepare to deal with a "one-child tornado" erupting from the therapy hour.

Special problems arise when the student informs his therapist that he is about to do something forbidden. In some instances the student says this simply in order to "let off steam" or else in the hope of ruffling the objective attitude and composure of his therapist—perhaps so as to test his seemingly rocklike strength, which is so important to the patient himself, as the following incident will show:

Case 52: The Reliable Therapist

An acting-out delinquent, who had been in therapy for nearly a year, remarked to his therapist that he impressed him like a ball of granite, without any chinks or cracks, and not susceptible of being "manipulated" either by cunning or by violence. He stated that this was very reassuring to him, partly because it helped him to vent his aggressions without any fear that he might thereby "destroy" his therapist and partly because it enabled him to respect and to trust the therapist, who could not be manipulated and cajoled like the "suckers" whom he despised.

THREATS OF PATIENTS

More important still is the fact that the student sometimes threatens to do something forbidden or risky solely in order to test his therapist's discretion. In other words, he does it in order to find out whether the therapist will "go running" to the unit supervisor or to the housemother, and "betray" his confidences, or whether he will adhere to his promise to safeguard the patient's privacy even under extreme circumstances. What the patient does not realize, of course, is that, in so doing, he is actually trying to find out whether the analyst has confidence in the student's own ability to behave reasonably. Indeed, nothing is more frightening to a patient than the realization that one is worried over him, since, if even his therapist is worried by his threats, the patient cannot but conclude that the storm raging within him is indeed diabolically destructive.

The way to handle such threats is at once simple and complicated, and the success of any maneuver will depend on the willingness of the therapist to assume responsibility for a "calculated risk." If the "threat" strikes him as being nothing more than a means of "testing" his discretion or stability, he will refrain from doing anything at all about it and will treat the matter as casually as it deserves to be treated. If the threat seems serious, but not conducive to irrevocable harm, he may—at the most—issue a "general storm warning" to the student's home unit. If, however, the student seriously threatens to commit either a genuine crime or else suicide, the therapist will have to do two things: First of all, he must explain to the student that the very fact that he reveals such intentions actually amounts to a "call for help," i.e., that he is asking his therapist to help him control his destructive and unmanageable impulses, thus revealing that he does not really wish to yield to them. An interpretation of this kind often appreciably increases the student's fundamental desire and inherent capacity to control his frightening impulses. In addition, the therapist will inform the student that, in further compliance with this implicit request for help, he will instruct his residential unit to keep him for a while under close supervision. If possible, the therapist should then telephone the home unit in the student's presence and issue appropriate practical instructions, but without revealing the nature of the patient's threats. If it is not possible to telephone the unit then and there, one may write a suitable note, which one shows to the student and asks him to deliver in person to his home unit. While one is admittedly taking the calculated risk that the student may not deliver this note, it is worth trying this approach in order to increase the student's confidence in his own ability to behave reasonably. If possible, one should not even telephone afterwards to the unit, to check up on whether the note has been delivered, except if the risk of irrevocable damage is unusually great or the student is temporarily acutely psychotic. Such a frank and above-board manner of handling the situation will increase the student's confidence in his therapist's discretion and in his ability to handle the student's anxiety-arousing impulses steadfastly and objectively. It will also reassure the student a great deal, by showing him that he will be given the help he needs in controlling his aggressions or his self-destructiveness. In addition, by taking full responsibility for the management of the crisis, and by providing practical suggestions, the therapist will increase the self-confidence of the unit staff, thus enabling it to handle the student with the calm consistency so greatly needed in situations of crisis. Last, but not least, he will materially improve the relationship between himself and the unit staff, thus doing his share in welding the various therapeutic specialists into a functional team.

STAFF RIVALRIES

This latter task is of great importance in all organizations having a relatively complex therapeutic pattern. We have seen that frictions between various categories of therapists occur even in hospitals, where the practitioner of the core technique, the physician, is also—by long tradition—the occupant of the core position in the organizational structure. Hence, it is inevitable that such difficulties should also arise in therapeutic schools, where the practitioner of the core technique—i.e., the therapeutic educator—is usually outranked by the practitioner of a peripheral technique—i.e., by the psychiatrist. Although, as stated above, conflicts explicitly rooted in problems of occupational prestige tend to be largely mitigated by the residual influence of the prestige system prevailing in extramural society, difficulties are bound to arise occasionally, regardless of how well a therapeutically educational institution is managed and regardless of how flexible its policies are. People are human, and never more exasperatingly human than when they can justify their human impulses, susceptibilities, and frailties by relating them to some phase of the organizational mores or ideology.[9]

While this linking of personal grievances, however mild they may be in well-managed organizations, with the organizational mores and ideology represents a general human tendency, it also gives a distinctive stamp to problems arising in such institutions. Specifically, such conflicts, while mostly narcissistic in origin, lend themselves almost too easily to a theoretical and intellectualistic phrasing. Hence, narcissistic rivalries between various classes of technicians often masquerade as "conflicts of principle" or as "technical differences." In a situation of occupational conflict the psychotherapist who practices an extramurally prestigeful but intramurally peripheral technique may insist that his advice must be followed, not because he practices a profession which enjoys a high status in society at large, but because psychiatry "has most of the answers." Conversely, the special educator may similarly deny narcissistic motives in stressing that it is he, after all, who practices the core technique which represents the chief means chosen by that organization for attaining its explicit goal, which is to help "exceptional" children through therapeutic education rather than through individual psychotherapy. These bilateral asseverations of "involvement purely in terms of principles," and the implicit or explicit denials of narcissistic involvement, explain at once the form assumed by such conflicts and the intensity of emotions which conflicts of a genuinely and purely technical order do not ordinarily mobilize. All this is very harmful to the students (*208*).

Much additional space could be devoted to a closer examination of such conflicts, as long as one views them from a purely negative

[9] The writer knows of a large plant, which also carries on research in basic science, in which there is considerable resentment among some of the engineers over the fact that they are made to "support" the research physicists. While the resentment itself is, in a way, understandable in logical terms, its intensity, in that particular plant, seems to be due to managerial inadequacies.

angle. However, quite often a deeper—and also more rapid—insight can be obtained into a seemingly deplorable situation, by seeking to analyze primarily its positive aspects.

THE PATTERNED APPROACH TO THERAPY

The problem confronting us may, therefore, be couched in somewhat the following terms:

1. As regards the psychiatrist, his willingness to work in a residential school, in which psychotherapy is a peripheral technique, clearly implies that he recognizes the value of therapeutic education. If he felt otherwise, he could easily find another kind of position. Hence, his complaints against therapeutic educators and milieu therapists must stem partly from his feeling of not being understood by them and partly from the conviction that, because of a lack of psychiatric sophistication, the other therapists do not practice their own techniques insightfully enough. If these complaints are legitimate—as they may well be in some instances—it seems reasonable to suggest that it is up to the psychiatrist, as practitioner of a peripheral technique, to interpret his work, both in general terms and in concrete situations, to the rest of the staff, and, by making his knowledge available to them, to increase their psychiatric sophistication and their ability to coöperate with him. In fact, sound intramural training in basic psychiatry for educational and milieu therapists invariably pays dividends, not only in the form of better care for the children, but also in the form of better teamwork and improved employee morale.

2. We stated that the educational or milieu therapist often feels that he is left "holding the baby"—the "baby" in question being a "one-child tornado" erupting from the therapeutic chamber, in a mood so explosive as to be almost unmanageable by routine educational and milieu-therapeutic means. In such crises it is humanly perhaps difficult, but technically highly necessary, for the educator or milieu therapist to ask himself precisely how and why that

particular child came to be in therapy in the first place. Once this question is asked, the answer becomes obvious: The child is in therapy simply because, even before therapy, it could not be managed by educational and milieu therapeutic means alone.[10] In other words, there must be a recognition of the role of individual psychotherapy in the therapeutically educational institution as a "court of last appeal"—as shock therapy may be a "court of last appeal" in a psychoanalytic sanitarium—i.e., as something whose effectiveness begins at a point which is beyond the effective reach of the educational core technique. It is hardly necessary to stress here once more something which is explained in detail in Chapter 12. Few cases are inherently either "simple" or "difficult" ones. What may be a "difficult" case for the educator may be a "simple" or "routine" case for the psychiatrist, and vice versa, of course. In other instances, a case which cannot be handled either by psychotherapy or by therapeutic education alone proves easily amenable to treatment by good teamwork. In brief, what is, and what is not, a "difficult case" is usually determined by the inherent limitations of a given technique, or pattern of techniques, for its treatment or management.

Hence, it is fairly obvious that, from the point of view of the core technique—regardless of what this technique may be—the peripheral technique is always a "trouble-shooting device." Furthermore, since, as stated previously, therapeutic schools, etc., are focused on "emergencies," the peripheral technique is, of necessity, an integral part of the therapeutic pattern. This view further implies that no single technique is, or can be, "an Iland, intire of it selfe." The same is true even of "routine-focused" organizations. Thus, although police procedure is a "peripheral technique" in our society, while the collecting of taxes is a nuclear process, the police could not exist without taxes and it may prove impossible to collect

---

[10] This view implies that in such cases psychotherapy is the most efficient but not necessarily the only suitable method.

taxes without the police. Once this interdependence of the various techniques, both nuclear and peripheral, is fully comprehended, so that an appeal to a peripheral technique is viewed as a result of a crisis situation wherewith the core technique is not prepared to deal, a self-justificatory interpretation of interoccupational friction, as resulting from a genuine "conflict of principles," becomes impossible, at least among people of good will, endowed with a modicum of emotional maturity and dedicated to the same objective.

In brief, where the core technique reaches its limits of effectiveness, there are two—and only two—policies open to an institution devoted to therapeutic education: an appeal to some peripheral technique such as psychotherapy, or the dismissal of the student. Since the latter is contrary to the basic objectives of that institution and represents a confession of institutional failure, as distinct from the failure of a particular technique, a final appeal to peripheral techniques is always justified. This, in turn, fully explains and vindicates the seemingly dysfunctional discrepancy between the rank ordering of the techniques used in the special school and the institutional and organizational hierarchy thereof.

....

OBSTACLES TO
THERAPEUTIC EDUCATION

It is the old story of human culture. As
soon as conditions get complex, man
fumbles, muddles and bungles.

ROBERT H. LOWIE

INTRODUCTION TO PART FIVE

The purpose of Part Five is to show that truly effective therapeutic education is beset by a variety of difficulties which have to be explicitly recognized in order to be overcome. Unless this is done systematically and skillfully, real therapeutic education is impossible and the so-called therapeutic school becomes either a kind of penal institution or a kind of pipe-dream paradise, utterly detached from reality—or, what is worse, a place fluctuating between irrational repressiveness and equally irrational and misguided over-leniency.

The difficulties are so many and so varied that they could not be fully discussed in anything short of a separate volume. Hence, we propose to discuss here chiefly some of the most important and most typical difficulties, related respectively to:

1. Society and its attitudes toward children in general and exceptional children in particular.
2. Parental influences in precipitating the illness of the child and in making the illness a permanent one.
3. Internal resistances of the therapeutic educators themselves to a truly creative and liberating program of helping exceptional children.*

* This last point is discussed repeatedly in the present volume, and more particularly in Chapter 5, under the heading "Counter Transference."

CHAPTER 14

....

Social and Cultural Attitudes Toward the Exceptional Child

The purpose of this chapter is to analyze the obstacles which traditional ways of viewing the exceptional child place in the path of effective therapeutic education. These attitudes are compounded of more primary traditional beliefs concerning (1) children in general and (2) mental disorders.

We will examine the first of these two attitudes and will then proceed to show in what manner traditional interpretations of disturbances in the behavior of children are at variance with the views underlying the whole philosophy of therapeutic education.

THE PROLONGED IMMATURITY OF THE HUMAN CHILD

Ever since Fiske (83) many of our most realistic insights into the "nature of human nature" have been derived from the realization that the crucial fact about mankind is the prolonged helplessness, immaturity, and dependence of the human child. Most of the behavior sciences, such as the psychology of learning, psychoanalysis, sociology, anthropology, and "culture and personality studies" assume this fact to be of fundamental importance (146, 190). It has also been noted that—generally speaking—as cultures become more complex, the longer and more complex will be the training necessary for earning a living and for making an adjustment to society. Hence, such societies increasingly delay the granting of a truly adult status to adolescents.

Thus, whereas among the Sedang head-hunters of Indo-China young Ndat, who was probably not over seventeen years old, managed to become a "leading citizen" simply by virtue of his personal maturity, economic competence, and ready tongue, in China a man never really grows up socially until his father dies, and even then remains, as Hsu expresses it, "under the ancestors' shadow" (121). In rural Ireland, even a fifty-year-old man is referred to as a "boy" if his father has not yet handed over to him the family farm, thus enabling him to get married (5, 6). In many societies this artificial prolongation of the immaturity of certain groups is systematically implemented by special social pressures or educational devices. For example, Dollard (68) has shown that the Southern whites not only define the Negro as an immature person but also force him to behave in an immature manner. This explains why Southerners address even adult Negroes as "boy," just as colonials call even elderly domestic employees by that term.[1] Victorian English middle- and upper-class society likewise systematically infantilized its women, by training them to be sexless, dependent, and helpless, thus completely reversing the trends of the Regency period, when duchesses cursed like mule skinners, society women were promiscuous and could be "bought," and a precocious maturity was practically forced upon adolescent girls.

In other societies the young are penalized both for an early and for a late maturity. Thus, it is said that when a debutante appeared at the Court of France she was made to drink deep from a golden goblet, whose inner surface was ornamented with scenes which became increasingly obscene as the level of the wine dropped in the cup. If the girl blushed, she was laughed at for being too inno-

[1] The equating of children with servants will be discussed further below.

cent, while if she did not blush she was ridiculed for being too sophisticated and knowing.

In many societies the "proper" rate of social maturation is judged by arbitrary standards. For example, according to Margaret Mead (166), one of the great social derelictions in Samoa is "presuming above one's age," while in other societies (166) children are systematically forced into a precocious maturity, in order to make them assume prematurely many of the burdens of adulthood —often without permitting them to enjoy at the same time also the privileges thereof. Child labor is a particularly striking example of this. In nineteenth-century Austria the parents' right to their children's earnings was so firmly established that, with the advent of the industrial system, a special law had to be passed to prevent parents from collecting at the pay window of the factory the salary of even their adult children. A moment's reflection will show that the same dual attitude inspires some of the most grotesque laws of our own society. For example, in some states the "age of consent"—i.e., the age at which a young girl may agree to have extra-marital sex relations without exposing her lover to prosecution for "statutory rape"—is much higher than the age at which the girl may—usually with the consent of her parents—contract a marriage. This implies that the girl is not deemed intelligent and mature enough to make decisions regarding a relatively temporary affair but is held to be mature enough to consent to marriage, which, in principle at least, involves a lifelong commitment. This has nothing to do with questions of morality, since it is ridiculous to assume that "wickedness" is less—rather than more—wrong in the case of adults than of children. The real basis of this law is the now almost obsolete conception of one's daughter's chastity as "valuable merchandise," useful in promoting economically or socially profitable marriages or in diminishing the dowry to be paid to a swain, who might ask for more money if he is expected to marry an unchaste girl. The same dual attitude also finds an ex-

pression in laws relating to the age of voting. The boy of eighteen
is deemed mature enough to lay down his life in defense of his
country, mature enough for the country to rely upon him for its
very survival in a life-or-death crisis—but not mature enough to
vote for a city dogcatcher, or to be elected to that responsible office
himself. Or, to take another example, some states still deem certain
children old enough to work for a living or to perform skilled
manipulations in the midst of machinery revolving at high speed
but not old enough to dispose freely of the fruits of their labors:
the pay check. We may well ask in connection with such anomalies
a question usually asked only in criminal investigations: *"Cui
bono?"* "Who profits by it?" The simple fact is that society treats
the young as adults when it suits its convenience, or when it is sufficiently exasperated, but treats them as children when that is what
benefits the adults most. Current controversies regarding juvenile
delinquency strikingly illustrate this point.

There is at present much agitation to hand over a child guilty
of a major crime not to the juvenile but to the criminal court, on
the grounds that its misdeed is a heinous one. This, of course, is
simply an attempt to revive a point of Roman law, which, even
though it gave child offenders special consideration on account of
their youth, nonetheless felt that, in extreme cases, *malitia supplet
aetatem*—"malice makes up for what the child is lacking in age"
(*141*). It is noteworthy, however, that society fails to be conse-
quent in this matter and therefore does not implement also another
principle, implicit in the first one, namely, that "maturity makes
up for what the child lacks in years," and therefore does not grant
full citizenship rights to eighteen-year-old heroes. Only a French
poet argued in favor of this view when he wrote: "Courage does
not wait upon the accumulation of years." (*La valeur n'attend pas
le nombre des années.*) As a result, fifteen-year-olds are sometimes
sentenced, under adult criminal law, to lifelong imprisonment.

Even in meting out punishment society applies a double standard to children. According to recent newspaper reports, an influential Philadelphia official came out in favor of the public whipping of juvenile delinquents. He apparently felt that, even though in most civilized states adults are no longer subjected to this degrading and bestial punishment, it is "good enough"—or, perhaps, "just right"—for juvenile delinquents.

In addition, corporal punishment continues to be resorted to in many "training schools" for delinquents, even in states where physical punishment is no longer administered to adult offenders.

PROLONGED PARENTHOOD

At this point we come to an extremely important corollary of Fiske's finding that man's prolonged immaturity deeply affects human nature and society. This corollary is that most people, sometime or other in their lives, function as parents, guardians, teachers, or persons having authority over children. This fact deeply affects man and society alike. It is very likely that the idea that one person has the right to lord it over another is directly derived from the fact that adults can pretty much do with children as they please, since children are neither physically nor intellectually a match for them.

The vocabulary of many languages substantiates this inference. The legal term "dependent"—so important at income tax times—which now denotes chiefly children, originally also included servants, poor relatives, and slaves. The Hungarian word for family, *"család,"* appears to be related to the word *"cseléd,"* meaning servant nowadays, but among peasants it originally meant also "child." Thus, a Hungarian peasant may address his small child affectionately as *"kis cselédem"*—"my little servant." Even in twentieth-century America a father can sue the man who impregnates his unmarried daughter for "damages resulting from the loss of the services of his daughter and servant." The Scottish term "clan" once denoted both children and dependents. The Sedang Moi slave addresses his master as "father" (*pa:*) and, since adult men wear their hair long, the slaves' hair is cut short—as short as the hair of children naturally is. This habit is so deeply ingrained in members of this tribe that, when the writer hired Sedang servants, one of them promptly cut his own hair, and the writer intervened just in time to prevent the others from doing likewise. We have already mentioned that the European colonial calls even an old manservant "boy," and to this day a woman, no matter how old, who works in a home as a servant is spoken of as the "maid"—i.e., as an unwed and immature woman. In Holland, which is an extremely title-conscious country, no female "superior servant," even if married, is entitled to be addressed *"Mevrouw"*—"my (married) woman." She can claim only the title *"Juffrouw"*—"miss." This term is related to the German word *"Jungfer"* denoting a female house servant, derived from the expression *"junge Frau"* (young woman). The latter, when written as a single word (*"Jungfrau"*), means "virgin" (= child). This practice jibes, in turn, with the legal and social minimization of the sanctity of a subordinate person's marriage. Thus, the highest, and most binding, form of marriage in Rome—by which the woman passed into the hands (*manus*) of her husband—was limited to the upper class, while the marriage of second-rate members of the Roman empire involved more equality for the woman but also less social recognition for the marriage (*137*). The feudal lord's right of access to the newly wed peasant bride (*jus primae noctis, droit du seigneur*) and his informal power to seduce the married peasant women also show how little even the religious marriage of serfs enabled them to achieve truly adult status[2] in medieval society.

We hold that *the adult's experience of having "total power" over another person—as in the parent-child relationship—is quite as important for human society, and therefore also for an understand-*

[2] This interpretation is not incompatible with the Freudian thesis that the *jus primae noctis* is derived from the "taboo of virginity" (*95*). The two interpretations are in different universes of discourse: Freud's is psychological, while the above one is sociological.

ing of "the nature of human nature," as is the child's experience of prolonged dependence on its parents. In fact, the one presupposes the other. Hence, it is very characteristic of man's emotionally determined blindness that, just as analysts have neglected the study of counter-oedipal impulses, and have concentrated instead on the oedipal urges of the child (57), so social scientists with a psychological bent have stressed chiefly the social relevance of prolonged childhood but, with rare exceptions (146), have systematically neglected the social relevance of prolonged parenthood.

How intimately these matters are articulated with social structure may be judged by the following fact. During the heyday of the Russian Revolution, when "maximum liberty" was an explicit goal, the government tried to abolish the family, to minimize marriage, to separate parents from children, to encourage free abortion and contraception, and to destroy parental power over the children. However, when Stalinism replaced early Leninism, and naked dictatorship became the avowed goal, it was realized that children trained for freedom, outside a patriarchal family, made poor communist robots. Hence, Stalinism gradually reëstablished the old patriarchal family. More recently, Khrushchev even assailed contraception and abortion as "uncommunistic" and "bourgeois" crimes.[3] The Russian Revolution has come full circle, and training for slavery begins now as early in Soviet Russia as it once did in feudal Europe: in the patriarchal family (60).

An understanding of the subordinate position of the child in our society is of crucial importance to the child therapist and educator. Only if he is fully aware of his own, culturally determined, biases on this point can he ever hope to treat the child entrusted to his care as a human being, instead of as so much clay. At the same time, he may just as well realize that he will get little enough assistance in this undertaking either from the child's parents or from society.

[3] We simply emphasize the grotesqueness of condemning as "bourgeois" something which is unlawful and morally condemned also in our society.

Case 53: Maternal Interferences with Therapy

A paranoid mother vented her unconscious hostility toward her daughter by bombarding the girl and the girl's therapist with a series of highly emotional letters, which almost disrupted the therapy. The wording of these letters was quite remarkable. The mother saw herself as a heartbroken and unremittingly vigilant parent, who shrank from no sacrifice to protect her immoral, rebellious, and ungrateful daughter from the inevitable consequences of her evil ways. Indeed, had the girl been what her mother "believed" (?) her to be, these letters would have been veritable monuments of maternal devotion. Actually, however, they simply showed how cunningly a paranoid individual can conceal destructive hatred behind a façade of "love." The girl was neither immoral, nor rebellious, nor ungrateful. She was simply a badly confused youngster who whole-heartedly coöperated with her therapist and did her best to overcome the tragic effects of her unhappy childhood.

This case, when taken in conjunction with the considerations which precede it, indicates that the real status of the child in society is profoundly influenced by what adults find convenient to believe about children. We must therefore devote some attention to certain prevalent ideas about the "nature of children and of childhood."

PRECONCEPTIONS REGARDING CHILDREN

THE CHILD: CHERUB OR KERUB?

We like to think of the small child as a "cherub," consisting exclusively of a halo, blond curls, a babyish face, dimpled arms and hands, and a pair of wings. However, if we seek to understand what we are trying to do to our children, that which this image of the cherubic child includes is far less important than is that which it so conspicuously fails to include.[4] The word "cherub" is related

---

[4] Conspicuous omissions, which practically clamor to be noticed, are also of paramount importance for the understanding of the latent content of dreams. Thus, the writer once had occasion to interpret a dream about three fishes named Mark,

to *kirubu,* which definitely designated not a sexless baby but the hypermasculine man-headed bull of Assyrian religious sculpture. In brief, the definition of the child as a cherub seeks to obscure the presence of sexual and aggressive impulses in small children. Not until Freud (*88*) and Hall (*110*) scandalized occidental society by describing the sexual impulses of small children did science officially take cognizance of something known to every nursemaid. Unfortunately, most parents continue to be haunted by the notion that children should be cherubs. Hence, when their own—quite human—children fail to display an angelic lack of sexual and aggressive impulses, an attempt is made to force them to approximate this inhuman ideal of perfection by punishing them for being human. In other instances certain children are defined as "cherubs" and other children as "kerubs." Thus, little girls are supposedly made of "sugar and spice and everything nice," while little boys are said to be made of "snippets and snails and puppy-dog tails."[5]

Of course, real children are neither cherubs nor kerubs, but something in between. They are human beings who crave love and try so hard to deserve it that sometimes they give up even their normal impulses and become neurotic, so as to meet the irrational expectations of their parents (see Chapter 15). In other instances the girl revolts against the parental denial of her uncherubic lower body by becoming provocatively "naughty," while the boy often accepts with appalling naïveté—and tragic results—his parents' belief that he is nothing but a bestial kerub, minus even the human head which such statues possess.

The harm which such fictions may cause can hardly be overestimated. They induce parents to expect the impossible from their

Matthew, and Luke. Since the fish was an early Christian symbol for Christ, it was obvious that the dreamer used the *Gestalt* of the four evangelists to attract attention to the omission of the fourth evangelist, John. The dreamer's associations rapidly proved that the dream actually concerned someone named John.

[5] Castrative impulses toward boys are revealed by the words "snippets" and "puppy-dog tails." Cf. the "Blackie test," in which castration anxiety is disclosed by the subject's reaction to a picture showing an ablation of a dog's tail.

children, and a child's failure to measure up to such irrational standards of perfection is interpreted as "badness," which calls for harsh and repressive punishment. By contrast, a constructive insight into the real nature of children and an understanding of their potentialities and limitations often suffice to protect the young both against overestimation, i.e., against impossible demands, and against underestimation, i.e., against condemnation. Otherwise expressed, only a realistic conception of the nature of children can protect the child against pathogenic punitiveness and equally pathogenic "spoiling."

Closely related to these destructive fictions are certain misconceptions regarding the role of childhood in the total life history of the individual.

THE MYTH OF HAPPY CHILDHOOD

Envious adults often remark that childhood is the happiest period of life. It is self-evident that only emotionally immature grownups, who still crave infantile gratifications, hold such a view. By and large, this envious attitude prevails chiefly in technologically advanced societies, where the child cannot contribute at an early age to the support of the family and is therefore viewed as a "luxury."

Needless to say, this myth sounds more convincing to the layman than to the serious student of child development. Unfortunately, it is a rather tenacious myth, since it appeals to our sentimentality, which, like most sentimentality, as distinct from real feeling, is but one of the protean masks of resentment, envy, and hostility.[6] Indeed, adults cling to the myth of happy childhood only in order to contrast it with the "burdens of adulthood." Parents who believe in this myth therefore often see to it that their chil-

[6] The three peoples which perpetrated the greatest cruelties during or since World War II—the Germans, the Japanese, and the Russians—are notorious for their sentimentality.

dren assume the "burdens of adulthood" at an early age—without, however, granting them also the privileges of adulthood.

We have stated that the myth of happy childhood is but an expression of the resentfulness of emotionally immature adults, who envy the gratifications which their children derive from being children only because they have never grown up sufficiently to prefer adult gratifications. Only persons who have never learned to enjoy work envy the child for not having to earn its living, and therefore see to it that the child does not have too good a time while it is engaged in learning those techniques by means of which it will eventually have to earn its daily bread.

Let us try to look at this factual description with creative naïveté. It obviously implies that some adults do not enjoy at all the fact that they have to work for a living and must support their wives and children. It means that such a man views work not as a blessing but as a curse; not as a deeply gratifying creative act but as a punishment for the "crime" of being adult and of enjoying adult privileges. Such infantile persons would like to have all the privileges of adulthood without its creative obligations. Now, it seems fairly evident that such a "pseudo adulthood" is not in the least adult. It represents a wholly infantile "program" or "daydream." It is this daydream of an irresponsible, uncreative "adult" (?) life which the adult unconsciously has in mind when he speaks of "happy carefree childhood." What is quite certain is that he is not speaking of real childhood.

Viewed psychoanalytically, this attitude clearly reveals the emotionally immature though physically mature "adult's" desire to be forever dependent upon a perennially bountiful mother, as well as his inability to take a creative attitude toward his work. Those who "have" such a perennial mother (the rich playboys) and those who brazenly "manufacture" such provident mothers (the exploitive psychopaths and their ilk) seek to create such a "happy carefree childhood" for themselves also in adult life (60).

How obviously such persons think of themselves not as real adults but as children is shown by their strangely offended and "hurt" attitude when—after committing some illegal act—they are taken to task in a manner befitting adults instead of mere juvenile delinquents. They seem to feel, in a way, that they deserve nothing more than a spanking.

Their second trait, their incapacity to experience work creatively, as a source of gratification and as a "sublimation" (*169*), is also a sign of immaturity, related to the myth of carefree childhood. Social and economic scientists, as well as industrial psychologists and, above all, Thorstein Veblen, have discussed the frustrations of the workingman's creativeness—of his so-called "instinct of workmanship" (*220*)—by work on the assembly line, where the worker never even sees the finished product. In fact, if he is one of those who do see it, he is usually not the one who actually made it. This argument, while partly true, is also so seductively plausible that it deserves being examined more closely.

The inference seems to be that "once upon a time" it was not so. This "once upon a time" is presumably one of those legendary "golden ages" (*189*) which continue to haunt the imagination of men throughout history and are referred to in Greek mythology, in the Old Testament, and in Near Eastern cuneiform tablets as well.[7]

Now, anyone who has taken the trouble to watch the daily routine of a primitive will soon realize (*181*) that it is a far from thrilling one, even if—as the writer can attest from experience—the Sedang Moi head-hunter does begin and complete his basket, and his wife does the same with the skirt she is weaving. The fact remains that basketry and weaving are as distinctly subsidiary occupations in this agricultural society as is, e.g., the woman analyst's

[7] The writer recalls his own childish resentment when, having at the age of eight developed a passionate interest in the derring-do of the Arthurian knights of the Round Table, he was "tactlessly" told by his father that the medieval knights were so small that a normal man of our own time could probably not even squeeze into the armor of one of these mythical giants.

knitting during the analytic hours. The Sedang himself is so clear in his own mind on this point that he refers to the drinking of alcohol during agricultural feasts as "paying our souls for the trouble they have taken while we worked." Yet, in this tribe, each person participates in all phases of agricultural work, which is, in a genuine sense, viewed not only as an economic but also as a ritual pursuit. A similar rite for rewarding one's souls for tedious and backbreaking toil came into being when Sedang villages had to furnish —in lieu of taxes—labor for road maintenance. In this case there was not only a frustration of the "instinct of workmanship" but also a lack of interest in roads and resentment over having to furnish labor gangs. Yet the "soul-paying rite" of road gangs and of sacred agricultural rituals is the same. This in itself proves that cultivation, too, is viewed as backbreaking toil.[8]

Yet, withal, the assembly-line worker does not find it easy to experience his work as creative and emotionally gratifying. The crux of the matter seems to be that the "soul-paying" agricultural feasts of the Sedang are integral parts of the whole working pattern, which includes not only the backbreaking and tedious teamwork of weeding but also the joys of the harvest feast. The contrast between old-time "cornhusking bees" and the dull chore of husking corn mechanically and alone is also of this order. There is nothing startling in this insight. Modern employers organize office parties and—in so far as possible—seek to make even factory work more like a cornhusking bee and less like the dehumanizing toil of nineteenth-century factories. There is ample proof of the human and economic efficiency of this approach (*185*).

[8] It may be objected, of course, that such characterizations are inapplicable to "romantic" economies, like Plains Indian buffalo hunting or Sedang slave raiding. We suspect, however, that buffalo hunting was largely romanticized by inherently sedentary professors of anthropology. And we know that Sedang slave raiding was quite unromantic to the Sedang themselves. When the French put an end to it, so that the Sedang had to perform their annual victory feasts without real victories, one of them remarked to the writer: "Of course, this way we have no slaves to sell— but, on the other hand, no one in the mock raiding party is getting hurt either." This remark speaks for itself.

Unless working conditions are exceptionally bad, any work whatsoever can, with a little imagination, acquire a meaning and become a source of gratifications and an outlet for sublimations. Hence, the fact that one considers work *per se* as a curse is proof positive of one's emotional immaturity. The adult person who, precisely because he is an adult, has creative needs, is, by definition, a person who needs work, in order to live a full and enjoyable life.[9]

It is the emotionally immature adult's inability to enjoy work which is responsible for the myth of happy childhood, which implies, in turn, the myth of adult drudgery.[10] Many parents transmit such unhealthy attitudes toward work to their children.

Case 54: The "Curse" of Work

The prosperous vice president of a bank, who had wanted to become a physician but had been forced to take over his father's old job at the bank, hated his work and never ceased telling his son how hard it is to earn a living. He urged him to enjoy his "happy carefree childhood" because "when you are grown up, the black bull of life will gore you." Needless to say, when the son decided to become a writer, the father tried to force him to become a banker, exactly as he himself had been forced to become one. However, the son refused to comply and, after many privations, became a well-known novelist. Yet, despite his successful rebellion, the son had so fully accepted his father's belief that one could only earn money by performing inherently odious and uncongenial tasks, that whenever he received a royalty check he felt the impulse to return it to his publishers. "It seems like money obtained under false pretenses. I seem to feel that one should only get paid for doing work—and writing novels does not seem like real work to me. I love to write, and work is something you hate to do—the way my father hated his work at the bank. Sometimes I think I made it hard for myself to succeed, because I felt I did not deserve pay for doing something which did not seem like 'honest toil' to me."

[9] The popularity of "do it yourself" hobbies may be due not only to the rising cost of labor but also to man's need to create something during his leisure time, if his regular work is too badly organized to gratify his creative urge.

[10] Cf. Veblen's antinomy: Exploit vs. drudgery (*219*).

This case is far from unique. Many parents systematically undermine the child's self-respect and interest in work, and exalt their
own labors by depreciating its efforts.

Case 55: A Child's Work Seems "Worthless"

An adolescent undergoing analysis reported that, at the age of thirteen, he worked after school in a store. "It gave me a funny sort of feeling to be paid for my work. I could not persuade myself that a mere
child's work could be worth $15.00 a week. I did all I was supposed to
do—and it still didn't seem right for a child to earn that kind of money.
(Therapist: You mean that only adults can do productive work?) I did
feel that way. My boss must have felt that I earned my pay since, during
the summer, he hired me full time. But I kept on feeling small and
young and incompetent—not at all like a person whose work would
warrant his getting paid for it. (Therapist: What made you feel that
way?) I don't really know. I do know that my father always brags
about how clever he is to earn a living, and he always depreciates everything I do. Maybe he wants me to think that he is something extra special, because he is able to earn a good living. Or maybe he is trying to
force me to be grateful to him. Anyhow, he made me feel that everything I did was worthless. He made me feel small. I often feel that
everyone except myself is grown up and clever and competent—that
only I am small and incompetent. No matter how hard I work, and no
matter how much money I earn, I never feel that my work is good
enough to warrant my being paid for it."

We have already stated that the myth of happy childhood seems
to prevail chiefly in industrial society, in which children are economically unproductive. In technologically more backward societies, where the child is an economic asset at an early age, neither
the myth of happy childhood nor the myth of wretched adulthood
seems to be prevalent. Many primitives are only too glad to be
adults and therefore neither encourage their children to remain
childish nor wallow in self-pity while contrasting their hard life
with the pleasures of childhood.

Thus, the Sedang (26) considers agricultural work so onerous that he finds it necessary to "reward his soul for its labors" by getting drunk periodically. On the other hand, he appears to enjoy such ancillary pursuits as making baskets, setting traps, and hunting. Above all, he does not contrast his lot with that of children, since even four-year-old Sedang girls take care of their younger siblings, bring water and firewood, and prepare dinner, while four-year-old boys herd the buffaloes, whose huge horns protect their small "guardians" against tigers and other dangers. The fact that children too are workers is so self-evident to the Sedang that every native character sketch of a child began in one of two ways:

1. "X is a baby. He is so young that all he knows is how to nurse, play, and void his stools and urine."

2. "Y is already working in the fields. He has intelligence and knows how to perform such and such tasks."

We stated in Chapter 2 that the native child derives satisfaction from identifying itself with its parents, by sharing their labors. Many tribes systematically encourage the child to grow up, by glorifying adult pursuits and by rewarding the child whenever it develops a new adult skill. Thus, when a Cheyenne Indian boy kills his first bird, he is a social cynosure for the day. His father presents a fine horse to some poor old person who, astride this steed, rides through the camp, announcing to all and sundry the little boy's feat (107). As regards the Sedang, the writer himself was present when a small boy took charge of the village buffaloes for the first time. He seemed to burst with pride as he sat astride the biggest bull, and "made a production" out of "driving" the herd to its habitual wallowing place in the jungle.

We do not imply that primitive children are never exploited or taken advantage of. A Mohave woman complained that in her childhood she had to carry around a young relative, who was far too heavy for her (39). To:a(ng), the writer's Indo-Chinese stableboy, was orphaned at an early age and heartless relatives sold him as a slave to a neighboring village. This, however, was actually a violation of native custom, and his relatives "managed to get away with it" only because To:a(ng) was still too young at that time to protect himself.[11] We recognize that the Arunta (213) boy must surrender to the old men the best part of the game which he has killed, that children in Alor (72) are not treated kindly, that Tanala (150) fathers and older brothers exploit the younger sons, and that, during periods of starvation, Australian (187) parents and older siblings eat the smallest baby. Likewise, when the writer gave a blanket to the shivering little son of the Sedang sorceress A-Rua, the mother took away her son's new blanket and gave him one of her own old blankets instead. In brief, even primitives abuse their children on occasion, but at least they do not pretend even to themselves that the child's lot is necessarily a happier one than is that of the adult.

One of the most important social consequences of the myth of happy childhood is that it provides a basis for parental counter-claims for a happy and secure old age. Indeed, if the drudgery of the parents is responsible for the happiness of children, then it seems only fair that the latter should toil in turn to provide a happy old age for their erstwhile benefactors. This is the psychological background of our laws which require even children deserted by their parents to support the latter in their old age.

We certainly do not deny that many primitive parents also expect their children to support them in their old age, on the basis of the parents' sacrifices. A tribe of Madagascar—which is obsessed

[11] To:a(ng) himself was fully aware of the fact that an injustice had been done to him, and planned to sue his relatives for damages as soon as he had earned enough money in the writer's service to acquire the status of a man of substance, who is not to be trifled with. Indeed, in that area a man can obtain justice only if he has relatives to back him up or is wealthy enough to command prestige. Since To:a(ng)'s claim was against his own relatives, he had to acquire wealth in order to make his claim "stick." The only exception to this rule are trespasses so outrageous that the gods take it upon themselves to punish the transgressor. In such cases there is a public outcry against the offender, which usually suffices to make him pay damages and a punitive fine as well.

with early toilet training—holds that the child owes compensation to its parents because, when it was a baby, it soiled them.[12] This case is especially revealing, since the claim is based on a childish "misdeed" which was especially unendurable to parents obsessed with soiling.

We recognize that some primitives profess to procreate children chiefly in order to have someone take care of them in their declining years. Thus, in the Torres Straits (4) the abortion rate decreased when there arose a demand for native laborers. Miller (172) even cites an African song to the effect that parents procreate children so as to make them work on their farms. Yet the myth of happy childhood seems absent even in tribes where parents expect their children to be a kind of "old age insurance" (50) because they took care of them during their early years. This may explain why the writer knows of no primitive tribe which forces a deserted child to support its delinquent parents in their old age. The primitive is admittedly quite often a very dutiful son, but apparently chiefly because he has been well treated by his parents. Thus, the Mohave (45) praised a man who was greatly devoted to his kindly stepfather, who had taken care of him in his childhood, but repudiated his real father, who had deserted him. By contrast, in some economically marginal tribes the decrepit old parents demand that their son kill them, since in such groups the adults must survive if the tribe is to go on (200). Hence, in such groups, adults and children are not expected to starve, so as to feed the aged. In many such tribes the "gift of life" is therefore not deemed to be a particular boon providing a basis for parental counterclaims, since the harshness of reality is too tangible and the struggle for survival too strenuous to make the mere "gift of life" seem like an especially meritorious act.

The point of this whole argument is that only parents who are emotionally too immature to enjoy the duties and labors of parent-

---

[12] Ralph Linton, personal communication.

hood feel that their "drudgery" alone is responsible for the "happy, carefree" childhood of their offspring and therefore view it as a basis for counterclaims. Parents who enjoy parenthood have no such feelings and therefore make no counterclaims. For example, it is reported that a Jewish man insisted on being a beggar, rather than live on the bounty of his well-to-do and devoted daughter (*127*).

INFANTILIZATION

Another important implication of the absence of the myth of happy childhood (as contrasted with a myth of adult drudgery) is that primitive parents seldom seek to prolong artificially the "(happy) child status" of their offspring.[13] One does not see among natives pubescent boys dressed in the equivalent of Little Lord Fauntleroy suits, which are so traumatic to children in our own society.

Case 56: Infantilization of an Adolescent

A European analysand made the following remarks: "I will never forgive my parents for making me wear socks and knee-length pants at the age of fourteen, when all the other boys in town already wore long pants. I hated to go out with bare knees and bare calves. They made me dress as though I were five years old, in order to humiliate me and make the girls laugh at me. It was part of their whole system of infantilizing me. At sixteen I was not even allowed to decide which shirt I would wear on a given day. I was not permitted to spend the money I earned tutoring other children, without asking permission, which often was denied. As a result, I did not know how to handle money. Hence, when I went away to college, I did not even know how to budget, and my adequate monthly allowance evaporated in two weeks. Yet, I did not spend money like a drunken sailor. I simply seemed to have been 'drunk with freedom,' because I never had a chance to develop the ability to

[13] There are exceptions to this rule. Among the Chaga (*182*) a mother may not bear children after her daughter begins to bear them. Hence, some Chaga mothers resort to various devices for delaying the puberty of their daughters.

control myself in any way. . . . It was not necessary for me to do so. My parents controlled me day and night, giving me no chance to develop some ego strength of my own."

This crippling type of infantilization, which leads to lack of self-control and of creative autonomy, appears to be almost unknown in primitive society. This may explain why, after searching the literature for twenty years for data on mental disorders in primitive society, the writer was able to locate only a very few instances of genuine impulsive character disorders.

In brief, the primitive child is neither encouraged nor taught to *be* a child (29). Even less is he taught to remain a child. He is simply permitted to be one (45). This fact is, in our opinion, of major importance to child psychologists. We strongly suspect that, just as it is obvious today that Charcot's "prize cases" of *grande hystérie* were systematically taught to actualize their inherent potentiality for developing this clinical picture, so that Charcot's theory of hysteria was largely based not on the observation of "genuine" hysterics but on that of "taught" hysterics, so parts of what child psychologists consider to be "the psychology of children" is not so much a genuine psychology of childhood as a psychology of chronologically immature persons who are taught to be children, the way "being a child" is defined by adults. We firmly believe that a true, comprehensive, and generalized "psychology of childhood" is impossible without a careful study of societies in which children are not taught and made to behave "like children," i.e., in accordance with (usually partly unconscious) adult ideas and expectations. This, rather than the direct influence of the culture pattern upon the behavior of children, explains why many "normal" primitive children so often behave very differently from our "normal" children. They behave like children, period. Ours behave to an appreciable extent in accordance with "childish behavior," as defined by adults.[14]

[14] Needless to say, the tendency to establish a conventional norm for "childlike behavior" is also a part of our culture.

We do not imply, of course, that primitives have no views about the nature of children, or that they invariably manage them with sagacity.

Case 57: A Spoiled Primitive Child

Little Nuo, a Sedang boy approximately four years of age, is rather neurotic and quite a domestic tyrant. This is not surprising, since his father is a rather weak and somewhat irresponsible but very intelligent man, while his mother is an industrious but depressive woman, prematurely worn out by domestic cares and numerous childbirths. Nuo was often quite hard to control. For example, he suddenly decided that he had to eat first, and thereafter refused to eat at all and displayed a great deal of temper if anyone else presumed to dip into the pot before he had his fill. The family meekly accepted his orders, since they did not dare antagonize their only surviving son.[15] Thus, Nuo had two parents and several older sisters to dance attendance upon him, because of the belief that, if one antagonizes a small child, its fragile soul, still only tenuously attached to its body, will take fright and flee, causing the child to die. When Nuo was slightly ill and more than usually fretful, the writer, whom Nuo knew very well indeed, was asked to take care of him. However, the boy flatly refused to take even an aspirin. When the writer tried to be firm about it, the family became frightened and begged him to desist, lest Nuo's offended soul take flight. This certainly differs from older European practices—if a sick child refused to take castor oil, sick or not, it received a spanking (Case 61).

While the Sedang way of educating a child is not an ideal one, it certainly does not have at its roots the conception that childhood is a particularly happy period of life. Instead, the child is defined as a highly vulnerable being, only incompletely attached to the earth. This latter belief is probably determined by a high ratio of infant mortality. Indeed, among the Mohave, where twin mortality

[15] This family lost so many children that, in order to make their newborn children seem less desirable to the evil spirits, they gave them, in accordance with Sedang custom, "repulsive" names. The older girls' names were variations on the word "stench." In the case of this only son, the parents went even further, and called him Nuo = urine.

is very great, twins are the only persons believed to be capable of dying at will and, until they marry, are thought to be only incompletely attached and committed to life on earth (32).

THE RANK OF THE CHILD

In our own society the child occupies a rank or status which is exceptionally low by any standards. This is not the case in many primitive societies. In the Marquesas Islands[16] the child's rank is automatically higher than is that of its parents, since the family's *mana* or magical power increases from generation to generation.[17] In order to make the following incident understandable, we have to add that in this society the head of a person is his most sacred part, which no person of inferior rank may touch, and that the name of the head is functionally "identical" with the head itself.

Case 58: A Small Marquesan Domestic Tyrant

One day a small boy became annoyed with his parents and, in order to punish them, named the family dwelling after his own head. The family had to move out immediately, so as not to desecrate the child's head, and camped in the yard until the little tyrant decided to relent and to remove the name of his head from the house.[18]

Of course, in many primitive societies the child is considered inferior to the adult. Thus, Miller (172) mentions that among some Africans the word "child" also means "negligible" or "unimportant." Among the Sedang the word "child" is also the only term meaning "small" and may even imply the additional meaning "in-

[16] Ralph Linton, personal communication.

[17] This point of view appears to be closely correlated with the aristocratic outlook on life. Thus, in Austria, a chamberlain of the Emperor had to have a certain number of noble ancestors. Hence, the *son* of a nobleman who lacked *one* noble ancestor could qualify as chamberlain, while his father could not. Napoleon himself is said to have ridiculed this outlook. One day he insisted that his son, the King of Rome (later on the Duke of Reichstadt), should enter the carriage before he himself did, "because his father is an Emperor, whereas mine [Napoleon's] was not."

[18] Ralph Linton, personal communication.

adequate," since, if a person declares that his field is "child" (= small) he implies that it is insufficient for his needs. However, as data cited in preceding paragraphs indicate, the child is certainly not despised among the Sedang, and is not denied the right of self-determination.

Case 59: Children's Ownership of Property

For example, when the writer tried to persuade a Sedang child to sell him his toys, for a collection which the writer was assembling for a museum of anthropology, the boy absolutely refused to do so, and an appeal to his parents to help persuade the child only elicited the remark: "The toys belong to him and we have no right to make him sell them."

The point we seek to make is that even where the child occupies a low rank in primitive society this does not automatically subordinate it to adults. The idea that the child owes automatic obedience to its elders is conspicuously lacking in many primitive groups.

In fact, native conceptions about the nature of children—even where these ideas include a liberal dose of notions about the inadequacy of the young—do not, as a rule, serve as a basis for justifying parental authority, but constitute a claim to parental leniency and protection.

Case 60: A Mohave Child's Temper Tantrum

An eight-year-old Mohave boy flew into a temper tantrum and assaulted his stepfather, who was one of the finest and gentlest persons the writer had ever met. The boy's mother—who was more acculturated than the stepfather—urged her husband to retaliate. The man only smiled and said: "Let him be! He is so small that he cannot hurt me." In fact, he allowed himself to be pummeled until the tantrum was over. It is hardly necessary to add that the boy adored his stepfather. When the stepfather was accidentally killed while the boy was in military service during World War II, the latter went into something resembling a genuine depression (38).

THE DISTURBED CHILD

In view of what we said about Occidental ideas concerning children, it is obvious that the emotional disturbances of a child will be defined first as "badness," which must be dealt with by punishment. In fact, punitive techniques may be resorted to even in connection with organic illness.

Case 61: Punishment of a Sick Child

A boy of eight reports as follows: "I was ill and my father, who believed in good old-fashioned remedies, put me on a table, made my mother hold me down, and tried to force me to swallow castor oil. The stuff made me gag so badly that I sprayed it all over my father's new Orlon suit. My father then hit me so hard on my bare bottom that his handprint was still visible an hour later."

Case 62: Punishment for Being Ill

An adolescent made this statement: "When I was six years old, I used to vomit after every meal. I just could not keep the food down. However, my parents felt that I was simply bad, and therefore, after every vomiting spell, beat me hard with a rattan switch. This went on for weeks, until it was discovered that I had chronic appendicitis and really could not keep the food down. I had to have an operation—and they never even had the decency to apologize to me for these undeserved beatings."

These cases are certainly in sharp contrast with the pleas of Nuo's parents that the writer desist from trying to make the reluctant boy swallow an aspirin (Case 57).

Similar punitive measures are also resorted to in strictly emotional disturbances, the severity of the punishment being usually proportionate to the inconvenience which the child's neurosis causes the parents. This explains why parents, whose own neurosis induces their children to become emotionally disturbed, welcome all "organicistic" explanations of neurosis, because they diminish their guilt feelings over the child's condition. Thus, when an eminent authority developed a new theory of the organic substratum of neuroses, many parents wrote him expressing relief over not having to blame themselves any longer for their children's neuroses. Interestingly enough, all of these parents conveniently overlooked the fact that this scientist specified that actual neuroticism is always triggered by traumatic events.

Be that as it may, the notion that the emotionally disturbed child is "bad" is so deeply ingrained that many parents who profess to believe in an organic causation of neurosis continue to consider punishment the proper way of dealing with the neurotic child.

Case 63: Punishment in Emotional Disturbances

An analysand finally developed sufficient ego strength to write a letter to his parents—who kept heckling him about the cost of his analysis—telling them calmly but firmly that he needed an analysis only because his upbringing had been a highly traumatic one. The parents replied indignantly that they had done nothing to cause him to become neurotic. "We are convinced that you were born bad—that you are congenitally unstable—and this forced us to deal severely with you." When the analysand wrote back that it seemed inappropriate to seek to remedy a presumably organic condition by beatings, his parents simply evaded the whole issue.

The tendency to deal with children's problem behavior at first punitively is of considerable importance to the psychotherapist, as well as to the therapeutic educator and the therapeutic school. By the time the child is referred to them, its neurosis usually has been greatly intensified by attempts to deal with it punitively. Indeed, psychotherapy and therapeutic education are still not thought of as "first aid," but only as "last resort" measures, after all other—usually punitive and constrictive—measures have failed. In many instances children are not put into treatment until it is almost too late. Also—significantly—people are less willing to pay as much for child therapy as for adult therapy, despite the fact that child therapy is usually the more difficult of the two.

CONCLUSION

It may be asked, perhaps, why so much attention was paid to the status of the child in our society, and why the difference between it and the status of the child in primitive society has been elaborated in such detail.

The answer is fairly simple. The therapist or therapeutic educator does not live in a social vacuum and is not immune to prevailing social attitudes. Despite his professional training, and despite the fact that "he knows better," he continues to live in a society and in a culture in which children, and the disturbances of children, are defined in a particular manner. Hence, one of the most eminent child analysts, Mrs. Berta Bornstein, felt it necessary to warn a psychoanalytic audience that even in child analysis one is often tempted to assume the attitude: "If I tell little so-and-so to get well, by golly, he had better get well!" (18)

It was therefore deemed necessary to emphasize the artificiality and destructiveness of many of our ideas about children and childhood, and to contrast them with different attitudes, in order to enable us to see the child as it is and not as we imagine it to be, and to encourage us to use techniques which are dynamically effective, instead of techniques whose sole claim to our attention is that they are "traditional ones." It is for this reason that every therapeutic educator should study the excellent anthropological accounts of child life in other societies which are listed in the Bibliography. He should, above all, read and reread that chapter of Lowie's book *"Are We Civilized?"* (156) which systematically contrasts the treatment of children in other societies with that prevailing in our own.

....

CHAPTER 15

The Wrong Patient

The most tragic difficulty of work with disturbed children is hard to define without sounding almost grotesque. Briefly stated, one usually has to treat or educate the wrong person.

SYMPTOMS VS. PSYCHOPATHOLOGY

This statement is understandable only if we differentiate between the underlying psychopathology of a patient and the outward manifestations of his psychopathology in the form of symptoms. Symptoms can be of different kinds: They may be primarily thought disturbances, such as delusions. They may be disturbances of the affective sphere: extreme emotions, such as tantrums, minimal emotions, such as the "flattened affect" of some schizophrenics, or inappropriate affect, not in harmony with the nature of the stimulus. There may be motor manifestations, some seemingly voluntary, as in handwashing compulsions, and some seemingly involuntary, as in hysterical convulsions. There may be psychosomatic symptoms, such as neurodermatitis. Finally, there may be a general distortion of the total behavior pattern and character, in which, naïvely expressed, "nothing in particular is wrong, and everything taken together is wrong."

The layman often confuses symptoms with illness, especially in mental disorders, though "fever" too is often viewed as an illness, instead of as a symptom. Indeed, fever is a rather good analogy for symptoms in mental disorders, since, like the latter, it is a manifestation not of the illness itself but of the organism's fight against illness, which in typhoid fever is a microbic invasion and in mental disorders a severe psychic injury.

The second point to be understood is that the strikingness, dramatic appearance, or "obvious severity" of the symptom is not necessarily proportionate either to the inherent severity of the illness or to the greatness or length of the therapeutic effort needed to correct it. The symptoms of a hysteric are often florid and dramatic —much more so than the quiet ruminations of an obsessive-compulsive neurotic. The violent behavior of some schizophrenic who —unless physically restrained—tears the ward apart in the acute stage of his illness, is certainly infinitely more "disturbed" than the colorless, drab, and dull existence of a "burnt-out" old schizophrenic, vegetating on a back ward for "chronic cases." Yet in each of these examples the more "obviously" ill patient is actually the one who is basically less ill than his quiet counterpart. His real self is less completely engulfed by his illness, and, above all, he is still struggling against it—and struggling hard. By contrast, the burnt-out schizophrenic has "thrown in the towel." He is "licked," and knows it. His personality has been swallowed up by his illness, all struggle has ceased, or nearly so, "the tail is wagging the dog," and prospects of recovery are slim or even negligible.

Now, it is a basic tenet of psychotherapy—and therefore also of therapeutic education—that the therapist must treat the illness and not the symptom. In fact, an uncomfortable symptom is often precisely what causes a good many patients to seek psychiatric help. Hence, as Freud pointed out, if we free the patient prematurely of his symptoms—which, especially in hysteria, is often quite easily done—the patient's chief motivation for enduring the far from pleasant process of seeing himself as he is and doing something about it—which is what psychotherapy amounts to—disappears.

THE SICK PARENT AND HIS NEUROTIC CHILD

Now, in the case of children, we are often confronted with the anomaly of having to treat symptoms instead of the underlying psychopathology, because it is sometimes not the child but the parent who is emotionally ill. The "obvious" illness of the child is often simply a vicarious manifestation of the hidden, but much more basic, illness of his parents. Crudely and almost grotesquely expressed: The parents have the psychopathology and the child has the symptoms. In fact, one reason why the parents often have no manifest symptoms is that they have unconsciously maneuvered the child into having symptoms on their behalf. This state of affairs is already described in the Bible: "The fathers have eaten sour grapes, and the children's teeth are set on edge" (Ezekiel 18:2).

In a sense this is often true even of adult patients but is something which—like many other unpleasant facts—"one does not mention in polite society." Thus, the writer recalls hearing an unusually able and sensitive chief psychiatric social worker remark: "When the relatives bring in a patient, one sometimes has the impulse to hospitalize the relatives and let the 'patient' go home." Hence, when the illness of an adult patient is very severe, a well-known psychiatrist refuses to treat him unless the most important member of his family also receives psychotherapy (*229*).

For obvious reasons the situation is even more acute in the case of children. Hence, many excellent child psychiatrists have drawn the inescapable conclusion and either insist that the parents too receive psychotherapy or, in other cases, give no psychotherapy at all to the child and take the parent into therapy instead. The writer knows of a case in which the neurotic stammering of a child was cured solely and exclusively by giving psychotherapy to the mother for six months. The child itself wasn't even seen by the therapist! In other words, in an exceedingly high proportion of cases the emotional disturbances of children are "situational" or "reactive." Their manifestly behavioral disturbances are not deeply rooted in the child's own intrapsychic conflicts. They are superficial disturbances, resulting from the impact of the emotionally ill—but relatively symptom free—parents' psychopathology on the child.

One proof of this is that often the mere removal of the child from the home to a therapeutic school results in startling improvements. A second, and even more telling, proof is that when such children are sent home for a vacation they often promptly experience a relapse—because they are literally maneuvered into a relapse by their parents. The following is a good example of such a surreptitiously and almost unconsciously engineered relapse:

Case 64: A Girl Is Made to Steal

A girl in her late teens, who had stolen both money and other things for several years, was placed in a therapeutic school where she received intensive psychotherapy. She soon improved to such an extent that she not only did not commit any further delinquent actions but even went out of her way to persuade other delinquents to refrain from misconduct. In addition, when the pocket money of one of the students was stolen by someone who could not be identified, this girl opened a subscription to replace the stolen money, chipping in from her own, very limited, resources to make up part of the loss. A couple of months later she went home on a vacation and, within twenty-four hours, stole a small sum from her father's wallet. The father promptly called the therapist long distance, informing him of this incident—and, while he was about it, doubling the actual amount stolen by his daughter. He also reproached the therapist with having given him the impression that his daughter had improved. The therapist was greatly struck by the fact that the father sounded as if he almost gloated over the "incorrigibility" of the girl. However, the therapist was quite unabashed and, instead of becoming defensive, asked the father bluntly whether the girl had been given spending money, in an amount compatible both with her age and with the economic status of the family. It turned out that this young woman had been left without one penny of spending money; she was practically forced to steal . . . presumably in order to confirm her parents' opinion that she was "incorrigible." When the therapist insisted that she be given adequate spending money, the father first tried to caricature this suggestion, by asking whether the girl should really get $20 a day pocket money. The therapist immediately realized that the amount named was deliberately preposterous. Had the girl actually received $20 a day, she would inevitably have drifted into irresponsible conduct—drinking and misbehaving. The therapist therefore replied that the girl should get about $15 a week, and was so firm about it that he managed to make his suggestion "stick." Significantly, the girl did not steal another cent during the rest of her stay at home and got into no trouble whatsoever.

The conduct of the father was quite striking: By refusing his daughter any pocket money at all he literally drove her to stealing. Otherwise expressed, he forced the girl to confirm her father's belief that she was "incorrigible." When the therapist demanded that he give his daughter some spending money, the father offered to give her too much, presumably in order to seduce her into other types of misconduct, which would also have "proved" that she was "incorrigible."

Hence, what mattered in this case was not the girl's delinquent behavior but the maneuverings of her father, who tried to force her to appear "incorrigible." The father's neurotic need to prove this point is fully understandable if one knows that—being at constant odds with his severely neurotic wife, who often humiliated him in public—the father felt the need to prove that his daughter came from "rotten stock," i.e., that she took after his wife.

It is hardly necessary to add that not only manifestly neurotic behavior in the child but even the normal (developmental) emotional upheavals of childhood—the Oedipus complex, for example —are also triggered by the parents' own emotional attitudes toward the child, i.e., in the case of the Oedipus complex, by their so-called "counter-oedipal complex" (57, 62).[1]

To return to our initial point, the child therapist, as well as the therapeutic educator, is often placed in the impossible situation of

[1] This point is so highly technical that its detailed discussion would lead us too far afield. It is therefore simply mentioned as a basic fact.

having to treat the wrong patient. He is expected to treat the child, whose reactive or situational neurosis is often but the symptomatic implementation of its parents' basic psychopathology. In brief, therapists and educators are forced to treat the wrong patient directly and the right patient—the parent—only indirectly. This is one reason why the wise management of the therapeutic school's relations with the children's parents is one of the most important therapeutic functions which such a school can perform.

Unfortunately, the parents cannot, as a rule, be subjected even to a careful diagnostic evaluation, lest they take offense. They can often be diagnosed only "at a distance," by a study of the child's illness. There is an almost tragicomical resemblance between this situation and the one said to have obtained in Mohammedan countries, where, if a properly secluded Mohammedan lady became ill, the attending physician was not even permitted to take her pulse directly. A silk thread was tied around the female patient's wrist. The thread was then passed to the physician, who, by pulling it tight, tried as best he could to count his patient's pulse.

We must not imagine that only "civilized" parents implement their own psychopathology through the symptoms of their children. It is true that our society does not reward the flamboyant kinds of disturbances which enable the primitive hysteric to assume tribal leadership as a magician or witch. Yet, even in primitive society, and in societies which are intermediate or transitional between the "primitive" and the "civilized" state, "training for neurosis," to meet pathological parental needs, is quite common.

Case 65: Mohave Transvestitism

To take a primitive example, Mohave Indian parents of the ipa: taha:na (real persons, i.e., elite) class sometimes encourage their boys to become transvestites, in order to protect them from death in warfare (161). Rich Blackfoot families have another "out" for their sons. They tell their boys to leave war to poor boys—who can only obtain the horses needed for status-enhancing rites by stealing them from the enemy's herds—and to take the horses needed for these rites from their own herds (232). Although this is a less neurotic "out" than is transvestitism, it nonetheless presupposes a culturally deviant subordination of war to intermediate economic goals and to final social self-enhancement and does not obtain therefore in other typical Plains tribes, such as the Sioux, Cheyenne, or Crow (50).

Case 66: A Guatemalan Girl

As regards a transitional society, Benjamin Paul (179) recorded with painstaking accuracy and considerable insight the almost classical case of a young Guatemalan Indian girl who was systematically trained by her father to become a neurotic and deviant in order to gratify certain pathological impulses of his own.

Case 67: Incest Among Swedish Farmers

As for civilized societies, Svend Riemer (184) describes in detail the process whereby the oldest daughter of an ailing Swedish peasant woman is gradually maneuvered into the position of having to become the "substitute wife" of her father.

The following case will illustrate the manner in which children actualize the conflicts of their elders.

Case 68: A Girl Dreams of Her Sister's Problem

Jane, who is twenty years old, has two younger siblings, Jack, aged six, and Mary, aged four. At the time the incident about to be described took place, the grandparents were visiting this family and were occupying Jane's room, so that Jane had to share the bed of her little sister, Mary. That same evening Jane became engaged to her boy friend—also named Jack—and set a date for the wedding. The engagement was sufficiently genuine for her to experience a considerable temptation to consummate the relationship at once. She refrained, however, and—tense but "walking on clouds"—went home to announce her engagement to her parents, who heartily approved of it. Jane then went to bed, joining Mary, who was already asleep. In the course of the night little Mary woke up and told Jane that she had just had the following dream:

"Jack got into my jewel box. He took my necklace."

The next day Jane, who had "no idea" what this dream meant, "just happened" to mention it to her fiancé, Jack, who, being a psychiatric resident, and an analytic candidate as well—and who, like his fiancée, had experienced the evening before the impulse to "jump the gun"—was quite startled by it. He realized that "getting into the jewel box" was a common dream symbol for intercourse and recalled that the evening before—apparently as a substitute for getting into Jane's "jewel box"—he had repeatedly inserted his hand under Jane's tight-fitting "choker-type" necklace. In brief, it seemed evident to him that little Mary had, in dream, satisfied symbolically her big sister's desire to consummate the relationship as soon as she became engaged. Hence Mary, who admired Jane and identified herself with her, dreamed that "Jack" got into her "jewel box," because Jane had felt tempted to let "Jack" get into "hers."

Jack, who knew that the writer did not believe in telepathy (56), immediately reported this dream to him, in order to disprove the writer's skepticism about such occurrences. The writer was not convinced, however, and urged Jack to talk to Mary herself, which he did the same evening. He was greatly surprised when, on telling Mary "I hear you dreamed *of me* last night," the little girl said, "I did not." When Jack reminded her that she dreamed of "Jack" getting into her jewel box, Mary replied, "Oh—that was my *brother* Jack, not *Jane's* Jack."

Despite this "mistaken identity," it is legitimate to ask just why little Mary dreamed precisely this night a dream which so obviously represented a symbolic gratification of her sister Jane's impulses. The precipitating factor appears to have been the unwonted presence in her bed of Jane, who felt erotically stimulated and therefore indulged in passionate "daydreams"—or, more properly, hypnagogic fantasies—before she fell asleep. Since children are extraordinarily sensitive to the moods of adults and—like schizophrenics, but also like exceptionally good analysts—can draw surprisingly accurate conclusions from their unconscious evaluation of people's posture and behavior,[2] even though she was asleep—or perhaps precisely because she was asleep, since while asleep her critical ego functions were more or less in abeyance[3]—Mary responded to the mood of her sister by having a highly appropriate dream.

So far, we have only explained what triggered this dream. The possibility of Mary's having such a dream must, therefore, also be explained.

1. The jewel box symbol is not the only one Mary could have used to "gratify" her sister Jane's impulses, especially since, unlike an older girl, she could not have known that "getting in the jewel box" is a colloquial expression for cohabitation. What determined the choice of this symbol is the fact that Mary is a somewhat vain and ostentatiously feminine little girl, who likes to adorn herself and is very proud of her jewel box. Hence, she chose, from among all other possible symbols, the jewel box, whose contents made her seem as adult and lovely as her admired older sister.

2. The necklace symbol cannot be interpreted with the same specificity, since we do not know enough about Mary to offer equally definite interpretations. A few suggestions must therefore suffice. The most obvious of these is the fact that necklaces are very obvious contents of a jewel box. In addition, since the necklace surrounds a columnar organ,[4] it is, like rings, a good symbol for the female parts. Last, but not least, little Mary happened to own a dime-store "choker" necklace, which resembled that of her sister Jane.

3. Brother Jack vs. fiancé Jack. The most important element of the dream is the confusion between the "two Jacks." Jane took it for granted that Mary dreamed about her fiancé Jack, whereas Mary was quite certain that she dreamed of her brother Jack. Of course, both were "right." Brother Jack was a "tease," who often kidded little Mary, the latter responding—as is typical of girls in the oedipal stage—in a

[2] The writer recalls an instance in which he did not grasp the hidden meaning of a patient's peculiar posture until he deliberately imitated it himself. At that moment its meaning became obvious to him.

[3] Aristotle pointed out that one sometimes dreams of an oncoming illness long before one feels ill in a waking state because in sleep one is more sensitive to minimal internal cues (7). This observation was recently substantiated by psychoanalytic findings (10).

[4] Cf. "The Song of Songs which is Solomon's."

highly feminine and seductive manner, or else with typically feminine tantrums. In addition, she was fond of her sister Jane's Jack. Helped by the identity of names, Mary was therefore able to have a dream which, from Jane's point of view, meant: "I wish Jack had ignored my objections—in fact, I can dream that he did ignore them." However, from Mary's viewpoint, it meant: "Jane wants her Jack. I too have a Jack of my own—my brother Jack."

Otherwise stated, Jane was right in unconsciously referring this dream to herself and in being sufficiently preoccupied with it to "just mention it" to her fiancé, so as to "egg him on" to disregard her future objections. She knew that even though she did not (consciously) understand this dream, Jack, who was in analysis, would understand it. Thus, from her viewpoint, the dream seemed "telepathic." It was also very convenient, since, in telling it to Jack, she could disclose to him the intensity of her passions without feeling "responsible" for what—"after all"—not she but Mary dreamed. She did not find it convenient to grasp that Mary had *her* dream."

By contrast, from Mary's point of view, the dream is not in the least telepathic. Mary was able to have this dream only because it dovetailed with her own oedipal impulses toward her older brother—and, by identification with Jane, also toward the adult Jack. Her dream was stimulated and made possible by her (unconscious) empathy with Jane's intense desires. However, she was able to respond with an appropriate dream, expressing her own (displaced) oedipal impulses, only because she had corresponding wishes of her own. These she symbolized by images specifically determined not by a "telepathic perception" of events which she had not witnessed but by her own personal preoccupation with jewelry, and by the similarity between her own necklace and that of Jane.

Returning now to our main argument, we do not say that parents would be able to induce their children to develop vicariously the symptoms of the parents' neurosis if the children did not have conflicts of their own, suitable for this type of vicarious symptom formation. The point we seek to make is that the neurosis of the

parents sets off and intensifies such conflicts in their children, causing them to develop suitable symptoms. Indeed, in the case just
cited we might take it for granted that Mary would never have had
such a dream—or, at least, not so transparent a dream—had her
preëxisting impulses not been both stimulated and "sanctioned" by
Jane's excitement and desires.

THE DEVELOPMENT OF CHILDHOOD NEUROSES

Broadly speaking, the development of many a child's neurosis
has four fairly distinct phases:

1. In the first phase the child's symptoms are vicarious and
simply implement the parents' psychopathology. The resulting distortion of the child's total behavior pattern then involves it in a
series of severe situational conflicts and difficulties, which pave the
way for:

2. the second phase of its evolution toward a genuine neurosis.
In this phase the child has what may be described as a "reactive" or
"situational" neurosis. From the psychodynamic point of view such
neuroses are not at all serious and usually cease as soon as the
pathogenic pressures are removed. This explains why children sent
to a therapeutic school at this stage of the game often show immediate and radical improvements. (Similar transitory reactive or
situational neuroses also occur in inherently normal adults who are
subjected to some abnormal or atypical strain for which they are
wholly unprepared.)

The important fact to remember in this context is that, in developing a reactive or situational neurosis, the child duplicates not
the conscious but the unconscious, inhibited, or repressed conflicts
and tensions of its parents. It does what the parents unconsciously
would like to do but prevent themselves from doing because they
would feel too guilty if they actually externalized their hidden
problems through overt behavior or symptoms. This, in turn,
means that the child's reactive neurosis will be particularly irritat-

ing to its parents, who are not able to tolerate these impulses in themselves. The child's conduct therefore consistently "rubs them in a sore spot" and they react to it with considerable vehemence. Yet, they usually do so in a manner unconsciously calculated to intensify, rather than to abolish, the child's "objectionable" conduct.

Case 69: Making the Child Dependent

Unconsciously dependent and passive parents, who fought these needs in themselves, developed a "reaction formation" and became over-efficient and domineering. As a result, any clumsiness or dependence exhibited by their small child unduly exasperated them and caused them to heckle and harass it constantly, "to make it efficient and independent." Nothing the child did satisfied them. All of its efforts were belittled and criticized. If it brought home a report card containing ten A's and one B, the parents only showed interest in this single B and accused their child of sloth or irresponsibility. These attempts to "make the child efficient and self-reliant" only undermined its self-confidence, made it more and more clumsy and dependent, and weakened its ego. This, in turn, enabled the parents to become even more overbearing than before, and to "justify" their condemnation of the child. In brief, the conduct of the parents, which was consciously calculated to strengthen their reaction formation against their own dependent and passive needs, by making their child equally "over-efficient," was unconsciously calculated to gratify their repressed desires to be dependent and passive via the child. This caused their child to become abnormally dependent, passive, and clumsy.

Such cases as this explain why domineering parents, who seek to force their child to become precociously self-reliant, usually end up with a withdrawn, passive, schizoid, and inefficient child, whose condition sometimes amounts to pseudo retardation or pseudo imbecility. If, furthermore, the child of such parents is actually more or less defective, it often becomes overtly psychotic, in addition to being feeble-minded. Thus, the process just described often simply actualizes a pathologically extreme form of the desire, harbored even by normal parents, that the child should have all that which its parents craved but could never obtain for themselves. In fact, the child is often explicitly viewed as a means for the fulfillment of the frustrated wishes of its parents. Where these wishes are realistic, the parents' educational efforts can produce excellent results; where they are neurotic or unrealistic, the results are usually tragic ones.

3. The third phase represents a stabilization and consolidation of the initially vicarious symptomatology and of the reactive or situational neurosis which it elicits. Indeed, any reactive or situational neurosis of sufficiently long duration gradually distorts the personality to a point where there develops a neurosis which is indistinguishable from, and is, in fact, an authentic "endogenous" or "autonomous" neurosis. In other words, after having at first certain vicarious symptoms, the child eventually develops an appropriate internal psychopathology, which provides a dynamic foundation for its symptoms.

4. The fourth and final phase of the child's neurosis often represents the complete gratification of the parents' unconscious needs, and therefore exasperates them a great deal on the conscious level. At this stage the child—who, by now, is often an adolescent or even an adult—does more than simply comply with his parents' unconscious expectations. It actually and systematically goes out of its way to maneuver its parents, relatives, and associates into the position of having to exhibit toward it a type of behavior which further justifies and "anchors" its neurosis. At this point there occurs a "mutual induction process" between the parents' neurosis and the complementary neurosis of the child. For example, as Case 37 indicates, the frequently beaten child may reach the point where it derives both an erotic pleasure and a guilt-assuaging relief from being beaten and will therefore "accidentally on purpose" behave in such a manner as to make further spankings "necessary."

When, as a result of therapy, the child ceases to maneuver its parents into gratifying its neurotic needs, the parents sometimes begin to display a strikingly different attitude toward their offspring.

Case 70: Change in Parental Attitudes

One of the writer's analysands was a young adult whose neurosis had incapacitated him to such a point that despite his great intelligence he was unable to finish high school or earn a living. He was the rather frail son of a big, somewhat primitive, fairly emotional, but not at all brutal father and of a typical Jewish matriarch, who ruled her family with the "tyranny of tears" and constantly threatened everyone by harping on the grief which they would feel once their ingratitude "drove her into an early grave."

Since the parents lived in a distant part of the country, the mother did not visit her son until after the latter had undergone one year of analysis. She was scheduled to arrive late in the evening, and, throughout the afternoon's analytic hour, her son agonized over her impending visit.

The next day, as the writer was driving to the office where he saw his analytic patients, the following thoughts flashed through his mind: "I know exactly what my patient will say today. Quite early in the hour he will tell me that his mother had changed a great deal." This prediction proved to be correct. The moment the patient lay down on the couch he exclaimed: "How my mother has changed! It bewilders me to realize how small a woman she really is. She is so much smaller than I am! She always seemed much larger to me. She showed none of the intimidating qualities which she formerly displayed toward me. She didn't boss me around at all. She seemed quite timid and left all decisions and plans up to me. I can't understand what has happened to her. Have I, perhaps, misunderstood her all my life? Etc." After listening to the patient for a while, the writer asked him whether he or his mother had been in analysis for a year. This sudden confrontation "drove home" with almost frightening intensity an insight which so startled the patient that he literally began to stammer, "You mean, of course, that not she but I have changed. Perhaps I let her, and even made her, treat me as a child. I did notice that she treated me yesterday as though I were the man of the family. It made me quite uncomfortable. Etc." In brief, the patient suddenly realized that his originally reactive neurosis had turned into an autonomously endogenous one, that his passivity and dependence had systematically incited his mother to treat him like a child, and that, now that he had partly grown up as a result of his analysis, she suddenly reacted to him as though he were an adult.

Case 71: A Tyrannical Mother Becomes Dependent on Her Daughter

An almost identical conversation took place between the writer and a woman analysand, who also had an octopus-like, "devouringly maternal" mother. The mother made her feel so childish that, even though the daughter was married, she called her domicile "the apartment," continued to refer to her parents' residence as "home," and readily admitted that she did not really feel like a married woman but simply like a little girl "playing house" with a boy. In this case, too, as soon as the daughter began to improve, the mother began to lean on her, asked her advice, allowed her to take the lead in various matters, and treated her as an adult.

These observations are susceptible of being generalized in the form of a broad principle for evaluating the progress of the child in therapy or enrolled in a therapeutic school: One tangible proof of the child's improvement—one proof of its budding maturity—is its feeling that those around it have "suddenly changed," regardless of whether these "changed persons" are smothering mothers, tyrannical and seductive fathers, unjust employers, exacting teachers, or "nosy" therapists.

PARENTAL INTERFERENCES WITH THERAPY

Unfortunately, it is more easy to promote this type of development in the adult patient, whose internal growth is more or less encouraged by society, than in children, in whose case society tends to encourage continued dependence, even to the point where it amounts to systematic infantilization.

The disturbed child's parents are often reluctant to allow the child to "grow up" in therapy or in the therapeutic school. They simply want the child to give up its more troublesome symptoms, but not all of its symptoms. It is almost as if the parents were afraid that, once the child is really cured, they will have to develop their own symptoms and display openly their own pathological conflicts and distorted impulses. Unconsciously they seem to want the child to remain emotionally ill, but without displaying too embarrassing or inconvenient symptoms.[5] This explains why children are so often prematurely taken out of therapy or withdrawn from the therapeutic school. Once the most troublesome symptoms are abolished, some parents declare themselves "satisfied" and deem further expenditures for therapy a "waste of money." Such decisions are apparently motivated by the unconscious feeling that, if the sick member of the family is absent for too long a time, someone else will have to take over the role of "deputy neurotic," so as to maintain the traditional dynamic balance obtaining within the emotionally disorganized family.[6]

The children themselves sometimes realize that their parents systematically maneuver them into relapses. Hence even children who profess to dislike the therapist or the therapeutic school are sometimes extremely reluctant to go home for a vacation. In such instances the school is often obliged to back up the parents' request that the child be sent home for its vacations, lest the parents become so panicked by the "competition" which the school offers them that they will decide to withdraw the child. Indeed, such parents interpret the child's reluctance to go home for a vacation as signifying that the child is drawing an invidious comparison between its parental home and the school. In such a situation the

[5] This, of course, is impossible, since "negativism" or "provocativeness" is an essential feature of symptoms (31).

[6] We suggested elsewhere (59) that society too may need such "deputy neurotics" or "deputy psychotics," in order to maintain its usual equilibrium, and that this role is assigned to the hysterical or otherwise disturbed shaman (medicine man), whose neurosis is systematically encouraged and rewarded (153) by society itself.

school simply has to prepare itself to receive, at the end of the vacation, a child who has temporarily lost ground, and whose conflicts have been revived by its stay at home.

Given this complicated setup, an almost superhuman level of maturity, warmth, and objectivity is needed on the part of the therapeutic educators and milieu therapists, who must offer the child a home which despite the parent centeredness of extramural homes is child centered and which, nonetheless, does not induce the child to reject its real home so utterly as to incite its parents to terminate prematurely its stay in the therapeutic school.

In view of these facts, it is not surprising that parents should sometimes (unconsciously) seek to prevent the recovery of their child by truly injurious "delaying tactics." Since the parents feel unconsciously guilty both for having caused the child's neurosis and also for seeking to delay its recovery, their maneuvers are often quite damaging to the whole family. The most striking examples of such maneuvers are those in which the parents' financial resources "just happen" to give out at the very moment when the child begins to improve. Sometimes such parents start this maneuver by warning the child via the mails that, due to a "sudden" financial crisis, its withdrawal from therapy or from the school may become unavoidable. While such economic setbacks are usually genuine enough, their timing and the fact that they are often the first setbacks of this kind ever experienced by consistently prosperous parents lead one to suspect that they were engineered by the parents themselves, "accidentally on purpose."

Case 72: Financial Reverses of a Mother

A hard-headed and consistently successful businesswoman, divorced from an ineffectual drifter of whom she lost track many years before, suddenly suffered the first reverses in her career. This happened at the very moment when her previously pathologically dependent son began to show signs of standing on his own feet.

Case 73: Psychosomatic "Illness" of a Father

A very successful, aggressive, and prosperous professional man, having no children of his own, adopted several daughters—presumably so as to be surrounded by a harem. This father developed a suspiciously psychosomatic seeming "illness," which forced him to reduce his standard of living quite radically, the moment his second daughter, who was undergoing an analysis in a therapeutic school, ceased to be promiscuous. This adolescent girl had become promiscuous precisely in order to conceal from herself the fact that "her heart belonged to daddy." As a result of these financial reverses the daughter had to be withdrawn from the school.

In other, less dramatic, instances the parents seductively pose as "ideal parents" and give their vacationing child so good a time at home that they undermine its therapeutically important relationship to the school. Thus, certain parents, who previously would not allow their adolescent children to date, suddenly encourage them to "go steady" even with "objectionable" boys or girls, whom they previously refused even to allow in the house. Such maneuvers are means of undermining the child's emotional commitment to the therapeutic school. Other parents commiserate with their children over school discipline, concur with their criticism of teachers and therapists, and "bend over backward" to "make it up to the child," by giving it more liberties than it can reasonably expect at its age or is prepared to handle rationally.

It is impossible even to begin to list the many subtle and unconsciously motivated maneuvers parents indulge in so as to delay the recovery and interfere with the therapeutic education of their children. They reveal the parents' need of the child's neurosis and express the parents' counter-oedipal impulses, which sometimes assume the form of "momism" or "dadism."

It is quite easy for parents to maneuver their children into resisting psychotherapy and therapeutic education, since the parents' latent opposition to their children's progress greatly strengthens the children's own neurotic resistances. The children themselves may be consciously quite unaware that their parents seek to disrupt their treatment, since the children's need to believe that their parents love them and are doing all they can to help them is so great that they readily persuade themselves that they, themselves, wish to terminate the treatment or their enrollment in the therapeutic school. However, their unconscious awareness that they are simply maneuvered into doing what their parents implicitly wish them to do often finds an expression in the preposterousness of their pretexts for breaking off the treatment.

Case 74: A Boy Is Manipulated into Breaking Off His Treatment

In the course of the last analytic hour preceding a brief vacation, the analyst confronted an adolescent with his need to deny that he was emotionally ill. The analyst explained that unless the boy admitted to himself that he was ill he would lack the necessary motivation for enduring the discomforts of the analysis. The next day the boy's father came and took him home for a brief vacation. During the first analytic hour following the vacation the boy angrily denied that he was ill. He said that he only had "problems" and insisted that he had already solved most of them. He declared that unless the analyst conceded this point he would break off his analysis. When the analyst refused to "make a deal," the boy told him that he was breaking off his treatment then and there—but did so in extremely vague language, full of "double talk" which reflected his unconscious reluctance to terminate his treatment. After the hour the analyst reported this fact to the clinical director, who replied that he was not in the least surprised, since he had seen the boy's father when the latter brought his son back to school and found him superficially most coöperative and unduly satisfied with the boy's progress, but unconsciously quite hostile to analysis. At that moment the telephone rang. The admissions officer of the school was calling the clinical director to inform him that the boy's father had just telephoned, requesting the immediate termination of the treatment.

Even the psychotherapy of adult children is sometimes sabotaged by the parents.

Case 75: Infantilization of a Daughter

A markedly schizophrenic girl showed little improvement after two years of shock therapy, insulin therapy, and superficial psychotherapy. She was therefore sent to Dr. M. L. Hayward, who specializes in the psychoanalytic treatment of ambulatory psychotics, and, at the time the incident about to be narrated took place, had been under his care for one year. When Dr. Hayward was about to go on his vacation, the girl's parents, who lived in another part of the country, came to take her home for the summer. Her therapist consented to this but insisted that, during her stay at home, the girl should be treated as an adult. The parents agreed to this and left the doctor's office accompanied by their daughter. Half an hour later the therapist saw the three of them in the street. The girl was walking between her parents hugging a huge penguin, which her parents had just bought for her, as though she were still a child (*114*).

Case 76: Infantilization of a Son

After about a year of analysis an adult analysand wrote his parents asking them not to address him any longer in their letters as "My dear little boy." He justified his request by explaining that the growing up of children requires certain readjustments in the earlier parent-child interaction pattern. The parents replied with a highly emotional letter, in which they protested their eagerness to do all they could to help him recover from his neurosis by treating him as an adult. In accordance with his request, they even signed this letter with their given names, instead of signing, as they had done before, "Mom" and "Dad." However, there was also a postscript, expressing their real feelings, which ran as follows: "We will do all you ask us to do—but in our hearts you will always be our little baby boy."

In the case of some adults it is not the parent but the spouse who sabotages the psychotherapy or psychoanalysis. A spouse may harass the patient with indiscreet and critical remarks about his psychotherapy, display an irrational jealousy toward the therapist, insist on constant conferences with him, or systematically sabotage the patient's attempts to achieve a more mature type of marital adjustment. In fact, like parents, the spouse of a patient may actually need the patient's neurosis because it complements the latent neurosis of the "normal" spouse. There is a great deal of wisdom in the somewhat facetious remark: "A sadist is someone who is kind to a masochist." Thus, a domineering or overly maternal wife may become quite anxious once her husband begins to improve and demands wifely, instead of maternal, love. A sober, staid woman, who displays the proverbial patience of a Griseldis and is pitied and admired by all for her devotion to her alcoholic husband, sometimes develops a neurosis or becomes quite shrewish the moment her husband ceases to drink.

In brief, members of one's family, be they parents, spouse, or siblings, are, because of the intimate relationship obtaining within the home, in a position to maneuver even adults into developing a type of neurosis which complements that of the dominant member of the family group, who, in this context, acts as the pathogenic agent. It is therefore not surprising that the impressionable and helpless child should prove particularly susceptible to such pathogenic maneuvers and should meet the neurotic demands of its parents more than halfway.

The preceding considerations indicate not only that we often have in therapy the wrong person but also that truly neurotic parents often do everything to delay or to prevent the recovery of their child. These are facts which have to be recognized if they are to be dealt with effectively. We hasten to stress, however, that a mere condemnation of the parents is therapeutically as sterile as is the spanking of a neurotic child. The parents do not make their children emotionally sick because they are inherently vicious or cruel but because their own parents made them sick—and so on, back to

Adam and Eve. Furthermore, we must realize that parental love, while "natural," is also a very complex and conflict-laden emotion in man. Among other mammals, where the helplessness of the young is less prolonged than in man, and where rutting is seasonal, the young are often sufficiently mature by the time the next rutting season comes around to be "on their own," thus protecting the mother animal from whatever may be the animal equivalent of "counter-oedipal impulses," or, to be more specific, from a simultaneous—and confusing—experiencing of both maternal and "wifely" impulses. Even in species where the young are not rejected by the mother as soon as they can fend for themselves, and where there occurs an occasional mating between the mother animal and her male offspring, by the time this takes place the mother ceases to have maternal impulses—or even a memory of former maternal impulses—toward her offspring. Hence, strictly speaking, there can be "incest" only where maternal and sexual impulses coexist at the same moment. As Lowie expressed it: The point is not whether the male ape ever cohabits with his daughter—but whether this makes any difference to him (157).[7]

MATURE PARENTAL LOVE

The most painful fact confronting parents who truly seek to love their child is that their love must be a "self-abolishing love." It must not be possessive but liberating. It must not chain the child to the parent but must enable it eventually to love another person. Ideal sexual love is possessive and seeks to perpetuate itself. By contrast, the desexualized tender love of good parents is liberating and self-abolishing. It enables the child to follow the Biblical dictum: "Therefore shall a man leave his father and his mother,

---

[7] Recent newspaper reports of an accidental marriage between brother and sister, who were reared apart and did not know of their relationship, are much to the point. No one seems to have condemned this couple, because their sexual feelings were not mingled with or superimposed upon a blood-kin type of love.

and shall cleave unto his wife: and they shall be one flesh" (Genesis 2:24).

There are many reasons for assuming that only parents who do truly "cleave to each other and become one flesh," because they love each other, can give their children a desexualized, non-seductive, and liberating kind of love. Otherwise stated, only parents whose need for love is sufficiently gratified by their marriage can give their child the tenderness which it needs.

Last but not least, we must bear in mind that parents are not always responsible for the emotional turmoils of their potentially normal children. Indeed, there is little a Jewish mother, caught in a pogrom, or a South Korean father, cowering with his family in a combat zone, can do to safeguard the child from a severe trauma. There is, likewise, not much the Negro tenant farmer can do to protect his children against continuous ego-weakening humiliations. The most such people can do is to give their children as much love and as much acceptance as possible—not an easy task for parents who are as severely traumatized by such external events as are their children. The emotional disturbances of children raised in concentration camps, or in camps for displaced persons, are also relevant in this context. The social tragedy is that such traumatized children will traumatize in turn their own children and will be "responsible" for their children's neuroses. Thus, in the psychiatric sense, not the sins but the traumatic misfortunes of the forefathers are visited upon their descendants, "unto the third and fourth generation" (Exodus 20:5).

DEALING WITH PATHOGENIC PARENTS

Neither in the case of parents made neurotic by their own parents nor in the case of parents traumatized by misfortunes is it appropriate or effective to heap "coals of fire" upon their heads. It is certainly not enough just to make them feel guilty, even if it is sometimes necessary to do so at first in order to crash through their psychological defenses, which blind them to what they have been doing, and may still be doing, to their children. The moment the parents consciously and genuinely accept their responsibility for their pathogenic actions, our attitude must become a therapeutic and supportive one.

We already have stated that, ideally at least, the parents of children in therapy should also undergo therapy at the same time. While this is not always possible, parents can be given a great deal of supportive guidance in the course of interviews with the therapeutic educators of their children, and also during admission procedures to the therapeutic school. In fact, the intelligent and objective, but also humane and understanding, attitude of the therapeutic school toward the children's families, implemented by a director for parent relations, is one of the most creative and most valuable therapeutic functions which such a school can perform, since, in helping the parents, one also helps the children. We have dwelled at some length upon the responsibility of the parents both for their child's condition and for the artificial prolongation of its neurosis, since we must know what we have to cope with, and what we have to be understanding about, before we can do our work efficiently. It may, at times, relieve one's emotions to exclaim against the parents, but once one feels sufficiently relieved to think intelligently and constructively once more, the next step is always to do something which will help the parents, and will enable them to allow us to help the child.

CHAPTER 16

....

The Child-Centered Home

On being asked why Greenlea, the unit of the Devereux Schools which he directs, is able to handle students who proved unmanageable in all other units, Mr. Joseph B. Ferdinand replied: "We give them a home." This characterization of the Greenlea program appears to take cognizance of two major needs of the exceptional child who is extruded from its home: (1) the need for a substitute home and (2) the need for a child-centered home, whose structure and dynamics are determined by the staff's willingness to adapt itself to the needs of the child, instead of requiring the child to adapt itself to the staff (cf. Chapter 8).

Both of these needs deserve a more detailed discussion.

THE SUBSTITUTE HOME: ROUTINE VS. CHALLENGE

The substitute home, if it is to be psychologically genuine, must have a truly homelike atmosphere, in which pressures and insecurities are minimized. It goes without saying that all good therapeutic schools minimize the pressure of specific demands made at specific times. To put it figuratively, in a therapeutic school fire is less hot, ice less cold, the knife less sharp, the demand pattern less taxing, and competition less acute than in the ordinary world. Every moment is less hard to "live through" than it is elsewhere. There is, however, also another type of security, which is at least as important as protection from too brutal an impact of reality here and now. We refer to the security which a sense of continuity provides, and which we might call "security in, and protection from, time." In more advanced units, which have a high turnover and a systematic program, friendships have to be formed with the expectation of being dissolved the moment the other child leaves the unit. There is a date set for examinations, etc. In brief, time is always "breathing down the necks" of the students.

The therapeutic alleviation of the pressure of time is, if anything, more difficult than is the alleviation of other pressures. It is often accomplished only at the cost of reconciling oneself to a purely custodial program, in which adaptation is achieved at the expense of (further) adaptability. Otherwise stated, the patient or the child simply learns to be a "perfect inmate" in a "land which time forgot," and ceases to develop in any way. This is a serious shortcoming of many therapeutic milieus, since, to our mind, the essence of sanity is not "adjustment" but the capacity for *re*adjustment (*50, 59*).[1] Of course, no individual's plasticity is unlimited. Thus, it proved almost impossible for the Plains Indian of the late nineteenth century to adjust himself to American culture, by learning to enjoy collecting money instead of scalps and war honors. Yet it is equally certain that, within limits, and especially in a rapidly changing culture—where psychic defenses and the techniques of adaptation which provided complete security yesterday may be grossly maladaptive in the wholly different world of tomorrow— the capacity for readjustment is a crucially important qualification for survival and for maintaining one's sanity.[2]

There are, of course, grossly defective children who can adapt to an environment only once, and then only by receiving constant

[1] The writer is indebted to Dr. Richard L. Jenkins for suggesting to him that the "perfect inmate," who learns to adjust so well to the hospital that he can never again function on the outside as a citizen, is a striking illustration of the writer's thesis that the crux of sanity is not adjustment but the capacity for *re*adjustment.

[2] We suggested elsewhere that one cause of schizophrenia may be the schizoid person's inability to "change with the times" (*29*).

guidance and help. In fact, in such cases every single demand, no matter how often it was made and met before, is experienced almost as a "new" and therefore perplexing problem. Hence, in helping the child to meet these recurrent demands one is, from the therapist's point of view, simply "maintaining adaptation to a constant milieu," while, from the child's point of view, which is determined by its intellectual defect and short memory span, one helps it to make constantly new readaptations. For example, whereas brushing one's teeth after washing one's face is—objectively speaking—a routine sequence, performed a thousand times before, from the defective child's viewpoint it is an "innovation," requiring it to shift from washing to toothbrushing. There is nothing startling about this observation, which fully dovetails with the well-established fact that feeble-minded workers find routine chores, which bore and frustrate the normal worker, interesting, satisfying, and challenging. To a normal cleaning woman there is nothing new or exciting about the fact that today a cup was left standing on the stove, whereas yesterday it was left standing on the mantelpiece in the living room. To the feeble-minded cleaning woman this is an "event" and therefore also a problem to be "solved." Needless to say, we are simplifying things here. However, the essence of our argument would be substantiated even by a more realistic, i.e., more complicated, example. One has only to listen to the meticulous accounts given by feeble-minded adolescents of small and commonplace occurrences in the course of the performance of routine chores to grasp how even the smallest change in routine seems "newsworthy" and challenging to them.[3] This, by

[3] Similar phenomena may be observed where the normal subject's environment is punitively or otherwise impoverished. For example, a medieval prisoner kept in a dungeon is said to have filled his empty days by focusing all his attention on spiders. Any account of explorers in isolated areas, such as the arctic wastes, proves that in such barren settings even the smallest incidents become unduly magnified. The whole problem is related to the human being's need for stimulation, which was stressed in particular by Chapple and Coon (22). It must be understood, of course, that where stimuli are inherently minimal they are affectively magnified out of all proportion with their inherent importance, so as to satisfy man's basic need

the way, may be one reason why psychotherapy with the feeble-minded is so exhausting to the therapist, who does not derive the same amount of stimulation from the incidents narrated by such persons as the latter do. Indeed, whereas a mislaid broom is a major event in the life of the grossly defective, and therefore elicits considerable affect, the therapist finds it humanly difficult to empathize with this affect quantitatively. This represents a major therapeutic difficulty, since, in any type of expressive psychotherapy, we are, of necessity, dealing more with affects and emotions than with thought *per se*.

We stated that the continuity and stability of the milieu—of its routine challenge and demand pattern—do alleviate the pressure of time, but usually at the cost of turning the "patient" into an "inmate." This happens invariably when routine becomes an end in itself, instead of remaining a means to an end. We know that brain-injured patients often organize their lives and environments very meticulously, so as to avoid surprises, with which they feel unable to cope (*104*). By contrast, routine can also be treated as a means to an end—for example, by simplifying unimportant tasks so as to have more time left over for important ones. As a critic once remarked, it is possible to be a genius and still keep order in one's desk drawers.

However, the most creative therapeutic use to which routine can be put is that it can be made to serve periodically as a refuge from the pressure of time, which is an integral component of any long-range pursuit. It is, hence, our thesis that continuity and stability need not necessarily imply stagnation, provided only that routine is treated as a means to an end. Thus, Benedict (*15*), who emphasized the continuity of cultural conditioning in primitive society

---

for variety and stimulation, without which there is a lapse into autism. Indeed, recent experiments—for an account of which the writer is indebted to Dr. John Lilly—indicate that persons made to float in tanks of warm water in dark and soundproofed rooms begin to hallucinate quite rapidly. Apparently hallucinations serve in such cases as substitutes for absent external stimuli.

and contrasted it with the discontinuities obtaining in "civilized society," did not imply that primitive culture was wholly aimless, stagnant, and stuck in the mud of barren routine.[4] The point is that the pressure of time can be blunted by building required routine around short-range objectives only, such as cleaning up the yard, changing body linen, etc., while at the same time making available, but without insisting upon them, also long-range objectives. When a child is in a disturbed or confused state or is "slowed down" temporarily, it may be permitted to "sink back" into a reality-cushioning and unchallenging routine. However, the moment it emerges from the doldrums, there must be made available to it the opportunity of becoming involved once more in long-range pursuits, such as schoolwork or psychotherapy. In fact, at such times it is often desirable to insist that the child take advantage of this second, more challenging, program, which coexists with the simpler program of mere routine. The crux of the matter is that both types of program must be available in the same unit, in order to create a sense of continuity, which is the chief characteristic of a truly secure and homelike atmosphere. Thus, while a child who is steadily improving and is therefore consistently ready to meet a consistently complex demand pattern may be advantageously transferred to a more advanced unit, children who are "unmanageable," precisely because they alternate between "the doldrums" and relatively good levels of performance, must have a "dual purpose" environment, in which they can feel at home and experience a sense of continuity, regardless of their current state. A sound therapeutic school needs not only a graduated set of units but also some "trouble-shooting" dual-purpose units for children who function alternatingly on two different levels and yet need a sense of continuity.

In an ideal unit of this type the child can, figuratively speaking, decide for itself whether it is Sunday or weekday. Its internal state

[4] There is, of course, some aimlessness also in primitive society. The relevant findings of Kroeber (143) for the Mohave were generalized elsewhere (61) for primitive society as a whole.

on any given day will determine whether it can "relax" in the timeless world of routine or must meet the challenge of long-range objectives. If a child is temporarily psychotic or acutely disturbed, or if a girl becomes sexually aggressive just before her menses, all nonroutine demands are to be suspended. When the "doldrums" are over, the child can return once more to its studies, projects, and the like. Thus, the hands of the clock and the pages of the calendar are not inflexible pace setters in a dual-purpose unit. "Internal clocks," running at the child's own current rate of "speed," set the pace. Routine and challenge, "easing up" and "bearing down," alternate in accordance with the child's changing condition.

In this manner, challenge and change—implying a pressure of time—are built upon a foundation composed of routine and continuity which minimize the pressure of time. Hence, even the child who is capable of real progress, but is temporarily disturbed, can feel at home in routine, which is all it has to conform to while it is not capable of meeting problems requiring not only adjustment but also readjustment. After it has had a chance to relax, and to get time "off its neck," such a child is usually ready to take advantage also of other available programs, involving distant goals. In such a unit, the child can withdraw from a project without censure and can return to it without a feeling that it "missed out" on something. The project will still be there, for it to participate in it; instruction still goes on from the point where it left off. While there may be "setbacks" from time to time—for example, when the child is assigned, during a period of semi-doldrums, to a lower grade—on the whole the progress is upward and forward, so that there is a turnover even in such a unit.

The philosophy underlying such a unit's program and policies is the assumption that the most important part of reality is the child's general state and its state at a given time, and not the "standard operating procedure" of the unit or the convenience of the staff.

This, in turn, implies that a therapeutic school must provide what we propose to call a "child-centered home," in which the adults perform a "child-focused role."

THE CHILD-CENTERED HOME

Now, there is a German quip that whereas it is easy to become a father it is quite difficult to be one. It aptly underscores the difficulties implicit in performing a "child-focused role," when it is so much easier for the possessor of superior physical strength, who is backed by social traditions, to structure the household around the adult members thereof, and in accordance with their needs and preferences. The remarks of a small boy indicate that children themselves are keenly aware of this.

Case 77: Bought vs. Given Love

I'd much rather visit my paternal grandmother than my maternal grandmother. It is true that my maternal grandmother is rich and can give me expensive presents all the time, while my paternal grandmother can afford to give me presents only on my birthday and at Christmas. But when I visit my paternal grandmother she entertains me. I can turn things upside down and play, if I wish, in a back room. When I go to see my maternal grandmother, I must sit in a chair and entertain her.

An important obstacle to the creation of a child-centered home is the infantile competitiveness for the position of "favorite child" between the parents and other children. We stressed elsewhere (61) the extent to which abortion is motivated not only by the desire to avoid the drudgery which parenthood entails but also by the prospective parents' reluctance to shift from the "child position" to the "parent position" in the family. In fact, the sentimentally exalted and authoritarian role which society assigns to parents, and which the latter accept with alacrity, is a means of compensating the parents for the drudgeries and renunciations of parenthood. The law is quite explicit on this point. If a girl living under her father's roof becomes pregnant, her father may sue her seducer for "damages" which he sustained by being deprived of the "services" of his "daughter and servant" during the latter's pregnancy and confinement. If a child is accidentally killed, some states permit the parents to sue the person at fault, to obtain compensation for the loss of the potential earnings of the child up to its twenty-first birthday. Certain states even compel deserted children, who received no support whatsoever from their parents, to support the latter in their old age. Many primitives explicitly state that they have children because they need someone to support them in their old age (Chapter 15). On a more subjective and more personal level, emotionally immature parents often extort "love," respect, and obedience from their children by constantly mentioning the sacrifices which they made for them.

SOCIAL OBSTACLES

The preceding comments indicate that the creation of a home, be it a home for one's own children or for children whom one has undertaken to foster and nurture, either privately or in a therapeutic school, requires considerable emotional maturity as well as tremendous resources of human warmth. It also requires, especially in a therapeutic school, a spontaneous capacity to establish a "child-centered home," for which there is hardly any precedent or pattern in the outside world. Specifically, it requires, on the part of the therapeutic educator and milieu therapist, the ability to improvise a social structure in harmony with certain scientific principles and insights and radically at variance with practices prevailing in the external world. How difficult it is to create a new type of family structure may be inferred from the legal, as well as internecine, difficulties experienced by the early Mormons, who evolved for themselves a family structure radically at variance with the family structure of the outside world.

The point we seek to stress here is that the establishment of a child-centered home in therapeutic schools is opposed not only by social tradition, but also by important psychological resistances on the part of staff members, who were raised in adult-centered homes. This latter point can be confirmed even by a cursory examination of relevant culture-historical data.

Thus, we strongly suspect that the Mormons did not end up by adopting monogamy—sanctioned by a new "revelation"—simply because they were subjected to great political and adminstrative pressures. Indeed, even in our own time a certain religious group chose to emigrate to South America rather than conform to the administrative practices of our society. The chief motive behind the modification of the Mormon marriage pattern was apparently the difficulty which persons raised in monogamous families experienced when they were expected to adjust to a deviant family system, while maintaining at the same time many of the other traditional values and patterns of Occidental society, from which they branched off.[5] Similar factors are presumably responsible for the gradual return of Soviet society to the patriarchal family pattern and for the current Soviet crusade against contraception and abortion.[6] The notorious contempt of gangsters for pimps (procurers) and madams also proves how tenaciously sexual and familial codes persist even among antisocial groups. This process can be generalized, by stressing the traditional tendency of revolutions to reverse only externally, without actually modifying their essence, the

[5] This last point is of considerable importance. On the basis of personal experiences in many countries, as well as on the basis of information obtained from a British psychoanalyst who, before moving to this country, had spent some time among natives in a British colony, we believe that it is much more difficult to adjust to a culture which is almost, but not quite, like that in which we were raised than it is to adjust to a radically different culture, whose value system and behavior pattern are so different from our own that no situation induces us to respond to it unthinkingly with behavior which is appropriate only in a wholly different cultural context. Gorer (106), too, points out how much, e.g., the American "necking pattern" confuses the European, who, unlike the American, expects such intimacies to "lead up to something."

[6] Cf. Khrushchev's recent speech, reported in the newspapers.

major sociocultural tenets of the very system which the revolution sought to abolish. One striking example of this may be found in Suetonius' *Lives of the Twelve Caesars.* Two emperors, who were elevated to that position only because their predecessors had been assassinated, apparently had nothing better to do than to punish the murderers of their predecessors—presumably in order to discourage future would-be regicides. Likewise, the official atheism of the French Revolution rapidly led to the cult of the "Goddess of Reason." Last, but not least, it is well known that where the basic family pattern of a society is destroyed by external pressures—for example, when missionaries force the natives to give up polygamy, bride purchase, and the like—society as a whole often disintegrates, and native codes of conduct are replaced not by an Occidental family system but by chaos of a type which Durkheim calls *anomie* (75).

REALITY TESTING AND SUBLIMATION

In brief, one of the greatest difficulties facing the therapeutic school which seeks to establish a child-centered home is the fact that we live in a society where the adult-centered home is the rule. It is but a hollow fiction that the "progressive" American home is child centered simply because children are permitted to make a nuisance of themselves. A child-centered home is not one where the child "can get away with murder" but one where its real needs are met systematically. One of these is the need for supervision and guidance, the objective of which is to satisfy the child's needs and not to suit the conveniences of the adult. The parent's or educator's responsibility for humanizing and ethnicizing the child is a fundamental one, and any repudiation of this task is an unforgivable dereliction. It is not a manifestation of great love, tolerant patience, and child centeredness but simply a roundabout way of destroying the child as surely as it can be destroyed by coldness, punitiveness, and adult centeredness. It results not from a sublimation of parental ambivalences toward the child but from what we call "hostile giving"—this time in the form of "hostile giving *in*" (Chapter 5). Since we would not dream of giving a child a man-eating tiger as a pet, neither should we deliver it up to the internal man-eating tiger of its conflicts, anxieties, and uncontrollable, partly *repressed* impulses.[7] Indeed, the child needs help in controlling its hostilities, which are mobilized by the unavoidable frustrations caused by living in society and in a real world. This world we have to accept as it is, since the laws of chemistry and of physics are as little subject to modification as is the legitimate though inconvenient appetite of a hungry wolf or the justifiable insistence of other persons upon their own rights. It does not help the child to be permitted to live in a "make-believe" world where fire does not burn, cats whose tails are pulled do not claw, and people unduly imposed upon do not retaliate. We must therefore neither inhibit punitively the child's frustration-actuated hostilities, so as to cause them to be repressed, nor constantly hover over it, to prevent tormented dogs and harassed people from retaliating. What we must do is help the child sublimate its hostilities, by teaching it that fire not only burns but also gives warmth and light, that, given half a chance, cats not only claw but also purr and play with children, and that adults not only get angry but also provide protection and love. In brief, in the child-centered home, where mature guidance is given to the child, education as well as reëducation and therapy promote sublimation and not mere repression leading to neurosis and to symptom formation. Mature guidance is neither punitively harsh nor destructively "lenient." It does not overemphasize either the clawing or the purring of cats and denies neither the "good" (agreeable) nor the "bad" (inconvenient) aspects of reality. On the contrary, it fosters reality testing and the acceptance of all of reality. These two

---

[7] This formulation does not contradict our inflexible repudiation of the thesis that children are fundamentally evil, and that instincts are "atom bombs." As Freud pointed out (92, 94) not instinct in its natural state but the repressed instinct only is "monstrous" and explosive.

activities, taken together, are the *conditio sine qua non* of both internal sublimations and external effectiveness and practicality.

The difficulty is that the personal conflicts of both the child's parents and the educators or milieu therapists often place unnecessary obstacles in the path of such a program, particularly since they can justify their resistances by an appeal to (destructive and unhealthy) child-rearing and educational tradition. Adult hostility toward the difficult child can express itself in an exaggeration of the harshness of the world, which the child allegedly "must learn to expect and to meet,"[8] quite as much as in exaggerating the "goodness" of the world—and particularly of adults—in a pollyanna-ish manner (Case 10). Reality is such as it is, and has to be accepted on its own terms, but only in order to learn how to make cats purr rather than claw. This requires simultaneously sublimation and reality acceptance. In fact, one is impossible without the other. If one fails to accept one part of reality, represented by the potential "goodness" of the world, one becomes a self-destructive pessimist or pseudo-efficient psychopathic confidence man. If one fails to accept another part of reality, represented by the tormented cat's capacity to claw, one becomes an equally unsublimated, naïvely and masochistically "sunny optimist," who is the self-appointed victim of every psychopath.

A child-centered home is one where sublimation, rather than repression, and reality acceptance, rather than the distortion of reality, are fostered. The most important aspect of reality in the child-centered home, and the one which must be most consistently and most tenaciously tested and accepted both by the child and by adults, is the child's own nature, such as it really is and not as it is "defined" by neurotic people, who either coo over the "little angel," or else—like Diderot—see it as a potential beast, lacking only the

---

[8] Compare the convenient and soothing "cultural bromide," that it is "good" for genius to starve in an unheated garret.

strength to act out its destructive impulses, who "must" be dealt with by not sparing the rod, so as not to spoil it.

In the truly therapeutic school the nuclear reality is the nature of the individual child, to which everything else has to be adjusted and subordinated. Since this is not the prevalent attitude in our society, the child-centered home of the therapeutic school and its attempts to achieve both reality acceptance and sublimation are often strenuously resisted by society at large, by the child's own parents, and sometimes even by the neurotic rigidities of "therapeutic" educators and milieu "therapists." Hence, the creation of a truly child-centered home is one of the most difficult and challenging of all therapeutically educational measures. Only if this fact is recognized is it possible to attain this goal.[9]

[9] Other internal conflicts of educational therapists, which interfere with therapeutic efficiency, are discussed in Chapter 5 under the heading "Counter Transference."

CHAPTER 17

··

The Road to Creative Objectivity

─────────────────────────────────────

Lest the therapeutic educator should think that the warnings contained in the preceding pages somehow reflect on his professional competence or human integrity, it seemed desirable to describe similar problems in the practice of analysis. A further purpose of this chapter is to interpret to the therapeutic educator the work of his psychiatric co-workers.

PERCEPTIVENESS

No one is supposed to engage in the therapeutic practice of psychoanalysis without having been analyzed even more exhaustively than are ordinary therapeutic patients. The purpose of the didactic analysis is to liberate the entire creative potential of the future analyst and to render him objective and perceptive toward all of his patients' latent problems, including even those which did not happen to play any significant role in the analyst's own development. In other words, the analyst must understand himself as fully as possible, lest he be unable to understand his patients and to see their problems from their viewpoint.

Let us imagine that an analyst somehow failed to obtain in the course of his didactic analysis an objective insight into the dynamics and meaning of his own adolescent difficulties with his father. Such an analyst, when treating a patient beset with similar problems, would impulsively "take sides" and fight once more his own ado-

400

lescent battles—this time through his patient. It is hardly necessary to state that this is bound to be very harmful to the patient, since the analyst would be fighting his own battles instead of those of the patient. Moreover, such an analyst, being still deeply—though unconsciously—resentful toward his own father, would not even realize that he was "siding with" his patient. He would not realize that he was indirectly attacking his own father when he thought he was "only encouraging the patient to emancipate himself." Of course, the patient should be helped to emancipate himself. However, when the encouragement is not a purely objective one but is unconsciously also a manifestation of the analyst's own unresolved conflicts, this will be sensed by the patient, who—often without realizing precisely why he feels that way—will, quite legitimately, resent being used as a pawn in the analyst's devious attempt to solve his own problems. The patient will therefore be unable to benefit even by "objectively sound" advice which the analyst gives for unconscious reasons of his own. For example, the patient may react not to the objectively sound confrontation: "You seem unable to emancipate yourself from your father," but to the analyst's unconscious hatred of all fathers which lurks behind this "benign" observation. Thus, though he hears: "You seem unable to emancipate yourself from your father," he may—rightly!—understand: "Kill the old so-and-so!" Now, this is precisely what one part of the patient's unconscious mind wishes to do, while the other part of his mind is trying to inhibit this impulse—thus causing him to develop a neurosis. Hence, the patient will react to the seemingly "moderate" advice of his analyst as though the latter were inciting him to parricide. This will throw the patient into a panic, thereby impeding his recovery. In brief, when the analyst's "good reasons" differ from his "real reasons"[1]—which happens whenever the analyst himself is insufficiently analyzed—the patient, as likely as

---

[1] The famous banker, J. P. Morgan, Jr., is said to have remarked that a man always has two reasons for doing anything: a good reason and a real reason.

not, will react not to the analyst's explicit statement but to what the latter says "between the lines."

The preceding example shows why the analyst, who always deals with deeply buried impulses, conflicts, and fantasies, must first come to terms with his own many-faceted unconscious problems before he can tackle therapeutically those of his patients without intruding his own personality and problems into them.

We do not claim, of course, that even the most exhaustive analysis can turn a rickety Ford into a brand-new Cadillac, nor is it necessary that this be done. Analysts are not and should not be supermen, lest they lose the capacity for saying, when confronted with the troubles of their patients: "Here, but for the grace of God"—and a successful didactic analysis—"go I!" The didactic analysis can, however, "rebuild" the broken-down Ford; it can enable the future analyst to become sufficiently objective about himself to allow himself to respond to the patient's statements with genuine understanding, without injecting himself and his own troubles into the patient's conflicts and into the analytic hour, and without asking the patient to gratify the analyst's own needs or to fight vicariously the analyst's unfinished battles.

In brief, it is the purpose of the didactic analysis to broaden the analyst's understanding of himself, in order to enable him to understand also the problems of others. It seeks to enlarge the analyst's perceptiveness and humanity and to help him develop a compassionate, but objective and clear-sighted, sense of human fellowship with his patient. Otherwise expressed, the didactic analysis seeks to enable the analytic candidate to live up to the noble maxim: *"Homo sum, humani nihil a me alienum puto."*[2]

SELF SCRUTINY

The analysis of one's patient also entails a continuation of one's own analysis. As one scrutinizes the patient's productions, as one

[2] I am a man, and therefore nothing human is alien to me.

listens to the reverberations of the patient's remarks in one's own unconscious, one constantly discovers new conflicts within oneself and learns to resolve them. Indeed, in a very genuine sense no analysis is ever finished. There simply comes a point where the didactic analysis may be terminated, because the analytic candidate has acquired the ability to continue it "on his own"—sometimes concurrently with the analysis of his patients.[3] Yet, precisely because analytic work constantly irritates some old "raw spots" in the analyst's psyche, Freud himself urged that practicing analysts be reanalyzed every five years or so (*101*). In brief, the efficient analyst is simply a person who is much more often objective and "right" than the reverse, and who, when he is wrong, (1) is not wrong with such intensity that it will disturb the patient and (2) is willing to admit, both to himself and to his patient, that he made a mistake in his interpretation—and why he made it.

In principle at least, every analysis is interminable as long as one is alive, because life's infinite variety constantly mobilizes analytically not yet explored and understood minor or residual conflicts. In general, the didactic analysis, apart from resolving major neurotic conflicts, seeks chiefly to give the candidate a complete understanding of his character, i.e., of his constant and recurrent reaction patterns, which can be observed even in the course of an analysis of limited duration. Indeed, even though the day-to-day experiences of the analysand during the period of his didac-

[3] When a candidate has been in analysis for some time, he is given one or more relatively easy cases to analyze under supervision. The manner in which he handles these cases is discussed in "control sessions" with a supervisor, who not only points out technical errors but, above all, gives the budding analyst an understanding of his unconscious motives for making such errors. Thus, the "control sessions" supplement the candidate's formal didactic analysis. The graduate analyst, who is no longer "in control," but analyzes without supervision, "controls himself" by analyzing his own reactions to his patient's productions. In some psychoanalytic institutes, such as that of the Philadelphia Association for Psychoanalysis, before an experienced analyst is appointed "training analyst"—i.e., as an analyst qualified to do didactic analyses—he must once more "go into control" with a senior training analyst, who belongs to another society and is therefore completely impartial, and who once more passes on the prospective training analyst's technical qualifications and also on his personal objectivity, as reflected in the manner in which he handles his patients.

tic analysis are not a "representative sample" of all that could happen to him[4] and therefore do not reveal all the specific, old, and hidden conflicts which some unusual event could mobilize in him, even the experiences of a perfectly ordinary day, when subjected to analytic scrutiny, will reveal the analytic candidate's standard reaction patterns, reflecting his character structure.[5] In brief, the "completely analyzed" analyst does not exist. The good analyst is simply someone who has overcome his definitely neurotic traits and has an understanding of his character structure, which determines his standard reaction pattern. This—together with the capacity to engage in a continuous self-analysis concurrently with the analysis of one's patients—suffices to insure the degree of analytic objectivity which is needed in therapeutic work.

HUMANE OBJECTIVITY

It is hardly necessary to stress that objectivity does not imply callousness to human suffering. The analyst must be able to empathize and sympathize with his patient's plight and with the patient as a person. He must feel his patient's sufferings and must understand the patient's inadequacies without supercilious "tolerance." Only then is he able to show creative objectivity. Similarly, a surgeon's heart may be wrung by the sight of the crippled child on the operating table, but he must know that he cannot operate efficiently if his eyes are dimmed by tears, and, at that point, the child needs the surgeon's clear-sightedness more than his compassionate but inefficiently eye-dimming tears. On the other hand, only if the surgeon is not only objectively dry-eyed but also compassionate will he be adequately motivated to do his best for his patient. Like the surgeon, the analyst too must learn to shed tears over his patient—but the tears must be shed inwardly, and not on

[4] For example, during his analysis the candidate is not likely to explore Africa, dangle from a parachute, live in a Siberian slave camp, etc.

[5] This view dovetails with Freud's remark that, theoretically speaking, the complete analysis of a single dream—which is technically impossible—would be the equivalent of a whole analysis.

the outside. In fact, in the case of the analyst compassion and human warmth are even more important therapeutically than in the case of the surgeon. His compassion, when coupled with human respect and a sense of human fellowship, has therapeutic value in itself, because the patient senses it and finds it helpful.

For example, when a patient has just managed to force himself to make some particularly humiliating admission and—still animated by infantile attitudes and memories—waits with bated breath for a thundering indictment, resembling that which his parents used to utter in similar circumstances, it is often useful to remark: "Do you think I could even understand what you are telling me if I myself were not human? Can a blind man really understand the meaning of the word 'white'?" Such a confession of one's capacity to empathize with the patient, such an admission of one's membership in the human estate, can be of tremendous help to the patient, who all too often defines himself as "the scum of the earth" and as "the only such monster in existence." It also encourages the patient, because, if his analyst could overcome such impulses, it will seem more probable to him that he, too, can eventually learn to cope with them.[6]

Unfortunately, such admissions are especially hard to make in work with children, precisely because adults are particularly vehement in their indictment of those childish "misdeeds" of which they themselves were once "most guilty." No one fulminates against the "heathen" as violently as does the new convert. No adult is as contemptuous of the five-year-old as the child of ten.[7]

[6] This type of admission should be made only when the patient is extremely anxious, and likely to become *panicky*. Where anxiety is less intense, it is sufficient to cite a similar case, or even some comparable primitive custom, to help the patient overcome the feeling that he is "unique in his 'depravity' and therefore past help— and not even deserving of help."

[7] Many progressive parents report that their older children, who have just entered the latency period, are particularly vehement in criticizing their younger siblings for their infantile sexual impulses. The same fact explains why those parents who experienced especially strong anxieties over their own infantile masturbatory impulses are the most fanatical in their attempts to inhibit the infantile sexuality of their own children.

Michael Arlen was right in saying that one did not know the best about a person until one knew the worst about him. As the really humane analyst listens to the private tragedies of his patients, he often marvels at the fact that any human being could endure such hardships—live through such bitter experiences, survive such cruel, wanton, and senseless injustices—and yet, somehow or other, be it but in a warped and twisted way, still "hold together at the seams," still have a sense of selfhood, still quest for health, still be human. A singularly competent analyst once told the writer that, when analyzing a man who had had a perfectly ghastly childhood, he said to the patient: "We can see now why you became neurotic. What puzzles me is that, despite all you had to endure, you did not become psychotic!"[8] This remark simply expressed a fine analyst's respect for every human being's inherent potentiality for health—for every human being's tenacious, if often warped and misguided[9] quest for wholeness, selfhood, and humanity. One must respect in particular the neurotic's willingness to become a patient, and to undergo a long, expensive, and painful "psychic surgery."[10]

THE CREATIVE THERAPEUTIC EDUCATOR

Our last task is to apply these insights to the problem of the relationship between educator and child. Ideally, in a Utopia, most

[8] Like all really humane and insightful remarks, this, too, had important therapeutic results. It led to an analytically important understanding of the beneficial role played in this patient's early life by a devoted grandmother.

[9] We agree with Nunberg that the patient's "wish to recover" often has very neurotic implications (*175*). This point had to be made but should not be overemphasized, since it is far from being "the whole story." Indeed, the wish to recover is a healthy one, though it can, in a neurotic, assume neurotic disguises. What stands in need of analysis is therefore the neurotic disguise or phrasing—not the wish itself.

[10] This is true even of patients who—as soon becomes apparent—enter analysis for the (often conscious) purpose of "defeating" the analyst's efforts, and of proving themselves "perfectly sane" or else "hopelessly incurable" as the case may be. On further analysis one always discovers in the deeper recesses of the unconscious minds of even such "defiant" patients a forlorn hope that it "might just work." It is often this forlorn hope—too "ridiculous" even to be voiced or allowed to enter the conscious mind—which masquerades as a defiant attempt to defeat the analysis.

teachers—and certainly most teachers in therapeutic schools—would be fully analyzed individuals. However, we cannot wait for Utopia and twiddle our thumbs in the meantime. Since we cannot have at this time a full loaf, we had better examine the possibilities of stretching our half loaf far enough to do—for the time being—the job of a full loaf. Suggesting means for accomplishing this end is a definite obligation of the very person who champions the thesis that all therapeutic teachers should be analyzed, just as increasingly large numbers of psychiatric social workers are nowadays analyzed.

The purpose of this chapter was to suggest some means for acquiring a certain degree of analytic objectivity toward the exceptional child, without having had a personal analysis. This, as is so often the case, can best be accomplished by means of a searching examination of the psychological factors underlying established cultural attitudes. Precisely because culturally inculcated attitudes are subjectively felt to be "impersonal," for which no personal responsibility has to be taken,[11] they provide man with excellent "secret hiding places" for his own quirks and psychological defects. As Edgar Allan Poe's story "The Purloined Letter" indicates, the best hiding place for a letter is the "obvious" letter rack.[12]

---

[11] A violently anti-Negro Northern intellectual would feel obliged to justify his prejudices, and would thereby indicate that he feels personally responsible for them. An equally violently anti-Negro Southerner, belonging to the lower middle class, not only would not feel it incumbent upon himself to justify his prejudices but would deem it silly and "subversive" if someone asked him to do so. In other words, he squarely repudiates personal responsibility for his prejudices, simply because they were furnished to him "ready made" by his culture.

[12] When, during World War II, an officer was training future intelligence agents in searching techniques, it was noticed that not one of them—not even the best—ever looked for, e.g., the "hidden" piece of chalk in the chalk box near the blackboard. A few of the less competent "forgot" to look for it there even after they were taught the trick of concealing objects by placing them where they "naturally belong."

CONCLUSIONS OF PART FIVE

Part Five seeks to alert the therapeutic educator to his ethnocentric preconceptions about children, and more especially disturbed children, and to make him realize that many of his most creative viewpoints are at variance with the attitudes of the community, so that his most effective efforts often elicit the most opposition.

In the contemporary world, in which real therapeutic education is nearly as great an innovation as was psychoanalysis in its time, the therapeutic educator must reconcile himself to the fact that he will often have to "go it alone" and will have to tolerate the unwarranted criticism which those who have "all the answers" based on tradition will heap upon him. At the same time, he must not become provocative in his opposition to obsolete attitudes and techniques, lest parents refuse to entrust to him the children who need his ministrations most. He must, above all, be realistic in his innovations, being "wise as a serpent and innocent as a dove." He must accept the necessity of contenting himself sometimes with giving the children in his care "half a loaf," lest, by insisting upon giving them a "whole loaf" despite social and parental opposition, he cause the children who need his help to receive nothing at all, by being entrusted to rigid, unenlightened, and punitive educators. In brief, he must be completely realistic, accepting both the ideal techniques of therapeutic education and society's traditional opposition to them. Only in this manner will he be able to help any child at all. And the real goal of the therapeutic educator must be to help the child within the limits of what is possible and permitted, rather than to uphold *combatively* an ideal of therapeutic education for its own sake, and without any hope of putting these techniques to an actual use.

Bibliography

1. Alexander, Franz, and French, T. M. *Psychoanalytic Therapy,* New York, Ronald, 1946.
2. Allport, G. W., *Personality,* New York, Holt, 1937.
3. Angyal, András, *Foundations for a Science of Personality,* New York, Commonwealth Fund, 1941.
4. Aptekar, Herbert, *Anjea,* New York, Godwin, 1931.
5. Arensberg, C. M., *The Irish Countryman* (rev. ed.), New York, Smith, 1950.
6. Arensberg, C. M., and Kimball, Solon, *Family and Community in Ireland,* Cambridge, Mass., Harvard University Press, 1940.
7. Aristotle, *De Divinatione per Somnum.*
8. Aumale, S. A. R., le Duc d', *Histoire des Princes de Condé* (7 vols.), Paris, Calmann-Levy, 1885–1896.
9. Bálint, Alice, Liebe zur Mutter und Mutterliebe, *Internationale Zeitschrift für Psychoanalyse und Imago* (1939), *24:*33–48.
10. Bartemeier, L. H., Illness Following Dreams, *International Journal of Psycho-Analysis* (1950), *31:*8–11.
11. Bastian, Adolf, *Der Völkergedanke im Aufbau einer Wissenschaft vom Menschen und seine Begründung auf ethnologische Sammlungen,* Vol. II, Berlin, Dummler, 1881.
12. Bell, E. T., *Men of Mathematics,* New York, Simon and Schuster, 1937.

13. Bender, Lauretta, and Blau, Abram, The Reaction of Children to Sexual Relations with Adults, *American Journal of Orthopsychiatry* (1937), 7:500–518.
14. Benedict, Ruth, *Patterns of Culture,* Boston, Houghton Mifflin, 1935.
15. Benedict, Ruth, Continuities and Discontinuities in Cultural Conditioning, *Psychiatry* (1936), 1:161–167.
16. Best, Elsdon, *Maori Religion and Mythology, Being an Account of the Cosmogony, Anthropogeny, Religious Beliefs and Rites, Magic and Folklore of the Maori Folk of New Zealand,* Wellington, Government Printer, 1924.
17. Bettelheim, Bruno, *Symbolic Wounds,* Glencoe, Ill., The Free Press, 1953.
18. Bornstein, Berta, lecture before the Topeka Psychoanalytic Society.
19. Bose, G., Psycho-Analytic Interpretation of Animal Behavior, *Samiksa, Journal of the Indian Psycho-Analytical Society* (1947), 1:209–230.
20. Brickner, R. M., and Kubie, L. S., A Miniature Psychotic Storm Produced by a Superego Conflict over Simple Posthypnotic Suggestion, *Psychoanalytic Quarterly* (1936), 5:467–487.
21. Burnham, James, *The Managerial Revolution,* New York, Day, 1941.
22. Chapple, E. D., and Coon, C. S., *Principles of Anthropology,* New York, Holt, 1942.
23. Czaplicka, M. A., *Aboriginal Siberia,* Oxford, Clarendon Press, 1914.
24. Davis, Kingsley, The Sociology of Prostitution, *American Sociological Review* (1937), 2:744–755.
25. Davis, Kingsley, A Case of Extreme Social Isolation of a Child, *American Journal of Sociology* (1940), 45:554–565.
26. Devereux, George, *Sedang [Hà(rhn)de:a(ng)] Field Notes.* MS, 1933–1934.
27. Devereux, George, Functioning Units in Hà(rhn)de:a(ng) Society, *Primitive Man* (1937), 10:1–7.

28. Devereux, George, L'Envoûtement chez les Indiens Mohave, *Journal de la Société des Américanistes de Paris* n.s. (1938), *29:*405–412.

29. Devereux, George, A Sociological Theory of Schizophrenia, *Psychoanalytic Review* (1939), *26:*315–342.

30. Devereux, George, A Conceptual Scheme of Society, *American Journal of Sociology* (1940), *54:*687–706.

31. Devereux, George, Social Negativism and Criminal Psychopathology, *Journal of Criminal Psychopathology* (1940), *1:*325–338.

32. Devereux, George, Mohave Beliefs Concerning Twins, *American Anthropologist* n.s. (1941), *43:*573–592.

33. Devereux, George, Motivation and Control of Crime, *Journal of Criminal Psychopathology* (1942), *3:*553–584.

34. Devereux, George, Primitive Psychiatry (Part II), *Bulletin of the History of Medicine* (1942), *11:*522–542.

35. Devereux, George, Social Structure and the Economy of Affective Bonds, *Psychoanalytic Review* (1942), *29:*303–314.

36. Devereux, George, The Social Structure of a Schizophrenia Ward and Its Therapeutic Fitness, *Journal of Clinical Psychopathology* (1944), *6:*231–265.

37. Devereux, George, The Logical Foundations of Culture and Personality Studies, *Transactions of the New York Academy of Sciences,* Series II (1945), *7:*110–130.

38. Devereux, George, The Function of Alcohol in Mohave Society, *Quarterly Journal of Studies on Alcohol* (1948), *9:*207–251.

39. Devereux, George, The Mohave Neonate and Its Cradle, *Primitive Man* (1948), *21:*1–18.

40. Devereux, George, The Social Structure of the Hospital as a Factor in Total Therapy, *American Journal of Orthopsychiatry* (1949), *19:*492–500.

41. Devereux, George, Catastrophic Reactions in Normals, *American Imago* (1950), *7:*343–349.

42. Devereux, George, Education and Discipline in Mohave Society, *Primitive Man* (1950), *23:*85–102.

412 **Bibliography**

43. Devereux, George, Heterosexual Behavior of the Mohave Indians, in Róheim, Géza (ed.), *Psychoanalysis and the Social Sciences,* Vol. II, New York, International Universities Press, 1950.

44. Devereux, George, The Psychology of Feminine Genital Bleeding: An Analysis of Mohave Indian Puberty and Menstrual Rites, *International Journal of Psycho-Analysis* (1950), *31:237–257.*

45. Devereux, George, Status, Socialization and Interpersonal Relations of Mohave Children, *Psychiatry* (1950), *13:489–502.*

46. Devereux, George, Cultural and Characterological Traits of the Mohave Related to the Anal Stage of Psychosexual Development, *Psychoanalytic Quarterly* (1951), *20:398–422.*

47. Devereux, George, Logical Status and Methodological Problems of Research in Clinical Psychiatry, *Psychiatry* (1951), *14:327–330.*

48. Devereux, George, Neurotic Crime vs. Criminal Behavior, *Psychiatric Quarterly* (1951), *25:73–80.*

49. Devereux, George, The Primal Scene and Juvenile Heterosexuality in Mohave Society, in Wilbur, G. B., and Muensterberger, Warner (eds.), *Psychoanalysis and Culture* [Róheim Festschrift], New York, International Universities Press, 1951.

50. Devereux, George, *Reality and Dream: The Psychotherapy of a Plains Indian,* New York, International Universities Press, 1951.

51. Devereux, George, Some Criteria for the Timing of Confrontations and Interpretations, *International Journal of Psycho-Analysis* (1951), *32:19–24.*

52. Devereux, George, Practical Problems of Conceptual Psychiatric Research, *Psychiatry* (1952), *15:189–192.*

53. Devereux, George, Psychiatry and Anthropology: Some Research Objectives, *Bulletin of the Menninger Clinic* (1952), *16:167–177.*

54. Devereux, George, Anthropological Data on Perversions, lecture delivered before the American Psychoanalytic Association, 1953.

55. Devereux, George, Cultural Factors in Psychoanalytic Therapy, *Journal of the American Psychoanalytic Association* (1953), *1:629–655.*

56. Devereux, George (ed.), *Psychoanalysis and the Occult,* New York, International Universities Press, 1953.

57. Devereux, George, Why Oedipus Killed Laius: A Note on the Complementary Oedipus Complex, *International Journal of Psycho-Analysis* (1953), *34:*123–141.

58. Devereux, George, Belief, Superstition and Symptom, *Samiksa, Journal of the Indian Psycho-Analytical Society* (1954), *8:*210–215.

59. Devereux, George, Normal and Abnormal, *Some Uses of Anthropology,* Washington, D.C., Anthropological Society of Washington, 1956.

60. Devereux, George, Charismatic Leadership and Crisis, in Muensterberger, Warner (ed.), *Psychoanalysis and the Social Sciences,* Vol. IV, New York, International Universities Press, 1955.

61. Devereux, George, *A Study of Abortion in Primitive Societies,* New York, Julian Press, 1955.

62. Devereux, George, A Counteroedipal Episode in Homer's *Iliad, Bulletin of the Philadelphia Association for Psychoanalysis* (1955), *4:*90–97.

63. Devereux, George, Acting Out in Dreams, *American Journal of Psychotherapy* (1955), *9:*657–660.

64. Devereux, George, and Loeb, E. M., Antagonistic Acculturation, *American Sociological Review* (1943), *7:*133–147.

65. Devereux, George, and Weiner, F. R., The Occupational Status of Nurses, *American Sociological Review* (1950), *15:*628–634.

66. Dodds, E. R., *The Greeks and the Irrational,* Berkeley, University of California Press, 1951.

67. Doll, E. A., Neurophrenia, *American Journal of Psychiatry* (1951), *108:*50–53.

68. Dollard, John, *Caste and Class in a Southern Town,* New Haven, Yale University Press, 1937.

69. Dollard, John, Auld, Frank, Jr., and White, A. M., *Steps in Psychotherapy,* New York, Macmillan, 1953.

70. Dollard, John, and Miller, N. E., *Personality and Psychotherapy,* New York, McGraw-Hill, 1950.

71. Donnan, F. G., Activities of Life and the Second Law of Thermodynamics, *Nature* (1933), *133*:99; Jeans, Sir James, *ibid.,* p. 174; Donnan, F. G., and Guggenheim, E. A., *ibid.,* p. 530; Jeans, *ibid.,* p. 612; Donnan and Guggenheim, *ibid.,* p. 869; Jeans, *ibid.,* p. 986; Donnan and Guggenheim, *ibid.* (1934), *134*:255.

72. DuBois, Cora, *The People of Alor,* Minneapolis, University of Minnesota Press, 1944.

73. Dupeyrat, R. P. André, Mental Disorders Among the Natives of Papua, lecture held at Winter VA Hospital, Topeka, Kansas.

74. Durkheim, Emile, *De la Division du Travail Social,* Paris, Alcan, 1893.

75. Durkheim, Emile, *Le Suicide,* Paris, Alcan, 1897.

76. Eilers, Anneliese, Inseln um Ponape (Kapinga-marangi, Nukuor, Ngatik, Mokil, Pingelap) in Thilenius, Georg (ed.), *Ergebnisse der Südsee-Expedition 1908–1910,* II, B, VIII, 1–464, Hamburg, Friedrichsen, 1934.

77. Ekstein, Rudolf, and Wright, Dorothy, The Space Child, *Bulletin of the Menninger Clinic* (1952), *16*:211–224.

78. Elkin, A. P., *Australian Aborigines,* Sydney, Angus and Robertson, 1938.

79. Ellis, William, *Polynesian Researches During a Residence of Nearly Eight Years in the Society and Sandwich Islands,* Vol. I, London, Bohn, 1853.

80. Elwin, Verrier, *The Muria and Their Ghotul,* Bombay, Oxford University Press, 1947.

81. Feldman, S. S., Notes on the "Primal Horde," in Róheim, Géza (ed.), *Psychoanalysis and the Social Sciences,* Vol. I, New York, International Universities Press, 1947.

82. Fenichel, Otto, *Collected Papers,* Vol. II, New York, Norton, 1954.

83. Fiske, John, *Outlines of Cosmic Philosophy,* Boston, Osgood, 1875.

84. Fletcher, J. M., The Wisdom of the Mind, *Sigma Xi Quarterly* (1938), *26*:6–16.

85. French, T. M., A Clinical Study of Learning in the Course of a

Psychoanalytic Treatment, *Psychoanalytic Quarterly* (1936), 5:148–194.

86. French, T.M., Reality and the Unconscious, *Psychoanalytic Quarterly* (1937), 6:23–61.

87. French, T. M., Reality Testing in Dreams, *Psychoanalytic Quarterly* (1937), 6:62–77.

88. Freud, Sigmund, Three Contributions to the Theory of Sex, *Nervous and Mental Disease Monographs,* New York, 1930 [1905].

89. Freud, Sigmund, Obsessive Acts and Religious Practices, *Collected Papers,* Vol. II, London, Hogarth, 1924 [1907].

90. Freud, Sigmund, The Sexual Enlightenment of Children, *Collected Papers,* Vol. II, London, Hogarth, 1924 [1907].

91. Freud, Sigmund, Contributions to the Psychology of Love, I: A Special Type of Choice of Object Made by Men, *Collected Papers,* Vol. IV, London, Hogarth, 1925 [1910].

92. Freud, Sigmund, A Note on the Unconscious in Psycho-Analysis, *Collected Papers,* Vol. IV, London, Hogarth, 1925 [1912].

93. Freud, Sigmund, A Case of Paranoia Running Counter to the Psycho-Analytical Theory of the Disease, *Collected Papers,* Vol. II, London, Hogarth, 1924 [1915].

94. Freud, Sigmund, Repression, *Collected Papers,* Vol. IV, London, Hogarth, 1925 [1915].

95. Freud, Sigmund, Contributions to the Psychology of Love III: The Taboo of Virginity, *Collected Papers,* Vol. IV, London, Hogarth, 1925 [1918].

96. Freud, Sigmund, The Uncanny, *Collected Papers,* Vol. IV, London, Hogarth, 1925 [1919].

97. Freud, Sigmund, *Group Psychology and the Analysis of the Ego,* London, Hogarth, 1922 [1921].

98. Freud, Sigmund, *Civilization and Its Discontents,* London, Hogarth, 1930 [1930].

99. Freud, Sigmund, The Acquisition of Fire, *Collected Papers,* Vol. V, London, Hogarth, 1950 [1932].

100. Freud, Sigmund, "Dreams and the Occult," *New Introductory Lectures on Psycho-Analysis,* London, Hogarth, 1933 [1932].

101. Freud, Sigmund, Analysis Terminable and Interminable, *Collected Papers,* Vol. V, London, Hogarth, 1950 [1937].
102. Fromm, Erich, *Escape from Freedom,* New York, Farrar and Rinehart, 1941.
103. Gitelson, Maxwell, The Emotional Position of the Analyst in the Psycho-Analytic Situation, *International Journal of Psycho-Analysis* (1952), *33:*1–10.
104. Goldstein, Kurt, *The Organism,* New York, American Book, 1939.
105. Gollancz, Victor, *Man and God,* Boston, Houghton Mifflin, 1950.
106. Gorer, Geoffrey, *The American People,* New York, Norton, 1948.
107. Grinnel, G. B., *When Buffalo Ran,* New Haven, Yale University Press, 1920.
108. Guggenheim, E. A. (see Donnan).
109. Guthrie, W. K. C., *The Greeks and Their Gods,* London, Methuen, 1950.
110. Hall, G. S., *Adolescence* (2 vols.), New York, Appleton-Century, 1904.
111. Han Wu Ti, Emperor, in *Gems of Chinese Literature,* no place, "The Progress," no date [also in Devereux, George, A Note on Classical Chinese Penological Thought, *Journal of Criminal Psychopathology* (1944), *5:*735–744].
112. Hartshorne, E. Y., *The German Universities and National Socialism,* Cambridge, Mass., Harvard University Press, 1937.
113. Hawke, C. C., Castration and Sex Crimes, *Journal of the Kansas Medical Society* (1950), *51:*470–473.
114. Hayward, M. L., and Taylor, J. E., A Schizophrenic Patient Describes the Action of Intensive Psychotherapy, *Psychiatric Quarterly* (in press).
115. Herzog, George, Linguistic Approaches to Culture and Personality, in Sargent, S. S., and Smith, M. W. (eds.), *Culture and Personality,* New York, Viking Fund, 1949.
116. Highet, Gilbert, *Man's Unconquerable Mind,* New York, Columbia University Press, 1954.
117. Hill, Gerald, and Silver, Gilbert, Psychodynamic and Esthetic

Motivations for Plastic Surgery, *Psychosomatic Medicine* (1950), 12:345–355.

118. Hoch, P. H. (ed.), *Failures in Psychiatric Treatment*, New York, Grune and Stratton, 1948.

119. Holt, L. P., Identification: A Crucial Concept for Sociology, *Bulletin of the Menninger Clinic* (1950), 14:164–173.

120. Howe [Holt] L. P., Some Sociological Aspects of Identification, in Muensterberger, Warner (ed.), *Psychoanalysis and the Social Sciences*, Vol. IV, New York, International Universities Press, 1955.

121. Hsu, F. L. K., *Under the Ancestors' Shadow*, New York, Columbia University Press, 1948.

122. Itard, J. M. G., *The Wild Boy of Aveyron*, New York, Appleton-Century, 1932.

123. Jaffe, Bernard, *Outposts of Science*, New York, Simon and Schuster, 1935.

124. Jeans, Sir James (see Donnan).

125. Jenkins, R. L., The Constructive Use of Punishment, *Mental Hygiene* (1945), 29:561–574.

126. Jenkins, R. L., and Glickman, Sylvia, Patterns of Personality Organization Among Delinquents, *The Nervous Child* (1947), 6:329–339.

127. Joffe, N. F., The Dynamics of Benefice Among East European Jews, *Social Forces* (1949), 27:238–247.

128. Jokl, R. H., Psychic Determinism and Preservation of Sublimation in Classical Psychoanalytic Procedure, *Bulletin of the Menninger Clinic* (1950), 14:207–219.

129. Jones, Ernest, *Freud, The Man and His Works*, Vol. I, New York, Basic Books, 1953.

130. Kanner, Leo, Exoneration of the Feebleminded, *American Journal of Psychiatry* (1942), 99:17–22.

131. Kardiner, Abram, *The Individual and His Society*, New York, Columbia University Press, 1939.

132. Kardiner, Abram, *The Psychological Frontiers of Society*, New York, Columbia University Press, 1945.

133. Karpman, Ben, *The Sexual Offender and His Offences,* New York, Julian Press, 1953.

134. Katz, Richard, *Heitere Tage mit braunen Menschen,* Berlin, Ullstein, 1930.

135. Keiser, Sylvan, Orality Displaced to the Urethra, *Journal of the American Psychoanalytic Association* (1954), 2:263–279.

136. Kennard, E. A., Hopi Reactions to Death, *American Anthropologist* n.s. (1937), 39:491–496.

137. Kiefer, Otto, *Sexual Life in Ancient Rome,* London, Routledge and Kegan Paul, 1934.

138. Kitto, H. D. F., *The Greeks,* Harmsworth, England, Penguin Books, 1951.

139. Köhler, Wolfgang, *The Mentality of Apes,* New York, Harcourt, Brace, 1925.

140. Krader, Lawrence, Buryat Religion and Society, *Southwestern Journal of Anthropology* (1954), 10:322–351.

141. Krafft-Ebing, Richard von, *Lehrbuch der gerichtlichen Psychopathologie,* Stuttgart, Enke, 1875.

142. Kroeber, A. L., Handbook of the Indians of California, *Bureau of American Ethnology, Bulletin 78,* Washington, D.C., 1925.

143. Kroeber, A. L., Olive Oatman's Return, *Kroeber Anthropological Society Papers* (1951), 4:1–18.

144. Kroeber, A. L., *The Nature of Culture,* Chicago, University of Chicago Press, 1952.

145. La Barre, Weston, The Cultural Basis of Emotions and Gestures, *Journal of Personality* (1947), 16:49–68.

146. La Barre, Weston, *The Human Animal,* Chicago, University of Chicago Press, 1954.

147. Lee, H. B., A Critique of the Theory of Sublimation, *Psychiatry* (1939), 2:239–270.

148. Levy, D. M., Primary Affect Hunger, *American Journal of Psychiatry* (1937), 94:643–652.

149. Linn, Louis, and Goldman, I. B., Psychiatric Observations Concerning Rhinoplasty, *Psychosomatic Medicine* (1949), 11:307–314.

150. Linton, Ralph, The Tanala, *Field Museum of Natural History Publication*, 317, *Anthropological Series*, Vol. XXII, Chicago, 1933.
151. Linton, Ralph, *The Study of Man*, New York, Appleton-Century, 1936.
152. Linton, Ralph, Culture, Society and the Individual, *Journal of Abnormal and Social Psychology* (1938), 33:425–436.
153. Linton, Ralph, *The Tree of Culture*, New York, Knopf, 1955.
154. Linton, Ralph, *Culture and Mental Disorders*, Springfield, Ill., C. C. Thomas, 1956.
155. Lowie, R. H., Takes-the-Pipe, a Crow Warrior, in Parsons, E. C. (ed.), *American Indian Life*, New York, Viking, 1925.
156. Lowie, R. H., *Are We Civilized?* New York, Harcourt, Brace, 1929.
157. Lowie, R. H., The Family as a Social Unit, *Papers of the Michigan Academy of Science, Arts and Letters* (1933), 18:53–69.
158. Lowie, R. H., The Professor Talks Back, *The Antioch Review*, Spring, 1942, pp. 317–321.
159. Macgregor, F. C., and Schaffner, Bertram, Screening Patients for Nasal Plastic Operations, *Psychosomatic Medicine* (1950), 12:277–291.
160. MacIver, R. M., *Community*, London, Macmillan, 1936.
161. McNichols, C. L., *Crazy Weather*, New York, Macmillan, 1944.
162. Malinowski, Bronislaw, *A Scientific Theory of Culture and Other Essays*, Chapel Hill, University of North Carolina Press, 1944.
163. Mandelbaum, D. G., Wolf Child Histories from India, *Journal of Social Psychology* (1943), 17:25–44.
164. Maurois, André, *Disraeli*, New York, Appleton, 1928.
165. Mauss, Marcel, "Une Catégorie de l'Esprit Humain: La Notion de Personne, Celle de 'Moi,'" *Sociologie et Anthropologie*, Paris, Presses Universitaires de France, 1950.
166. Mead, Margaret, *From the South Seas*, New York, Morrow, 1939.
167. Mead, Margaret, The Swaddling Hypothesis: Its Reception, *American Anthropologist* (1954), 56:395–409.

168. Menninger, K. A., *Man Against Himself,* New York, Harcourt, Brace, 1938.

169. Menninger, K. A., *Love Against Hate,* New York, Harcourt, Brace, 1942.

170. Menninger, W. C., Facts and Statistics of Significance for Psychiatry, *Bulletin of the Menninger Clinic* (1948), *12:1–25.*

171. Meyer, J. J., *Sexual Life in Ancient India* (2 vols.), New York, Dutton, 1930.

172. Miller, Nathan, *The Child in Primitive Society,* London, Kegan Paul, 1928.

173. Munshi, Abdullah, *The Autobiography of,* Singapore, Methodist Publishing House, 1918.

174. Myerson, Abraham, Theory and Principles of "Total Push" Method in the Treatment of Chronic Schizophrenia, *American Journal of Psychiatry* (1939), *95:1197–1204.*

175. Nunberg, Herman, Practice and Theory of Psychoanalysis, *Nervous and Mental Disease Monographs,* New York, 1948.

176. Orlansky, Harold, Infant Care and Personality, *Psychological Bulletin* (1949), No. 46, pp. 1–48.

177. Pareto, Wilfredo, *The Mind and Society* (4 vols.), New York, Harcourt, Brace, 1935.

178. Parsons, E. C. (ed.), *American Indian Life,* New York, Viking, 1925.

179. Paul, Benjamin, Mental Disorder and Self-Regulating Processes in Culture: A Guatemalan Illustration, in *Interrelations Between the Social Environment and Psychiatric Disorders,* New York, Milbank Memorial Fund, 1953.

180. Popov, A. A., The Receipt of the "Shaman's Gift" Among the Vilyuysk Yakut, in *Yakut Ethnographic Sketches,* New Haven, Human Relations Area Files, 1953.

181. Provinse, J. H., Cooperative Ricefield Cultivation Among the Siang Dyaks of Central Borneo, *American Anthropologist* n.s. (1937), *39:77–102.*

182. Raum, O. F., *Chaga Childhood, A Description of Indigenous Edu-*

cation in an East African Tribe, New York, Oxford University Press, 1940.

183. Reider, Norman, The Concept of Normality, *Psychoanalytic Quarterly* (1950), *19:*43–51.

184. Riemer, Svend, A Research Note on Incest, *American Journal of Sociology* (1940), *45:*566–575.

185. Roethlisberger, F. J., and Dickson, W. J., *Management and the Worker,* Cambridge, Mass., Harvard University Press, 1939.

186. Róheim, Géza, *Animism, Magic and the Divine King,* London, Kegan Paul, 1930.

187. Róheim, Géza, Psychoanalysis of Primitive Cultural Types, *International Journal of Psycho-Analysis* (1932), 13:1–224.

188. Róheim, Géza, Women and Their Life in Central Australia, *Journal of the Royal Anthropological Institute* (1933), *63:*207–265.

189. Róheim, Géza, The Garden of Eden, *Psychoanalytic Review* (1940), *27:*1–26, 177–199.

190. Róheim, Géza, *Psychoanalysis and Anthropology,* New York, International Universities Press, 1950.

191. Rosen, Harold, and Erickson, M. H., The Hypnotic and Hypnotherapeutic Investigation and Determination of Symptom-Function, *Journal of Clinical and Experimental Hypnosis* (1954), *2:*201–219.

192. Rosen, J. N., *Direct Analysis,* New York, Grune and Stratton, 1953.

193. Rowland, Howard, Friendship Patterns in a State Mental Hospital, *Psychiatry* (1939), *2:*363–373.

194. Russell, Bertrand, *Principles of Mathematics,* New York, Norton, 1938.

195. Schurtz, Heinrich, *Altersklassen und Männerbünde,* Berlin, Reimer, 1902.

196. Sears, R. R., *Survey of Objective Studies of Psychoanalytic Concepts,* New York, Social Science Research Council, 1943.

197. Sewell, W. H., Infant Training and Personality of the Child, *American Journal of Sociology* (1952), *58:*150–159.

198. Shipley, James, and Blair, Clay, Jr., *The Hydrogen Bomb*, New York, David McKay, 1954.

199. Simmons, L. W., *Sun Chief*, New Haven, Yale University Press, 1942.

200. Simmons, L. W., *The Role of the Aged in Primitive Society*, New Haven, Yale University Press, 1945.

201. Singh, J. A. L., and Zingg, R. M., *Wolf-Children and Feral Man*, New York, Harper, 1942.

202. Smith, M. W., Wolf Children and the Principle of Reinforcement, *Child Development* (1954), 25:115–123.

203. Spindler, G. D. (ed.), *Education and Anthropology*, Stanford, Stanford University Press, 1955.

204. Spitz, R. A., Hospitalism, *The Psychoanalytic Study of the Child*, Vol. I, New York, International Universities Press, 1945.

205. Spitz, R. A., The Role of Ecological Factors in Emotional Development in Infancy, *Child Development* (1949), 20:145–156.

206. Spitz, R. A., and Wolf, K. M., Anaclitic Depression, *The Psychoanalytic Study of the Child*, Vol. II, New York, International Universities Press, 1946.

207. Spock, Benjamin, *The Commonsense Book of Baby and Child Care*, New York, Duell, Sloan and Pearce, 1947.

208. Stanton, A. H., and Schwartz, M. S., *The Mental Hospital*, New York, Library of Behavior Sciences, 1954.

209. Stewart, Kilton, *Pygmies and Dream Giants*, New York, Norton, 1954.

210. Stouffer, Samuel, Intervening Opportunities: A Theory Relating to Mobility and Distance, *American Sociological Review* (1940), 5:845–867.

211. Strauss, A. A., and Lehtinen, L. E., *Psychopathology and Education of the Brain-Injured Child*, New York, Grune and Stratton, 1947.

212. Strecker, E. A., *Influence of Mental Defect upon Civilization and Culture* (6 pp.), Devon, Pa., Devereux Foundation, 1943.

213. Strehlow, Carl, *Die Aranda und Loritjastämme*, Frankfurt-am-Main, Städtisches Völker-Museum, 2 vols., 1907–1908.

214. Suetonius, *The Lives of the Twelve Caesars.*

215. Tönnies, Ferdinand, *Fundamental Concepts of Sociology,* New York, American Book, 1940.

216. Tredgold, A. F., *Mental Deficiency,* New York, William Wood, 1924.

217. Vajda, G., Juifs et Mussulmans Selon le Ḥadīt, *Journal Asiatique* (1937), *229:*57–127.

218. Van Loon, F. H. G., Amok and Lattah, *Journal of Abnormal and Social Psychology* (1926), *21:*434–444.

219. Veblen, Thorstein, *The Theory of the Leisure Class,* New York, Macmillan, 1899.

220. Veblen, Thorstein, *The Instinct of Workmanship,* New York, Viking, 1918.

221. Vercors, *You Shall Know Them,* Boston, Little, Brown, 1953.

222. Waelder, Robert, Presidential Address, Philadelphia Association for Psychoanalysis, July, 1954.

223. Waller, Willard, Social Problems and the Mores, *American Sociological Review* (1936), *1:*922–933.

224. Warner, W. L., *A Black Civilization,* New York, Harper, 1937.

225. Webster, Hutton, *Primitive Secret Societies,* New York, Macmillan, 1933.

226. Westermarck, Edward, *Ritual and Belief in Morocco* (2 vols.), London, Macmillan, 1926.

227. Wexler, Milton, The Structural Problem in Schizophrenia: Therapeutic Implications, *International Journal of Psycho-Analysis* (1951), *32:*157–166.

228. Wexler, Milton, The Structural Problem in Schizophrenia: The Role of the Internal Object, *Bulletin of the Menninger Clinic* (1951), *15:*221–235.

229. Whitaker, C. A., and Malone, T. P., *The Roots of Psychotherapy,* Philadelphia, Blakiston, 1953.

230. Whiting, J. W. M., *Becoming a Kwoma,* New Haven, Yale University Press, 1941.

231. Whorf, B. L., *Collected Papers on Metalinguistics,* Washington, D.C., Department of State, 1952.

232. Wissler, Clark, The Social Life of the Blackfoot Indians, *American Museum of Natural History, Anthropological Papers,* Vol. 7, Pt. 1, New York, 1911.

233. Wissler, Clark, *Man and Culture,* New York, Crowell, 1923.

234. Zaidens, S. H., Dermatologic Hypochondriasis: A Form of Schizophrenia, *Psychosomatic Medicine* (1950), *12:*250–253.

INDEXES

INDEX OF CASES
INDEX OF NAMES
INDEX OF SUBJECTS

INDEX OF CASES

427

INDEX OF NAMES

Lenin, Nikolai, 36, 343
Levy, D. M., 127, 418
Lilly, John, 390 n.
Lincoln, Abraham, 12
Lindner, Robert, 6, 234
Linn, Louis, 73, 418
Linton, Ralph, 10, 16, 81, 94, 176, 234, 237, 268, 287, 290, 353, 354, 358, 378, 419
Liszt, Franz, 150, 290
Livia, Empress, 52
Loeb, E. M., 226, 290, 291, 413
Loeb, L. B., 150
Louis XIII, King, 185
Louis XV, King, 43
Louis XVI, King, 43
Lowie, R. H., 31, 33, 218, 290, 335, 362, 384, 419
Lyautey, Marshal L. H. G., 42

Macgregor, F. C., 73, 419
MacIver, R. M., 8, 419
McNichols, C. L., 368, 419
Mach, Ernst, 15
Malinowski, Bronislav, 95, 419
Malone, T. P., 247, 365, 423
Mandelbaum, D. G., 14, 419
Maurois, André, 257, 419
Mauss, Marcel, 288, 419
Mazzanti, Vincent, 247
Mbra:o, 10
Mead, Margaret, 94, 339, 419
Medici, Lorenzo de', 11
Menninger, K. A., 221, 273, 347, 420
Menninger, W. C., 182, 420
Meyer, J. J., 33, 420
Miller, Nathan, 354, 358, 420
Miller, N. E., 114, 413
Molière, J. B. P., 144
Montgomery of Alamein, Field Marshal Viscount, 235
Moses, 365, 384, 385
Mozart, W. A., 7, 8, 9, 89, 289
"Mulvaney, Terrence," 230
Munshi, Abdullah, 33, 420
Myerson, Abraham, 293, 420

Napoleon I, 103, 168, 358
Napoleon II, 358
Neumann, John von, 21
Nunberg, Herman, 406, 420
Nuo, 357

Orlansky, Harold, 241, 420

Pareto, Vilfredo, 294, 420
Parsons, E. C., 296, 420
Paul, Benjamin, 368, 420
Pericles, 11
Peters, Henry, 262
Phryne, 12
"Pirard, Abbé," 132
Plato, 25, 35, 37, 39, 40, 239, 240
Poe, Edgar Allan, 407
Poincaré, Henri, 20
Poncelet, J. V., 103
Popov, A. A., 281, 420
"Procrustes," 189
Provinse, J. H., 347, 420

Raum, O. F., 355, 420
Reichstadt, Duke of, see Napoleon II
Reider, Norman, 260, 281, 421
Reik, Theodor, 269
Riemer, Svend, 368, 421
Roethlisberger, F. J., 347, 421
Róheim, Géza, 23, 67, 188, 272, 321, 337, 347, 353, 421
Rosen, Harold, 74, 421
Rosen, J. N., 247, 421
Rousseau, Jean-Jacques, 41, 211
Rowland, Howard, 280, 421
Russell, Bertrand, 78, 95, 322, 421
Rutherford of Nelson, Lord, 21

St. Augustine, 229
St. Mark, 285
St. Paul, 238
Sand, K. L., 232
Schaffner, Bertram, 73, 419
Schiller, Friedrich von, 144
Schoeck, Helmut, 256
Schubert, Franz, 149
Schumann, Robert, 150
Schurtz, Heinrich, 239, 421
Schwartz, M. S., 330, 422
Schweitzer, Albert, 150
Sears, R. R., 256, 421
Sewell, W. H., 241, 421
Shakespeare, William, 87
Shipley, James, 21, 422
Silver, Gilbert, 73, 416
Simmons, L. W., 14, 354, 422
Singh, J. A. L., 14, 422

INDEX OF SUBJECTS

p34
p52
p 94-95 * Presential – Idiosyncratic
ordinal – Social